P9-DFZ-595

iPhone® OS Development

Your visual blueprint™ for developing apps for Apple's mobile devices

by Richard Wentk

WILEY

Wiley Publishing, Inc.

iPhone® OS Development: Your visual blueprint™ for developing apps for Apple's mobile devices

Published by
Wiley Publishing, Inc.
10475 Crosspoint Boulevard
Indianapolis, IN 46256

www.wiley.com

Published simultaneously in Canada

Library of Congress Control Number: 2010921247

ISBN: 978-0-470-55651-1

Manufactured in the United States of America

10 9 8 7 6 5 4 3 2 1

Trademark Acknowledgments

Contact Us

For general information on our other products and services, please contact our Customer Care Department within the U.S. at 877-762-2974; outside the U.S. at 317-572-3993; or fax 317-572-4002.

For technical support, please visit www.wiley.com/techsupport.

TianTan, the Temple of Heaven

Designed in harmony with numerology and ancient symbolism, Beijing's Temple of Heaven was built around 1420 during the reign of Ming Emperor YongLe. As both the image of heaven and the site of an annual ritual believed to ensure a bountiful harvest, the Temple complex surpasses the Forbidden City in size.

Reflecting the ancient Chinese perception of heaven, the Temple buildings are round, with rectangular foundations that represent the earth. An avenue 360 meters long takes visitors up a barely perceptible incline to the sacred Hall of Prayer for Good Harvests, symbolizing the progression of life toward heaven.

Discover other ancient Chinese monuments in *Frommer's Beijing, 6th Edition,* available wherever books are sold or at www.Frommers.com.

WILEY

Sales

Contact Wiley
at (877) 762-2974
or (317) 572-4002.

Credits

Acquisitions Editor
Aaron Black

Project Editor
Christopher Stolle

Technical Editor
Jesse David Hollington

Copy Editor
Lauren Kennedy

Editorial Director
Robyn Siesky

Business Manager
Amy Knies

Senior Marketing Manager
Sandy Smith

Vice President and Executive Group Publisher
Richard Swadley

Vice President and Executive Publisher
Barry Pruett

Project Coordinator
Katherine Crocker

Quality Control Technician
Rebecca Denoncour

Proofreading and Indexing
Henry Lazarek
Potomac Indexing, LLC

Media Development Project Manager
Laura Moss

Media Development Assistant Project Manager
Jenny Swisher

Media Development Associate Producers
Josh Frank
Shawn Patrick
Doug Kuhn
Marilyn Hummel

Layout
Carrie A. Cesavice
Andrea Hornberger
Jennifer Mayberry

About the Author

Richard Wentk has more than 10 years of experience as a developer and more than 15 years in publishing. Richard is also one of the United Kingdom's most reliable technology writers. He covers Apple products and developments for *Macworld* and *MacFormat* magazines and also writes about technology, creativity, and business strategy for titles such as *Computer Arts* and *Future Music*. As a trainer and a former professional Apple developer returning to development on the iPhone, he is uniquely able to clarify the key points of the development process, explain how to avoid pitfalls and bear traps, and emphasize key benefits and creative possibilities. He lives online but also has a home in Wiltshire, England. For more on iPhone development, technology blogging, and other projects, visit Richard's website at www.zettaboom.com.

Author's Acknowledgments

This book is dedicated to my HGA: *ad pulchritudinem tria requiruntur — integritas, consonantia, et iterum claritas.* Without whom …

I'd like to thank Aaron Black, Christopher Stolle, and the entire team at Wiley for their hard work in making this book possible and Mark Hattersley at *Macworld* for the initial suggestion.

Software development has become a communal activity, and particular appreciation is due to the countless bloggers, experimenters, developers, and problem-solvers on the web whose generosity and creativity have made so much possible in so many ways.

Very special thanks are due to the EuroTribe for continued support, education, challenges, and entertainment and for being some of the finest people in the world and also to the L&Fers, particularly Rachel, Alexa, and Hilary — with gratitude and appreciation.

How to Use This Book

Who This Book Is For

This book is for advanced computer users who want to take their knowledge of this particular technology or software application to the next level.

The Conventions in This Book

❶ Steps

This book uses a step-by-step format to guide you easily through each task. Numbered steps are actions you must do and indented steps give you the result.

❷ Notes

Notes give additional information — special conditions that may occur during an operation, a situation that you want to avoid, or a cross reference to a related area of the book.

❸ Icons and Buttons

Icons and buttons show you exactly what you need to click to perform a step.

❹ Extra

An Extra section provides additional information about the preceding task — insider information and tips for ease and efficiency. An Apply It section takes the code from the preceding task one step further and allows you to take full advantage of it.

❺ Bold

Bold type shows text or numbers you must type.

❻ Italics

Italic type introduces and defines a new term.

❼ Courier Font

`Courier` font indicates the use of scripting language code, such as statements, operators, or functions, and other code elements, such as objects, methods, or properties.

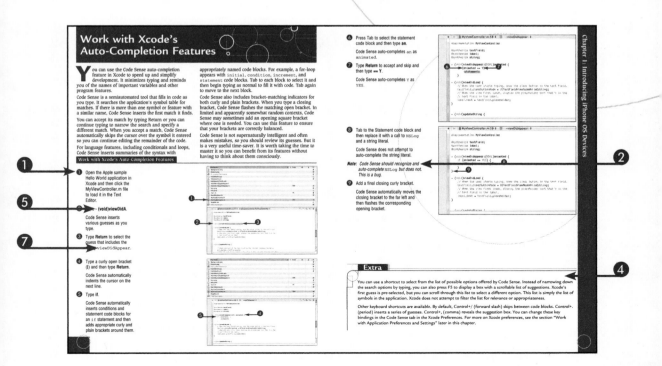

TABLE OF CONTENTS

5 ENRICHING THE USER EXPERIENCE 106

6 CREATING AND USING TABLES 124

TABLE OF CONTENTS

Introducing iPhone OS Devices

The iPhone, iPod touch, and iPad combine innovative new computing technologies with a completely new business model. Technologically, developing for the iPhone family is challenging but rewarding. The development environment is loosely based on the Mac, with some extensions and limitations, but the user environment is innovative and encourages creative and novel experiences.

If you are a Mac developer, you will find many concepts familiar and can likely start iPhone development after a brief reorientation. If you are new to the Apple development environment, give yourself a few weeks to master the principles and programming models. This book includes key concepts with worked examples. Combined with Apple's documentation, they will enable you to move rapidly toward understanding and creating your own applications.

The iPhone OS documentation lists thousands of objects, message definitions, and function calls. The biggest challenge for new developers is learning which messages are used to signal which event. The second-biggest challenge is mastering the syntax of each call to the OS. Every message type uses a different syntax, with different data structures and access methods.

Fortunately, Apple's code samples include generous amounts of boilerplate code. When you begin developing applications, you can copy this boilerplate to your own projects and reuse it with minor edits. As you gain experience, you can begin to customize it and extend it to meet your own requirements. You will also learn how to add custom messages and message handlers of your own design.

The App Store Advantage

Apple's App Store is a key advantage because Apple distributes your app and does significant marketing for you. The ideal iPhone application is simple and elegant, and its development is tightly focused, which means development cycles can take months as opposed to years. Therefore, you see the benefit from your development work more quickly than you would from a typical desktop product, and the cost of entry in both time and capital is significantly lower.

Apple's iPhone SDK is free. To download it, you must sign up as a developer at http://developer.apple.com/iphone. Registrations are typically approved within 24 hours. If you decide to distribute or sell your applications through the App Store or test them on your own iPhone rather than the SDK Simulator, you must pay Apple $99 to join the Standard Developer Program. Individuals should allow a month for signup. Small businesses should allow two months.

The App Store model is not perfect. You must allow two weeks for testing of each submitted application, and not all applications are accepted. There is no way to check if your application will be approved ahead of submission. In the past, Apple has blocked applications that compete with its own products because its air-time partners have refused to support them or for other reasons that remain inscrutable. However, most applications are accepted. Many are profitable. Some become very profitable indeed.

Web Apps and Native Apps

This book includes information about developing native applications. However, web applications remain an interesting option on the iPhone. When the iPhone was first released, no native SDK was available. All applications were developed as web apps for the iPhone's Mobile Safari browser, which was optionally supported by server-side data management.

Web apps blend HTML, CSS, JavaScript, and AJAX to create an interface that mimics the iPhone's native interface. Flash is not supported. Web apps are not listed in the App Store, but you can submit them to Apple, which lists them in a dedicated area on the Apple web site. You can also direct users to your web app within Mobile Safari via a standard URL.

If you are familiar with web technologies and if your application is relatively simple, you will find it is easier and faster to create an iPhone web app than a native application. The disadvantages of apps are limited performance and limited support for the iPhone's enhanced hardware features. Unlike stand-alone applications, most web apps do not work offline. Web apps are not covered in detail in this book. They remain a legacy option for projects that aggregate and summarize web information and manage user interaction with web data.

The iPhone OS Product Range

iPhone OS devices include the iPhone, iPhone 3G, iPhone 3GS, iPod touch, and iPad. All share a thin form factor with a unique high-resolution display and a multi-touch interface. The iPod touch is identical to the iPhone series but lacks phone and mobile data features, a camera, a microphone, and GPS. The accelerometer, Mobile Safari web browser, and Wi-Fi networking are included.

However, the iPod touch is much more than a crippled iPhone and remains a popular product with buyers and developers. Approximately 95% of applications in the App Store are compatible with the iPod touch. It is also more affordable than an iPhone. For developers, it is possible to develop, test, and sell complete applications on an iPod touch. An iPhone is not essential unless you intend to develop for iPhone-specific hardware features, such as the camera, GPS, compass, and so on.

With the iPhone 3GS comes an improved camera with video capture, voice control, a compass, enhanced Open GL 2.0 graphics acceleration, and a faster processor than the base 3G model. There is a small but increasing market for premium applications for the 3GS, offering extra features and performance at a premium price. As long as Apple continues to sell the 3G and the 3GS, developing exclusively for the 3GS will limit your application's market. However, you can assume that most users will upgrade within 12 to 18 months of each new model's release date. The latest iPod touch range includes the same enhanced graphics and a faster processor.

The iPad extends the iPhone OS family in a new direction with a larger touch screen, faster processor, and additional OS features. The core programming model remains largely unchanged, but the interface supports new options. For details, see Appendix C.

Memory Limits

The iPhone does not support virtual memory. There is no page file and no option for disk swapping. When your application runs out of memory, there is no more memory available. Your application must manage memory errors effectively. Otherwise, it may be terminated by the iPhone OS without notice, it may crash, or it may force a complete reboot of the iPhone. All your applications must include basic memory-error handling because they may be run on an iPhone with limited free memory. You must carefully design applications that use large media files to avoid exceeding memory limits.

Battery Life

The iPhone and iPod touch have limited battery life. You must take care to manage power by suspending software features in your application when they are not needed. Hardware features such as the camera, GPS, and accelerometer generate waste heat, which dramatically decreases battery life. It can also make the iPhone uncomfortable to hold and affect its reliability. These hardware features should never be left running when they are not required.

The iPad offers improved battery life, and power management is not quite so critical. However, your application should still suspend non-essential features whenever possible.

User Expectations

The iPhone programming model assumes that only one application is active. Although the iPhone OS is a variant of Unix, there is no official support for multi-tasking or background execution. Users expect applications to launch almost instantly, with an equally instant suspend-on-demand feature. Applications should save and restore their states automatically, and interfaces should be simple and elegant and follow Apple's design guidelines.

You can support users by relying on the standard Cocoa Touch interface library to manage scrolling, text input, and other interface essentials. Applications should not include features that require a complex manual, and operation should be as intuitive as possible.

Install the iPhone SDK

You can get started with iPhone development by downloading and installing the iPhone SDK. The SDK includes the latest version of the Xcode development environment as well as a full set of documentation for the current version of the iPhone OS. You do not need an iPhone to develop with the SDK. Xcode includes a simulator on which you can test applications. The only prerequisite is an Intel Mac and the most recent version of OS X.

Apple provides three levels of access to the SDK and its contents. Anyone can read web versions of the documentation included in the SDK. Useful outline descriptions of the development cycle and the documentation for the iPhone's libraries are available online. However, access to sample code and examples is not available.

To download the full SDK, you must register with Apple's Developer Connection. Registration is simple and free but requires confirmation from Apple. Currently, development is open to almost anyone who expresses interest.

Once registration is confirmed, you can download the SDK package. Installing the SDK gives you access to sample code and the development environment. You can develop and test applications on the Simulator, but you cannot install them on your iPhone, share them with others, or upload them to the App Store unless you pay a fee and enroll in the Standard Developer Program. You can then *provision* your iPhone with a unique digital access key supplied by Apple to confirm it as a valid development target in Xcode, submit your applications to Apple for possible inclusion in the App Store, and create a limited testing program with up to 100 users.

Corporations developing applications for internal distribution can join the Enterprise Developer Program for $299. This supports in-house development only. The program does not allow App Store distribution.

Install the iPhone SDK

① Open a web browser and navigate to http://developer. apple.com and then follow the links to find the most current enrollment page.

Note: *Apple regularly modifies its developer pages, so the current URL may be different from the URL shown here.*

② Click Continue and then follow the instructions that walk you through the complete signup process.

Note: *You must wait until Apple confirms your application before you can complete the signup process.*

③ If you plan to develop applications for the App Store, select the Standard Developer Program.

④ Pay for and activate your chosen program.

Note: *Steps 3 and 4 are optional. You can download and install the iPhone SDK as soon as Apple confirms your application.*

⑤ Navigate to the download location for the SDK.

⑥ Select your OS and then download the compatible SDK release.

Note: *The download may be between 2GB and 5GB.*

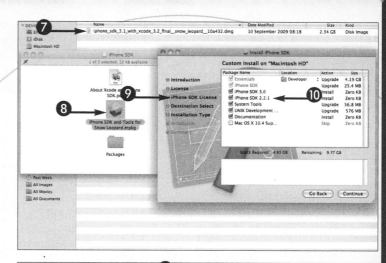

7 The SDK download is a standard DMG file, so double-click it to mount it.

8 Double-click the MPKG installer to begin installation.

9 Step through the License Confirmation and Destination pages.

10 Select the elements to install.

Note: *You can leave most defaults unchanged. You can choose not to install older versions of the SDK.*

11 Choose Macintosh HD→ Developer to open the installed Developer folder.

12 Add the Developer folder to the Places sidebar for ease of navigation.

13 Open the Applications folder to reveal Xcode. Optionally, add Xcode to the Dock for ease of navigation.

14 Create a new folder you can use to keep your projects in one location.

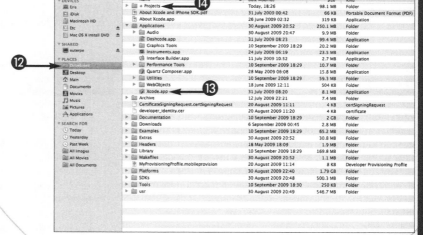

Extra

The current cost of professional developer enrollment is $99 for individual developers and small businesses. Company enrollment requires legal verification of business status and takes two to four weeks to process. You must fax a copy of your incorporation documents to Apple on demand. Individual enrollment takes one to two weeks; business enrollment is likely to take four to six weeks.

One of the benefits of the Standard iPhone Developer Program is that it is likely — but not guaranteed — to provide early access to beta versions of the iPhone OS, including updates to the SDK. You will have a head start of two to three months over non-enrolled developers. This gives you time to update your apps to make sure they are compatible with the new iPhone OS when it is released.

Beta versions are a moving target for developers. It is good practice to investigate new OS features when they arrive in beta and to consider new apps that support them but not to commit application code until the beta OS has stabilized and Apple mandates a move to the new OS.

Introducing Xcode and the iPhone SDK

You can develop applications for the iPhone and iPad with Xcode — Apple's iPhone and Mac development environment. Xcode requires an Intel-compatible Mac running the latest version of OS X. It does not require an iPhone or iPad because a simulator is included.

Most but not quite all of the iPhone's software and hardware features are modeled in the Simulator. Xcode includes a complete suite of tools for application development, including a compiler and editor, interface designer, web app tool kit, performance profiler, and the Simulator.

When you sign up for the iPhone development program, you receive download links for the latest version of Xcode. Do not use the version on your OS X installer disk. It will not be up to date and is likely to include bugs that have been fixed in the most recent version.

The iPhone version of Xcode includes both Mac and iPhone development tools. These offer a similar development environment but use different tools and libraries. Code developed in one environment is not guaranteed to run successfully in the other. There are significant differences between the Mac and iPhone programming models, and you will not be able to reuse code without changes.

Interface Builder

Interface Builder is a visual interface design tool. It includes a selection of tools that manage links between visual interface objects, such as buttons and sliders, that appear on the iPhone's display and the software objects and message handlers defined in your code. Interface Builder is not a complete visual development environment. It is a hybrid tool that includes visual features but also displays lists of objects and methods. You must define these objects and methods in your code before you can use them in Interface Builder.

Interface Builder includes a library with instances of all the standard iPhone interface objects, including buttons, sliders, text fields, tables, and pickers. More generic interface objects, including windows and views, are also part of the library. These provide a background for the interface and make it possible to add custom objects to an application.

The Simulator

The Simulator appears on your desktop as a virtual iPhone or iPad. The screen is clickable, and there is a double-touch feature for testing multi-touch interfaces. There is no GPS, camera, or accelerometer, but limited work-arounds for some of these missing features are available. For example, you can select images from the Simulator's photo library in place of direct camera capture. A limited selection of Apple applications with preset data are built into the Simulator, including Photos, Contacts, Settings, and the Safari browser. Other applications are not available.

When you compile an application, it is installed on the Simulator and runs immediately. Old applications are not deleted, but you can rearrange and delete applications just as you can on the iPhone. The Simulator runs Intel x86 code and not code compiled for the ARM processor used on the iPhone. Simulator performance is not a guide to performance on a real iPhone, and running speeds may be very different. Applications that rely on real-time graphics and sound or other performance features should be tested on real hardware.

Xcode and GCC

Xcode is based on a modified version of the Gnu Compiler Collection (GCC) and includes support for all the C variants, including Objective-C, which is the default language for Mac and iPhone development, and for other languages that are not relevant to iPhone development.

Most of the iPhone libraries are written in Objective-C. Some features of the OS still use conventional C calls. It is sometimes faster and more efficient to define C functions in your code than to create complete Objective-C class definitions. Xcode can handle either option.

Apple's editor and asset manager was developed around GCC and is unique to Xcode. It adds useful windowing, asset listing debugging, and auto-completion features and includes hooks for the Simulator, performance monitoring, memory integrity checking, and other performance-oriented features.

Behind the Xcode interface, the compiler remains a recognizable variant of GCC, expanded with extra Apple libraries. Although GCC is not a fast compiler, iPhone applications are often small, so compilation speed is rarely a problem.

Xcode Instruments

Instruments add code profiling and memory management to increase efficiency and eliminate memory errors — one of the prime causes of application crashes on the iPhone. The package is based on Sun's DTrace toolset and can provide a comprehensive view of activity inside your application. Use it to monitor object allocation, animation and graphic performance, and memory leaks as well as to record sequences of user actions for testing your applications in the Simulator.

Advanced Xcode

Xcode includes too many features to list here in detail. This book introduces an essential subset of features, but as you develop more complex applications, you will need to manage your projects in more sophisticated ways. Apple's *Xcode Project Management Guide* includes a detailed summary of Xcode's file and source tree management features. The guide is available online in the Developer Connection area of Apple's site. Because Apple changes some of its URLs regularly, doing a web search is the easiest way to locate it. You should work through this guide as soon as you start reusing code in your projects and when branching projects.

For advanced developers, Xcode includes scripting and automation features that use Apple's Automator plug-in, which is built into all current versions of OS X. Automator can simplify development with scripted file and asset management. Mastering Automator will save you significant development time on larger projects.

Dashcode

Dashcode is Xcode's web app development tool. Web apps use similar technology to Apple's OS X dashboard widgets, so Dashcode can also be used to develop widgets. Two template modes select either iPhone or widget targets. For the iPhone target, the included templates mimic the iPhone's native interface features. The Run button in Dashcode creates a web page that loads in Mobile Safari in the Simulator. Web apps are not compiled into separate applications and are not installed on the iPhone. Dashcode is a legacy development tool and is not described in further detail in this book.

Explore the Sample Code Libraries

You can use the sample code libraries to gain a head start on effective development. To speed up development, you can reuse code from the libraries in your own applications. You can also use the libraries as worked examples that demonstrate how to solve coding problems and implement the iPhone's unique features.

The iPhone's documentation is updated with each new release of the OS. Prior to Xcode 3.2, documentation was organized in sections that matched each OS release. After Xcode 3.2, the presentation was streamlined. Reference material, tutorials, and links to sample code appear in a single browser-like window.

In Xcode 3.2, you can find links to the sample code library at the top left of the documentation window, under the Resource Types tab. The main Documents window also lists links to the sample code, and you can create a list of links by clicking the Resource Types sort header in the title bar and then scrolling down to view the list.

However, neither list is comprehensive. You can find further links to source code on the Class Reference pages. See Chapter 2 for details. You can also find incomplete code snippets in some of the reference sections. You cannot usually use this code as is without significantly expanding it.

All the sample code listed on the main reference library page and in the Class Reference is packaged as a complete Xcode project. You can download this project and then load it into Xcode, and it should compile and run immediately without changes. However, some code samples are saved with legacy settings and may generate errors. You can usually eliminate the errors by setting a new target environment by using the drop-down menu at the top left in the main Xcode window — for example Simulator - 3.1.2 | Debug — or by saving the main files, closing Xcode, and then reloading the project.

Explore the Sample Code Libraries

1 Open the Documentation Library by choosing Help→Developer Documentation.

2 Choose iPhone OS Library from the Home drop-down menu.

3 Click Sample Code under the Resource Types header in the left-hand pane.

● A list of sample code examples appears in the Documents pane of the Reference Library window.

4 Optionally, you can click the Resource Type sort tag in the Documents pane to sort all the documents by type and group the sample code content together.

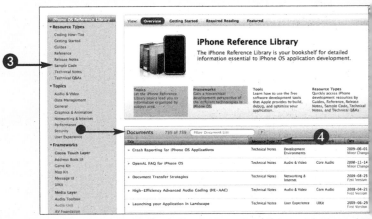

⑤ Review the list of sample code examples.

⑥ Optionally, click Title to sort the examples by name.

⑦ Optionally, click Resource Type, Topic, Framework, or Date to re-sort the examples by the corresponding criteria.

⑧ Optionally, scroll down to review the rest of the list and then select an example by clicking its title.

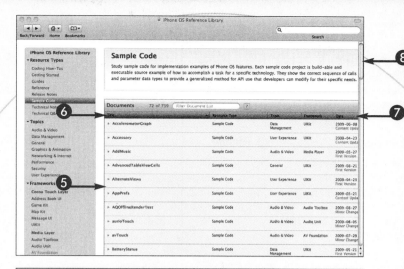

⑨ Review information about the example, including the version number and build requirements.

⑩ Optionally, you can view one or more of the files included in the example project by choosing it from the View Source Code drop-down menu.

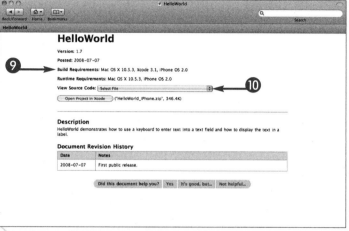

Extra

Further examples of source code are available from various sources online. One of the most useful is the iPhone Developer site at www.theiphonedev.com. The Source Code tab on the site lists about 50 applications with links to source code. Most applications are relatively simple, but some are more adventurous and push the limits of what is possible on the iPhone.

Unlike the Apple sample code examples, these applications are more or less complete. Although you can reuse or repurpose their code, this does not mean the code is in the public domain or that you can use it as you want. Most applications are licensed under one of the many open-source licenses that cover open code. If you add this code to your own projects, you must accept the restrictions in the license.

Introducing Xcode's Work Areas

Ⓐ File Name

The file name displays the name of the file currently being edited. Project files often have very similar names. Use this to double-check that you are editing the correct file.

Ⓑ Toolbar

The Toolbar includes the main Build and Run tool that compiles a project. The Info tool displays information about a selected item. Click the Tasks button to stop an active operation. The Action pop-up menu displays a smart list of actions relevant to a selected item.

Ⓒ Search Field

Enter a search string to search the Detail View for a match. The search field does not search the Text Editor. You can use it to search for groups and files in a project but not for symbols in code.

Ⓓ Detail View

The Detail View shows the item or items selected in the Groups & Files list, with summary and status fields for each. From left to right, the summary fields are File Name, Build Status, Code (which lists file sizes), Build Errors, Build Warnings, and Target Membership (which specifies whether the file is included in the current build target). These icons are not named, and there is no hovering screen tip to remind you of their function.

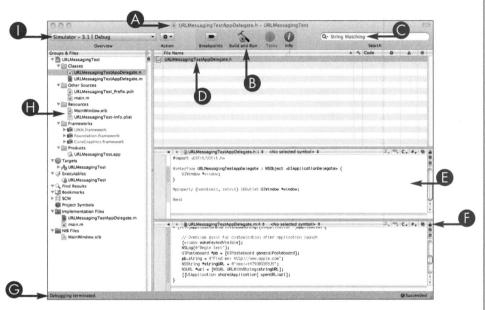

Ⓔ Text Editor

Use the Text Editor to edit the code of the file you have selected in the Detail View or in the Groups & Files list. The text area includes a complex navigation bar at the top, with features that aid speedy navigation and code management.

Ⓕ Text Editor Navigation Bar

Use the Previous and Next arrows and the File History menu to move through your edit history. The Function Menu displays a list of code sections. On the right, from left to right, the Bookmarks, Breakpoints, Class Hierarchy, and Included Files icons open drop-down menus when clicked. Counterpart button swaps between header and implementation files, and a Lock button prevents editing. You can split the Text Editor to view multiple files by clicking the Split icon under the Lock button.

Ⓖ Status Bar

The status bar displays a confirmation message if the compilation was successful or an error count if the compilation failed. It also displays information about the status of the current run once an application has been installed in the Simulator or in an attached iPhone.

Ⓗ Groups & Files List

The Groups & Files list displays a complete summary of all files and other information associated with a project, including a complete file list, a class summary, a list of included frameworks, compile targets, and other resources.

Ⓘ Compilation Configuration

Choose options from the Configuration drop-down menu to run the compiled application in the Simulator or on an attached iPhone. This menu also summarizes active targets and sets debug or final release status.

Understanding Xcode's Work Areas

The Groups & Files List

The Groups & Files list is the key to managing an Xcode project. It summarizes all the components of a project and defines the compilation products and targets. However, many of its features are not intuitive or obvious, are not immediately visible, or are simply confusing.

You can use the Classes folder to review the list of classes in your project. Projects that use the Xcode Templates list all the pre-included classes here. However, if you add a new custom class, it is not moved to this folder automatically. You must move it manually.

You can load most source code files into the Text window by clicking them. However, you must double-click to open nib files, which are used in Interface Builder, because Interface Builder is a stand-alone application and is not built into Xcode. If you double-click a source code file, it opens in a new maximized floating Text Editor window.

You often need to add a framework to a project. The menu option for adding a framework is not included in the main menu tree. To add a framework, right-click on the Frameworks folder, choose Add→Existing Frameworks, and then select one or more frameworks from the floating list that appears. See Chapter 3 for more on frameworks.

Symbolic Links and Real Files

One of the more confusing features in Xcode is that the list of files in the Groups & Files list may not mirror the corresponding files in a project folder. If you delete a file from the Groups & Files list, the file is removed from the project, but it remains in the project folder. Similarly, if you rename a file in Xcode, the original name on disk is not updated. If you move a custom class so it appears in Classes folder, it is not moved to the corresponding folder on disk.

The file names in the Groups & Files list are *symbolic links* to real files. If you right-click on a file and then choose Get Info from the pop-up menu, you will see a name and path specification. The name appears in the Groups & Files list and can be changed to anything. The path specification points to the real file.

Smart Groups

The Implementation Files and Nib Files at the bottom of the Groups & Files window are examples of Smart Groups. You can use Smart Groups to automatically group project files according to search criteria that you define. Choose Project→New Smart Group to add a group. Select Simple Filter Smart Group to add files with a simple file name search and the Regular Expression option to include files using a regular expression search.

Further Features

Xcode includes a rich set of further features, with corresponding windows, in its menu tree. Xcode's many debugging windows are described in Chapter 1. To use the Class Model tool, choose Design→Class Model→ Quick Model, and it displays a graphical view of the relationships between project classes and lists their properties and methods. For more on properties and methods, see Chapter 2. You can view a Class Browser by choosing Project→Class Browser. This lists all the classes used in the project, including those imported from frameworks.

Build a Sample Application

Y ou can use Xcode's features to quickly build and test the sample code applications included in the documentation. Compilation is a one-click process in Xcode. You do not need to know anything about Objective-C, frameworks, or other features of the iPhone OS to build and test the sample applications. The only prerequisite is an ability to use the Finder to create and name folders while saving files and to select a target platform in Xcode.

There are two ways to build a sample application. The first is to use the sample code found in the documentation. This includes a quick link. Clicking the Open Project in Xcode button and choosing a Save As location loads the project into Xcode. Behind the scenes, a compressed version of the project is decompressed and copied into the directory you nominate. The project files are then loaded into Xcode — ready to be built.

If you are downloading a project from an online collection, the files are usually compressed into an

archive that includes a complete directory tree for the project. You will need to uncompress the archive manually before you can load the project and optionally copy the files to a working directory. From there, you can load the project into Xcode by double-clicking the file with the .xcodeproj extension.

For convenience, you may find it helpful to keep all your applications in one or more subfolders of a main project or archive folder.

To select a target platform, click the Compilation Configuration drop-down menu. By default, only the iPhone Simulator option is available. You can also choose a debug configuration for testing or a release configuration to create a leaner application that requires less memory. You can install a release build on your own iPhone, but you cannot upload it to the App Store. For information about creating a configuration suitable for distribution via the App Store, see Appendix 1.

Build a Sample Application

① Select a sample application from the documentation.

Note: *See the section earlier in this chapter for more on finding sample source code.*

② Click Open Project in Xcode.

③ Select a target folder.

④ Optionally, click New Folder to create a new target folder.

Note: *You do not need to create a folder for the project itself. It is automatically created in a new subfolder.*

⑤ Click Choose to confirm your selection.

The sample application is copied to the target folder, decompressed, and then automatically loaded in Xcode.

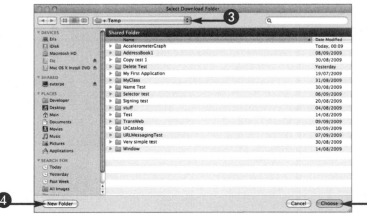

⑥ Select the Simulator option from the Compilation Configuration menu.

⑦ Click Build and Run to build and run the application.

⑧ Review the status of the compilation process in the status bar.

The application is automatically installed in the Simulator.

⑨ Use the Simulator to test and explore the features of the sample application.

The Simulator runs the application as if it were installed on an iPhone.

Note: Optionally, you can quit the Simulator when done by choosing iPhone Simulator→Quit iPhone Simulator. You can also leave the Simulator running. You will be asked to confirm that it should quit and reload if you recompile.

Extra

To test applications on a real iPhone, you will need to *provision* it. To provision a phone, you must sign up for the full iPhone Developer Program, register, be accepted, and pay a fee. You can then set up Xcode with a set of provisioning keys and also add further keys for specific handsets.

The provisioning process is complex. You create three software keys — one for yourself or your managing corporate entity, one for each developer in the project, and one for each handset. You must copy the first two keys to your project folder, install the handset key on the iPhone, and then add it to the Provisioning Profiles tag under the iPhone Development tab in Xcode's Organizer window. You can view the Organizer by choosing Window→Organizer in Xcode.

You can find detailed walkthrough instructions for the provisioning process on the developer pages of your Apple account once you have been accepted into the program.

Choose a Project Template

You can speed up the development process by beginning a project with one of the Xcode project templates. Each template includes a minimal set of files and features and implements an application with a certain type of interface. For example, the View-based Application template creates a blank screen, which is an example of an iPhone *view* — a screen that you can fill with settings and information. The Utility Application template creates an application with two views as well as buttons to flip between them. For more on views, see Chapter 3.

Templates are not complete sample applications. If you compile and run them, they either do nothing at all or very little. Many of them do not respond to user actions. But they do offer a skeleton for an application. You can

fill out this skeleton by adding further features to create a working application. Templates are built into the Xcode workflow and are not an optional feature. Whenever you create a new project, you begin by selecting one of the templates. Although it is possible to create an application from scratch without using templates, this is not straightforward and is not recommended.

Many of the templates include features that have been commented out. You can add extra features to your application by removing the comments. However, even with commented sections, the list of features included in the templates is minimal. In a typical application, you will need to add further features by hand. You can save further development time by creating custom templates to your own design. There is no limit on how complex a template can be.

Choose a Project Template

① Open Xcode.

② Choose File→New Project.

③ If it is not already selected, click Application.

④ Choose a template.

⑤ Review a brief description of the template and its features.

⑥ Click Choose to confirm your selection.

A Save As dialog box appears, allowing you to specify a file location for the new project.

⑦ Navigate to the folder in which you would like to save your new project.

Note: *You may find it useful to create a Temp folder for quick experiments and tests — separate from your main Project folder.*

⑧ Type a name for the new project.

Note: *The project is saved inside a folder with the new name.*

⑨ Click Save to create the new project.

The project is created by using the selected template and is automatically loaded into Xcode.

⑩ Review the list of files in the project. Optionally, you can build and run the project.

The project is now ready for editing.

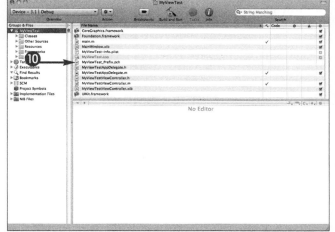

Extra

You can get the most from templates by creating your own. With custom templates, you can move beyond the minimal features included in the standard templates to create skeleton applications with a more comprehensive set of features.

In Xcode 3.2, the template files are available in /Developer/Platforms/iPhoneOS.platform/Developer/Library/Xcode/Project Templates/Application.

Each folder in this directory appears in the Xcode's Template window. To create a custom template, drag+copy one of the folders to create a duplicate — for example, Navigation-based Application 2. Open the folder to find the __ PROJECTNAME__.xcodeproj file. Double-click this file to open it in Xcode. You can then edit source code, add further source code or Interface Builder files, include custom icons, and so on. To rename the template, rename its folder.

Do not change the __PROJECTNAME__ and __PROJECTNAMEASIDENTIFIER__ labels. These labels are automatically replaced when you create a new project.

Work with Xcode's Auto-Completion Features

You can use the Code Sense auto-completion feature in Xcode to speed up and simplify development. It minimizes typing and reminds you of the names of important variables and other program features.

Code Sense is a semiautomated tool that fills in code as you type. It searches the application's symbol table for matches. If there is more than one symbol or feature with a similar name, Code Sense inserts the first match it finds.

You can accept its match by typing Return or you can continue typing to narrow the search and specify a different match. When you accept a match, Code Sense automatically skips the cursor over the symbol it entered so you can continue editing the remainder of the code.

For language features, including conditionals and loops, Code Sense inserts summaries of the syntax with appropriately named code blocks. For example, a for-loop appears with `initial`, `condition`, `increment`, and `statement` code blocks. Tab to each block to select it and then begin typing as normal to fill it with code. Tab again to move to the next block.

Code Sense also includes bracket-matching indicators for both curly and plain brackets. When you type a closing bracket, Code Sense flashes the matching open bracket. In limited and apparently somewhat random contexts, Code Sense may sometimes add an opening square bracket where one is needed. You can use this feature to ensure that your brackets are correctly balanced.

Code Sense is not supernaturally intelligent and often makes mistakes, so you should review its guesses. But it is a very useful time-saver. It is worth taking the time to master it so you can benefit from its features without having to think about them consciously.

Work with Xcode's Auto-Completion Features

① Open the Apple sample Hello World application in Xcode and then click the MyViewController.m file to load it in the Text Editor.

② Type **- (void)viewDidA**.

Code Sense inserts various guesses as you type.

③ Type **Return** to select the guess that includes the string `viewDidAppear`.

④ Type a curly open bracket (**{**) and then type **Return**.

Code Sense automatically indents the cursor on the next line.

⑤ Type **if**.

Code Sense automatically inserts conditions and statement code blocks for an `if` statement and then adds appropriate curly and plain brackets around them.

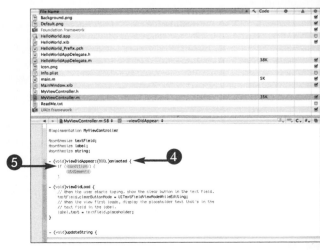

6 Press Tab to select the statement code block and then type **an**.

Code Sense auto-completes `an` as `animated`.

7 Type **Return** to accept and skip and then type **== Y**.

Code Sense auto-completes `Y` as `YES`.

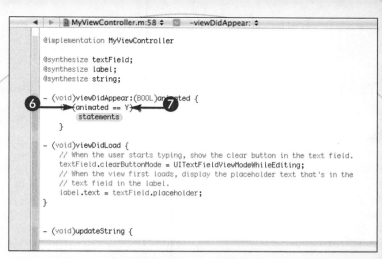

8 Tab to the Statement code block and then replace it with a call to `NSLog` and a string literal.

Code Sense does not attempt to auto-complete the string literal.

Note: *Code Sense should recognize and auto-complete* `NSLog` *but does not. This is a bug.*

9 Add a final closing curly bracket.

Code Sense automatically moves the closing bracket to the far left and then flashes the corresponding opening bracket.

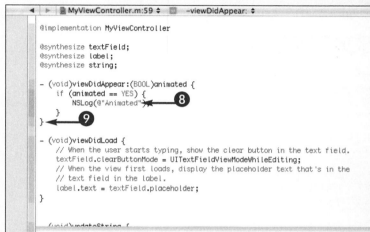

Extra

You can use a shortcut to select from the list of possible options offered by Code Sense. Instead of narrowing down the search options by typing, you can also press F5 to display a box with a scrollable list of suggestions. Xcode's first guess is pre-selected, but you can scroll through this list to select a different option. This list is simply the list of symbols in the application. Xcode does not attempt to filter the list for relevance or appropriateness.

Other keyboard shortcuts are available. By default, Control+/ (forward slash) skips between code blocks. Control+. (period) inserts a series of guesses. Control+, (comma) reveals the suggestion box. You can change these key bindings in the Code Sense tab in the Xcode Preferences. For more on Xcode preferences, see the section "Work with Application Preferences and Settings" later in this chapter.

Speed Up Editing with Pop-Ups and Bookmarks

Xcode includes three navigation shortcuts. All appear in the navigation bar at the top of each file window in the Text Editor. The File History menu shows a pop-up list of recently edited files. Pop-up lists for each project are managed independently.

The Function menu shows a list of function, variable, and method definitions in the current file. You can extend this list and add custom locations to it by adding `#pragma` directives to your code. These directives do not affect compilation. They work exclusively with this menu.

You can use the Bookmarks menu to remember the current cursor position in each file. When you select a bookmark, the cursor moves to the saved location. The bookmark list for each file is independent.

However, the Bookmarks group in the Groups & Files pane shows a complete list of project bookmarks. You can use this list to move quickly between bookmarked locations in different files.

You can also click the Bookmarks group to reveal a bookmark editor page. This list is designed for renaming bookmarks rather than for quick navigation. Single-clicking each item selects the relevant file but does not position the cursor. Double-clicking an item moves the cursor to the correct position — but in a new Text Editor window.

Speed Up Editing with Pop-Ups and Bookmarks

① Open Xcode and then load the Hello World application.

② Click HelloWorldAppDelegate.m.

The contents of HelloWorldAppDelegate.m appear in the editing window. The file is automatically but invisibly added to the file history list.

③ Click MyViewController.m.

④ Click the File History pop-up menu.

The two files appear in the recent history list.

Note: *You can use the Forward and Back arrows to move through the recent history list.*

⑤ Click the Function menu to reveal a list of variables, methods, and functions.

Note: *Until you select an item, the Function menu title is <No selected symbol>. You can display the menu by clicking this text.*

⑥ Click the –viewDidLoad method.

Note: *The cursor is not placed at the start of the method. If you begin typing without moving the cursor, the method name is deleted and replaced.*

⑦ Add a `#pragma` directive to any location in the file.

⑧ Click the Function menu again. The label for the pragma mark appears in the list.

Note: *You can add as many pragma marks to a file as you need. When you click a label name, the cursor moves to the label and the entire label is selected.*

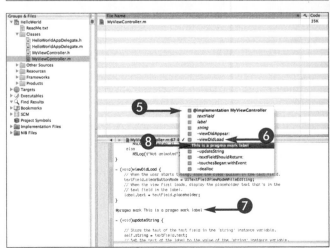

9 Move the cursor to any location in the file.

10 Choose Edit→Add to Bookmarks to add a bookmark.

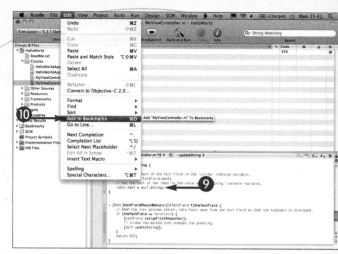

11 Click Bookmarks in the Groups & Files pane.

The bookmark appears in the Bookmarks list. An editable list of bookmarks appears in the Detail View.

12 Click the Bookmark icon in the Text Editor navigation toolbar.

The pop-up list appears with the new bookmark added. You can move the cursor to the bookmarked location by clicking the bookmark.

Extra

In addition to bookmarks and navigation shortcuts, Xcode includes a Favorites feature. To show the Favorites toolbar, choose View→Layout→Show Favorites Bar. The toolbar appears as a blank gray area below the main Xcode toolbar. You can drag items from the Groups & Files pane and then drop them on the toolbar for quick access. To remove an item, drag it back to the Groups & Files pane. Do not delete it — this deletes it from the project.

The Favorites feature is a simple file selector. It does not include positioning information, so you cannot use it to move quickly to a specific location in a file.

The bookmarks list in the Groups & Files pane is the only feature in Xcode that can move between different locations in different files. Unfortunately, there is no way to undock the Bookmarks feature and open it in a separate window.

Debug
Your Code

You can use Xcode's debugging features to eliminate errors in your code. The debugging environment is unusually sophisticated. You can set breakpoints at line numbers or at specific symbols. You can single-step through the code after a breakpoint, and you can monitor variables. You can also set breakpoint actions, which force Xcode to perform various actions when it reaches certain breakpoints.

Xcode includes four separate but related debugging windows. You can debug directly in the Text Editor, setting breakpoints and single-stepping through code. You can use the mini debugger, which is a floating window that summarizes the application state. There is also a full debugger window, which provides more detailed information about variables and execution status. Finally, there is a general-purpose console window. It provides runtime status messages, including crash dumps. You can also send messages of your own to the console window. The console is independent of the main

iPhone display. Messages sent to it are not visible to iPhone users. It is equivalent to sending the stdout stream to a terminal in Unix.

Identical debugging features are available on the Simulator and on an attached iPhone. You can monitor execution on a real iPhone, check variables, and receive crash dumps and other real-time status information.

To use the debugging features, choose the Debug option from the Compiler Configuration drop-down menu. When you build and run, your application is generated with a full symbol table and other debugging information. Remember to select the release setting for a final build run. Otherwise, your application will use more memory than it needs to and will run slowly.

Advanced developers can use further features, such as conditional breakpoints, breakpoint templates, breakpoint actions, and watchpoints. For details, see "Managing Program Execution" in the "Xcode Debugging Guide" section of the Xcode documentation.

Debug Your Code

① Open Xcode and then load the Hello World application.

② Click the MyViewController.m file to open it in the Text Editor window.

③ Scroll down to the updateString method declaration and then place the cursor at the start of the last line before the closing curly bracket.

④ Choose Run→Manage Breakpoints→ Add Breakpoint at Current Line.

An arrow appears next to the selected line of code to indicate that a breakpoint has been added.

⑤ Choose the Debug build option from the Compiler Configuration drop-down menu.

⑥ Click the Breakpoints switch to select it if it is not already selected.

⑦ Click Build and Debug to create a debug build and then install it in the Simulator.

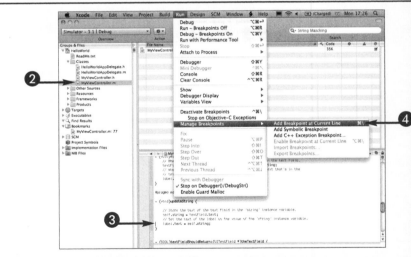

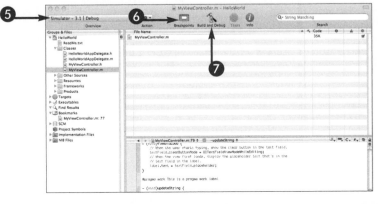

⑧ Type a test string into the application in the Simulator to trigger the breakpoint.

Note: *In this example, the debug breakpoint is triggered when you attempt to update the string. But the breakpoint can be placed anywhere in the application and triggered at any point.*

⑨ Review the changes that appear in the Text Editor window.

The breakpoint location is highlighted, an arrow appears next to it, and the navigation bar changes to display pause, resume, single-step, and other debugging icons.

⑩ Choose Run→Debugger to open a new debugging window.

⑪ Review the list of functions and methods in the Overview pane.

⑫ Click the updateString method to highlight it and show its variables.

⑬ Click self in the right-hand variable viewer to show the variables used in the `updateString` method and to reveal the string variable that has been updated with your new test value.

You can now review other variables and use the Step Over, Step Into, and Step Out buttons at the top of the window to continue testing and debugging.

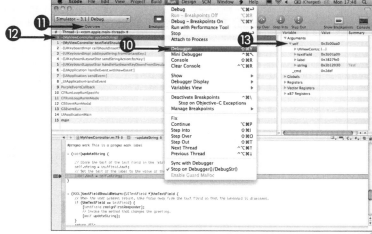

Extra

Xcode's console is usually hidden. You can show it by choosing Run→Console in Xcode. To send messages to the console, add NSLog statements to your code. For example:

```
NSLog(@"Hello, iPhone Console!");
```

This prints Hello, iPhone Console! on the console, with an associated time stamp.

You can use console messages to debug applications that are difficult to manage using the standard debugging tools. Multi-threaded applications can be particularly challenging. Adding a conventional breakpoint can disrupt the interaction between threads. You can use NSLog to display the status of variables and program execution without disrupting thread interaction.

You can also use it to monitor simpler status messages generated by a single thread. However, the other debugging tools offer more sophistication for problem-solving at this level.

NSLog works in both debug and release builds. For best performance, you should remove all NSLog statements from an application before final release. You should also select the Release build option for a final build so debugging information is not unnecessarily included.

Profile and Improve Your Code

You can use Xcode's Instruments to monitor features of operation of your application in real time; for example, you can watch memory allocations, check processor activity, and monitor file accesses. Instruments do not use the debugging system and do not require a debug build. You can use Instruments with a release build. You can run them on the Simulator or on an iPhone handset. These two environments create different results with different features and options. But the principles of profiling an application's features using one or more Instruments are the same for both.

The Instruments display is split into four areas. A toolbar at the top shows key settings. Under it, the Instruments timeline displays important changes in the status of the settings and features you select for monitoring. Beneath the timeline is a detailed view pane, which shows relevant variables and other monitored settings.

To the left of the detailed view is a control pane. Use this to select between the different options that can appear in the detailed view.

To use Instruments, build an application using the Build feature, choose Run→Run with Performance Tool, and then choose from the list of available instruments in the drop-down menu. The list of instruments available for iPhone development is a small subset of those available on the Mac. The tools do not always distinguish between Mac and iPhone monitoring, so you should use caution when viewing and interpreting the results.

You can save an Instruments run to review it later or to compare it with other runs. Saving it saves the timeline and the current detailed view. You cannot scroll back to watch changes in the detailed view, but you can move the timeline play point backward and forward to watch a summary of changes in a run.

Profile and Improve Your Code

① Open Xcode and then load the Hello World application.

② Scroll down to find the line with the `[dViewController release];` statement and then comment it out.

Note: *This deliberately creates a memory leak in the code.*

③ Choose Build→Build to build the application without running it.

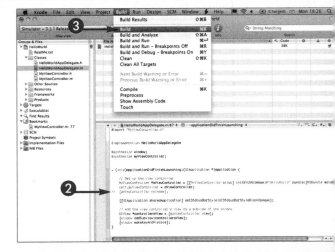

④ Choose Run→Run with Performance Tool→Leaks to load the memory leak profiler.

The Simulator loads the application and runs it, and the Leaks and Object Allocation Instrument window automatically appears.

5 Review the timeline in the Leaks and ObjectAlloc window.

Note: *The Hello World application includes a small memory leak, which is visible in the Leaks timeline. This is a bug in the Simulator.*

6 Review the memory allocations shown in the detailed view.

Note: *This is a complete list of all the memory allocations in the application.*

7 Type a test string in the application in the Simulator to trigger a deliberate memory leak.

8 Review how the allocations listings are updated as memory is assigned.

9 Watch as the bar graph display flags the leak with a red indicator and a step change in the bar height.

The Leaks instrument gives a clear indication of memory leaks in the application.

Extra

The Instruments tool is modular. The presets listed in the Instruments menu display one or two monitoring tools from a wider selection of options. You can assemble a list of tools to suit your own requirements. To add a monitoring tool to the list, click the gear icon in the bottom-left corner of the Instruments window, choose Add Instrument from the pop-up menu, and then select an instrument from the list that appears next to it. Some of the instruments are designed for the Mac environment and either do not work on the iPhone or do not display useful information. To remove an instrument from a collection, drag it to the Trash.

Advanced developers can build their own monitoring tools. Choose Instrument→Build New Instrument to view an Instruments development panel. You can use this to create a tool to monitor a selection of various system and runtime events and states.

Work with Application Preferences and Settings

You can customize many of the features in Xcode by using the Preferences feature. You can set the preferences to modify the working environment to suit your own coding style and to reveal some of the features in Xcode that are not visible with the default settings. For example, you can change the debugging preferences so Debugger and Console windows automatically appear during a debugging run.

The full list of preferences is long and detailed. For example, you can change the colors and fonts in the Text Editor, modify some of the features of the Code Sense auto-completion tool, change the key bindings in the menu tree, set up distributed builds on a network, and load extra documentation. You can also set up source code repositories for shared online development.

In addition to Xcode's preferences, each project features a separate collection of settings. You can use these to define the files and folders that are part of the project and to specify build targets, including the final name for the application. Unlike the Xcode preferences, project settings are not collected in a single location. The programmer name and company copyright tag are not set in Xcode — they are automatically read from the default user card in the Contacts database.

To view and change the other project settings, right-click on the Targets icon in the Groups & Files pane and then choose Get Info from the pop-up menu. Click the Build tab to view general project compilation options. You can typically leave these options unchanged. Advanced developers familiar with all the features of the GCC compiler can fine-tune the compilation process by modifying them and saving custom settings to create specialized compilation templates.

Work with Application Preferences and Settings

① Choose Xcode→Preferences to view the Xcode Preferences dialog box.

② Click one of the preferences categories to view and change the settings.

③ Click apply to make a change and leave the dialog box open to make more changes. Click OK to make a change and close the dialog box. Click Cancel to undo the last change, if any, and close the dialog box.

④ Use the scrollbar to scroll horizontally through the complete list of preference groups.

⑤ Click any group to make changes.

⑥ Click or double-click individual items to make changes.

Note: *In the Fonts & Colors group, you can Shift+click the entire list of text types to select them all and then double-click the list to show a text size and font selector.*

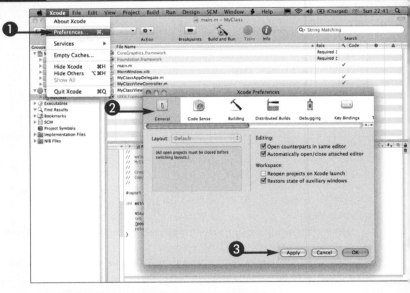

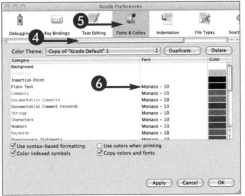

7 Scroll through the complete list of preferences to review their features.

8 Select optional features to suit your preferences — for example, to load non-essential documentation libraries.

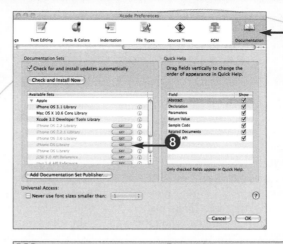

9 Click Targets to reveal the application target.

10 Right-click on the application target and then choose Get Info from the pop-up menu.

11 Review the Application Preferences and then click through the tabs.

12 Click the Build tab to reveal the build settings and then scroll down to review the complete list of all build settings.

You can now change the build settings if you desire.

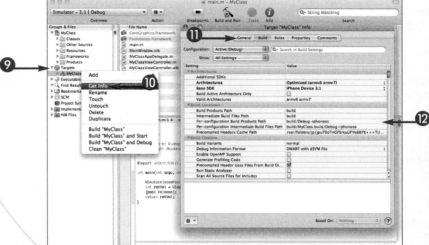

Extra

Xcode does not include features for copying or renaming projects. You can typically copy a project by copying its folder to a new folder with a different name. By default, the links in the Groups & Files window are created so they are relative to the folder root. This is not always the case. To avoid editing a file from the original project by accident, you should double-check that the links have been updated correctly.

Xcode 3.2 includes the Rename tool for renaming application targets. Choose Project→Rename. You can use it to change the name that appears under the application icon in Springboard. This feature does not rename any of the other files in the project. It is also buggy and might delete your project file.

There is no easy way to rename an entire project in one click, including all the source files. One work-around is to create a template from your project using placeholder template names for key files. Alternative semiautomated solutions are available online. For example, see http://mohrt.blogspot.com/2008/12/renaming-xcode-project.html.

Introducing Objective-C and Cocoa Touch

You can use the iPhone's Objective-C development environment to create applications that make full use of object-oriented programming (OOP) techniques and also include the advanced features available in the Cocoa Touch library.

Traditional programming languages, such as C and Assembler, are procedural. Program execution flows from start to finish, occasionally diverting into loops and subroutines. Objective-C is an object-oriented language and uses a different development model.

You can think of the iPhone's operating system as a virtual machine that sends messages to your application whenever a specific event happens — for example, when an application loads successfully, when a user touches the screen, or when a memory error occurs. As a developer, you must decide which events your application responds to. You can then write message handlers that define its response to each event.

Messaging is so fundamental that almost every line of code you write is likely to include one or more messages. Even simple data assignments in Objective-C may use messaging.

The iPhone OS documentation lists thousands of system messages definitions. The biggest challenge for new developers is learning which messages are used to signal which event. The second-biggest challenge is mastering message syntax. There are many different message types with different syntax, data structures, and access methods.

Apple's code samples include plenty of boilerplate code. When you begin developing applications, you can copy this boilerplate to your own projects and then reuse it with minor edits. As you gain experience, you can begin to customize and extend it to your own requirements. You can also start to create custom messages and handlers for your own projects.

The History of Objective-C

Objective-C was developed in the early 1980s by Brad J. Cox. The initial release added features and concepts from an earlier object-oriented language called SmallTalk-80 to the C language. In 1988, NeXT Software licensed Objective-C and created a development environment for the NeXT system called NeXTSTEP. This was standardized in 1994 to create OpenStep. This is still available under the GNU license as GNUStep and on Linux as LinuxSTEP.

In 1996, Apple acquired NeXT Software, and the NeXTSTEP/OpenStep system was further developed to create a foundation for a new operating system called OS X. The development API for OS X is called Cocoa. Because of the NeXTSTEP legacy, calls to the core features in the Cocoa API start with the letters NS (such as `NSLog`). In 2007, Apple announced a new version of Objective-C, called Objective-C 2.0. This extended the core language with new features, such as improved memory management and automated garbage collection, and simplified message syntax. The current iPhone development environment includes all the syntax and most of the runtime features available in Objective-C 2.0.

Objective-C and Cocoa Touch

The NeXT/Apple extensions to Objective-C, which interface with the OS X environment, are called Cocoa and are available to developers on both the Mac and iPhone platforms. The iPhone version of Cocoa is called Cocoa Touch and is a subset of the full OS X environment. Some of the enhanced features available in the full version of OS X, including garbage collection, are missing from Cocoa Touch. Other features have been added to provide developer support for the iPhone's hardware, including the camera, the accelerometer, and the multi-touch panel and display.

Moving from C, C++, and C# to Objective-C

If you are an existing developer — with Windows, Linux, or any other smartphone experience — you should find the move to Objective-C straightforward, apart from a few caveats. Objective-C is a strict superset of C. This means that all valid C code is valid in Objective-C. However, the programming model is more like that of C++, with some important differences. Typing and methods are dynamic and can be changed at runtime, and it is possible to send messages to objects, which forward them or ignore them deliberately.

Typically, Cocoa features are used instead of C functions. For example, C's string pointers and operations are supported, but NSString in Cocoa provides an enhanced set of string handling features, including UTF-8 encoding, and should be used instead. Similarly, the NSLog method in Cocoa should be used instead of printf(), and file management should use Cocoa's file-handling features.

Objective-C's messages are very similar to methods in C++ and C#, but the syntax is different. The default syntax uses square brackets. For example:

```
SomeType *someType = [[SomeType alloc] init];
[someType someTypeMethod:usefuldata];
```

is equivalent to

```
SomeType someType = new SomeType();
someType.someTypeMethod(usefuldata);
```

Like C++, Objective-C requires separate declaration and implementation definitions. This may feel limiting if you are used to C#, but it is an essential part of Cocoa development. It helps maintain clarity of code and design and promotes reusability.

Moving from Java to Objective-C

Although code syntax is often different, Java and Objective-C are built on a similar OOP model, and moving from one to the other is relatively straightforward. An important difference is that Objective-C's method definitions are less terse and more explicit than those of Java, and message nesting can make code and definitions harder to read. Clarity improves with experience. Initially, it can be useful to write out complex definitions from the Cocoa documentation as Java method signatures until translation becomes automatic and second nature.

A key difference in Objective-C is dynamic typing. In Objective-C, you do not have to explicitly define or even know the type of object you are working with. When you invoke a method by sending a message, the target object will always respond, as long as it recognizes the message. If it does not recognize the message, your application will crash.

Finally, Objective-C on the iPhone lacks Java's memory management and garbage collection. Memory management uses reference counting and manual allocation and de-allocation. It is very easy to forget to do this or to do it incorrectly. Good coding practices minimize the chances of memory leaks, and the Xcode development suite includes a tool that tests for memory integrity.

Moving from the Mac to the iPhone and iPad

iPhone OS is not quite a pocket version of OSX. Cocoa and Cocoa Touch are similar, but there are significant differences in the development model, the user interface, the features available in the hardware, and the foundations and frameworks that support development. For example, there is no support for floating windows. Instead of windows, developers must use views, which are introduced in Chapter 3. Memory is managed manually. Cocoa bindings are not included in Interface Builder. Instead of mouse and trackpad handlers, Cocoa Touch includes touch-screen methods that can receive and track multi-touch events.

Introducing Objects, Classes, Methods, and Messages

You can use classes and objects in Objective-C to organize your code and to access the features in Cocoa Touch.

A *class* is a template with a list of attributes and methods. *Attributes* define the data in a class and how it is structured. *Methods* define what your application can do to the data and the different ways in which the class can respond to outside requests. Classes are a convenient way to create data structures and associate them with pre-packaged tools for reading, setting, and processing data.

For example, in a driving game, a car is likely to feature attributes such as color, position, and velocity. Associated methods are likely to include reading and setting the position and velocity of the car. With a car class, you can package these attributes and methods into a single collection. You can then create instances of it whenever you need to add a new car to your game.

Objects and Classes

Once you have written a class definition, you can create and delete instances of the class. Each instance is called an *object*. You can add cars to a game by creating a new instance of the car class. Each car includes the same full set of attributes, also known as instance variables or `ivars`. When you create an object, you must give it a unique name — for example, `carOne` or `carTwo`. You can then access its attributes through a unique pointer: `carOne*`, `carTwo*`. You can control a car and set or read its instance variables by sending a message to it. For example, `[carOne setVelocity:0];`.

Methods, Accessors, and Properties

Objective-C is message-based. Objects spend much of their time messaging each other. Methods define the messages that a class responds to. For a car, these might include stopping, accelerating, or turning. To implement these features, your class must include a method definition for each possible action.

A *method definition* is a block of code that responds to a named message and implements a response. For example, a `stop` method would set a car's velocity to zero. You can add as few or as many methods to a class as you choose to. You can extend a class with further methods at any time.

By default, class attributes are private. To make them public, you must define *getter* and *setter* methods — also known as *accessors* — to read and set their values. They can also be declared as *properties,* which allows more nuanced access — for example, attributes can be declared read-only — and includes simple memory management features. Class attributes that lack a getter, setter, or property declaration remain invisible to other code. For more, see Chapter 7.

The Object Life Cycle

Objects typically follow a create, initialize, message, release life cycle. Your application begins the cycle by creating an instance of a class with a unique name and pointer. This creates a named object. Next, it sends this object an `init` message to preset its properties to useful defaults and to prepare it to receive messages.

Your application can now set other properties and send the object messages to trigger any of its methods. It can repeat this set/message subcycle as often as you need to. Finally, it releases the object to delete it. This erases its properties and removes the object from memory. Your application will crash if it tries to access the object's pointer, properties, or methods after release.

Class Methods and Class Properties

It is sometimes useful to send messages to classes instead of to specific objects — for example, to request a new instance of an object or to access a class property, such as a count of the number of objects that have been created. Class methods are typically used for object management as well as to report and set class features and active settings. In Objective-C, class methods are prefixed with + and instance methods with –.

Objective-C includes a small number of pre-defined class methods, which are called automatically by the runtime environment. You can implement them by including suitable code in your class definition.

Custom Classes and Prewritten Classes

You can define as many custom classes as you need in your application. However, the iPhone SDK includes a vast library of prewritten classes. You can use them to simplify application development. You must access all the iPhone's key features — including the touch screen; interface objects, such as tab bars, buttons and lists; and hardware, including the camera and accelerometer — through these prewritten classes.

Thousands of classes and messages exist, and it is impossible to remember them all. You can simplify

development by understanding how classes and messages are organized into *layers* and *frameworks*. Frameworks are prewritten code libraries. Layers are groups of frameworks, and provide low-, mid-, and high-level access to the features of the iPhone OS. Each layer and framework includes classes, objects, and messages that can solve or manage a specific problem. For example, the high-level UIKit framework includes all the classes and messages that manage the user interface. For more on layers and frameworks, see Chapter 3.

Inheritance and Subclasses

Classes can be assembled into hierarchies. For example, the iPhone OS library grows from a generic class called NSObject. NSObject manages object creation and deletion, handles object messaging, and includes useful memory management methods. Most other objects are subclasses of NSObject. A *subclass* is a customized and extended version of an existing class. It inherits all existing features but adds further methods and properties. Subclasses are typically less general than their original class and are tailored for specific applications.

A *superclass* of an object is any class that is closer to the root object. One of the powerful features of Objective-C is

that any system object includes all the methods and properties defined in its superclasses up to NSObject.

Objects can be subclassed indefinitely. You can create subclasses for any class you define yourself. You can also subclass the system classes to customize and extend them.

Another powerful feature of Objective-C is that your application can override methods and properties by redefining them locally. You can use this very useful feature to modify the behavior and performance of any of the system classes — for example, to extend them with custom methods of your own or to modify existing methods to suit your application's requirements.

Delegation

You can use delegation to add new features to your code without changing the object hierarchy or creating new subclasses. Although you can implement delegation in your own classes, it is more typically used in the prewritten classes to implement optional features.

A delegate object implements a bundle of optional methods — called a *protocol* — for another object. In practice, this means that you must adopt the protocol in the delegate object's header by adding the protocol name between angle brackets to the start of the header. You can then add custom code to implement some or all of the methods in the protocol.

Delegate methods are often used to define how an application responds when a significant event is about to happen, is happening, or has just happened. Many prewritten classes do not work correctly unless you implement at least some of their delegate methods.

You can nominate any object as a delegate. However, for simplicity, the delegate is often self — the calling object is its own delegate — and you implement the optional methods within it.

Create a Custom Class

Y ou can use classes and objects in Objective-C to keep your code organized and to benefit from the advantages of Objective-C's class system. You can also use Cocoa features to integrate your own classes with the iPhone operating system. This guarantees that your application creates and releases custom objects properly and manages their memory correctly.

Classes are defined with a public interface and a hidden implementation. The *interface* defines and names the properties and methods that are visible to other code. The *implementation* defines the code for the properties and methods and may include private variables that are not visible to other objects.

The standard approach to creating a class is to define the interface in a header file with a .h suffix and the implementation in a separate file with a .m suffix. By

default, Xcode creates this pair of files for you when you add a new item to your project.

However, you can create class definitions without using separate files. In fact, you can define an interface and implementation with inline code almost anywhere in your application. This is not usually considered good practice, but you can use this technique to extend an existing class — for example, to define private methods within a class that are not visible to other objects.

Properties are defined using an optional @property declaration. This includes a selection of optional parameters that include atomic||nonatomic and copy||retain||assign. atomic creates a lockable property that is guaranteed to return a valid value, even in a multi-threaded environment. copy and retain are used in memory management. assign is a simple pointer assignment. See Chapter 3 for more on copy and retain.

Create a Custom Class

① Create a new project in Xcode by using the Window Application template.

② Click File→New File.

③ Click Cocoa Touch Class and then click the Objective-C class.

④ Click Next.

A dialog box appears with a pre-selected file name.

⑤ Name the file MyNewClass.m and then save it.

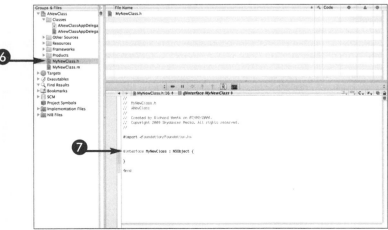

⑥ Click the MyNewClass.h header file to load it in Xcode.

⑦ Locate the @interface statement, which holds the new class attributes.

Note: *By default, new classes are defined as a subclass of Cocoa's master* NSObject *class. To declare your class as a subclass of a different object, change the class name here.*

8 Add code to declare two `ints`.

9 Add code to declare a class method to print the class name.

10 Add code to declare a collection of object methods.

Note: This example includes a new `init` method, which overrides the default `init` method included in `NSObject`.

11 Optionally, use the `@property` directive to declare the two `ints` as class attributes, making them visible to other objects.

12 Click MyNewClass.m.

13 Add a `@synthesize` directive for each class property.

14 Add code to implement the `printClassName` method.

15 Add code to implement the custom `init` method.

16 Add code to implement the `setfirstInt`, `setsecondInt`, and `sum OfTwoInts` methods defined in the class header.

Note: Every method declared in a class header must have a corresponding implementation. If you are not yet ready to write a full implementation, a stub — an empty named code block — is sufficient.

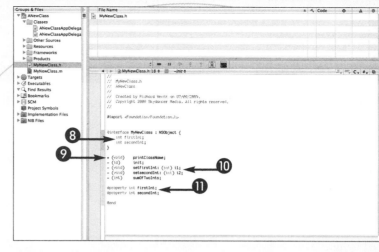

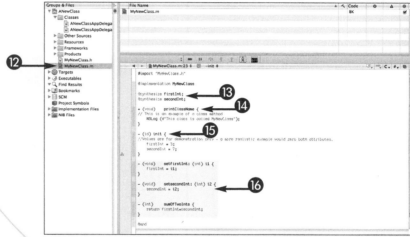

Extra

The relationship between accessors and properties can seem confusing. Writing an explicit method to access every variable seems wasteful. A simpler solution is to declare variables as properties in the header and then add a convenient Objective-C directive called `@synthesize` to the implementation. This automatically generates setter and getter code for properties.

After a `@synthesize` directive, you can use simple assignments to read and set the property. You do not need to create explicit setter and getter methods. You can also use the familiar dot syntax from traditional C-type languages. For example:

```
myObject.property
```

becomes equivalent to

```
[myobject property]
```

Explicit setter and getter implementations are best reserved for cases where accessing an attribute triggers extra code, such as a complex initialization sequence that does not need to be visible to the rest of your application.

Work with Messages

Y ou can use messages to create, control, and delete objects in your application as well as to read and set their attributes. When you send a message to an object, the object looks for a method in its class definition with a matching name. If it finds a match, it runs the method. If there is no matching method, your application crashes.

Messages are similar to named function calls, but they emphasize the object-oriented nature of Objective-C. Code does not run sequentially but rather in blocks that are triggered by user actions as well as by application states and events. The syntax for sending a message to an object is [object message];. If the message returns a result, you can assign it in the usual way:

```
result = [object messageThatGeneratesAResult];
```

Messages can also be nested:

```
[object1[object2messageThatGeneratesAResult]];
```

If there are parameters, the syntax uses colons to separate them:

```
[object parameterOne:dataOne
 parameterTwo:dataTwo];
```

Many Cocoa calls use complex nested messages or long chains of parameters. It is good practice to enhance readability by splitting these so there are never more than two messages on a line.

An object can send messages to itself by using self:

```
[self someMessage];
```

This triggers the someMessage method in the calling object. This is widely used, especially in interface programming. An object can also send a message to its super object by using super:

```
[super someMessage];
```

This sends someMessage to the object above self in the object hierarchy.

Work with Messages

Note: *This example uses the* MyNewClass *definition from the preceding spread and adds code to test the features of the new class to the application delegate file. The tests run as soon as the application loads.*

❶ Click ANewClassAppDelegate.m.

❷ Add a #import directive to add the features of MyNewClass to the code.

❸ Add code to the applicationDid FinishLaunching method already included in the template to test the printClassName class method.

❹ Add code to create an instance of the MyNewClass object.

❺ Add code to allocate memory for the new object and then initialize it with the custom init method.

Note: *This line uses standard boilerplate code. Use equivalent code whenever you create and initialize objects.*

❻ Add code to use NSLog to display the result of calling the sumOfTwoInts method on myObject by using the default parameter values set by init.

Note: `[NSString stringWithFormat:]`; *is the Cocoa method used to create a formatted string.*

7 Add code to demonstrate how to set values by using the explicit setter methods defined in `MyNewClass` and then print the sum to the console.

8 Add code to demonstrate how to set values by using synthesized properties and then print the sum.

9 Click Build and Run to compile the application and install it in the Simulator.

10 Click Run→Console to display the console.

11 Review the output of the application in the console window.

The results of the test messages sent to `MyNewClass` and `myObject` appear in the window.

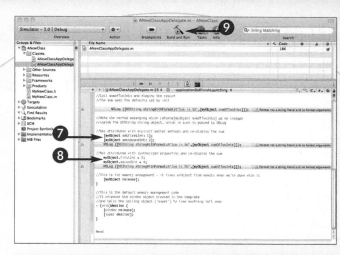

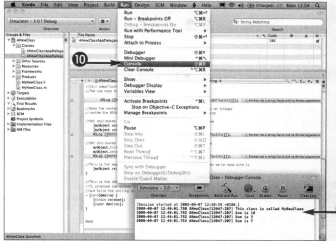

Extra

One of the most powerful features of Objective-C is runtime flexibility. Method calls do not have to be fixed. They can be selected at runtime by using a *selector*, which works like a pointer to a method or an indirect function call. For example:

```
[self performSelector
  @selector(someMethodName)];
```

This calls `someMethodName`.

You can also use a string to choose a selector:

```
[self performSelector:
  NSSelectorFromString(someString)];
```

This calls whichever method name is stored in `someString`.

Class attributes can be accessed by name by using *key-value coding* (KVC). A selection of KVC methods are available for use with any Cocoa object. For example:

```
[object valueForKey:@"someAttribute"];
```

This returns the value of `someAttribute` by using the `valueForKey` method. Similarly:

```
[object setValue:@"thisIsMyNewValue"
  forKey:@"someAttribute"];
```

This sets `someAttribute` to `thisIsMyNewValue` by using the `setValue:forKey:` method. KVC is generic, and you can set any attribute in a class as long as it has a name. You do not need to define a setter or getter method or declare it as a property.

Introducing Frameworks, Foundations, and Layers

You can use the code libraries built into the iPhone OS to communicate with the OS and to add special features to your applications. The code libraries are split into groups called *layers*. Layers are literal layers of software and features that were added as the Mac and iPhone operating systems evolved. Because each layer was added at a different time, there is no standardization. As a developer, you must use different coding techniques and programming models to access the features in each layer.

Each layer provides access to a unique collection of iPhone features. For example, the Cocoa Touch Layer manages the user interface and links your application with important system events. The Core OS Layer provides a selection of low-level Unix operating system calls and includes basic math functions and data networking features.

Frameworks

Each layer is split into frameworks. For example, the Cocoa Touch Layer includes the UIKit framework that manages the interface, the Message UI framework that can send email from the iPhone, and others. Each framework uses its own exclusive collection of data structures and data types. For example, the CGPoint data type in the Core Graphics framework stores a pair of coordinates that define a screen position.

The framework system can appear confusing initially, but in reality, it is easy to navigate. An obvious but useful orientation aid is each feature in a framework starts with the same two-letter abbreviation. For example, CG is used for all the data types and features of the Core Graphics framework and UI for all UIKit features. The one exception to the rule is the Foundation framework, which uses the NS two-letter code as an abbreviation for NeXTSTEP.

Using Frameworks

Frameworks are not standardized. Different frameworks use different programming models, and they also manage data in different ways. For example, all the Cocoa Touch frameworks use the class and messaging model built into Objective-C. To access Cocoa Touch features, your application creates and deletes Cocoa objects and communicates with them by sending and receiving messages. The Core OS System framework is more primitive and uses traditional C-language function calls.

To include the features of a framework in your own applications, you must read the documentation to find the right programming model. You must add the framework to your project — typically by right-clicking on Frameworks in Xcode and then choosing Add→Existing Frameworks from the pop-up menu — and you must also add #import directives to make sure that the relevant headers for each framework are loaded into Xcode. For example, to use the UIKit framework, you must add a #import <UIKit/UIKit.h> statement to at least one file in your project.

Overlapping Frameworks

There is a certain amount of overlap between the features and data types used in different frameworks. A particular source of confusion is the relationship between the Foundation and Core Foundation frameworks.

For example, the NSString data type is used in the Foundation framework to store and manipulate strings. It appears very similar to the CFString data type available in

the Core Foundation framework, but there are important differences. Although many of the features of NSString and CFString are related, NSString is more sophisticated and offers more features. It also includes convenient memory management options. As a rule, you should use Foundation data types and objects where possible. However, in some applications, the low-level Core Foundation functions may provide a more efficient solution.

The Cocoa Touch Layer

The most obvious feature of the Cocoa Touch Layer is the UIKit framework. This is one of the key iPhone libraries and is responsible for managing visible objects on the iPhone's display as well as for taking photos with the built-in camera. The framework includes object definitions that match the objects available in Interface Builder and can be grouped on the display when designing an application interface.

The Game Kit framework in Cocoa Touch adds networking features to an application by using the Bluetooth protocol. It was developed for peer-to-peer gaming but can be used for general-purpose data sharing. It can also provide direct voice communication between two or more iPhones for short-range walkie-talkie communication or in-game chat.

Other frameworks in the Cocoa Touch Layer include Map Kit, which enables your application to embed and work with Google Maps; Message UI, which creates and sends email messages; and Address Book UI, which makes it possible to read information from the iPhone's Address Book contacts database and copy it to tables, lists, or other interface objects.

The Media Layer

The Media Layer offers a mix of media frameworks that can create custom animations and playback and record audio and video. The OpenGL ES framework is ideal for custom animations, including games that rely on perspective shifts, fast animations, morphing objects, or other advanced game graphics. The simpler Quartz Core framework is better suited to simpler object animations, such as screen flips and button bounces. It can also be used for simple tile-based or sprite-based game design.

The Core Graphics framework is designed for general color control, PDF rendering, gradient and path-based graphics, and very simple image output, including support for basic image files, fonts, and text effects.

The Core Audio framework handles basic audio recording and playback on the iPhone. There is also a separate Audio Toolbox framework for streamed audio, including basic support for streamed data types. The Audio Unit framework supports the development of audio processing plug-ins and effects.

The Core Services Layer

The Core Services Layer features the Foundation and Core Foundation frameworks that add useful low-level data management features to the iPhone, including support for complex data types, such as arrays, trees, strings, dates, character sets, time zones, URLs, and others. It also features Dictionaries, which provide simple management of data objects associated with named keys.

This layer implements direct access to the Address Book database through the Address Book framework. It also features the Core Location framework, which interfaces with the iPhone's GPS receiver, and the Store Kit framework, making it possible to sell content from a server via the App Store.

The Core OS Layer

The Core OS Layer includes a collection of low-level frameworks. The System framework provides access to the underlying Unix features of the iPhone OS and includes useful basic math library functions, such as trig features and simple random numbers. The Security framework manages the iPhone's keychain and can also provide crypto-ready random number generation.

The CFNetwork framework manages low-level access to networking services, including web, FTP, and Bonjour services, and BSD socket connections. Finally, the External Accessory framework manages direct hardware access to custom-designed accessories for the iPhone that connect via Bluetooth or the external 30-pin connector.

Master the Apple Developer Documentation

You can use the Developer Documentation to understand how to add features from the various Apple frameworks to your application. Being able to use the documentation effectively is critical to iPhone development. It provides a master reference for all iPhone OS features and includes links to sample code and introductory tutorials on all aspects of iPhone development.

To open the documentation window, choose Help→Developer Documentation in Xcode. From Xcode 3.2 onward, documentation appears in a browser-like window. You can click the Bookmarks button to create a list of bookmarks for browsing.

The documentation includes three elements: the iPhone OS Library, the Max OS X Library, and the Xcode Developer Tools Library. You can choose them from the Home drop-down menu at the top of the Documentation window.

The iPhone OS Library is the definitive guide for iPhone development. The Xcode Developer Tools Library offers useful information about Xcode under the Tools link, but most of the other information is optional. The Mac OS X Library is largely redundant for iPhone developers.

The most productive way to approach the documentation is to first find the framework that includes the feature(s) you are planning to add to your application. If a Framework Reference is available, select it to find the classes, protocols, and functions included in the framework. Review the Class and Protocol references to find the specific item in the framework that matches your requirement. You can then add relevant objects and method calls to your application by copying their syntax from the reference.

Master the Apple Developer Documentation

① Choose Help→Developer Documentation to open the documentation window.

② If the iPhone Reference Library page is not visible, choose iPhone OS 3.0 Library from the Home drop-down menu.

③ Scroll down to view a full list of Topics, Frameworks, Tools, and Resource Types in the left-hand pane.

Note: *You can also use the quick summary links in the main Reference Library overview pane.*

④ Optionally, explore the Getting Started, Required Reading, and Featured panes to reveal introductory essays.

⑤ Click the Cocoa Touch Layer link to view a list of relevant documentation for this layer.

⑥ Click the Title, Resource Type, Topic, Subtopic, Framework, and Date headers to sort the list of topics and subtopics by using various ordering criteria.

⑦ Click the Details radio button to show short summaries for each topic and deselect it to hide them.

⑧ Find the ABPeoplePickerNavigation Controller Class Reference and then click it.

⑨ Review the summary box for information about the AbPeoplePickerNavigation Controller class and its relationship to other files and classes.

Note: *In addition to the key details listed here, some classes also include useful links to sample code and companion guides in this summary box.*

⑩ Review the class Overview for a brief text description of the features and functions of the class.

⑪ Review the Tasks section to view the definitive list of properties and methods for the class.

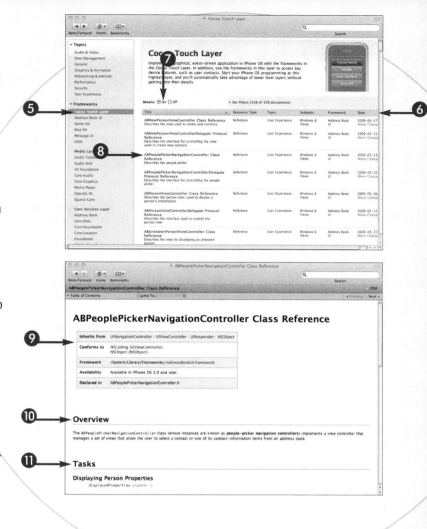

You do not have to use the search or browse options to find symbol details. The documentation includes useful shortcuts for quick access. To search for documentation for a symbol, right-click on it and then choose Find Text In Documentation from the pop-up menu to run a search. The results appear automatically. The equivalent keyboard shortcut is Command+Option, followed by double-clicking the symbol.

You can also press Option and then double-click the symbol to reveal a floating Quick Help summary window. It shows a single-line description of the symbol, its syntax, and a list of links to related symbols, with further links to sample code where available. The Quick Help window remains open until you close it. To update it with information for a different symbol, double-click the symbol. A dual-monitor system is indispensable for development. You can use one monitor to display code in the Xcode window and another to display documentation. Unfortunately, from Xcode 3.2 onward, you no longer have the option to view multiple documentation windows at once.

Developing iPhone Applications

The iPhone is not a desktop computer, and it is limited in obvious ways. However, it is unexpectedly powerful in other ways. Some developers emphasize the limitations, but you can turn them into benefits by creating a compelling and satisfying experience for users. Capturing user interest and enthusiasm is a key goal of application design on the iPhone. You do this by creating applications that are useful, elegant, creative, and exceptionally easy to understand.

Design for Clarity

Because the iPhone is not a desktop platform, the interface cannot support standard desktop software features. Instead, you can use the features in Xcode and Interface Builder to create minimal but powerful interface designs for your applications. Apple's built-in applications are good examples. They offer users a clearly stated benefit and present a concise list of features in straightforward and intuitive ways. Your applications should follow the same design principles.

An ideal iPhone application does not need a manual. Key features should be clearly visible and easy to understand. It is not always possible to create this level of simplicity, and a single help page may be necessary. However, if your users cannot immediately understand your application's key features, consider simplifying the design.

Create Beauty

iPhone applications should have a simple, clean interface that is pleasing to look at. Even if you are not artistically gifted, you can improve the visual impact of any application with simple but effective enhancements. If you are using standard Cocoa Touch interface elements, arrange them on the iPhone's display to maximize symmetry and proportion. If you are using custom design elements, add rounded glassy buttons or subtle reflective highlights. Aim for a unified and consistent visual style.

For more creative projects, consider delegating some or all of the visual design to a professional artist or designer. Do not underestimate the value of visual elegance on the iPhone, especially in comparison with other platforms. A modest application with strong graphics will be at least as successful as a more powerful application with a confusing interface and a mediocre look and feel.

Devise a Plan

Making a detailed plan of your application before you begin coding can simplify and speed up the development process. Include a mockup or sketch of the main interface elements and a diagram of their relationships. Make a list of the different screens that will appear, and define how your user will navigate through them. Do not design the implementation at this stage. Concentrate on minimizing the number of screens, and sketch a simple and clear interface for each screen. Iterate this stage until your application is as uncluttered as possible.

Do not start sketching class definitions or writing code until you are sure you have optimized your design. Once you have sketched the interface, you can use it to define which code blocks you will need and how they will respond to each other. Sketch out the data structures and classes you will use as well as the methods and protocols associated with them.

Once your skeleton is complete, create headers and implementation outlines in Xcode and then fill in the remaining code. Never begin coding from the bottom up without a clear structure or plan.

Develop for the iPad

The iPad environment is slightly richer and more complex. It offers simplified handling of touch gestures and more options for interface design. However, the rest of the programming model remains unchanged, and the development workflow is largely unchanged. For more, see Appendix C.

The Application Sandbox

An iPhone application runs in its own sandbox, with limited memory and a local file system. This memory area is strictly private. Application data and methods cannot be shared, and applications do not have access to each other's file areas. This makes the iPhone a secure platform but complicates development. The sandbox model abstracts the file system for each application. Applications do not have direct access to the iPhone's directory tree. Read and write operations are only allowed to a single unique document directory, which is accessed indirectly through operating system calls, and to select iPhone data, such as the Address Book.

For the developer, the iPhone programming model assumes task switching rather than full multi-tasking. Only one application can run at a time. An incoming phone call or text message can suspend an application temporarily, but this feature is reserved for the iPhone operating system. Your application cannot suspend another application. However, applications can start multiple independent threads; for details, see Chapter 9.

Limited Interaction

Although applications are isolated from each other, a work-around is available. Very limited messaging and file sharing are available through a strictly limited set of Cocoa calls. These messages can switch execution to a second application and then send it a limited block of data. Unfortunately, there is no simple return facility. This feature is limited to simple task-switching operations, such as launching the Safari browser with a custom URL just before your application quits. However, you can use this *URL scheme* feature to pass information to a second application or to a dedicated web server. For more on URL schemes, see Chapter 10.

Cocoa Touch includes interface objects that can read or write some but not all of the user data stored in Apple's own applications. Not all applications are equally accessible. Calendar data is not accessible at all, but Address Book data — the database managed by the Contacts application — includes a sophisticated API for reading, editing, adding, and removing entries.

Application Bundles

An application bundle includes all the code, support graphics, sounds, plists, and settings that are used by the application. Bundles are created automatically when you develop your application in Xcode.

Bundles also include a digital signature. This is created during development and distribution. It locks the application so it cannot be modified or copied to a different phone.

You can examine the contents of any application on your iPhone by synchronizing your iPhone to iTunes to back it up and then selecting the Applications tab under Library.

Right-click on an application and then choose Show in Finder. You will see a list of application files with the .ipa extension. Copy one or more of these to a different folder.

The .ipa format is a renamed .zip file. Rename the extension to .zip and then use Stuffit Expander or an equivalent application to extract the contents. You will see graphics and sound files, application resources — including .nib Interface Builder files — and other information. This content is copyrighted, so you are not allowed to use it in your own projects, but you can examine it for insights into the creation of another application.

Understanding Design Patterns

You can use *design patterns* to simplify development by solving problems in standardized ways to create code that is easy to understand, maintain, and reuse. Certain design patterns are built into Cocoa and Cocoa Touch. For example, Apple's Interface Builder application relies on a design pattern called Model-View-Controller (MVC). It also uses a pattern called Delegation. You can override these patterns in your own custom code or ignore them altogether. You will usually find that development goes more smoothly and successfully if you follow these patterns.

Using Design Patterns

Initially, design patterns can seem like wasted effort — which adds extra complication — but with experience, you will find that problems break down naturally into sections. This makes development simpler. You can limit your attention to smaller blocks of code with clean interfaces. You can also create code that can be recycled or repurposed more easily. Many iPhone applications use boilerplate code that can be copied and reused between applications. This is particularly true of interface development; for example, the same basic interface skeleton can be reused for a series of games. With design patterns, you can avoid code that is difficult to read and understand.

This does not mean that design patterns are the definitive top-level key to iPhone development. Design patterns are helpful coding models. They offer useful guidelines that are closely related to some of the features of the iPhone's development environment. However, to develop successfully on the iPhone, you also need to have a good understanding of the iPhone's other features, including the object hierarchy built into Cocoa Touch, the resource hierarchy, the view system, and the messaging and event system.

Delegation

Instead of subclassing an object to implement new methods, you can forward messages to an associated object called a *delegate*. The delegate implements a *protocol* — a list of optional methods for which you can write your own custom code. If you do not add custom code to implement a method, it is ignored. The delegate can be any object, but for convenience, it is often `self` — and delegation is used as an indirect way to add optional methods to an existing object. Delegate methods typically add optional features; for example, you can use them to include code that runs just before or just after a significant event or user action, such as a tap on the screen, a screen update, or a handset rotation. A standard example is the application delegate, which is included as a file in most of the Xcode application templates. This delegate handles top-level, application-specific messages, such as `applicationDidFinishLaunching`. If you add code to the `applicationDidFinishLaunching` method, this code runs as soon as the application starts. A key point is that some objects do not function correctly unless one or more essential delegate methods are implemented.

To use a delegate effectively, you must know the full list of messages included in its associated protocol. The examples in the application templates do not include every possible message and cannot be used as a reference. You can find detailed information about delegate options and protocols in Apple's documentation.

Model-View-Controller

The Model-View-Controller (MVC) design pattern is an important feature of development on both Mac and iPhone platforms, but it is not always obvious how you should use the design pattern in practice.

On the iPhone, the MVC pattern means the iPhone display is handled by two kinds of objects — *view objects* that appear on the screen and *controller objects* that manage them. View objects are the visible view element of MVC. Controller objects create the controller element. They work behind the scenes in code.

When a user touches view objects, they send messages to the iPhone's operating system. Controller objects respond to these messages and process them. They can also send messages back to the view objects to update their appearance.

The model is the rest of the application and includes the underlying data structures and application logic. All persistent data belong in the model. It is the application's core database and data processor.

In the MVC design pattern, a model and a view never communicate directly. Messages and data are always routed through a controller, which translates them.

A key benefit of MVC is data abstraction. The view does not need to understand the model's data structures or access them directly. This makes it possible to create generic views, such as lists and tables, which can be reused between applications with only minor changes. Another key benefit is efficiency. A view can and should show a small subset of the underlying model data. This is perhaps the simplest way to understand MVC. A web browser (view) does not attempt to display the entire Internet (model).

Similarly, some Cocoa objects recycle views, such as table cells, to save memory. Using MVC, it is possible to display a table with tens of thousands of entries using a handful of recycled visible objects that are refreshed dynamically as the table scrolls. This is far more efficient than pre-allocating a view for every entry and keeping all the views in memory simultaneously. A common error is to assume that model, view, and controller code should be split into separate files or classes. This is ideal but not always possible. In a very simple application, model data is often managed directly from within controller objects. Creating and maintaining separate classes adds development overhead. The benefits of separate classes with clean interfaces become more obvious on larger, more complex applications.

Target-Action

Target-Action means that when an event such as a button tap occurs, it can select an *action* — that is, trigger a method — in a *target object*. You can use target-action in two ways. When you design an interface using Interface Builder, you connect events to actions as well as actions and objects by dragging links between them.

However, you can also set or change targets and actions for certain objects directly from code. To set an action, use a *selector* — a standard Objective-C data type that specifies a method call. Typical code looks like this:

```
[anInterfaceObject setTarget: anotherObject];
[anInterfaceObject setAction:
  @selector(aMethod)];
```

When the user interacts with `anInterfaceObject`, it triggers `aMethod` in `anotherObject`.

A key benefit is that you can change targets and actions at any time. However, more advanced techniques are possible. For example, a function called `NSSelectorFromString:` converts any string into a selector. You can use this feature to convert button labels or other visible text directly into a selector. Actions must be implemented; in this example, if `aMethod` is not implemented in `anotherObject`, the application crashes. Also, `aMethod` and `aMethod:` are not identical. The latter takes a parameter; the former does not. In Objective-C, these methods are completely distinct.

Managed Memory Model

The iPhone does not include *garbage collection* — automated memory management. Memory for objects must be allocated and released explicitly. On the iPhone, this is done by counting references to each object. The count is managed semiautomatically. You do not have to manage a counter for each object, but you must always include memory management methods that maintain the count accurately. Memory management is described in detail later in this chapter.

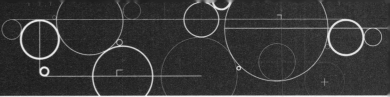

Introducing
Interface Builder

A Document Window

The Document window lists the objects in this nib interface file. Right-clicking on or double-clicking any object displays event and messaging links to and from the object.

B View Window

The View window displays a preview of your iPhone interface. Drag objects from the Library window to add them to your interface design. Drag them within the View window to reposition them.

C Interface Objects in a View

Edit objects by selecting them. Right-clicking on them reveals outlets and events for linking by using Interface Builder's link tools.

D Selected Object

Select an object by clicking it. In interfaces with multiple layers, you may need to click and hold to drill down through the interface layers to select an object. A selected object displays its properties in the Attributes window.

E The Inspector Window

The Inspector window has four selection tabs — from left to right, Attributes, Connections, Size, and Identity. Use them to view object attributes and traits, link objects, set object size and position, and define miscellaneous class information. Click the tabs to display information panes relevant to each feature. The name at the top of the Inspector window always shows the selected item.

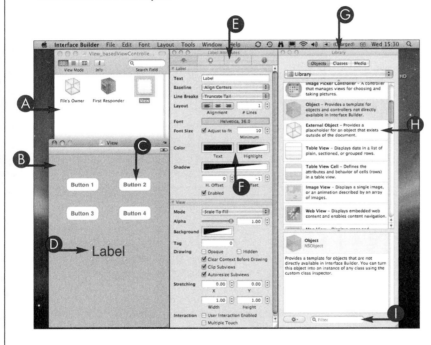

F Object Attributes

Attributes define display options for an object, including color, transparency, justification, and shadow. Each object type has different attributes.

G The Library Window

The Library window displays the object, class, and media libraries. The object library lists all standard Cocoa Touch interface objects, object controller classes, and custom interface objects. The class library lists every class in the application. The media library displays custom graphics, icons, and other media resources.

H Library Objects

Scroll through the Library to review the list of objects and to see a brief description of each one. Drag objects from the Library to the Document window or View window to add them to a design.

I Library Options

Use the Filter control to find by name or by searching for keywords in a description. Click the Settings icon to display verbose or terse object descriptions and to add or remove custom objects from the Library.

Introducing Nib Design in Interface Builder

Y ou can use Interface Builder to design the visual interface for your application. By convention, the files created in Interface Builder are called nib files, even though the extension is .xib and the format is XML. They are part of your application's file bundle. You can view them by clicking your application's Resources folder icon in Xcode. Interface Builder is not a complete visual development tool, and it does not produce the code for a skeleton application. Developing an interface on the iPhone is a complex process with many stages, and Interface Builder and Xcode are used equally. For clarity, follow this summary:

- Create an application skeleton in Xcode, either from a template or manually. You will need an application delegate and at least one controller class.

- Add IBOutlet and IBAction definitions to your controller class. These create placeholder objects and methods that can be linked to messages and objects in your interface.
- Load Interface Builder and then lay out a selection of objects from the library to create an interface. Add controller objects and then assign your controller class(es) to them.
- Create links in Interface Builder to the IBOutlet and IBAction definitions in your code.
- Save the interface as a nib file.
- Load Xcode and then add the rest of the application logic.

Each item is described in detail in the remainder of this chapter.

Understanding Nib Loading

When a nib file loads, it creates instances of the objects inside it. The main application nib is loaded automatically. When you create a new project, Xcode automatically creates a main nib file with the same name as your application. Optionally, you can load a different nib by changing the Main nib file base name field of the application's plist.

You will usually include at least one controller object in the main nib. Typically, this is an instance of a UIViewController object. When a UIViewController object loads, it attempts to find and load another nib with the same instance name. For example, MyViewController will look for MyViewController.nib. This nib file can contain further view controller objects in turn. Potentially, you can extend this hierarchy indefinitely, adding as many UIViewController objects and their corresponding nibs as your application requires.

Lazy Loading

Optionally, you can also load nib files under program control. It is good practice to load nibs only when they are needed and to unload them when they are not visible. This is called lazy loading and uses memory efficiently. For an example, see Chapter 4.

Introducing
Windows and Views

You can use views to manage user interaction and to split your application into functionally distinct pages. Only one view is visible at a time. When the user selects a different view, the old view disappears and a new view replaces it. This is called *view switching*.

You use *view objects* to create a view. Plain and color backgrounds, images, maps, tables, text panels, scrolling areas, and embedded web pages are available in the Interface Builder Library. You can add further interactivity with buttons, sliders, and other objects from the Library.

You can add a tab bar or toolbar view object at the bottom of the screen to your interface or a navigation bar at the top to allow users to switch views. You can also allow users to switch views by dragging a finger or by shaking or rotating the iPhone.

View Trees and Subviews in Interface Builder

Views are arranged in *view trees*. These include a root view object that creates a background canvas for the view and other visible interface objects, such as buttons, sliders, text, and so on. You can add other objects to the tree by dragging them from Interface Builder's Library and dropping them on the view object. Objects in a tree appear indented. The list is drawn from the bottom up, so objects at the bottom of the list appear to cover the objects above them. You can change the draw order in Interface Builder by dragging objects up and down the list.

As you design your view, drag these objects onto a view object to create a tree. You can edit their size, position, and other properties to create an aesthetic design. The view tree is often saved as a separate nib file to allow lazy loading.

To create *subviews* — views below the current view in the hierarchy — add further view objects to the top-level view. For example, you can add a collection of UIImageView objects to display custom tiles or player tokens in a game. Clipping, transparency, and dynamic resizing of view objects are all supported. You can also manage view switching with subviews; for example, a menu view object can remain on-screen while subviews are switched behind it.

Windows and Views

Every iPhone application must include one instance of a UIWindow object at the top of the Interface Builder object tree. This window does not appear on the screen, but it creates the software framework that draws and manages view trees. All Xcode application templates include a window with prewritten code to manage it. If you use a template, your code does not need to manage the window directly.

Interface Builder Object Messages and Traits

Interface objects, including buttons, labels, sliders, and switches, offer a collection of 17 preset messages. Whenever the user interacts with an object, the interface generates one of these messages automatically. Typically, your code only needs to respond to one or two messages from each object — for example, TouchDown from a button object, which is sent when the user touches a button. Other messages can be ignored.

All visible objects have a list of associated properties called *traits*. Your application can update any visible object's appearance by changing its properties. You can also initialize traits to useful defaults in the Inspector window in Interface Builder.

Introducing the Screen

The screen of the current version of the iPhone and iPod touch is 320 × 480 pixels in the default portrait mode and 480 × 320 pixels in landscape. The iPad screen is 768 × 1024 pixels. Apple offers design guidelines for the size and position of menu, status, and navigation items within this area. You should follow these guidelines because users expect them and are already familiar with them.

In both portrait and landscape modes, point 0,0 is at the top left of the screen. The x-coordinate increases to the right of the screen. Less conventionally, the y-coordinate increases toward the bottom of the screen. Coordinates are floating point numbers, not integers. x,y coordinate pairs use the `CGPoint` data type from the Core Graphics framework — a key library of iPhone graphics functions.

Views have local coordinates. The `UIView` class includes convenient translation methods that can convert between local view coordinates and the background view. You can use the `pointInside` method to check if a given coordinate is inside a given view.

The OpenGL ES graphics subsystem uses different coordinates. Point 0,0 is at the bottom left of the screen. You can combine OpenGL ES and Core Graphics in a single application, but maintaining two different coordinate systems can become a challenge, so applications should typically exclusively use one system.

Screen Standards

The dimensions for applications include a status bar and a navigation bar at the top of the screen, an application area in the middle of the screen, and a toolbar or tab bar at the bottom. These areas have standard sizes. The status bar is 20 pixels high, and the navigation bar is 44 pixels. In portrait mode, the application area is 372 pixels high. In landscape mode, this is 212 pixels. The lower toolbar/tab area is another 44 pixels. You will find it useful to take screenshots of standard interfaces and use them as templates for your own interface designs.

Rotation and Auto-Rotation

When the user rotates the iPhone, the operating system sends a message to your application. You can ignore these messages and support only the standard portrait orientation — except on the iPad, where all orientations must be supported. If you implement rotation, you can use the auto-resize options in Interface Builder or you can create a custom view that is swapped in for each rotation. Apple's guidelines suggest that inverted portrait mode should not be used on the iPhone because users may be confused when an incoming call arrives. For more, see Chapter 4.

Screen Sizes

In theory, all applications should be able to work at arbitrary resolutions and screen dimensions. In practice, this is difficult to achieve, and the user benefits will not be obvious on current hardware.

A more practical strategy is to develop your application for the standard screen size, but you should make the interface modular enough to allow for a fast redesign. Current screen dimensions can be read as properties of the `UIWindow` object or included as constants in the code with a single declaration point.

The iPad supports dual screens. It also features a new `UIScreen` class, which can be used to read screen dimensions.

Create a Hello World Application

Y ou can use the Xcode View-based Application template to explore nib design and begin creating your own views. The template includes boilerplate code and sample nib resources. When you create a new project by using this template, Xcode automatically creates the files for a complete skeleton application.

You can compile and run this skeleton application successfully without editing it. It does very little but includes all the key building blocks for a complete view-based application.

The skeleton includes a delegate file, a view controller, associated headers, and two nibs. The nibs include an application window, a view controller, and a view tree. Instances of a window and view controller object appear in the main nib. A minimal view tree with a single view object is included in the second nib.

Two nibs may seem redundant and unnecessary for a simpl application. But this template is a practical example of the MVC design pattern. The view controller owns the second nib. It loads it automatically after the controller is loaded from the main nib and then displays the view inside it.

When you compile and run the template, it creates an empty view with a gray background. It does not respond to user actions.

To create a Hello World example, you can extend this blank application to display a line of text. You could do this unde program control. However, in this introductory example, you will use Interface Builder to modify one of the nib files

To add the text, drag a single `UILabel` object from Interface Builder's Library to add it to the second nib and then save the nib. When the application launches, your edited nib loads automatically. The new text appears on the iPhone's display on the original gray background.

Create a Hello World Application

① Create a new project in Xcode by using the View-based Application template and then name it HelloWorld.

Note: *See Chapter 1 for how to choose an application template.*

② In the Project window, click HelloWorld at the top left to reveal a list of project files.

③ Double-click HelloWorldViewController.xib to load the nib file in Interface Builder.

Note: *You can find the HelloWorld project on the website for this book: www.wiley. com/go/iphonedevelopmentvb.*

④ Click the Objects tab in the Library window in Interface Builder to reveal a list of interface objects.

Note: *If the Library window is not visible, you can reveal it by choosing Tools→Library.*

⑤ Scroll down to find the Label object.

⑥ Drag the Label object from the Library window and then place it on top of the View object in the Document window.

● You can also place it on top of the view.

The label is added to the view's view tree.

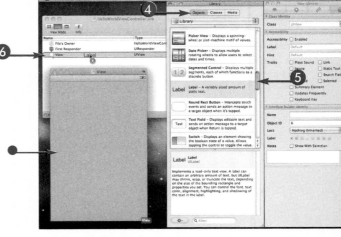

7 Double-click the Label object to make it editable.

8 Type in some arbitrary text, such as **Hello, World!**

9 Optionally, change the label's traits by clicking the Attributes tab in the Inspector window and then modifying any of the trait settings.

● For example, you can click the centering button in the Layout options to center text within a label. To change the font and size, click the Font field to display a font-editing window.

10 Save the nib file, but do not change its name.

11 In Xcode, click Build and Run to compile and run the application.

● The Simulator loads automatically, and the modified view with the new Hello, World! label appears on the display.

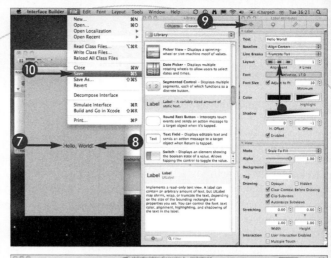

Apply It

To set an object's traits in Interface Builder, double-click the object in the Document window and then click the Attributes tab at the top left of the Inspector window. The object's traits appear, ready for editing. You can set traits for the UIView object in the same way — for example, to change the background color. You can change the size and color of the label, set different letter sizes and justification options, and define the maximum number of lines of visible text.

You can auto-center an object by clicking the Sizing tab in the Inspector window and then opening the View Size panel. Use the Placement options at the bottom of the panel to center an object horizontally or vertically. If you select a group of objects, you can use the Alignment options to align their centers. Top, center, and bottom alignment modes are available.

Design a View in Interface Builder

You can design a complex view in Interface Builder by adding a selection of objects from the Interface Builder Library window to the minimal default view included in Xcode's View-based Application template. This template includes two nibs. The main nib is a placeholder with a window object and a controller object that loads the second nib.

The second nib is the minimal default view. It includes a single `UIView` object set to display a plain gray background. Treat this view like a blank canvas. You can create a view design in Interface Builder by adding objects to it to create a view tree.

To add objects to a view tree, drop them on the root `UIView` object. When you release the mouse, the new object should appear indented under the root. If it is not indented, delete it and then try again. Otherwise, Interface Builder treats the dropped object as the root of a new tree. This changes the drawing order of all objects on the display and also modifies how they generate and handle messages.

A view tree works in a somewhat similar way to a Finder folder. The top-level object can be opened and closed in Interface Builder to show or hide the objects inside it. Do this by clicking the triangle icon next to the object. In a complex view, you can use this feature to save screen space and hide objects when you are not editing them.

You can nest view trees. This is useful when you design a view with subviews. Each subview can include an object tree of its own.

Design a View in Interface Builder

① Create a new project by using the View-based Application template and then name it DesignAView.

Note: *You can find the DesignAView project on the website for this book: www.wiley.com/go/iphonedevelopmentvb.*

② Double-click the view controller nib to load it in Interface Builder.

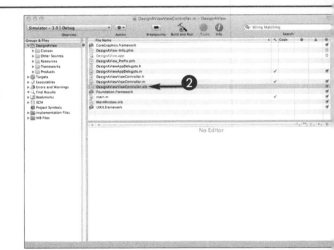

③ Drag and drop a Round Rect Button object from the Library to the view.

④ Double-click it and then label it Button 1.

⑤ Drag another Round Rect Button object to the view, double-click it, and then name it Button 2.

⑥ Use the alignment guide lines that appear to align it horizontally with the first button.

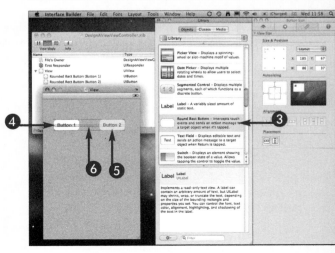

7 Shift+click Button 1 and Button 2 to select them.

8 Click the Sizing tab in the Inspector window and then click the horizontal alignment Placement option to center both buttons as a pair.

Note: *Click View Size under the Inspector window tabs if the Placement option is not visible.*

9 Press Option+click, drag, and release to copy the buttons, aligning them with the vertical guide lines.

10 Name the copies as Button 3 and Button 4.

11 Drag a Label object to the view, center it, and then give it any name.

12 Select the view tree in the Document window. All objects should be single-indented under the root view.

Note: *If an object is not indented, drag and drop it on top of the root View object.*

13 Save the nib file and then compile and run the application.

● The complete view appears in the Simulator. Buttons respond to clicks but are not yet linked to the application. The application ignores them.

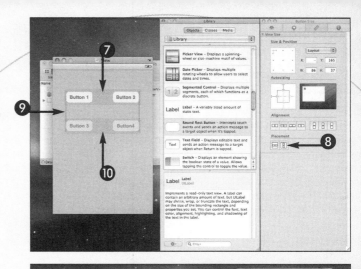

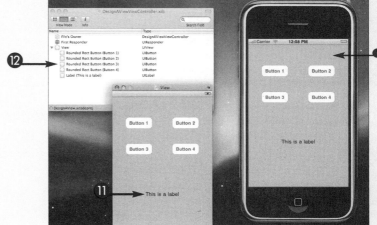

Define IBOutlets and IBActions in Xcode

You can create a view that is responsive by connecting objects in the view to methods and properties in your code. Creating connections is a complex process with at least three stages. You can begin this process by declaring *outlets* and *actions* in your code. Outlets link objects in code to objects in the interface, while actions link messages from the interface to methods in the code. When all the stages are complete, your application can recognize user actions and control the appearance of the objects in the view.

It would be logical to guess that because Interface Builder is a visual tool that it can output information about objects you add to a view and that Xcode can somehow capture this information and automatically generate declarations for them. In fact, the process is not automated at all. You must begin it in Xcode by manually

declaring the objects and methods that represent the view. When you next load Interface Builder, it scans your application for these declarations. When it finds them, it makes them available for *linking* — the process of connecting objects in the interface to outlets and actions. Until you create links and save them in the view's nib file, your application cannot communicate with the view. You must create these links manually by using linking tools included in Interface Builder.

The syntax for these declarations is standard Objective-C, with the difference that you must add an `IBOutlet` tag to declare a view object that will be changed or read by your application. Methods that handle messages from the view must be declared with the `IBAction` type. In this example, you add declarations to a simple application. The linking process is described in the next example.

Define IBOutlets and IBActions in Xcode

① Load an application with a completed view in Xcode.

Note: *You can reuse the application from the previous spread for this example.*

② Click Classes to reveal the application delegate and view controller files.

③ Click the View Controller header file.

● The contents of the file appear in the editing window.

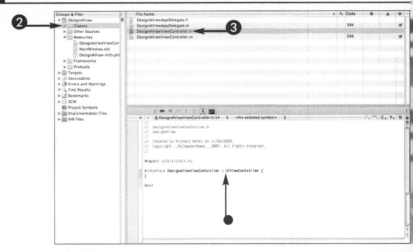

④ Add code to declare an outlet to a `UILabel` object.

⑤ Declare a named pointer to the object.

⑥ Add a property declaration for the label object and its pointer.

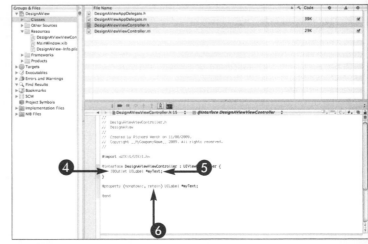

7 Add code to declare a new IBAction custom method.

8 Give the method a descriptive name and remember to add the (id) sender parameter.

Note: *The (id) sender parameter passes a pointer from the interface object touched by the user to the receiving method so the method can read and set its properties. This parameter should be included in every IBAction declaration.*

9 Save the header file.

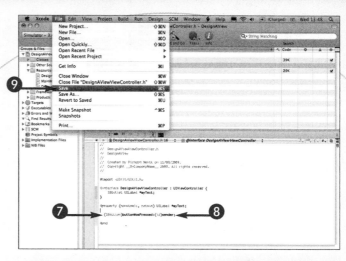

10 Click the implementation file for the view controller.

● The contents of the file appear in the editing window.

11 Add code to synthesize the name of the label object declared in the header.

12 Add a placeholder stub for the method handler.

13 Save the implementation file.

Object and method declarations are now ready for linking in Interface Builder.

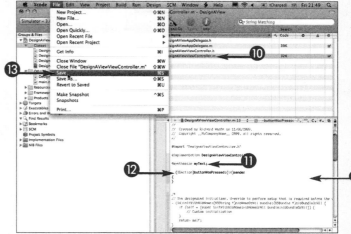

Extra

When declaring outlets, each live object in a view that you plan to control from your code must have a corresponding object declaration in the code. For example, if a view includes a label object, you must add a UILabel declaration; a slider object requires a UISlider declaration; and so on. You must also include a pointer with a unique and appropriate name to make the object's properties accessible.

Designing a view and connecting it to your code is a process that typically requires at least three stages. First, lay out the view in Interface Builder. Next, add method and property declarations to support it in Xcode. Then, return to Interface Builder to add links to them. If you sketch out your design beforehand, you may be able to avoid the first stage by making a list of objects and methods before you add them in Interface Builder. More realistically, you will iterate through the cycle as you develop and refine your interface.

Link Objects to Outlets in Interface Builder

You can use Interface Builder's link-making tools to make a view live and allow communication between view objects and your application code. Until you create links, your application cannot respond to user actions or update the appearance of view objects.

Begin by loading the nib file of an application with outlet and action declarations in Interface Builder. As Interface Builder loads the nib, it scans it for declarations.

To see a list of outlets, select a controller object in the Document window and then click the Connections tab in the Inspector. To add a link to an outlet, click the empty circle icon next to an outlet. Drag a line from the circle to one of the objects in your nib. When you release the mouse button, the outlet is linked to the object and the list in the Inspector window is updated.

To link an event to a method in your code, select an object that generates events, such as a button. A list of available events appears in the Connections window. Drag a link from an event to the object that includes the `IBAction` method declaration. Release the mouse. A list of the `IBAction` methods declared in the controller appears. Click a method to select it as the target for that action.

Your link target should be the nib's view controller. However, the view controller is usually in a different nib, so you must use the File's Owner icon as a stand-in. It is not a real object. It works as a convenient placeholder for the object that loaded the nib. Similarly, First Responder is a proxy for your application's responder chain. In a complex application, it offers a convenient single point of entry for messages sent from the view.

Link Objects to Outlets in Interface Builder

① Load an application with a completed view and outlet declarations in Xcode.

Note: You can reuse the application from the previous spread for this example.

② Double-click the view controller nib file to load it in Interface Builder.

Interface Builder pauses as it loads to scan the file for outlet declarations.

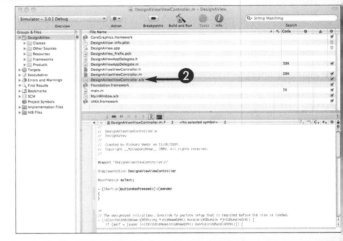

③ Click the List View Mode button in the Document window.

④ Click File's Owner.

⑤ Click the Connections tab in the Inspector window.

● The myText outlet and the buttonWasPressed: action declared in the code appear in the Inspector window, ready for linking.

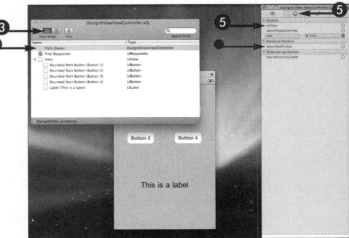

Note: *If the Connections tab is not selected in the Inspector window, click it to open it.*

6 Click the myText outlet and then drag a line to the UILabel object in the view window.

Note: *You can also drag the line to the label object icon and description in the Document window.*

7 Release the mouse.

● A link is created between the outlet and the label.

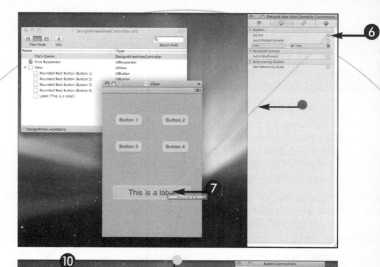

8 Click Button 1 in the Document window.

● A list of events that can be generated by the button appears in the Inspector window.

9 Click the circle next to the Touch Down event and then drag a link to File's Owner.

10 Release the mouse and then click the floating buttonWasPressed: target that appears.

11 Repeat these steps for Buttons 2, 3, and 4 and then save the nib file.

● The application and the view are now linked.

Note: *You can confirm the links by clicking File's Owner in the Document window and then clicking the Connections tab in the Inspector window to view the connections.*

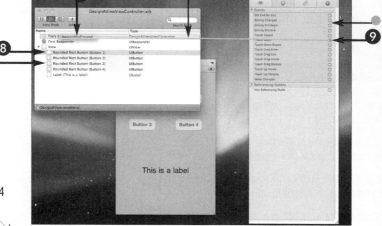

Extra

If your declarations do not appear in Interface Builder, check their syntax. Then, check them again against an application that is correct, such as an Apple example. Xcode does not always report syntax errors in outlet and action declarations, and Interface Builder always ignores declarations with errors.

When you change your class headers, you can sometimes load them into Interface Builder without restarting it by choosing File→Reload All Class Files. This feature often works but is not completely reliable.

You can see a list of available outlets and events for any object by right-clicking on it. This can be a useful shortcut when you are deleting a link. It is not so efficient when you are creating links because it does not display all the available outlets in a view. You must select the view controller or the File's Owner proxy to see all the outlets declared for the view.

Many objects use a standard list of events. For example, `TouchUpInside` is sent when a user releases a touch from an object, and `TouchDown` is sent as soon as a user touches an object.

Note: You can link more than one event to a method, but this is rarely useful or necessary.

Handle Messages from a View

You can create a finished user experience by adding message and object handlers to your code. Once you have linked your code and view, you can begin adding code that defines how your application responds when the user touches the objects on the screen and how it updates the view in response.

Typically, this means adding code to the IBAction methods declared in your view controller. This code updates the appearance of objects in the view and may also change data in your application's model.

Messages arrive at each IBAction method with an id(sender) object that includes information about the name and current state of the object that sent the

message. In a simple interface, you can assume that the object is in the normal state and read [sender titleForState:UIControlStateNormal]; to return the object's name. You can then add conditionals or switch statements so your application responds to each button in a different way. In a more complex interface, objects can be in the highlighted and selected states, and you must add extra code to handle each state differently.

All interface objects feature a rich set of properties that you can update. The full list for every object appears in its Class Reference documentation. You can use this information to update visible objects in creative ways to display a clear and intuitive interface.

Handle Messages from a View

① Load an application with outlet declarations and links in Xcode.

Note: *You can reuse the application from the previous spread for this example.*

② Double-click the ViewController.xib method file to load it in Interface Builder.

● The view controller code appears in the editing window.

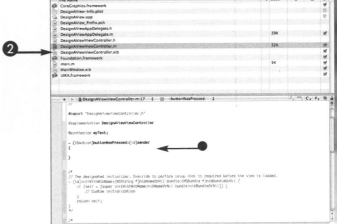

③ Add code to the IBAction stub to create a string to hold the received button label.

④ Add code to read the button label into the string.

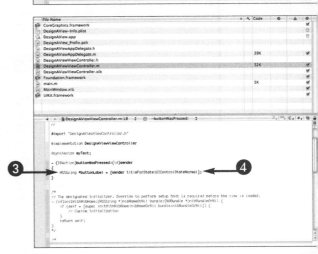

5 Add code to check if either Button 1 or Button 2 was pressed by reading the returned button label and then comparing it to test strings.

Note: *In Cocoa and Cocoa Touch, you must use* `isEqual:` *to compare strings.*

6 Add code to set the text property of the `myText` label with the name of the button and a brief message.

7 Add code to handle messages from the other two buttons and then update the label with a different message.

8 Click Build and Run to build and run the application and then confirm file saves when asked.

9 Click each button in the Simulator to test your application.

● Each button updates the label with a different message.

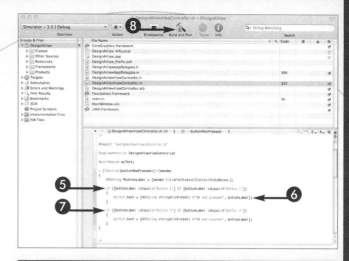

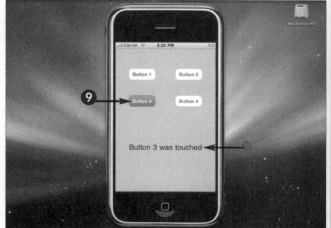

Extra

In this example, the four buttons in the view are linked to a single method. The method handles messages from all the buttons and chooses a response by reading the button name. It would be just as valid to add four separate methods and link each button to its own method in Interface Builder. The best approach to method management is the one that minimizes and simplifies the code.

If your application has distinct states or if the objects in it have distinct states, you can often simplify it by writing private custom methods for each state and including them in your controller object. First, add the following to the top of the implementation file, not the header:

```
@interface MyControllerName()
-(void)someMethodToSwitchToAState:aListofParameters;
@end
```

Next, write a full implementation elsewhere in the file. You can then call the method whenever you need it to update a set of objects when the state changes:

```
[self someMethodToSwitchToAState:someParameters];
```

Manage Memory Effectively

You can avoid application crashes by managing memory effectively. Memory management is not automated. Internally, the iPhone assigns a memory counter to each object. When the object is created or referenced, the counter is incremented. When an object is released, the counter is decremented. When the counter reaches zero, the object is destroyed, and its memory is released. If your application tries to reference the object again, it will crash.

Remember that object references are pointers, not memory blocks. Copying a pointer to another does not duplicate an object in memory. If the memory is released, both pointers become invalid. Use the alloc and copy methods to create an object and claim ownership. Use retain in your code to reference an object and release to release it. If your application is crashing, you may need to add extra retain statements. If you are not sure when an object will be released, use autorelease. This enables the operating system to release the object later. Avoid this if possible

because it creates a performance penalty and because objects can be released without notice.

To manage memory, balance every alloc and retain with a release. In practice, it is not always obvious when to release an object. For transient objects, such as alerts, call the release method immediately after the object appears. For persistent objects within a class, include a release for every object in a catchall dealloc method in the class implementation.

Your application must also include a memory warning message handler, which releases memory when the operating system requests it. At a minimum, you should implement a handler for the didReceiveMemoryWarning method in your application delegate.

The final memory management feature uses *convenience methods*. These create temporary objects without an alloc call that are managed and released automatically. You can use convenience methods for local variables and system objects but not for class properties.

Manage Memory Effectively

① Copy or make a note of all the objects declared at the start of a class implementation.

② Find the dealloc stub declared for the class.

Note: *This is included in the Xcode application templates. You will need to add it to your own custom classes.*

③ Paste the objects and then add a release message for every object.

④ Add the super dealloc method as a catchall for objects remaining in the superclass.

⑤ Add this code when you need to create an object by using the alloc method.

⑥ Balance the alloc with an immediate release as soon as the object is no longer needed.

⑦ Add this boilerplate code to release an old object and retain a new object whenever you declare a setter method for a custom class.

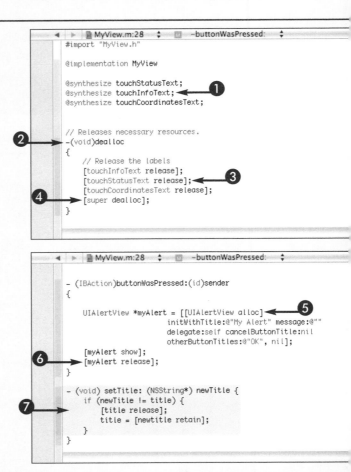

```
#import "MyView.h"

@implementation MyView

@synthesize touchStatusText;
@synthesize touchInfoText;                    ①
@synthesize touchCoordinatesText;

// Releases necessary resources.
-(void)dealloc                                ②
{
    // Release the labels
    [touchInfoText release];
    [touchStatusText release];                ③
    [touchCoordinatesText release];
    [super dealloc];                          ④
}
```

```
- (IBAction)buttonWasPressed:(id)sender
{
    UIAlertView *myAlert = [[UIAlertView alloc]    ⑤
                    initWithTitle:@"My Alert" message:@""
                    delegate:self cancelButtonTitle:nil
                    otherButtonTitles:@"OK", nil];
    [myAlert show];
    [myAlert release];                        ⑥
}
- (void) setTitle: (NSString*) newTitle {
    if (newTitle != title) {                  ⑦
        [title release];
        title = [newtitle retain];
    }
}
```

8 Add this standard code idiom to create a temporary object, such as an `UITouch` object, without an `alloc` call.

9 Add this standard method call — called a convenience method — whenever you need to create instances of any subclass of `NSObject`, such as `NSString`.

Note: Convenience objects are automatically added to the release pool and do not need a separate release call.

10 Add this boilerplate code to set up an auto-release pool for your application in `main()`.

Note: All Xcode application templates already include this code. If you are using a template, you do not need to add it again or modify it.

Objects in the auto-release pool are released just before the application quits.

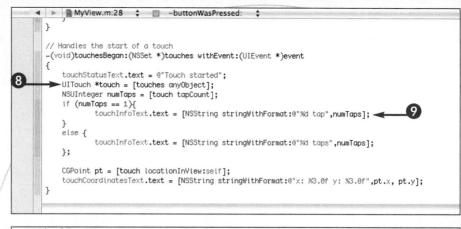

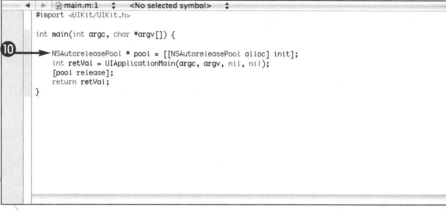

Extra

Your options for dealing with a memory warning from the operating system are likely to be limited. If your application uses a data cache, clear it. Otherwise, you may have to save your application's state, display a warning, and quit. A quick fix for memory crashes that you cannot trace is to set object pointers to `nil` after they have been released. This traps references to released objects and prevents a crash. Ideally, you should work through your code methodically to eliminate all memory problems. This may not always be possible or you may decide to use this `nil` pointer trick as a temporary fix while you concentrate on other problems.

Two useful tools include the Object Allocations Performance Tool and NSZombie. The allocations tool, under Run→Run With Performance Tool, lists all objects by type. Use it to monitor object allocations and de-allocations and check for leaks.

NSZombie lists de-allocated objects. Select your application under Executables in Xcode, click the blue Info button, and then click the Arguments tab. Add `NSZombieEnabled` and then set the value to `YES`. When your application crashes, you will see information about the de-allocated object that caused the crash.

Handle System Messages

Y ou can add system message handlers to your application to enable it to respond to system events and to user actions that are independent of a view. For example, your application can run a block of code as soon as it loads, when it is about to quit, or when it is about to run out of memory. Similarly, you can add code that runs when a view appears, disappears, loads, or unloads or when the iPhone is rotated.

Your application should always handle memory error messages, but you can choose the other messages it responds to. To respond to a message, you add a method for it, usually in the application delegate or the view controller. The application delegate handles application-level messages, and the view controller handles view-level messages. If you do not create a method for a system message, it is ignored.

Method stubs for some messages are already included in each file in the Xcode application templates. However, the templates do not include a comprehensive list, and you cannot use them as a guide. For a full list of messages, review the documentation. Application-level messages are listed in the UIApplicationDelegate Protocol Reference documentation. View-level messages are in the UIViewController and UIView Class Reference documentation. The list of all possible messages for every object is very broad, and you may find yourself imagining new features for your applications as you become familiar with the features offered by system messages.

To implement a method, you can often copy and paste its definition directly from the documentation. Add a pair of curly brackets {} to create a method stub. As your application develops, fill in the stubs to add message-specific features to your own design.

Handle System Messages

① Open the Xcode Documentation window.

Note: *You can open the window by choosing Help→Developer Documentation from the Xcode menu.*

② Search for "UIApplication."

③ Double-click the UIApplicationDelegate Protocol Reference entry in the list of search hits.

④ Scroll down to find a list of Tasks.

This displays the definitive list of methods in the protocol.

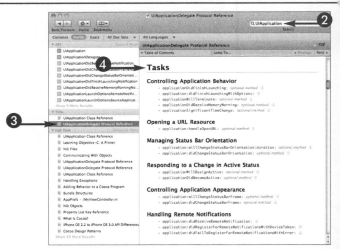

⑤ Click a method to review its features and syntax.

⑥ Select a method to add to your code by dragging a highlight over it and then choosing Edit→Copy from the main Xcode menu.

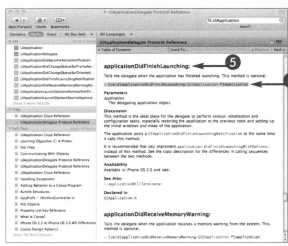

7 Paste the method into the application delegate implementation file and then modify or fill in any extra parameters if they are needed.

Note: The order in which methods are declared in your code is not important.

8 Add curly brackets and optionally a comment to create a stub.

9 Repeat the previous steps for other methods you plan to implement.

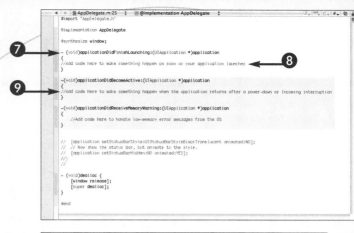

10 Add code to each method to implement the features or responses it triggers in your application — for example, a low memory alert.

11 Repeat the entire sequence for your root view controller, adding one or more of the methods listed in the UIViewController Class Reference documentation.

Your application now responds to a selected range of system messages.

Extra

Your application can be interrupted by incoming calls, SMS messages, and calendar events. The application state is suspended automatically, but you can add further optional save and restore features — for example, to save essential data to the solid state disk — by implementing the `applicationWillResignActive` method in your application delegate. If needed, implement the `applicationDidBecomeActive` method to add recovery features. If the user decides to accept certain interruptions or in other circumstances, such as serious memory errors, `applicationWillTerminate` is called. This can happen at any time without warning, so your handler for this method should be able to save an application state and release memory.

An extra set of messages is handled directly by the `UIApplication` class and defined in main.m. If you use a template, you can leave this code unchanged. However, you can also use `main()` to nominate a custom application delegate:

```
int retVal = UIApplicationMain(argc, argv, nil, @"NameOfYourDelegateGoesHere");
```

Handle Single-Touch Events

When a user touches the iPhone screen, touch messages are sent to your application. You can create a simple touch-tracking application by implementing standard methods to handle these messages in your code. Begin by designing a view to display information about touch messages. Next, add the methods that respond to touch messages and display touch status, tap status, and current touch position. Finally, add a button to demonstrate how touch events and button events interact.

Touch messages are part of the UIResponder system, which manages the iPhone's touch screen and also recognizes movement gestures, such as shakes. As a user moves a finger around the screen, UIResponder sends a stream of messages with information about touch status, position, and number of taps. Touch messages are independent of event messages sent by objects in a view.

The three standard touch messages are touchesBegan:, touchesMoved:, and touchesEnded:. Each is sent at a different *touch phase*. For example, touchesBegan: is sent whenever a new touch is recognized. An additional system-generated touchesCancelled: message is sent when an application is interrupted by an incoming phone call or text message. To handle these messages in your application, add a method for each one.

You do not need to create links or declare outlets for touch messages in Interface Builder. The links in this example are specifically included to handle label updates, not to manage the touch message themselves. Similarly, the custom myView class in this example is optional and is included solely to save memory and simplify the resource tree. A standard view controller object can also handle touch messages.

Handle Single-Touch Events

① Create a new project by using the Window Application template.

② Add a new custom view controller class called MyView.

Note: See Chapter 2 for instructions on how to create a custom class.

③ Edit the MyView.h file to convert the class to a subclass of UIView.

④ Add a class declaration to the app delegate to register the new MyView class.

Your MyView class is ready for use as a customized view controller.

⑤ In Xcode, add IBOutlet declarations for three labels and an IBAction declaration for a button message to MyView.h.

⑥ Load Interface Builder, add a UIView object to the UIWindow, and then add three labels and a button to the UIView.

⑦ Click the UIView object and then change its class to MyView by selecting this class from the drop-down menu in the Class Identity pane in the Inspector window.

The custom myView class is designated as the view controller.

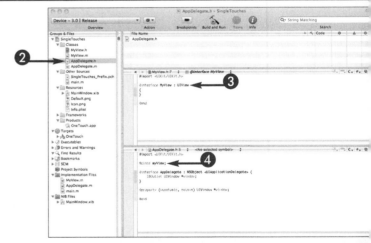

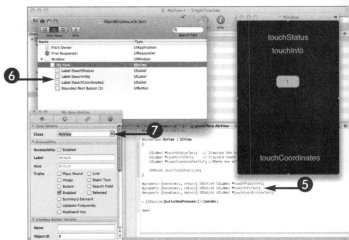

8 Link the labels and the label declarations in Interface Builder.

9 Link the TouchDown button message to the IBAction button message handler in Interface Builder.

The labels in the view are now ready to display touch information, and you can begin to add method declarations to handle touch messages.

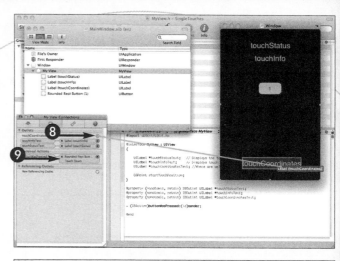

10 Add a `touchesBegan:` method to `myView` to handle initial touch events.

Use this boilerplate method header without changing it.

11 Add code to set the touch status label to show `Touch started` and to read the touch object returned by the touch message.

12 Add code to read the number of taps and update the touch info label.

13 Add code to read the touch position and update the position label to display touch coordinates.

Note: The labels in this example are for display only. You can display and process touch information in whichever way is most useful in your application.

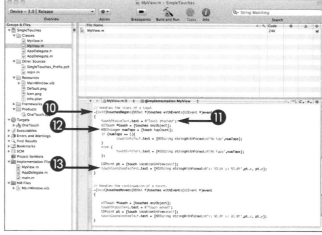

Extra

This example demonstrates a simplified resource tree. It relies on a re-classing trick available on the iPhone. The single nib includes a view tree inside a window. The root `UIView` object is re-classed as an instance of `MyView` — a specially written custom controller class. This creates a hybrid object that appears on the screen, works as a controller, and includes the properties and methods declared in the custom class. Only `UIView` objects can be re-classed in this way.

In a simple application, this saves memory at the cost of access to the full range of system messages sent by the OS to a separate `UIViewController` object. Either approach responds to touch messages.

You can click and deselect the Multiple Touch check box in the Attributes pane in the Inspector window to turn multi-touch features on and off, respectively, for a view. It is a good idea to turn off multi-touch responses in a single-touch application. You can also change this setting under program control by sending `[nameOfMyView setMultipleTouchEnabled:Yes|No]` to a view.

continued ➡

While the syntax of the touch methods can seem complicated, it is, in fact, concise and fairly simple. However, there are standard tricks and idioms you should be familiar with. Touch messages arrive with two associated data structures. The first is an NSSet object. It includes a collection of all the current touch objects, a total touch count, and tap status. Each touch object is an instance of the UITouch.

You can use a standard method called [touches anyObject] method to read the current touch from the NSSet. A single-touch interface will always send a set with a single touch, so you can use this message as a convenient catchall without having to specify the first and only touch. For convenience and clarity in your code, copy this touch object to a local instance of UITouch.

To extract the coordinates, call the locationInView method to copy the coordinates to an instance of the Core

Graphics CGPoint object and then read point.x and point.y:

```
UITouch *aTouch = [touches anyObject];
CGPoint pt = [aTouch locationInView: self];
```

The [aTouchtapCount] method (added on the previous page) returns the current tap status. Use this to identify single- and double-tap events. The UIResponder system does not generate distinct double-tap messages, so you must check for double-tap events in the touchesBegan: method.

The second data structure that arrives with touch messages is a UIEvent object. It includes useful but optional information about event timing and also specifies which view sent the message. Potentially, you could use this information to calculate touch velocity or t check for touch events from a specific view. This simple example ignores the UIEvent data.

Handle Single-Touch Events *(continued)*

⑭ Add a touchesMoved: method.

⑮ Add code to read the current touch object and to update the touch status label.

⑯ Add code to read and update the touch coordinates.

```
    };
        CGPoint pt = [touch locationInView:self];
        touchCoordinatesText.text = [NSString stringWithFormat:@"x: %3.0f y: %3.0f",pt.x, pt.y];
}


// Handles the continuation of a touch.
-(void)touchesMoved:(NSSet *)touches withEvent:(UIEvent *)event
{
    UITouch *touch = [touches anyObject];
    touchStatusText.text = @"Touch moved";
    CGPoint pt = [touch locationInView:self];
    touchCoordinatesText.text = [NSString stringWithFormat:@"x: %3.0f y: %3.0f",pt.x, pt.y];
}

// Handles the end of a touch event.
-(void)touchesEnded:(NSSet *)touches withEvent:(UIEvent *)event
{
    touchCoordinatesText.text = @"";
    touchStatusText.text = @"No touch";
    }
```

⑰ Add a touchesEnded: method.

⑱ Add code to clear the coordinate label and to reset the touch status label.

```
-(void)touchesMoved:(NSSet *)touches withEvent:(UIEvent *)event
{
    UITouch *touch = [touches anyObject];
    touchStatusText.text = @"Touch moved";
    CGPoint pt = [touch locationInView:self];
    touchCoordinatesText.text = [NSString stringWithFormat:@"x: %3.0f y: %3.0f",pt.x, pt.y];
}
// Handles the end of a touch event.
-(void)touchesEnded:(NSSet *)touches withEvent:(UIEvent *)event
{
    touchCoordinatesText.text = @"";
    touchStatusText.text = @"No touch";
    }

-(void)touchesCancelled:(NSSet *)touches withEvent:(UIEvent *)event
{
    touchStatusText.text = @"Touch cancelled";
    touchCoordinatesText.text = @"";
}

@end
```

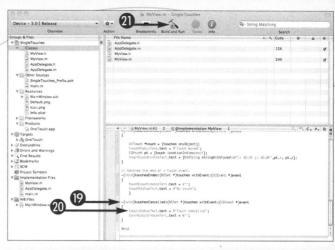

19 Add a `touchesCancelled:` method to handle interruptions.

20 Add code to update the touch status and coordinate labels.

21 Click Build and Run to build and run the application.

22 The application recognizes single touches and updates the display with touch status, tap count, and position information.

Note: *You can find the SingleTouch project on the website for this book: www.wiley.com/go/iphonedevelopmentvb.*

Apply It

You can test for swipe movements by storing the initial position of a touch in the `touchesBegan` method and then comparing it to the current position in `touchesMoved`. If the change is longer than a set length, call your swipe method. Swipes are either horizontal or vertical, so you must split the x and y components of the movement and test them separately. For extra precision, constrain the opposite coordinate; for example, insert this code into `touchesMoved` to test for a horizontal swipe:

```
CGFloat deltaX = fabsf(touchStartPosition.x - touchCurrentPosition.x);
CGFloat deltaY = fabsf(touchStartPosition.y - touchCurrentPosition.y);

if (deltaX >= kMinSwipeLength && deltaY <= kMaxConstraint) {
  [swipe Horizontal]; //This is the swipe handler
}
```

Handle Multi-Touch Events

You can use the multi-touch interface to create an application that tracks two touches, displays the distance between them, and then processes this information to recognize pinch and stretch actions.

Multi-touch interfaces are not standardized, and there is no definitive multi-touch metaphor or model. However, pinch and stretch actions are almost as familiar to iPhone users as drags, taps, and swipes. You can use the multi-touch message system to recognize these actions in your applications by measuring the distance between two multi-touches and comparing them to a trigger value. If the distance shrinks to less than a trigger value, your application can call a pinch method. If it is outside the trigger value, it can call a stretch method. If you filter out touch events with more than two touches, you can assume that distance tracking will always be valid and useful.

This sample includes a simple C-language function to calculate the distance between two points. You could write a custom class to implement a complete point geometry library, but classes are only efficient when complex data structures are associated with a rich method library. A pair of coordinates is not a complex data structure, and the overhead needed to create and manage a class for a single-distance calculation would be unreasonable.

Single-touch and multi-touch applications use the same methods and data structures. The iPhone interface does not send different messages when multi-touch is active. It sends the same `touchesBegan:`, `touchesMoved:`, and `touchesEnded:` messages with extra touch events in each. You can use the same methods in your code, modifying them to read more than one touch message from the `NSSet` data structure.

Handle Multi-Touch Events

① Load an application that already includes single-touch support.

Note: *You can reuse the application from the previous spread for this example.*

② Choose File→New File to create a new file in Xcode.

③ Click the Mac OS X C and C++ tab.

④ Click C File, confirm by clicking Next, and then save the file as CGDistance.c.

The CGDistance.c file and a corresponding header file are added to your project.

⑤ Add code to CGDistance.h to import the Core Graphics library.

⑥ Add code to CGDistance.h to define a prototype for a distance function between two CGPoint coordinates.

⑦ Add code to CGDistance.c to implement the distance function.

The distance function is now ready for use in your project.

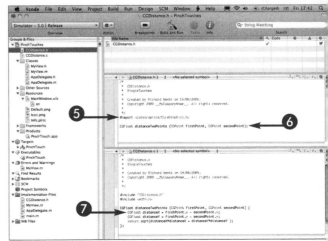

8 Add constant definitions for minimum and maximum pinch trigger distances to `myView.h`.

9 Declare two new label objects for the view: one object to display a second pair of coordinates and another to display distance.

10 Add a second CGPoint start point and then add floats for initial distance and current distance.

11 Add a new property declaration for each new object and then declare the new labels as IBOutlets.

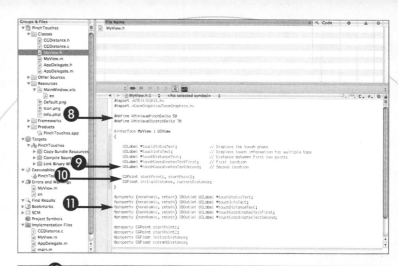

12 Double-click the nib file to load it in the view.

13 Add a new label to display distance.

14 Add a new label to display a second-touch position coordinate.

15 Link both new labels to their corresponding outlets.

The revised view is ready to display a new pair of coordinates and a label that displays distance.

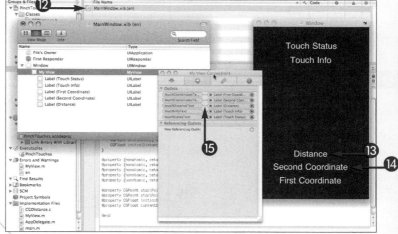

Extra

This example triggers discrete pinch and stretch messages when they cross a threshold. This is a good solution for an application with discrete zoom in and zoom out features, such as a game. An alternative approach to double-touch design is dynamic scaling. Instead of triggering pinch and stretch methods, this maps distance to a zoom factor directly.

Ideally, a user should be able to touch an object and have it follow his or her fingertip as he or she pinches and stretches. This is not easy to do precisely, but a reasonable approximation is often useful enough. Apple's own applications use this model, and it is a more intuitive solution for any application that features graphic data.

You can implement dynamic scaling by reading distance from the touch events and then adding code to the `touchesMoved:` method to shrink or stretch a view object. See Chapter 8 for more on view scaling with affine transforms.

To enable multi-touch support, you must check a view's multi-touch enabled attribute in the Attributes pane in the Inspector window in Interface Builder.

continued →

Handle Multi-Touch Events (continued)

I n a multi-touch interface, the NSSet object generated by a touch event may arrive with more than one touch object. A convenient way to read this information is to copy the NSSet object to an NSArray. Your application can then read each object in turn by indexing through the array.

You can create more reliable and responsive triggers by using separate values for pinches and stretches. Fixed constants are adequate for current iPhone variants, but if an iPhone with a different screen size becomes available, you may want to define the triggers as percentages of the screen dimensions.

Touches are persistent, but user actions may not be. If a user touches three fingers to the display and then lifts the middle one, the order of objects in the array may change. Alternatively, some objects may return nil pointers and be unavailable for reading. You should usually split your code with conditionals to handle one, two, and more touches. This entry-level application tracks single and dual events and uses a simple conditional check to filter out three and more active touches. It does not attempt to track a full set of touches; it only selects the first two.

You may find it useful to add further functions to return the angle between the two points. You could potentially use rotation and other derived information to add further interaction options to an interface design, such as a twist action to rotate a view.

Handle Multi-Touch Events *(continued)*

⑯ In MyView.m, add a conditional check to touchesBegan: to run a separate code block when there are two touches.

⑰ Add code to copy both touch objects to an NSArray.

⑱ Add code to read the first touch object from array index 0, extract its position, and then update the first coordinate label.

⑲ Add code to read the second touch object from array index 1, extract its position, update the second coordinate label, and then calculate and display the initial distance between the points.

Note: This code calls the distanceTwoPoints *function defined earlier.*

⑳ In touchesMoved:, add a similar conditional check and code to update the status label.

㉑ Add code to copy the two touches to an NSArray, extract the coordinates, and then calculate the distance.

Note: *You can copy this code from* touchesBegan: *and then update it with minor changes.*

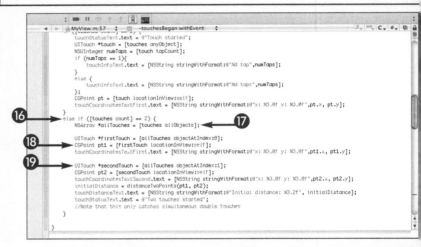

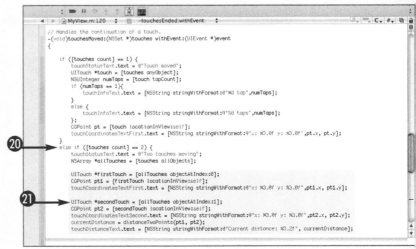

㉒ Add code to `touchesMoved:` to compare the current distance with the starting distance, and trigger pinch or stretch methods as appropriate.

㉓ Add code to track changes in distance and report pinch events.

㉔ Add code to `touchesEnded:` to reset the view's text labels.

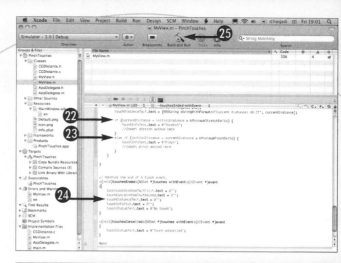

㉕ Click Build and Run to build and run the application.

Hold down Option while clicking in the Simulator to simulate double-touch events.

㉖ The application displays two touch coordinates as well as the distance between them and then updates the status label when it recognizes pinch and stretch movements.

Note: *You can find the MultiTouch project on the website for this book: www.wiley.com/go/iphonedevelopmentvb.*

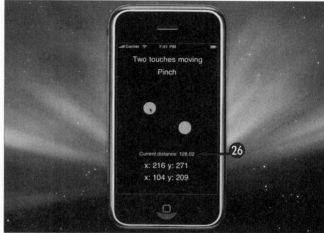

Extra

Touching a button, slider, or other interface object will not send touch events. Conversely, you can drag a finger over a button without generating a button event. Because of this ambiguity, it may not be clear to users how touch events and interface objects will respond if they share the same screen space. A good design guideline is to separate touch areas from other interface objects. You can mix touch areas and objects on a single view in a nib file, but you should keep them visually separate and clearly distinct as well as include interface logic to separate their responses.

An alternative idiom for touch management is enumeration and dispatch. Instead of copying the NSSet data to an NSArray, you can use a counter to cycle through all the touches and then dispatch each to a custom handler — which, for example, might check if the touch is within one of a list of views:

```
UITouch *touch = [touches anyObject]
NSUInteger touchCount = 0;
For (UITouch *touch in touches){
 [self someDispatchMethodGoesHere forTouchNumber: touchCount];
 touchCount++;
 }
```

Views and View Navigation

Views typically offer a selection of visible objects, including buttons, sliders, and features. Applications usually offer more than one view. You can assemble a complete interface by creating views in Interface Builder and adding view-switching options so users can move between them.

The Object library in Interface Builder lists the visible objects and controllers you can add to a view. It also offers optional extra objects to implement view switching. You can use this list of objects to create iPhone interface designs with a unified look and feel and familiar navigation features. You can also create your own customized navigation options — for example, switching views when the user taps part of the screen or shakes the handset.

The View and View Controller Hierarchy

The iPhone's view switching system is complex but flexible. Typically, an application includes a collection of controller classes with associated nib files arranged in a hierarchy. Top-level controllers are often loaded permanently and load, unload, display, or hide the controllers the user sees. You can arrange the controller hierarchy in various ways — for example, to create an application with a permanently visible button bar that switches the views behind it.

Each view is built from an array of items, each of which may contain *subviews*, arranged in a tree. The view above a subview is the *superview*. When you design a nib file, subview trees are created automatically as you add buttons, tab bars, and other elements and saved in the nib.

Typically, you design a view by creating a custom view controller class in Xcode by choosing New File→UIViewController, clicking the With XIB for user interface check box to create an associated nib file, and then populating the nib file with the features you want to appear in the view. The controller class manages messages from the objects in the nib and also controls their settings and properties.

You can then switch views in two ways. For simple, manual view switching, allocate a view controller and initialize it with its nib file, release the old superview, and then insert the new view at `Index: 0` in the view array. You can also add and remove objects from the view tree without using a nib by adding code that allocates and releases them, and inserts and removes them from the array. Use the `addSubViewAtIndex:` method to insert a view. Use the `removeFromSuperview:` method to delete a view. There is no `deleteSubviewAtIndex:` method — you must call `removeFromSuperview` on a view's superview. To change the index of a view, use `exchangeSubviewAtIndex:`. This swaps two views at two given indices.

The second view switching method is used for more complex effects, managed by the iPhone's tab bar and navigation controllers. These load and release view controllers directly to show their associated views. Tab bar controllers switch controllers when you tap a button, and navigation controllers implement a stack; to load and release views, you push and pop them from the stack.

Navigation Controllers

Navigation controllers add named buttons to a navigation bar at the top of the interface to implement a Forward/Back multiview interface. When the user touches the right-hand button, the controller slides in a new view, adds it to the top of the stack, and then creates a Back button. When the user taps the Back button, the controller pops the previous controller from the stack. Navigation controllers work well with cell-based *table views* — see Chapter 6 — but can be used independently for customized results. The buttons can trigger any feature in your application.

Toolbars

Toolbars are more flexible than tab bars — you can add buttons and icons, with optional spacing — but they do not include automatic view switching or animation. Toolbar buttons glow momentarily when tapped. They do not include radio button features, and the user cannot customize the layout. You can use toolbars for navigation or to add a palette of features to an application.

Tab Bars

Tab bars appear at the bottom of the screen. They function like radio buttons, giving the user a choice of views or features. Unlike navigation controllers, they do not create a Forward/Back breadcrumb trail. Users can tap the buttons on a tab bar to move directly to different views. Optionally, you can include a More button that includes a built-in customization feature that allows users to modify the tab bar, selecting visible buttons from a longer list.

Customized View Controllers

You use generic instances of `UIViewController` to manage subviews, but it is often easier to create custom subclasses — for example, `firstViewController`, `secondViewController`, and so on. You can use this feature to create views with different options, controlled by unique code in each subclass. For example, `firstView Controller` could handle touch events in one way, while `secondViewController` could handle them differently or ignore them altogether.

Xcode includes a shortcut to speed up the creation of custom view controller classes. Choose File→New File and then choose Cocoa Touch Class. Click the UIViewController subclass, and make sure to click the With XIB for user interface check box. Click Next to name your subclass and then save the file. You will need to manually move the class header and implementation file to the Classes folder and the nib file to the Resources folder.

Switching Views

You can switch views in two ways. If you have implemented lazy loading, you can allocate a new view controller on demand and then load it with a new view by using the `initWithNibName:` method. You can then remove the current view from its parent superview and insert the new view at `Index: 0` in the view — not the view controller — hierarchy with this code:

```
[oldViewController.view removeFromSuperview];
[self.view insertSubview:
  newViewController.view atIndex: 0];
```

Alternatively, you can load the entire view stack when the application starts and then use the `exchangeSubviewAt Index:` method to move the new view to the top of the stack.

Sharing Information

Views and view controllers must be able to exchange information. For example, a subview that sets an application's preferences must be able to share its settings with the rest of the application.

You can share information in two ways. The first is to define `IBAction` target methods in a root view controller and then link them to interface objects in subviews. The subview objects can then trigger update methods in the root controller directly.

Another solution is to make the properties and methods included in the root view controller directly accessible to subview controllers. You can do this by routing messages through the application delegate. Create a local pointer to the delegate in one of the subview controllers:

```
theNameofMyAppDelegateFile *appAccessPoint =
  (theNameofMyAppDelegateFile *)[UIApplication sharedApplication] delegate];
```

You can then use `appAccessPoint` to send messages to any object in the application and to set its properties. For example, `[appAccessPoint.viewController aMessage];` sends `aMessage` to the root view controller and triggers the `aMessage` method.

`appAccessPoint.viewController.someProperty = aNewValue;` changes `someProperty` to `aNewValue`. If you use the View-based Application template, the root view controller is named `viewController` by default, so you can use this name to access its properties.

Touch methods are passed up the responder chain automatically. To process touch messages from any subview, add touch methods to the root controller. Do not add them to the subview — unless you want them to be processed by the subview.

For more sophisticated handling of application preferences, you can use the `NSUserDefaults` object described in Chapter 7.

Create a Multiview Application with a Tab Bar

Y ou can use a tab bar to create an application with simple automated view switching. Xcode includes a Tab Bar Application template that generates a complete two-view application. The template is very easy to use. When you build and run the application, it automatically switches between two views when the user taps the buttons at the bottom of the screen. You do not need to add further code to switch views. The tab bar controller manages the views for you.

To use the template effectively, you must understand how it is constructed. The default MainWindow.xib file includes the root tab bar controller, a visible tab bar view object, and two view controllers.

The two view controllers work differently. The first controller, with its view tree, is included in the MainWindow.xib file. The second controller is set up to load a separate nib, called SecondView.xib. The Nib Name

is set in a drop-down menu on the Attributes pane in the Inspector window.

You can add further buttons by dragging and dropping tab bar items from the Library in Interface Builder onto the tab bar. Each item adds a button and a controller. You can change the name of the button in the Title field in the Attributes pane in the Inspector window. You can also set the button to show one of a selection of preset names, with associated icons. For example, Search shows a magnifying glass, Recents shows a clock, and Favorites shows a star.

When you add a new button, it does not add an associated view. To add a new view, create and save it in a new controller class in Xcode and then choose its nib from the Nib Name field in the View Controller Attributes pane in the Inspector window. If the view does not need a controller, you can also create and save a new nib by using Interface Builder and then choose the name directly.

Create a Multiview Application with a Tab Bar

① In Xcode, choose File→New Project.

② Click Tab Bar Application and then click Choose.

③ Save the new project as TabBar.

Note: *You can find the TabBar project on the website for this book: www.wiley.com/go/iphone developmentvb.*

④ Optionally, click the Build and Run button to build and run the project.

The new project creates a template with a tab bar controller, two buttons in the tab bar, and two views. The views are automatically switched by the controller.

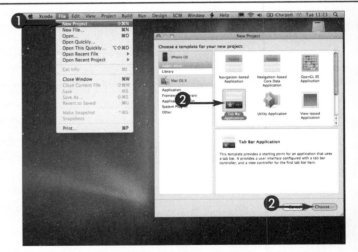

⑤ Choose File→New File.

⑥ Click Cocoa Touch Class.

⑦ Click UIViewController subclass.

⑧ Click the With Xib for user interface check box and then save the file as ThirdController.

Files for a new ThirdController class are added to the project, with a ThirdController.xib nib.

9 Double-click MainWindow.xib to open it in Interface Builder.

10 Drag a View Controller from the Library to the Tab Bar Controller's view tree. Drag it so it appears under ViewController (Second), with the same indentation.

Note: *A Tab Bar Item is automatically added.*

11 Click the new Tab Bar Item.

12 In the Attributes pane, set the Tab Bar Item's name to Third.

13 Click the new view controller.

14 In the Class Identity panel in the Attributes pane, set the Class to ThirdController.

Note: *This links the third view controller to the code in the* ThirdController *class files.*

15 In the Attributes pane, set the NIB Name to Third Controller.

Note: *This selects the nib file loaded when the third button is tapped.*

16 Click Build and Run to build and run the project.

A third button appears on the tab bar. When the user taps it, this button selects the new ThirdController.nib.

Note: *The default ThirdController nib displays an empty view. To build a finished view, add visible objects to it in Interface Builder and then add supporting code in the ThirdController.m and ThirdController.h files.*

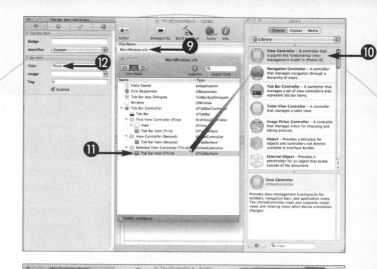

Extra

You can add an almost indefinite number of buttons in Interface Builder. However, a maximum of five will be visible when the application runs. If your application offers more than five buttons, a More button appears automatically. When the user taps this button, a scrollable text list appears, showing the names of the buttons. The user can tap items in this list to reveal the views controlled by the other buttons or tap an Edit button to display a Configure screen, with the option to select the visible buttons from a list.

The More button feature is built into the tab bar controller, but you will need to add code to implement it by using methods defined in the UITabBarDelegateProtocol.

By default, only the first view controller has an associated controller class that you can customize with your own code. The other controllers are plain instances of UIViewController with default features. Even after you create a new subclass, its code is ignored until you assign it to a view controller in the main window nib. To do this, use the Class Identity drop-down menu in the Inspector window. It is easy to forget this step. If a view controller is ignoring your code, verify that you have made this assignment.

Create a Toolbar

You can add a `UIToolBar` toolbar object to your application to display a list of buttons that can trigger various application features. The toolbar itself is cosmetic; it functions as a placeholder for one or more buttons. You can specify one of three graphic styles: Default, Black, and BlackTranslucent. The latter style enables translucency. The toolbar's Attributes pane in the Inspector window includes a tint feature for adding color. You can change these attributes in code by using the `tintColor` and `translucent` properties.

The toolbar is a placeholder for instances of the `UIBar Button` class. Buttons can show custom text or a range of preset graphics, including a trash can, magnifying glass, play/pause/record controls, and others. Optionally, you can import a custom graphic. There are three button styles: Plain, Bordered, and Done. The Plain style glows when tapped and displays large text or graphics. The Bordered style is a simple button with a border. The Done style is for buttons that complete a task or switch views.

A toolbar does not implement view switching or other automated features. Buttons do not send event messages, such as `TouchUpInside`. Instead, they are connected directly to methods in a view controller. You must link a method to a selector attribute in Interface Builder. When the user taps a button, the method is triggered.

You can control the layout of the buttons on the toolbar by inserting variable and fixed spacers. Without spacers, buttons are left-justified. To spread out the buttons on the bar so they appear at the far left and far right, insert a variable spacer. For manual spacing, use fixed spacers.

Create a Toolbar

① In Xcode, create a new project by using the View-based Application template and then save it as ToolBar.

Note: You can find the ToolBar project on the website for this book: www.wiley.com/go/iphonedevelopmentvb.

② Click ToolBarViewController.h.

③ Add a `UILabel` object with an outlet and an associated property.

④ Add two `IBAction` methods — `incrementCount:` and `decrementCount:` — and then save all open files.

⑤ Double-click ToolBarViewController.xib to open it in Interface Builder.

⑥ Drag a Toolbar object from the Library to the view and then drag it to the bottom of the view.

⑦ Drag two Bar Button Items from the Library and then drop them on the Toolbar in the view.

⑧ Drag a Flexible Space Bar Button Item and then drop it between the two buttons.

The Flexible Space automatically pushes the two buttons to the far left and right.

⑨ Drag a UILabel from the Library, drop it on the view, and then optionally increase the font size.

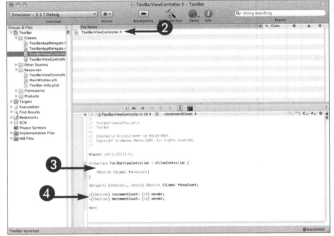

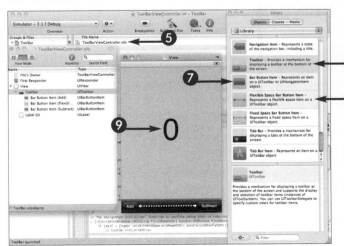

0 Select one of the Bar Button Items, change its title to Add in the Attributes pane in the Inspector window, and then change the title of the other Bar Button Item to Subtract.

1 Drag a link from the showCount outlet in File's Owner to the label in the view.

2 Drag a link from the Subtract button to the decrementCount action.

3 Similarly, create a link from the Add button to the incrementCount action.

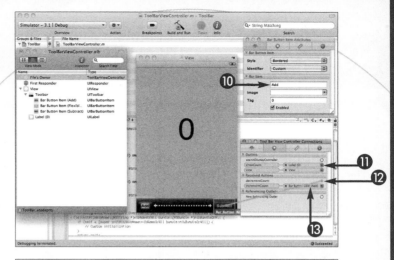

4 In ToolBarViewController.m, add an integer counter variable and then synthesize the showCounter label.

5 Add code to implement the incrementCount: and decrementCount: methods that update the label.

6 Click Build and Run to build and run the application.

The toolbar buttons trigger the increment and decrement methods when tapped, updating the label.

Note: In this example, the toolbar style has been set to BlackTranslucent in the Attributes pane in the Inspector window.

Extra

Toolbars are ideal for creating a dock-like selection of menu choices for an application and for adding transport controls to media applications. You can implement a drag-to-trash feature in your application by placing a trash icon on the toolbar and then using touch methods to monitor when items are tapped, dragged, and released. A successful toolbar design is intuitive and adds features that the user can immediately understand.

The selector attribute in Interface Builder is usually linked to methods in an application's root view controller via File's Owner. However, if you have a number of views with associated controller classes, you can link the buttons to methods in the other controllers. UIBarButton items include a target and action property. You can use these to change the messages that are sent and the objects they are sent to at any time. Target objects must include the methods specified; otherwise, the application will crash when the user taps a button.

Switch Views with a Navigation Controller

You can use a `UINavigationController` object to create semiautomatic navigation between two or more views. A navigation controller is associated with three visible objects: a `UINavigationBar`, a `UINavigationItem`, and one or more `UIBarButtonsItem` buttons. The navigation bar is the visible representation of the controller and displays a blank bar at the top of the window. The `UINavigationItem` adds a title to the bar and manages title updates.

The bar button items implement Forward and Back buttons. Typically, a user moves through a hierarchy of views by tapping these buttons. When the user taps a button, it triggers a method in the root view controller. To implement view switching with a navigation controller, you must call `pushViewController` on the navigation controller within this method, passing it a pointer to the next view: `[self aNavigationController] pushView Controller: nextViewController animated: YES];`.

When the navigation controller receives this message, it adds the view controller to the top of the stack, displays the view with an optional animation, and then automatically creates a Back button. When the user taps the Back button, the view is popped from the stack and the original view is restored, with its original title and button configuration.

One of the unusual features of navigation controllers is that they are persistent. Typically, they are added to the MainWindow nib rather than to a subview. Subviews appear and disappear behind the navigation bar, which is always visible. Unusually, this means placing the controller in the MainWindow nib file rather than a subview.

This example uses the Navigation-based Application template in Xcode to create a minimal two-view application. The template uses a table view object, which is ideal for navigating through more complex applications. Here, the table view is unnecessary. It is deleted and replaced with a simpler view.

Switch Views with a Navigation Controller

① In Xcode, choose File→New Project.

② Click the Navigation-based Application template.

③ Click Choose.

④ Save the file as SimpleNav.

Note: You can find the SimpleNav project on the website for this book: www.wiley. com/go/iphonedevelopmentvb.

The template creates a new project.

⑤ Click RootViewController.h.

⑥ Add an `import#` directive to load the header for a new class called `SubViewController`.

⑦ Add an instance of the new `SubView Controller` class and then declare it as a property.

⑧ Add a new `IBAction` method called `show SubView` and then save all open files.

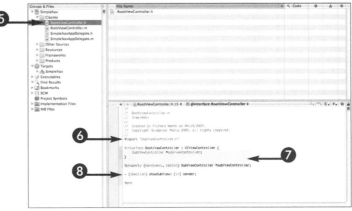

9 Choose File→New File.

10 Click Cocoa Touch Class.

11 Click UIViewController subclass.

12 Click the With Xib for user interface check box.

13 Click Next and then save the new class as SubViewController.

Note: This creates the files for the new `SubViewController` *class.*

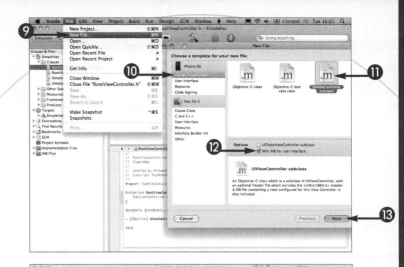

14 Double-click RootViewController.xib to open it in Interface Builder.

15 Drag a View from the Library to the Document window, drop it under First Responder, and then drag a Label from the Library and drop it on the new view.

16 Optionally, change the font size of the label, center it, and set the text to 1.

Note: The text is arbitrary. You can customize this view to your own design.

17 Delete the Table View object and then save the file.

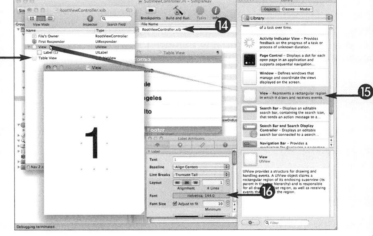

Extra

You can use `UINavigationBar` objects without a navigation controller. On its own, a navigation bar is equivalent to a simplified toolbar object. It can be used for navigation or for managing other features and options. You can drag bar buttons to the left and right of the bar as well as assign any method to them in Interface Builder. You can also add a segmented control to the center of the bar. The bar does not implement stack management, and it does not create Back buttons automatically. To implement these features, you must add them in code.

Because the iPhone offers more than one option for navigation, it is good practice to consider which controller type presents the views in your application in the most intuitive way. As a guide, tab bar controllers are ideal for applications with a small number of distinct views. Toolbars are a good choice for applications with features that may not be view based, such as transport controls in a media player. Navigation controllers are an ideal solution for complex hierarchical menus with many options.

continued ➡

Switch Views with a Navigation Controller (continued)

This minimal two-view navigation controller example uses familiar techniques to handle user interaction. A root view controller class handles interaction for the root view and a subview controller for the subview. Both are subclasses of UIViewController. The root view controller is included in the Navigation-based Application template. You must add the subview controller with an associated nib by hand. The subview is loaded with the root view in its viewDidLoad method.

The button in the navigation bar is linked to a showSubView method in the root controller. To implement lazy loading, you could move the subview load code to this method. It includes code that asks the navigation controller to push the subview onto the stack. The controller generates a Back button and handles the corresponding pop event when the user taps it. These features are automated; you do not need to write code to implement them.

The navigation controller reads the title of the view from its title property. You must set this property explicitly; otherwise, it remains nil and no title appears. Add the following to the viewDidLoad method in every relevant view controller:

```
self.title = @"A Title";
```

Navigation bars display large text. The size of the bar is fixed, as is the size of title text. This limits the available space, so you should keep titles as short as possible. This example includes optional code that hides and reveals the navigation bar when the user taps the display. The navigation bar does not cover the underlying view; it pushes it toward the bottom of the display. When you hide the bar, the view moves upward. Your view designs should take this into account. You may need to offset visible items vertically to keep them centered in the display.

Switch Views with a Navigation Controller *(continued)*

⑱ Click RootViewController.m.

⑲ Synthesize the subViewController instance variable.

⑳ Add code to implement a showSubView: method, calling pushViewController: on the subview controller to switch from the root view to the subview.

㉑ Add code to ViewDidLoad to set a title for the root view, preload the subview controller's nib, assign it to the subview controller, and then save all open files.

㉒ Double-click MainWindow.xib to open it in Interface Builder.

㉓ Drag a Bar Button Item from the Library and then drop it on the Navigation Item.

Note: *It should appear indented under the Navigation Item.*

㉔ In the Attributes pane in the Inspector window, set the Identifier to Play.

Note: *This displays a play icon in the button. Alternatively, set a Custom identifier and then give the button an arbitrary title. These settings are cosmetic and do not affect the button's operation.*

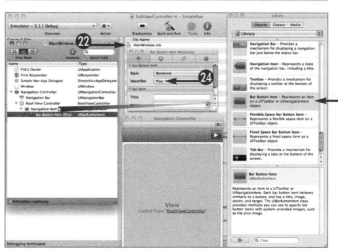

㉕ Click the Connections tab in the Inspector window to show the Bar Button Item's connections.

㉖ Drag a link from the selector field to RootViewController.

㉗ Click the showSubView: method when it appears.

㉘ Save the file.

The button is linked to the showSubView method and will trigger it when tapped.

㉙ Double-click SubViewController.xib to open it in Interface Builder.

㉚ Add a Label to the view and then optionally change the text and font size.

Note: *These changes are cosmetic. You can use them to make the subview visually distinct from the root view.*

㉛ In Xcode, click SubViewController.m and then add code to viewDidLoad to set the subview title.

㉜ Optionally, implement a touchesBegan: method with a Boolean variable to show and hide the navigation bar when the user taps the screen.

㉝ Click Build and Run to build and run the project.

Note: *You can add an identical touchesBegan: method to RootViewController.m to show and hide the bar when the root view is visible. This feature is optional.*

The project switches between a root view and a subview when buttons on the navigation bar are tapped. The Back button in the subview is created automatically.

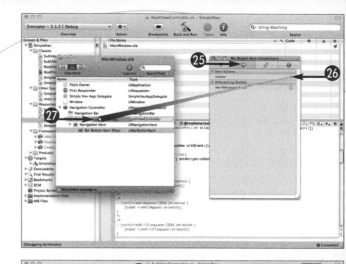

Extra

You can hide and reveal the navigation bar by calling the setNavigationBarHidden: Animated: method. The method takes two Booleans. The first hides and reveals the bar. The second enables and disables a simple sliding animation. The navigation bar takes up significant space, and you can use this method to slide it out of sight when it is not being used — for example, to create a full-screen mode in a video player. Toolbars offer an equivalent method: setToolBarHidden: Animated:.

Navigation controllers work well with table views — lists of text items that are often used as a substitute for drop-down menus in iPhone applications. You can see an example of table view navigation in the iPhone's Settings application. Table views are somewhat complex to initialize and manage, and they use screen real estate you may prefer to reserve for other features. They are unnecessary in a two-view application but are a good way to implement a more complicated hierarchy. For more on table views and how to use them for navigation, see Chapter 6.

Add a Page Control

Y ou can use a *page control* to present a series of views in a linear sequence. The control appears on the display as a series of small dots. The user moves through a fixed series of views by tapping the dots. The sequence of views is fixed, and the user must move through it linearly, one view at a time. The Springboard home screen uses this feature for navigation.

Page controls are not popular with users because they are unintuitive. Users often guess they can skip to any view in the sequence by tapping the corresponding dot. This is not what page controls do, so the experience is often frustrating. The active area of the control is very limited, and the control feels unresponsive, creating further frustration.

Page controls are also unpopular with developers because they do not offer automated view switching. A page control counts dots and displays them and then sends a `Value Changed` message to its application when tapped. It has no other features.

Even with this limited range, a page controls can be useful as a display object. If your interface includes some other view-switching option, such as a drag or a swipe, you can use a page control to show which view is visible — as long as your application is a list of sequential views. Page controls are not suitable for hierarchical view structures.

This example demonstrates how to receive messages from a page control and how to read its status to find the number of the current dot. It does not implement view switching, which is described in the next example.

Add a Page Control

① In Xcode, create a project by using the View-based Application template and then save it as PageControl.

Note: *You can find the PageControl project on the website for this book: www.wiley.com/go/iphonedevelopmentvb.*

② Click PageControlViewController.h.

③ Add IBOutlet instances of a page control and a label and then declare them as properties.

④ Add a pageChanged: IBAction method.

⑤ Click PageControlViewController.m.

⑥ Synthesize the label and the page control instances.

⑦ Add code to implement a pageChanged: IBAction method, which reads the current page from the control and copies it to the label, and then save all open files.

Note: *You can read the current page from a page control's* currentPage *property.*

8 Double-click PageControlViewControl.xib to open it in Interface Builder.

9 Drag a Page Control from the Library to the view.

10 Optionally, set the number of pages in the control in the Page Control panel in the Attributes pane in the Inspector window.

11 Drag a Label from the Library to the view and then optionally center it, change the font size, and set the default text to 0.

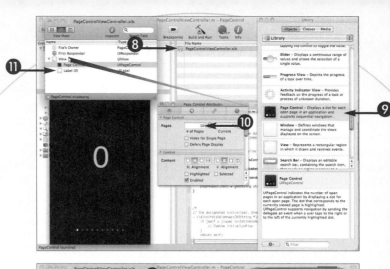

2 Click the Page Control.

3 Click the Connections tab in the Inspector window.

4 Drag a link from the Value Changed message to File's Owner and then select pageChanged: as the target.

5 Drag another link from the Referencing Outlets to File's Owner and select pageControl to create a link.

6 Click the Label and then drag a link from a Referencing Outlet to File's Owner and select pageNumber.

7 Click Build and Run to build and run the application.

When the user taps the page control, the label shows the number of the current page.

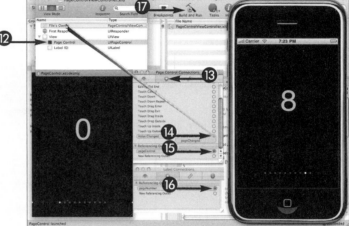

Extra

The default page control in Interface Builder's Library has three page dots, set in a relatively small frame. If you increase the number of pages in the Attributes tab in the Inspector window, the frame does not expand automatically. As a result, the control can appear clipped and only the middle dots are visible. You can avoid this by resizing the frame to expand the page control across the full width of the display.

Although it is possible to squeeze 20 dots into the page control in portrait mode, the maximum practical limit that leaves a reasonable margin at the side of the control is 16 or 17. A more realistic limit is 10 dots. Moving through views sequentially does not create a satisfying user experience, so you should limit this number to avoid user frustration.

Switch Views Manually

Y ou can switch views manually by using general-purpose code that can be triggered from any user action, including a screen tap, shake, tilt movement, or even a GPS position update. The core of all view-switching code is the simple swap, introduced earlier in this chapter:

```
[oldViewController.view removeFromSuperview];
[self.view insertSubview: newViewController.
 view atIndex: 0];
```

This is a minimal implementation that works with lazy loading. It hides the `oldViewController` view and releases it from memory. To prepare for the swap, you must allocate an instance of the new view controller and then load it from a nib file by using:

```
aViewController *newController =
 [[aViewController alloc] initWithNibName:
 @"aNibFile" bundle: nil];
```

To swap in a default view when the application first runs, add similar code to `viewDidLoad` in the root view controller, loading the default view's nib. An alternative solution is to create a view hierarchy of every view in your application in Interface Builder and then use the `exchangeSubviewAtIndex:` method to shuffle views up and down the stack to show them and hide them. You can extend this simple code to add animation effects and improve the sophistication of the view-switching effect. For more on animation, see Chapter 5.

This example swaps two views when the user taps the screen. The root view controller — `ViewSwitcherView Controller` — includes code to load nibs on demand and swap the views in a `touchesBegan:` message.

Switch Views Manually

① In Xcode, create a new project with the View-based Application template and then save it as SimpleViewSwitcher.

② Create a new controller subclass by choosing File→New File.

③ Click Cocoa Touch Class.

④ Click UIViewController subclass.

⑤ Click the With XIB for user interface check box.

⑥ Click Next and type in a file name to save the new subclass as FirstController.

⑦ Repeat steps 2–6 to create another subclass called SecondController.

FirstController and SecondController, with source files and nibs, are added to the project.

Note: You need to manually drag the files to the Classes folder and the nibs to the Resources folder.

⑧ Double-click FirstViewController.xib.

⑨ Add a label and other features to create a view.

⑩ Double-click SecondViewController.xib and then add a label and other optional features to create a view that is recognizably different from FirstViewController.xib.

⑪ Choose File→Save to save both views.

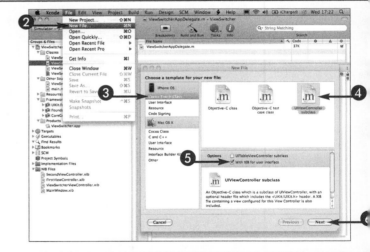

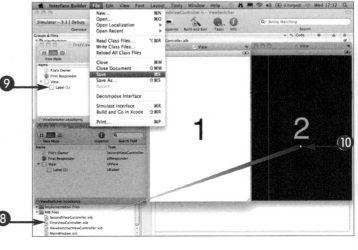

12 Click ViewSwitcherViewController.h.

13 Add @class directives for both of the new controller classes.

14 Add instances of each class and then declare them as properties.

15 Click ViewSwitcherViewController.m.

16 Import the class headers and then synthesize the new controller classes.

17 Find viewDidLoad, uncomment it if necessary, and then add code to load an instance of FirstController and its nib, replacing the default blank view loaded automatically from ViewSwitcherViewController.xib.

Note: This example uses the split-screen feature to show the header and the implementation file at the same time.

18 Add a touchesBegan method and then add code to implement lazy loading of each of the view controllers and their associated nibs.

19 Add code to swap the views.

Note: This code automatically releases the views when they are not visible.

20 Click Build and Run to build and run the application.

The application swaps between two views when the user taps the screen.

Note: You can find the SimpleViewSwitcher project on the website for this book: www.wiley.com/go/iphonedevelopmentvb.

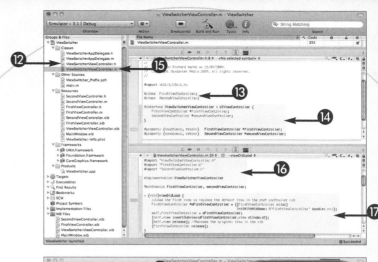

Extra

The advantage of lazy loading is that it minimizes an application's memory requirements. It is also slightly faster, and you can add optional code to initialize incoming views as required — for example, loading an application's preferences and then initializing a view so it shows them when it is switched in.

If your application uses no more than four or five relatively simple views, you can use the simpler approach of preloading all the views into the application's nib file and then swapping them up and down the hierarchy to display them. With this technique, use a root view controller to manage all user interactions instead of scattering them among different view controllers.

The simplest possible application uses a single root view controller and a nib with a stack of views but no separate controllers or controller classes. The controller manages all application events and shuffles the views to update the interface. This is a practical solution for a simple project but can become unwieldy in a complex application where subviews have different visible objects and need to be handled in different ways.

Create
an Alert

You can use alerts to ask users for a decision and to inform them of application errors or other problems. Alerts use the `UIAlertView` class. To display an alert, create an instance of this class, set the messages it will show, and then call the `[show]` method. You should use `[release]` immediately after `[show]` to free the alert object's memory.

Alerts include a title, a message, and at least one button. The title is shown in bold at the top of the alert. The message is a subtitle, shown in a lighter font. You can add two kinds of buttons — Cancel and Other — with distinct properties.

A Cancel button is optional. When the alert appears, the Cancel button is rendered in a darker color. You can add any number of Other buttons, with different titles, but

you must add `nil` to the end of the list to terminate it. By default, alerts display two buttons in a row, so you must keep the title strings short. Cancel and OK should always fit on a single line. Longer titles may not. Three or more buttons can use longer text because they appear in a column.

Because the `UIAlertView` object has so many options, you can make your code more readable by splitting initialization across multiple lines. For example:

```
UIAlertView *anAlert = [[UIAlertView alloc]
 initWithTitle:@"Alert title"
 message: @"Alert message"
 delegate: self
 cancelButtonTitle: @"Cancel"
 otherButtonTitles: @"OK", nil];
```

Create an Alert

① In Xcode, create a new project with the View-based Application template and then save it as Simple Alert.

Note: *You can find the Simple Alert project on the website for this book: www.wiley.com/ go/iphonedevelopmentvb.*

② Optionally, add a label to Simple_ AlertViewController.xib for clarity.

Note: *This step is optional and is for appearance only. It has no effect on the alert code.*

③ Click Simple_AlertViewController.m.

④ Add a `touchesBegan:` method.

⑤ Add code to create an alert object and then initialize it with a title, a message, a Cancel button, and an OK button.

⑥ Add code to show the alert and to release its memory.

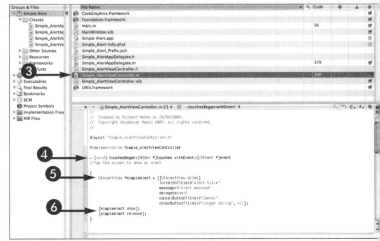

7. Click Build and Run to build and run the application.

● An alert appears when the user taps the screen. It displays the initialized values.

8. Optionally, change the `otherButtonTitles` list to show two or more buttons.

9. Click Build and Run to build and run the application.

● The alert shows the Other buttons in a column rather than a row.

Extra

You can use the `setNumberOfRows` method to arrange buttons vertically rather than horizontally. This solves the problem of short button titles, but it is an undocumented feature. If you submit an application to the App Store and it uses this option, Apple will almost certainly reject it. But this may change in the future, and it is a useful option if you are developing applications for your own needs.

To set the number of rows, call `setNumberOfRows` on the alert object before showing it. For example:

```
[anAlert setNumberOfRows:3];
```

If your user needs to select between three or more different options, use `UIActionSheet` instead. `UIActionSheet` displays options in a column automatically and includes extra color-coding. It is a better choice for showing a group of menu-like options.

Get User Input with an Alert

A user can respond to an alert by canceling it or by selecting another option from the list of other buttons that you choose to show. You can use this feature in your application to allow users to choose a response to an error or another application state.

The UIAlertView object includes a delegate field. To read responses, set the delegate to self and implement the alertView clickedButtonAtIndex: method. For example:

```
- (void) alertView: (UIAlertView *) alertView
  clickedButtonAtIndex: (NSInteger) buttonIndex
{ //Code goes here
}
```

You can test buttonIndex to find the button the user clicked. The index starts at zero with Cancel and then increases by one for each extra button. With a two-button alert, the index will be 0 for Cancel and 1 for OK.

This example uses this information to display a second alert automatically, confirming the user's selection. It creates another UIAlertView object, sets up the display details by using the response from the previous alert, and then displays it.

The delegate is set to nil in the second alert. If the delegate were self, the alertView method would call itself indefinitely, creating a loop.

The UIAlertViewDelegate protocol lists other optional methods that may be useful. willDismissWithButton Index: and didDismissWithButtonIndex: are called before and after the alert is dismissed.

You can use dismissWithClickedButtonIndex: to automatically dismiss an alert. The user does not need to respond; the alert disappears when the method is called, returning the specified index automatically. You can use this feature to implement a time-out.

Get User Input with an Alert

① Create a new project with the View-based Application template and then save it as AlertWithInput.

Note: *You can find the AlertWithInput project on the website for this book: www.wiley.com/go/iphonedevelopmentvb.*

② In AlertWithInputViewController.m, add a touchesBegan method to create an alert with OK and Cancel buttons when the user taps the screen.

③ Add an alertView method to process the return from the alert.

Note: *This method is triggered when the user dismisses the alert.*

④ Add code to read the buttonIndex to discover which button was pressed on the alert.

⑤ Add code to use the buttonIndex value to set a new title string.

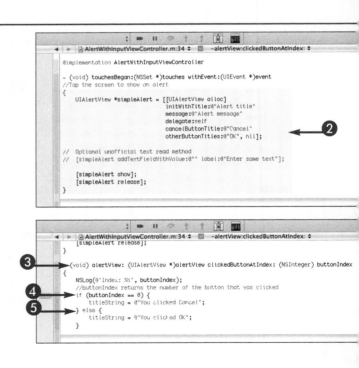

6 Add code to initialize a second alert.

7 Set the title to the new title string.

8 Set a nil message, nil Cancel button, and a fixed other button title.

9 Add code to show the alert and release its memory.

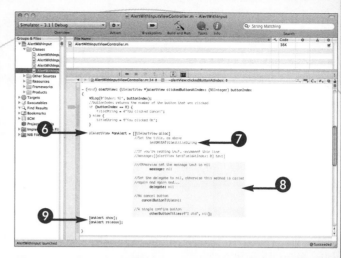

10 Click Build and Run to build and run the application.

● The application shows a second alert that reports the button pressed in the first alert.

Extra

You can add text input to alerts by using an undocumented feature. As with all undocumented features, using this option is likely to disqualify your project from the App Store. However, this is a useful feature that you can add to private applications not intended for public distribution.

To add a text field, call `addTextFieldWithValue:` on an alert before showing it. This displays the alert with a keyboard and adds a text field for the user to type in. The text can be filled with a default return or with a grayed-out hint. For example:

```
[anAlert addTextFieldWithValue:@"This is a preset value" label:@"Enter some text"];
```

`Value` sets the default: `This is a preset value`. If the user taps OK without typing anything, this default is returned.

`label` sets the grayed-out hint. The default return is `nil`. The hint disappears as soon as the user begins typing. If `Value` is non-nil, the label is ignored.

To read the returned text, add `[[alertView textfFieldAtIndex: 0] text];` to `alertView clicked ButtonAtIndex:` This is a standard string and can be read, displayed, and compared in the usual ways.

Create a Sliding Action Sheet Menu

The `UIActionSheet` class is related to `UIAlert` but is optimized for use as a pop-up menu. You can use action sheets to offer the user a selection of choices. Unlike alerts, action sheet buttons are stacked vertically and can display longer title strings.

Like alerts, action sheets are modal. They appear as a view that slides on top of an existing view. While they are visible, other features in the interface are locked, and the user cannot interact with them. When the user makes a selection, the action sheet slides out of sight, and the rest of the interface is unlocked.

To make an action sheet appear, create an action sheet object, initialize its settings, and call a show method on it to display it. The show method specifies a view explicitly. You can use `self.view` in a view controller to select the view that the user is currently interacting with:

`[anActionSheet showInView self.view];`.

You can also make the action sheet appear from a tab bar or a toolbar by using two alternative show methods that animate the sheet in slightly different ways:

`[anActionSheet showFromTabBar: aTabBarView];`
`[anActionSheet showFromToolBar: aToolBarView];`

Action sheets use a delegate that calls the `actionSheet: clickedButtonAtIndex:` method. You can read the number of the selected button from the button index.

In addition to Cancel and one or more Other buttons, you can also specify a Destructive button. This appears in red and should be used for destructive actions, such as file deletions. The Destructive button appears at the top of the sheet, with index 0. Other buttons appear under it, in order, with an increasing index. Cancel appears at the bottom, with the highest index. If there are more than six items, `UIActionSheet` automatically creates a scrolling table view.

Create a Sliding Action Sheet Menu

① Create a new project with the View-based Application template and then save it as ActionSheet.

Note: You can find the ActionSheet project on the website for this book: www.wiley.com/go/iphonedevelopmentvb.

② In ActionSheetViewController.h, add the `UIActionSheetDelegate` protocol to the interface.

Note: This adds the Action Sheet Delegate methods to the view controller.

③ In ActionSheetViewController.m, add a `touchesBegan:` method to respond to taps.

④ Add code to create and initialize an action sheet object, with a nil title, a Cancel button, a Destructive button, and four other buttons.

⑤ Optionally, add code to change the appearance of the action by setting the action sheet style property.

⑥ Add code to show the action sheet in the current view and to release its memory.

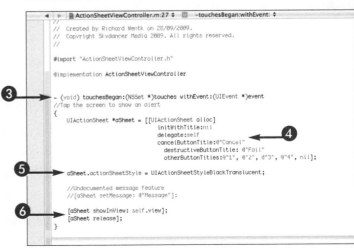

7 Add an `actionSheet: clicked ButtonAtIndex:` method to read the index of the button tapped by the user.

8 Add code to convert the `buttonIndex` into a title string.

9 Add code to create an alert message to display the button index, with a nil message, nil delegate, nil Cancel button, and a single OK button.

Note: *This example illustrates one possible way to use* `buttonIndex`. *The alert is for demonstration only. You can customize the* `actionSheet` *method to your own requirements.*

10 Click Build and Run to build and run the application.

● When the user taps the screen, an action sheet menu appears. When the user taps a button, an alert is generated, with the button index.

Note: *Buttons are numbered from top to bottom. The index numbering is sequential and does not distinguish between Cancel, Destructive, and other buttons.*

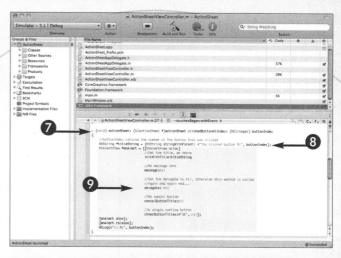

Extra

You can use an optional action sheet style property to change the visual appearance of the sheet:

```
anActionSheet.actionSheetStyle = UIActionSheetStyleBlackTranslucent;
```

There are four preset styles: Automatic, Default, BlackTranslucent, and BlackOpaque. The differences are not dramatic. BlackTranslucent is darker than the others but not — apparently — very translucent.

You can use an undocumented property to give the action sheet a subtitle. This appears under the main title in a slightly larger font. The main title is smaller and less visible than perhaps it should be, so you can use this feature to replace the official title property with a more visible alternative. Set the `initWithTitle:` property to `nil` to make it disappear and then use `[anActionSheet setMessage: @"This is an alternative title"];` to display the alternative. If your application uses this feature, it may not be accepted in the App Store, which is in line with Apple's policy on undocumented features.

Display an Activity Indicator

Y ou can use an activity indicator to let users know that your application is busy. UIKit includes a UIActivityIndicatorView object that can display one of three minimally different activity indicator styles.

The styles are pre-defined as constants, with a UIActivityIndicatorViewStyle prefix. The Gray and White styles are small. You can see examples of this size when the iPhone is booting and shutting down. The WhiteLarge style is larger and less subtle. All the sizes are preset, so you cannot change them.

You can add an activity indicator to any nib in the usual way. However, indicators are often used to display a temporary application state, which may not have an associated nib. To display an indicator in the current view

without a nib, create an instance of UIActivityIndicator View and then initialize it with your chosen style. Use [self.view addSubview: myIndicator]; to show it and [myIndicator removeFromSuperview]; to hide it and release its memory. You can move it to any point on the display by setting its center property.

Activity indicators are very simple; they have only a handful of properties and methods. The [start Animating] and [stopAnimating] methods start and stop the spinning action. Objects and methods can use [isAnimating] to check the spinner's status. You can also set [hidesWhenStopped] to hide the indicator automatically when it is not spinning. This hides it on the display but does not remove it from the view hierarchy.

Display an Activity Indicator

① Create a new project with the View-based Application template and then save it as ActivityIndicator.

Note: *You can find the ActivityIndicator project on the website for this book: www.wiley.com/go/iphone developmentvb.*

② In ActivityIndicatorViewController.m, add an instance pointer to UIActivityIndicatorView.

③ Add a Boolean, which is used internally to set the spin status.

④ Add a touchesBegan: method to respond to taps on the screen.

⑤ Add code to test the Boolean and to toggle its status when the user taps the screen.

⑥ Add code to allocate an instance of UIActivityIndicatorView.

⑦ Add code to position the indicator at the center of the display and to set it spinning.

⑧ Add code to insert the indicator in the view tree and then add code to remove it from the view tree and to release it when the user taps the screen a second time.

⑨ Click Build and Run to build and run the application and then test it by tapping/clicking the screen.

● A small spinner appears when the screen is tapped once and disappears when it is tapped again.

⑩ Optionally, change the spinner style to UIActivityIndicatorViewStyle WhiteLarge.

⑪ Click Build and Run to build and run the application and then tap/click the screen.

● A larger and more visible spinner appears.

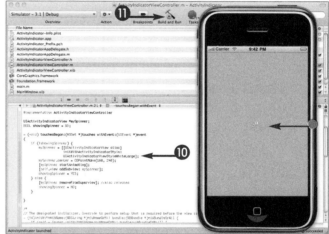

Extra

You can give users more on an application's status by combining a spinner with a progress bar or with an optional text field to indicate time remaining or the percentage of a task left to complete. A spinner on its own says "Wait," but it does not specify how long. A short wait of a minute or two is acceptable. When the wait is longer, you should give users more information.

You can also use the spinner as a generic indicator that something is happening. For example, the Maps application uses it to show that the position is being continually updated.

To use a spinner as a floating activity indicator, attach it to a subview box with an optional frame and display the subview with an opacity of 7 or 8. This simulates some of the translucency of an alert box and helps draw attention to the spinner. Calculating time remaining can be a challenge. Although it is very easy to create a spinner, you may need to add a separate thread to your application to manage a time-consuming task and then pass information between the threads to update the time remaining. For more on threads, see Chapter 9.

Add a Slider and Progress Bar

You can use sliders in your interface to give the user an analog-style control option for setting parameters. You can also set the slider value in code to use it as an indicator. However, a separate progress bar indicator is also available and provides a better solution.

UISlider appears very simple but offers extra features that are not obvious. By default, you can use instances of UISlider to send Value Changed messages to your application. In Interface Builder, you can set the slider range to any pair of floats as long as the maximum is greater than the minimum. You can also toggle a Continuous property. When enabled, the slider sends messages whenever it is moved. Otherwise, it sends a single updated value on release. Slider graphics, including both sides of the track and the moveable *thumb*, can show customized images.

For simple progress bars, you can use the UIProgress View class. You cannot customize progress bars, but you can select from two standard designs: a default option, which is similar to a slider without a thumb, and a thinner and more visually sophisticated bar style, with a black and silver color scheme. You can set the displayed progress by writing a float to the view's progress property, in the range from 0.0 to 1.0. This range is fixed. If your source range is different, you must add code to normalize it.

If you are using Interface Builder to design a view, you cannot rotate a slider or progress bar; the orientation is always horizontal. However, you can change the rotation in code to create vertical sliders and progress bars by applying an affine transformation. For more on affine transformations, see Chapter 8.

Add a Slider and Progress Bar

① Create a new project with the View-based Application template and then save it as SliderProgress.

② In SliderProgressViewController.h, add IBOutlets for a UISlider, a UIProgressBar, and a UILabel to the interface.

③ Add an IBAction sliderWasChanged method.

④ Add property declarations for the objects in the interface and then save the file.

⑤ In SliderProgressViewController.m, synthesize the objects in the interface.

⑥ Add an implementation for the sliderWasChanged method.

⑦ Add code to read the slider value.

Note: sender *is the sending object. In this method, the sending object is the slider.*

⑧ Add code to convert the slider value to a string, to copy it to the label, and to set the progress bar's position to match the value and then save the file.

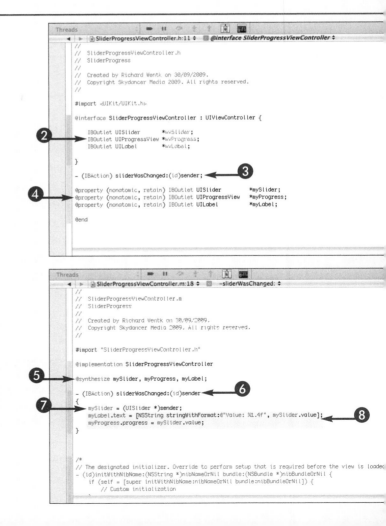

9 Double-click SliderProgressViewController.xib to open it in Interface Builder.

10 Add these to the view: a slider, a progress bar, a label for the slider, and a label for the progress bar.

Note: This example shows the `Bar` slider style. You can set the style in the Attributes pane in the Inspector window.

11 Create links between the progress bar label, the progress bar, and their corresponding outlets.

Note: The outlet for the slider is not used in this example — the application reads the slider value but does not write to it.

12 Create links between the slider's Value Changed message and the sliderWasChanged method in First Responder and then save the nib.

13 Click Build and Run to build and run the application and then test it by moving the slider with your finger or dragging it with the mouse in the Simulator.

● The progress bar tracks the slider value, and the label reports the value numerically.

Note: You can find the SliderProgress project on the website for this book: www.wiley.com/go/iphonedevelopmentvb.

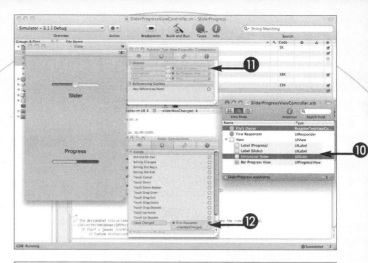

Extra

You can customize a `UISlider`'s graphics to create original slider designs. The slider effect is created from three elements: a minimum track image that draws the area to the left of the track, a maximum track image that draws the area to the right, and the thumb marker itself. In the default slider design, the left area is colored and the right area is plain. You do not have to copy this effect. For example, you can create a more sophisticated result by switching between a selection of different images as the slider moves — for example, to create a slider that changes color from left to right.

You can set the left and right areas in the Attributes pane of the Inspector window. You can also set them in code by using `setMinimumTrackImage:`, `setMaximumTrackImage:`, and `setThumbImage:`, each pointing to a `UIImage` object.

Optionally, you can add minimum and maximum images — fixed graphics that appear to the left and right of the slider, beyond the track area. You can use these to hint at the slider's function — for example, with images of a hare and a tortoise to indicate speed.

Add Toggle Switches and Segmented Controls

You can add toggle switches and segmented controls to your application to provide clear feedback about preferences and application settings. The UISwitch toggle switch is one of the simplest and least customizable objects in the Cocoa Touch library. You cannot change the text — the two options are preset to On and Off — or the color. The size is also fixed.

UISwitch sends a Value Changed message when the user toggles it. It does not send any other messages. You must connect this message to a receiver method in Interface Builder. It has a single on property that you can toggle from your application — for example, to manage a bank of synchronized switches with code to simulate a radio button effect.

UISegmentedControl switches have many more features, although they do not include the smooth toggle animation

effect available with UISwitch. They offer customizable text, color, and graphics, and a built-in radio button feature. You can also use them as momentary nonlatching switches. However, the height is fixed and is set by the three available styles: Plain, which is a larger style with a fixed blue selection color; Bordered, which adds a thin black border; and Bar, which is a narrower option with customizable features. The Bar option works well when added to a toolbar or a navigation controller.

A segmented control sends a Value Changed message when the user taps it. You can link the message to a receiver method for processing in Interface Builder. Segments are indexed starting from 0. To read the number of the selected segment in a linked IBAction method, use [sender selectedSegmentIndex];. Elsewhere, replace sender with the name you set for the control.

Add Toggle Switches and Segmented Controls

① Create a new project with the View-based Application template and then save it as Switches.

② In SwitchesViewController.h, add IBOutlets for two UILabels to the interface.

③ Add property declarations for the objects in the interface.

④ Add IBAction switchChanged: and segmentChanged: methods and then save the file.

⑤ Synthesize the label instances.

⑥ Implement the switchChanged: method and then add code to read the sender object into a local UISwitch object.

⑦ Add code to test the on property and then set the corresponding label text in the view.

⑧ Implement the segmentChanged: method, add code to read the segment index and copy it to the corresponding label in the view, and then save the file.

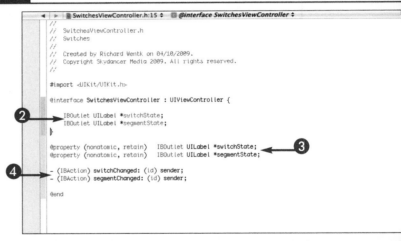

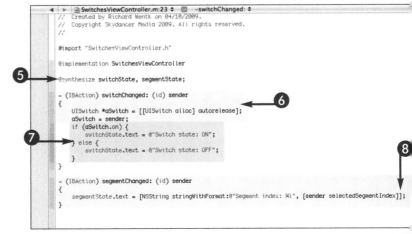

9 Double-click SwitchesViewController.xib to open it in Interface Builder.

10 Add a UISwitch, a UISegmentedControl, and two UILabels to the view by dragging and dropping them from the Library.

11 Optionally, center them and resize the text by using the features in the Attributes pane in the Inspector window.

12 Select the UISegmentedControl, click the Attributes tab in the Inspector window, and then set the number of segments to 3. Select each segment in turn by using the drop-down segment menu and then give each one a unique title.

13 Link the labels to the segmentState and switchState outlets in File's Owner and then link Value Changed messages from both switches to the corresponding methods in First Responder.

14 Click Build and Run to build and run the application and then test it by clicking the switch and the segmented control.

● The labels are updated with the current state of the controls as you click/tap them.

Note: You can find the Switches project on the website for this book: www.wiley. com/go/iphonedevelopmentvb.

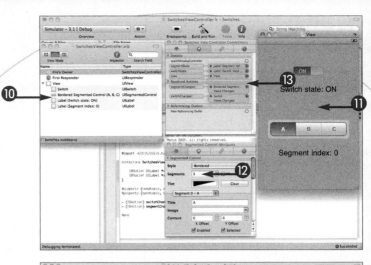

Extra

You can set the target object and method of a segmented control from code:

```
[nameOfSegmentedControl
addTarget: self
action:@selection(aMethod:) forControlEvents:UIControlEventValueChanged];
```

This sets the target object from `addTarget:` — `self` in this example — and specifies that `aMethod` should be triggered when the user taps the control. Typically, this code is placed in `viewDidLoad` in the root view controller.

You can set the color of a bar-segmented control by changing the tint in the Attributes pane in the Inspector window. However, this option is only semi-customizable. The selected segment uses the same tint as the rest of the bar but is automatically made slightly darker. You cannot set it to a different color or alter its relative brightness. This limits the workable brightness range for the bar. For good results when tinting, set the brightness slider in Interface Builder's Color Control to between 50% and 75%.

Add a Search Bar

You can add a search controller to your application by displaying a *search bar*. A search bar is a visible object that displays a text entry bar with a magnifying glass. When clicked anywhere, it reveals a keyboard and text entry area, with a Clear option and a Cancel button. You can add optional *scope buttons* to the search. These preset tags appear under the search bar and can be clicked to narrow the range of a search; for example, if you are searching the Address Book, you can set scope buttons to specify friends, family, or coworkers. Similarly, you can search From, To, Subject and All fields in the Mail app.

You can also select one of the preset iPhone keyboards for search string entry. The default text keyboard is ideal for text searches, but you can also select a phone keypad

to search for numbers or specify numeric, email, and URL keypads. The search can be prompted with grayed-out placeholder text that disappears when the user starts typing or filled with a default search string. Optionally, you can give the search box a title and select one of three graphic styles: the default light gray, a darker gray, or a glassy opaque black.

The search bar does not actually perform the search. It passes search strings from the user, with information about user interaction with the scope buttons and other features, to a delegate object. To implement a search feature, you must add search code to the delegate.

Search bars are often combined with table views. Typically the search feature is used to select one or more items from a visible table based on the search string. The table can be updated continuously as the search string is entered.

Add a Search Bar

① Create a new project with the View-based Application template and then save it as SearchBar.

② In SearchBarViewController.h, add the `UISearchBarDelegate` protocol to the interface.

③ Add an `IBOutlet` for a label.

④ Declare the label as a property and then save the file.

⑤ In SearchBarViewController.m, synthesize the label.

⑥ Add a `searchBar: textDidChange:` delegate method and then copy the search text to the label.

Note: *This method is triggered every time the user changes the search text, updating it as the user types.*

⑦ Add a `searchBarSearchButtonClicked` delegate method and then add code to clear the search string.

⑧ Add code to hide the search keyboard by calling `resignFirstResponder` and then save the file.

Note: *This is the standard technique for dismissing a keyboard when the user no longer needs it.*

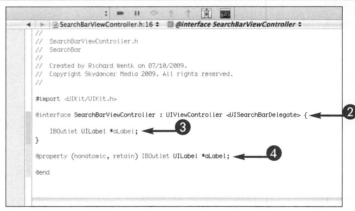

⑨ Double-click SearchBarViewController.xib to open it in Interface Builder.

⑩ Drag and drop a search bar and two labels from the Library onto the view.

⑪ Move and center the labels toward the top of the view and then set fixed text for the top label in the Attributes pane in the Inspector window.

⑫ Select the search bar and then drag a link between its delegate outlet and File's Owner in the Connections pane in the Inspector window.

⑬ Drag a link between the lower label and its corresponding outlet in File's Owner and then save the nib.

⑭ Click Build and Run to build and run the application and then test it by clicking the search bar, entering text using the keyboard that appears, and clicking the Search button to dismiss the search keyboard.

● The label displays search text as the user types, and the keyboard is dismissed when the user taps the Search button.

Note: In this example, the search string is not retained when the keyboard is dismissed.

Note: You can find the SearchBar project on the website for this book: www.wiley.com/go/iphonedevelopmentvb.

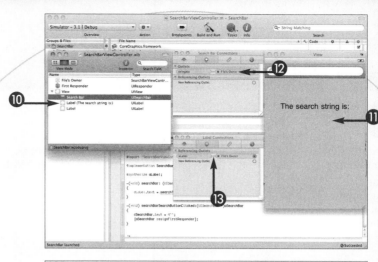

Extra

The list of messages sent by a search bar is listed in the UISearchBarDelegate Protocol Reference in the documentation. `searchBar:TextDidBeginEditing:` is sent when the user begins editing text and `searchBar:TextDidEndEditing:` when the user finishes. `searchBar:textDidChange:` is sent whenever the text changes. You can implement this method to create live searches that update as the user types.

You can implement searches in many different ways. A comprehensive set of search options is built into the `NSString` class in the `rangeOf:` methods. These return the position of a search string within a target string, with eight possible search options, including literal, backward, and case-insensitive. For details, see the NSString Class Reference in the documentation.

Add a Background Image

By default, `UIView` objects display a fixed color background. You can improve the appearance of your application by adding a background image. You can then place buttons, sliders, and other elements on top of the background image.

You can use this feature creatively — for example, by creating a background image with a perspective that creates an illusion of depth. You can also use it as a visual design aid. For example, you can split a view into two or more color-coded functional areas, with optional frames. To save memory, you can create your own static button graphics in the background image and then read the coordinates of touch messages to check whether the user tapped them.

To fill the screen, background image dimensions should be 460 × 320 pixels. The height is 20 pixels smaller than

the full 480-pixel height of the display because the top of the screen is reserved for the status bar. However, for a completely customized look, you can hide the status bar by adding `[[UIApplication sharedApplication] setStatusBarHidden: YES animated: no];` to `viewDidLoad` in your root view controller. You can then design and load your custom background image to fill the full 480 × 320 screen.

To display the background, you must first add your image to your Xcode project by dragging it into the project folder in the Finder, right-clicking on Resources, choosing Add→ Existing Files from the pop-up menu, navigating to the file, and then clicking Add. You can then add a `UIImageView` object to your view in Interface Builder. The Attributes for `UIImageView` include an image selection drop-down menu. All images included in your project appear in this list. When you select an image, the `UIImageView` object is updated to show a preview.

Add a Background Image

① In Xcode, create a new project from the View-based Application template and then save it as ShowImage.

Note: *You can find the ShowImage project on the website for this book: www.wiley.com/go/ iphonedevelopmentvb.*

② In an image editor of your choice, create a 460-pixel × 320-pixel image.

③ Save it to your new project's folder as background.png.

   The image is saved to the folder but is not yet part of the project.

④ Right-click on the Resources folder and then choose Add→Existing Files from the pop-up menu.

⑤ Click background.png.

⑥ Click Add and then click Add in the second dialog box. Do not change the default options.

7. Double-click ShowImageViewController.xib to open it in Interface Builder.

8. Drag an Image View object from the Library and then drop it on the view.

Note: It should appear indented under the view.

9. Click the Attributes tab in the Inspector window.

10. Choose background.png from the Image drop-down menu and then save the nib file.

   The view preview changes to show the new image.

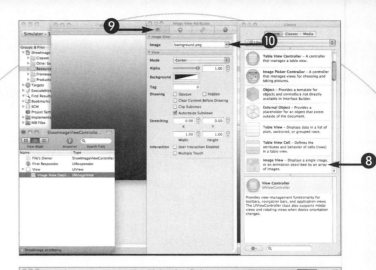

11. Click Build and Run to build and run the project.

● The background image appears in the view.

Extra

You can use `UIImageView` to display images in other contexts — for example, to add moveable tiles and buttons to your application. `UIImageView` is a subclass of `UIView`, so all of `UIView`'s features are available. For a full list, review the UIView Class Reference in the documentation. For example, you can move images by setting their center properties. You can also scale them. To check whether a user has touched an image, use the `hitTest` method.

`UIImageView` supports flip-book animation. You can load the `animationImages` property with an `NSArray` of `UIImage` objects, which are shown in sequence over a specified duration. Animation is not supported in Interface Builder, so you must add it in code.

`UIImage` objects offer more direct access to image data. You can load them from a file, from images produced by one of the graphics frameworks, or from an array of raw image data calculated mathematically. `UIImageView` is optimized for static images and for images that respond to user interaction. `UIImage` is optimized for image processing. You can load any `UIImage` object into `UIImageView` by setting the latter's image property.

Create a
Custom Button

You can make your application more visually appealing by replacing the default Rounded Rect Button type with custom button graphics. Creating appealing custom graphics is a graphic design challenge rather than a coding problem. Beginners in Photoshop or Gimp can copy a popular look, such as the glass button effect, relatively quickly. Simple step-by-step tutorials are easy to find online.

This example uses a pair of very simple gradient fill PNG files to demonstrate how to replace the default button graphics in Interface Builder. You must save your custom button art as a PNG file. To add rounded corners, save the file with transparency. The active area of the button — the area that responds when tapped — is set by the full width and height of the file, including the transparent area. You

can use this feature deliberately to expand the active area of a small button. However, making the area much larger than the visible graphic may confuse users.

Buttons have two basic states: default and highlighted, which is triggered when the button is tapped. You must create different button art for each. There are also two optional states: Selected and Disabled. The Selected option is used for buttons that toggle between two states. The Disabled state is used to indicate a button that is not available and will typically be grayed-out. If you do not design and select files for these optional states, Interface Builder assigns one of the other two files by default.

Changing the button graphic does not change the operation of a button. A custom button sends the same messages as the default Rounded Rect Button and must be linked to a receiver method in the usual way.

Create a Custom Button

① In Xcode, create a new project with the View-based Application template and then save it as CustomButton.

Note: *You can find the CustomButton project on the website for this book: www.wiley.com/go/iphonedevelopmentvb.*

② In an image editor of your choice, create two custom PNG files with optional transparency: one for the default state and one for the highlighted state.

Note: *Buttons can be resized in both dimensions in Xcode. Custom graphics do not have to be actual size.*

③ Save both files to the CustomButton project folder.

Note: *The file names are arbitrary. You can include the words default and highlighted for clarity, but this is optional.*

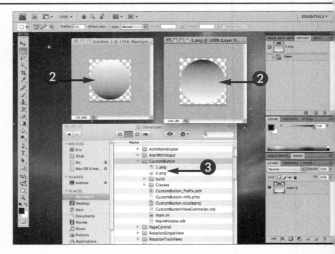

④ Right-click on the Resources folder in Xcode and then choose Add→Existing Files from the pop-up menu.

⑤ Navigate to the CustomButton project folder and then select both PNG files.

⑥ Click Add and then click Add in the import dialog box. Do not change the default settings.

The graphic files are added to the project and appear in the Resources folder.

7 Double-click CustomButtonViewController. xib to open it in Interface Builder.

8 Drag a Round Rect button object from the Library and then drop it on the view. Optionally, resize it by dragging the corner markers.

9 Click the Attributes tab in the Inspector window and then set the Type to Custom and select the Default State Configuration from the Type menu.

10 Click the Background drop-down menu to choose a button graphic for the Default state.

● The view preview shows the new button image.

11 Choose Highlighted State Configuration from the Type menu.

12 Choose the other button graphic from the Background menu.

Note: *The view preview does not show the highlighted button state.*

13 Optionally, change the text color.

Note: *The default highlighted text color is white, which may not be suitable for your custom button art.*

14 Save the nib file.

15 Click Build and Run to build and run the application.

● The default custom button art appears on the display, and the button automatically displays the highlighted art when tapped.

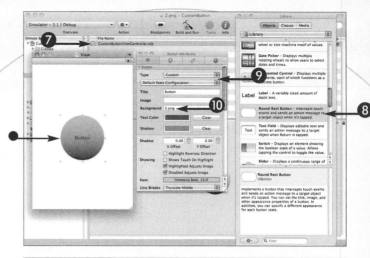

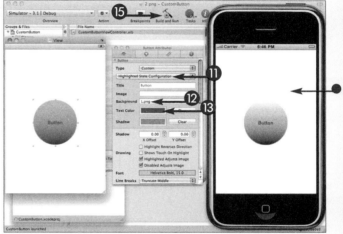

Buttons can be stretched and squashed in Interface Builder. Your art is automatically resized to fill the area you select. However, Interface Builder does not always preview this correctly, so you must check the results in the Simulator. If you select a button title, it appears on top of your art. By default, the Default state shows the title in dark blue, and the highlighted state shows it in white. For most custom graphics, you need to change the highlighted text color to dark blue.

Buttons do not have to be round or rectangular. The rounded glassy button has become a design cliché; you can make your application more visually interesting with other shapes and icons. More advanced developers can use the features in the Core Graphics framework to create custom buttons that use the iPhone's graphics library. You can use this option to create buttons with automated reflection effects, to turn photos from the camera into buttons or icons, or to produce completely original effects. Under code control, you can add any UIImageView object to a button — including a flip-book animation effect.

Create a Webview

Y ou can use a webview object to add a customized web browser to your application. A webview UIWebView object has all the features of a UIView object but can be loaded with a URL to display a web page. The web display is minimal. It supports scrolling, zooming, and pinching, but it does not support bookmarks, Forward and Back buttons, a URL bar, or other features of a full browser. However, you can implement these by adding extra toolbars, tab bars, labels, and other visible objects to the view tree.

Webviews have a limited selection of built-in methods. You can load a URL with an optional MIME type. You can also load a request, which is an instance of an NSURLRequest object. You must preload the request object with a URL object, which must in turn be preloaded with this URL string:

```
NSURL *url = [NSURL URLWithString: @"http://
www.someurl.com"];
NSURLRequest *requestObject = [NSURLRequest
requestWithURL: url];
```

To load the request into the webview, use [webView loadRequest: requestObj];.

This tells the webview to download and display the selected URL. If you add extra Forward and Back buttons — for example, on a toolbar — you can send goBack: and goForward: messages to the webview to navigate through a series of pages. A history is maintained automatically. A webview can automatically recognize telephone numbers and can show them as clickable links that load the phone application. You can enable this option in the webview's attributes in the Inspector window or send a bitmask loaded with UIDataDetectorType constants to the dataDetectorTypes property.

Create a Webview

① In Xcode, create a new project with the View-based Application template and then save it as WebView.

Note: *You can find the WebView project on the website for this book: www.wiley. com/go/iphonedevelopmentvb.*

② Click WebViewViewController.h.

③ Add an IBOutlet with a named UIWebView object.

④ Declare the webview object as a property.

⑤ Click WebViewViewController.m.

⑥ Synthesize the webView instance variable.

⑦ Add code to viewDidLoad to create a URL Request object from a URL object pointing to www.apple.com.

⑧ Add code to load the request into the webview. Save all open files.

9 Double-click WebViewViewController.xib to open it in Interface Builder.

10 Drag and drop a Web View from the Library to the view.

11 Click the Connections tab in the Inspector window.

12 Drag a link from a New Referencing Outlet to File's Owner and then select webView from the floating menu that appears.

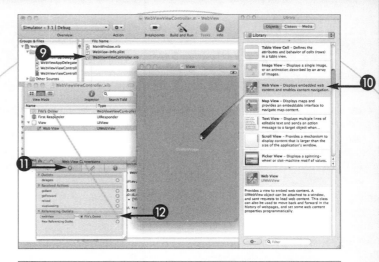

13 Click Build and Run to build and run the project.

● The webview displays the Apple website. Links in the content work, but the webview does not offer a URL bar, Forward and Back buttons, or other browser features.

Extra

Webviews are ideal for directing users to a web page while keeping them within your application — for example, to load a support page for an application. You can also use them to display formatted help pages, with optional images, in your application. A webview parses Cascading Style Sheets (CSS), with styled text, in exactly the same way as the iPhone's Safari browser. Use the `loadHTMLString: baseURL:` method to load a local file.

`UIWebView` supports JavaScript, with limitations. The `stringByEvaluatingJavaScriptFromString:` method returns the result of running a script. However, the execution time is limited to 10 seconds, and the available memory is limited to 10MB. When JavaScript is running, it monopolizes your application's execution thread. The ten-second limit ensures that JavaScript cannot lock the iPhone.

Create an
Auto-Rotating View

You can use *auto-rotation* — also known as *auto-orientation* — to create interfaces that rotate automatically when the user rotates his or her handset. By default, auto-rotation is disabled, and the display is fixed in portrait mode. But you can enable auto-rotation with just a few lines of code.

To implement auto-orientation, add a method called `shouldRotateToInterfaceOrientation:` to your application's view controller. This method is included in the View-based Application template in Xcode but is commented out. To enable this feature, uncomment it.

When the user rotates the device, the operating system triggers `shouldRotateToInterfaceOrientation:`, passing it the new orientation of the handset. When the method returns YES, the view is rotated automatically. If it returns NO, nothing happens. The four possible rotations are `Portrait`, `PortraitUpsideDown`, `LandscapeRight`, and `LandscapeLeft`. They are pre-defined as constants in UIKit, with the `UIInterfaceOrientation` prefix — for example, `UIInterfaceOrientationPortrait`.

To support every orientation, add a single line of code: `return YES`. However, according to Apple's guidelines, users may be confused by the `PortraitUpsideDown` orientation if they receive an incoming call. To disable `PortraitUpsideDown`:

```
return (interfaceOrientation != UIInterface
    OrientationPortraitUpsideDown);
```

This returns NO for `PortraitUpsideDown` and YES for the other orientations. You do not need to add further code to `shouldRotateToInterfaceOrientation:`.

To ensure that a view rotates correctly, you must enable auto-centering for every object in a view. Otherwise objects rotate about their corners, destroying the view's layout. When auto-centering is enabled, objects automatically rotate correctly. You can preview rotations in Interface Builder by clicking the Rotation icon at the top right of the view window. You can also rotate views in the Simulator. However, to test the full range of orientations, including `PortraitUpsideDown`, you must test the application on a real handset.

Create an Auto-Rotating View

① Create a new project in Xcode with the View-based Application template and then save it as RotationSingleView.

Note: You can find the RotationSingleView project on the website for this book: www.wiley.com/go/ iphonedevelopmentvb.

② In RotationSingleViewViewController.m, find `shouldAutorotateToInterface Orientation:` and then uncomment it.

③ Add code to return YES for every orientation except `PortraitUpsideDown`.

④ Double-click RotationSingleViewViewController.xib to open it in Interface Builder.

⑤ Add a text label by dragging it from the Library and dropping it on the view. Optionally, edit the text.

⑥ Click the Alignment tab in the Inspector window.

⑦ Click both Placement icons to center the label in the view.

⑧ Click the label.

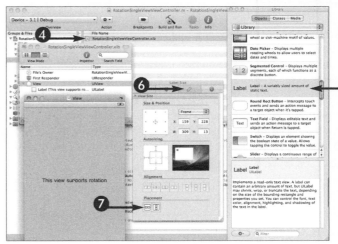

⑨ In the Autosizing box, click the top and left-centering options to disable them.

Note: *When disabled, the centering options are shown as dashed lines. All four should be disabled.*

⑩ Test the layout by clicking the rotation preview icon.

The layout rotates, and the label remains centered in the view.

⑪ Optionally, experiment by adding other items to the view, turning off their centering, and rotating the layout.

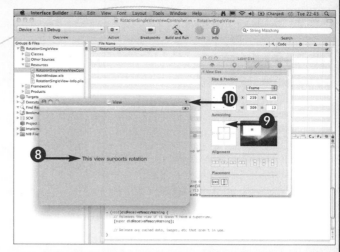

⑫ Click Build and Run to build and run the application.

⑬ In the Simulator, test the orientation by choosing Hardware→Rotate Left and Hardware→Rotate Right.

Note: *The Simulator does not model the* PortraitUpsideDown *orientation.*

The view rotates to match the orientation.

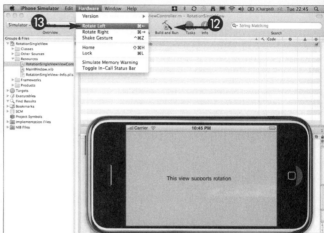

Extra

Auto-rotation is a powerful feature. You can use it to create views that rotate automatically with little or no extra design effort. But it is not a complete solution. If your view uses large buttons, text fields, or other larger visible objects, they may overlap when the view is rotated. You can solve this problem by rearranging the objects to avoid overlap. Alternatively, you can also create two or three different views and then swap them in when the orientation changes. For details, see the next example.

Text fields — including buttons, toolbars, switches, and labels — need special handling. By default, text is left-justified. Text fields positioned on the center line of the display should be center-justified. Other text fields may need center- or left-justification, depending on the position of the text field and the length of the text. You can center-justify text in the Inspector window by clicking the Layout Alignment buttons near the top of the Attributes pane.

Use Orientation Events to Switch Views

Auto-rotation is an ideal solution for rotating simpler views. However, applications sometimes need more sophisticated rotation options. You can use orientation events to swap between two or more distinct views and to implement other rotation-based features. For example, you can run code before or after a rotation event to enable or disable application features that are unnecessary while a view is rotating. You can also set or reset zoom levels, update scroll positions, or trigger sounds and animations.

There are four rotation events. To implement them, add them to your view controller. They are pre-defined as optional methods in the `UIViewController` class.

`willRotateToOrientation:` is triggered before rotation begins. It passes the new orientation, with a duration that specifies how long the rotation sequence will take.

`willAnimateFirstHalfofRotationToInterface Orientation:` is called before an animation begins.

When you use rotation events to switch views, you can add optional animations, as described in Chapter 5. The animation is done in two stages. The first stage switches the main views. The second stage animates pending rotation of any header and footer views. A `willAnimate SecondHalfofRotationToInterfaceOrientation:` method is triggered just before the second part of an animated rotation, when the header and footer views are about to slide into place. You can also handle animation in a single step with `willAnimateRotationToInterface Orientation:`. This is called before animation begins and replaces both the `FirstHalf` and `SecondHalf` methods.

You can use any of these methods to swap views. A single-view design may not be suitable for auto-rotation, so you can use these methods to swap between two views, with appropriately placed buttons and other features.

Use Orientation Events to Switch Views

① Create a new project in Xcode with the View-based Application template and then save it as RotationTwoViews. Choose File→New File in Xcode to create a new class.

② Click UIViewController subclass and then click the With Xib for user interface check box.

③ Click Next and then save the new class as FirstViewController. Repeat steps 2 and 3 to create another class and nib called SecondViewController.

④ In Interface Builder, add a label to each view, edit it to show distinct text, and then save both views.

⑤ In Interface Builder, select the view in the second nib file and then use the rotation preview button to rotate it. Check its rotated layout. Turn off auto-sizing for every element in the view but not for the view itself.

⑥ Click the view.

⑦ Click the Size tab in the Inspector window, turn on the auto-sizing feature for the view on all four sides, and then save the nib file.

⑧ In RotationTwoViewsViewController.m, find `shouldAutorotateToInterface Orientation:` and then uncomment it.

⑨ Add code to return `YES` for every orientation except `PortraitUpsideDown`.

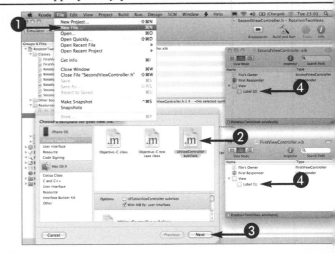

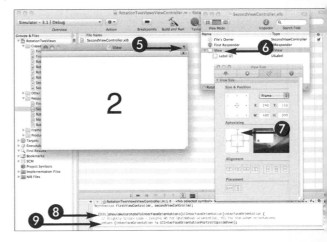

Note: All four sides should show solid lines. These steps guarantee that the nib will remain anchored to the center of the screen when it is switched in. Only the second view needs to appear rotated — the first view disappears automatically when the handset is rotated.

🔟 Find `viewDidLoad` and then add code to load and show the first nib.

⑪ Add a `didRotateFromInterface Orientation:` method.

⑫ Add code for lazy loading of the two views.

⑬ Add code to switch between the two views.

⑭ In RotationTwoViewsViewController.h, add class definitions for `FirstViewController` and `SecondViewController` and then add instance variables and properties for each.

⑮ In RotationTwoViewsViewController.m, synthesize the properties.

⑯ Click Build and Run to build and run the application.

⑰ In the Simulator, test the orientation by choosing Hardware→Rotate Left and Hardware→Rotate Right.

Note: The Simulator does not model the `Portrait UpsideDown` orientation.

The views are switched automatically when the handset is rotated.

Note: You can find the RotationTwoViews project on the website for this book: www.wiley.com/go/iphonedevelopmentvb.

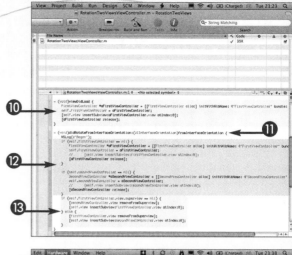

Extra

View-switching with rotation does not create a smooth transition. The views are in different orientations when they are switched, and the effect is disjointed. You can create a smoother effect by animating the transition. Movement-based animations, such as pushes and spins, are even more confusing for the user. But a cross-fade, which fades out the opacity of one view while fading in the other, is ideal for this application. Because the rotation can be split into two halves, you can use three views: the original view, a gray or black transition view, and the second target view. Fading to gray or black creates a smoother feel. For more on creating animations, see Chapter 5.

Although this example uses view-switching, the second view is also auto-rotated. By using auto-rotation, you can reuse either or both of the views for two opposing rotations. Your application can display three or even four completely different views selected by orientation, but users typically only need to see portrait and landscape options.

Enriching the
User Experience

You can use the iPhone's advanced graphics, sound, and animation features to create a more dynamic, interesting, and creative user experience. A key feature of the iPhone is that interfaces are not static. They can be animated, updated, and transformed in real time. Unlike a desktop application with fixed menus and dialog boxes, an iPhone application can be made more dynamic with movement, action, and change. This helps maintain user interest and also gives a user extra information about the state of an application.

Animation and dynamic features are optional but can enhance almost any project. For example, changing views in Springboard triggers a subtle bounce effect. Springboard's designers could have implemented simple view switching, but the bounce effect gives the impression that the iPhone is tactile and responsive and that objects on the display have a physicality that would be missing in a simpler interface. Adding simple animations is easy on the iPhone and creates obvious user benefits.

Animation

The Core Animation library on the iPhone offers a rich set of animation features. Objects can be animated in two ways. They can have their properties modified directly; for example, changing an object's `center` property updates its position on the display. Objects can also be linked to animation objects to create animation effects. Some classes, including modal views, offer a small collection of pre-defined effects. More complex animations can be created under program control and applied to a wider range of objects.

Your application can use either or both of these techniques to modify position, scaling, rotation, and clipping, among other properties. Optional *keyframing* — fine multistep control of animation timing and events — is available for more complex effects.

Animation timing can be handled automatically. Your application does not need to create an update loop or calculate the intermediate steps in an animation; however, it can still use this technique for exceptional and unusual effects. More typically, you can use the animation features built into the `UIView` class. Because all display objects are subclasses of `UIView`, your application can use the same set of features to animate any visible object.

Transforms are a key part of Core Animation. Using transforms, animations can change an object's visible appearance without changing its properties. Objects can be squashed, stretched, rotated, or moved on the display. These are purely visual effects — their true position and size are not modified.

Sound and Vibration

The iPhone features a selection of audio frameworks, grouped into a collection of features called Core Audio. Adding complex sound playback that can mix multiple sound files is a relatively advanced project, but you can easily add simple sounds and alerts via the `AVAudioPlayer` class to trigger playback of sounds bundled with an application. Source files can be compressed MP3 or AAC files or uncompressed WAV or AIFF files.

Your application can use sound for alerts, as feedback, or to implement application features. For example, the DTMF (dual-tone multi-frequency) tones used in the iPhone application are stored as preset sound files and triggered when the user touches the numeric keypad. You can also add vibrate alerts to your application — with or without sounds. The vibrate feature uses the System Sound interface, which is also part of Core Audio.

A key concept in interface design is the view hierarchy, introduced in Chapter 4. The view hierarchy manages complete view trees, including complete views created in Interface Builder. It also manages individual view objects, which can be moved up and down the view hierarchy at any time to show them or hide them.

Animation adds another feature to the view hierarchy. A selection of preset animations can be applied directly to views and view objects. More complex animations require *layers*. A layer holds graphic information. Layer features are part of the Core Graphics library and can be used for drawings and other graphic effects.

A simple `[layer]` method can be run on any view or view object to convert it to a layer, ready for animation, automatically including all its subviews. You can use this feature to animate complete views, with all their visible objects, by using just a few lines of code.

Targets and Actions

The `touches` methods introduced in Chapter 3 are a subset of the available features for managing user interaction. All views and view objects can have targets and actions reassigned dynamically. For example, in Chapter 3, you created a view in Interface Builder by linking a button to a `buttonWasPressed:` method.

This link is not fixed. Your application can detach the method from the button and reassign an alternative method under program control, optionally updating the title to show the button's new status. You can use the features in the `UIControl` class to handle assignment and reassignment of targets and actions for all visible objects. `UIControl` also includes multi-touch management features.

Creating Interfaces without Interface Builder

You do not have to use Interface Builder to create interfaces. Your application can add and remove objects from a view under code control. You can use this feature to create complete views and view controllers, with associated actions and targets. Almost any Cocoa object included in the UIKit framework can be created, displayed, modified, and released as your application runs.

You can use this powerful feature to create dynamic interfaces, with elements that move or adapt according to a user's requirements. You can also use it to create grid-based interfaces. Designing a layout with 40 buttons is difficult in Interface Builder but relatively simple in code. Objects can also be moved and rearranged under program control.

Interface Builder remains a good visual design tool for relatively simple views. Layouts can be designed by eye — helped by Interface Builder's alignment, centering, and grouping tools. It is more difficult to create an attractive layout under program control because the size and spacing of objects must be calculated from scratch. If you use dynamic views regularly, you will find it helpful to create centering and alignment methods to simplify your code.

You can also create hybrid views in which part of the interface is created in Interface Builder and the rest is managed dynamically. This can be a good solution for simple games, where a game area with tiles or other view objects is managed dynamically to create movement or color changes and a standard tab bar and navigation bar manage the rest of the application. For an example, see a section later in this chapter.

Create an Animated Modal Pop-Up View

ne of the simplest enhanced interface options is an animated pop-up. Pop-ups are ideal for information views and for dialog boxes and settings. Users dismiss the pop-up when they have finished with it, revealing the original view. Pop-ups are *modal* — they take full control of the application interface when they appear. You must include explicit touch methods and interface features in the modal view controller; otherwise, the user will not be able to dismiss it.

The animation options for modal pop-ups are fixed. You cannot change the duration of the animation, and three fixed *transition* modes set the animation type: CoverVertical, which slides up from the bottom of the screen; FlipHorizontal, which rotates the view; and

CrossDissolve, which fades between the two views. Each type creates a different experience for a user. CoverVertical is the default and creates the best pop-up effect. FlipHorizontal and CrossDissolve create the feeling of a more permanent switch. You can minimize this by including an obvious Return icon or button in the modal view so the user can see how to dismiss it.

This example uses the touchesBegan: method to switch between views. The user taps the screen to show the alternative view by using the presentModalView method and taps it again to dismiss it by using dismissModalView. The second view is kept in a separate nib file and loaded on demand. The second view controller includes a minimal touchesBegan: implementation to dismiss the view.

Create an Animated Modal Pop-Up View

1 Create a new project by using the View-based Application template and then save it as ModalViewSwitcher.

Note: *You can find the ModalViewSwitcher project on the website for this book: www.wiley.com/go/iphonedevelopmentvb.*

2 Choose File→New File in Xcode to create a new class.

3 Click the UIViewController subclass and then click the With Xib for user interface check box.

4 Click Next and then name the new class as FirstViewController.

5 Repeat steps 2 and 3 to create another class and nib called SecondViewController.

6 In Interface Builder, edit both of the new nib files to create two distinct views and then save the files.

Note: *In this example, the two views are numbered with large labels.*

7 Click ViewSwitcherViewController.h.

8 Add instances of both new classes to the class interface.

9 Add the same instances of both new classes to the class property list.

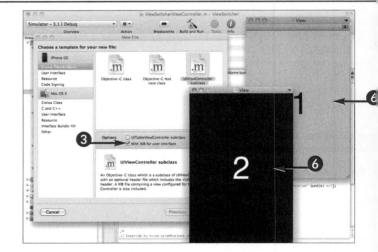

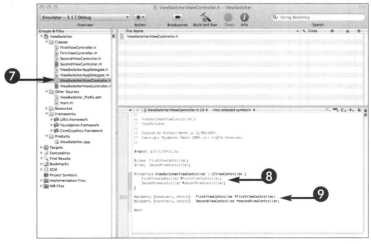

0 Click ViewSwitcherViewController.m and then synthesize both new view controller classes.

1 Uncomment the `initWithNibName:` and `viewDidLoad` methods to enable manual nib loading.

2 Add code to `viewDidLoad` to load and display the `FirstViewController` nib.

Note: *You do not need to specify the .xib file extension for the nib.*

3 Add a `touchesBegan:` method, with code to load the `SecondViewController` nib, set up a transition animation, and then call `presentModalViewController:` to display the second view.

4 Click SecondViewController.m.

5 Add a `touchesBegan:` method to monitor screen touches.

6 Add code to dismiss the second view by using the `dismissModalViewController Animated:` method.

Note: *The animation transition cannot be changed. It is always the inverse of the animation used to display the view.*

7 Click Build and Run to build and run the application.

The application shows the first view, reveals the second view with an animated transition when the screen is tapped, and then restores the first view when the screen is tapped again.

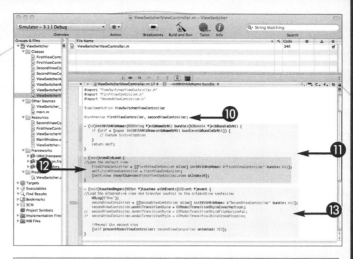

Extra

This example adds a single pop-up view, but you can stack pop-ups indefinitely. This is rarely necessary and is likely to confuse a user. A single pop-up is straightforward and intuitive. A stack of pop-ups is harder to understand and more difficult to navigate.

One possible exception is game design. You can use pop-ups to slide in different sets of controls and reveal different player options. This works best when the pop-ups do not fill the screen and a main game area remains visible. You cannot use modal views to implement this because modal views always fill the screen and are opaque. Instead, you must create or load a custom subview and then explicitly animate it by using techniques described later in this chapter.

Pop-ups use the same view hierarchy and stack as other views. When your application displays a pop-up, it is added to the stack in the usual way. When it is dismissed, it is removed. You can dismiss multiple pop-ups by calling `dismissModalViewControllerAnimated:` on one of the pop-up views lower in the stack. This removes the top-most view, using its transition animation, and deletes intermediate views without animating them.

Create Flip and Curl Animations

Y ou can animate views with flip and curl animations to add interest to your application. Although you can create flip effects for modal views by using the `presentModalViewController` method, these animations are completely preset. You cannot set their duration or modify other settings. To animate a curl effect in a smaller area, such as a photo in a border, you must use a different technique.

The `UIView` class includes a collection of preset animation methods. You can use these to create a slightly more flexible class of animations. Two effects are available: horizontal flip and page curl. These animations are still limited compared to the much wider range of effects that are possible via other animation techniques. But they are easy to use and are slightly more programmable than the modal view effects.

To use `UIView` animations, you must specify the incoming and outgoing views as well as setting up the animation duration and keyframe curve, which controls how the animation develops. You must also give the animation a name — this is necessary, even though the name is rarely used — choose one of the two transition effects, and set a direction.

Animations are run by using the `commitAnimations` method. This creates the animation effect by using the settings you have chosen. It does not add or remove views from the hierarchy, so you must include extra code for this.

`commitAnimations` is a class method and is run on `UIView` itself rather than on a specific view. Animation settings are added to a queue that is part of the master `UIView` class. The class runs the animations when it receives a `commitAnimations` message.

Create Flip and Curl Animations

① Create a new application by using the View-based Template and then save it as AnimatedViewSwitcher.

② Create two new classes based on UIViewController: FirstViewController and SecondViewController.

③ Create nib files and labeled views for each controller class.

④ Add instances of both controller classes to the interface and properties of ViewSwitcherViewController.h.

⑤ In ViewSwitcherViewController.m, import the new classes and then synthesize them.

⑥ Optionally, uncomment the `initWithNibName:` method.

Note: *This is only necessary if you plan to add extra features to nib loading.*

⑦ Uncomment the `viewDidLoad` method. Add code to load the first nib into an instance of the first view controller class. Assign it to the main view controller and then add it to a view hierarchy so it appears on the display.

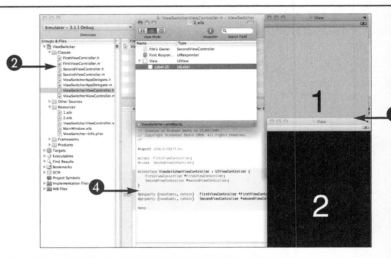

8 Add a `touchesBegan:` method to respond to user taps.

9 Add code for lazy loading of the two nibs.

10 Add code to begin setting up the animation as well as setting an animation name, a preset transition curve, and a duration.

11 Add further code to `touchesBegan:` to create incoming and outgoing transition pointers and then set them to specify which views will appear and disappear.

12 Add code to select one of the preset animations.

Note: The animations in this example switch direction alternately. This suggests to users that the second view is temporary and leads back to the first when it is dismissed.

13 Add code to set the animation transition, switch the views in the hierarchy, and then run the animations.

14 Click Build and Run to build and run the application.

Tapping the screen switches between two views, with an animated up-and-down curl effect.

Note: You can find the AnimatedViewSwitcher project on the website for this book: www. wiley.com/go/iphonedevelopmentvb.

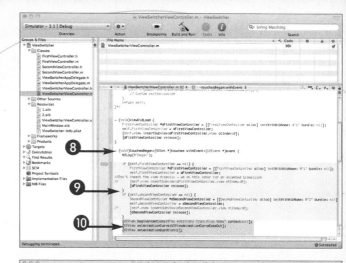

Extra

When you switch views under program control, it is up to your application to send view management messages to the incoming and outgoing views. Specifically, you can choose to send the `viewWillAppear` and `viewDidAppear` messages to trigger appropriate methods in the receiving views. You can use these features for cleanup or to start and stop animations, timers, and other processing as views appear and disappear. In practice, you should add

```
[incoming viewWillAppear: YES];
[outgoing viewWillDisappear: YES];
```

before the transitions and

```
[incoming viewDidAppear: YES];
[outgoingViewDidDisappear: YES];
```

after them. You can then implement these methods in the relevant views to add view-based features as needed.

Create a Swipe Animation

You can create more sophisticated and open-ended animation effects by including Core Animation features in your application. You can use the Core Animation framework to customize animations with control over duration, keyframing, and animation type.

Core Animation offers a different collection of preset animation movements, with some duplication of effects available via other techniques. Curls are not available, but cross-fade, push, move, and reveal effects are included. Flip effects are available, but these use the `oglFlip` animation type, which is not officially documented or supported.

The cross-fade effect is a simple transparency blend, identical to the modal `CrossReveal` effect. The move and reveal effects slide the new layer in or out over the old layer and are similar to the modal `CoverVertical` effect. However, with Core Animation effects, you can set the

direction of the animation by using a subtype variable to create views that slide upward, downward, or sideway. Unlike modal effects, Core Animation effects include a built-in transparency blend feature. As a view disappears it loses opacity and brightness.

To create a swipe effect, use the push type. This literally pushes one view in from the top, bottom, or side of the screen and replaces it with another. Types and subtypes are set via constant declarations. These are listed in the CATransition Class Reference in the Apple documentation.

Although Core Animation effects are sophisticated, they are easy to work with. Animation details are set in the properties of an animation object and run on a layer object instead of a view. You can convert any view into a layer by using a `[self.view layer];` message. This tells Core Animation to treat the current view as a layer. To run animations, use the `addAnimation` method on the layer.

Create a Swipe Animation

1. Create a new application by using the View-based Template and then save it as CAViewSwitcher.

2. Create two new classes based on UIViewController: FirstViewController and SecondViewController.

3. Create nib files and labeled views for each controller class.

4. Add instances of both controller classes to the interface and properties of ViewSwitcherViewController.h.

5. Uncomment `viewDidLoad` and then add code to load the first nib.

6. Add a `touchesBegan:` method and then add code to implement lazy loading of both nibs.

7. Create two pointers to implement view controller switching.

8. Add code to create an animation object, declared as an instance of the CATransition class.

Note: *This object holds information about the type, subtype, duration, and other properties of an animation.*

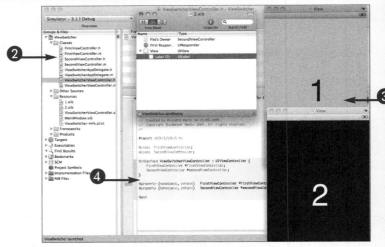

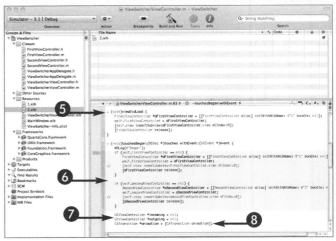

9 Add code to initialize the animation's properties, including the duration and type, and a nominal delegate — usually `self`.

10 Add code to set a timing function.

Note: The timing function uses keyframe definition presets, such as `EaseIn`, to control how the animation develops.

11 Add code to set an animation subtype to control the direction of the animation.

Note: For a swipe animation, set the left or right direction to match the direction of the swipe. You can also create up or down swipes.

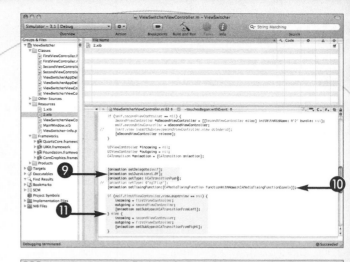

12 Add code to swap the views and then run the animation by using the `addAnimation` method to call the animation object.

Note: The key is arbitrary.

13 Click Build and Run to build and run the application.

The application shows a swipe animation, switching between two views when the screen is tapped.

Note: You can find the CAViewSwitcher project on the website for this book: www.wiley.com/go/iphonedevelopmentvb.

Extra

Springboard uses swipe animations to switch between pages, with extra features. The controller estimates finger velocity and uses it to set one of a small number of preset animation durations. This makes the views feel more physical and tactile and creates a responsive effect.

You can measure finger speed in `touchesMoved` by using the timer information supplied with each touch event. Each touch event is an instance of a `UIEvent` class and includes a time stamp property that is an instance of `NSTimeInterval`, which is a counter that runs continually and returns the time in seconds since system startup.

The interface also includes a subtle keyframed bounce effect, described in more detail later in this chapter. Changing the animation duration automatically speeds up or slows down the bounce.

Control Animations with Preset Timing Functions

You can use preset *timing functions* to control how animations develop over time and to create different effects for the user. Timing functions are purely cosmetic but can make your application seem more polished and responsive.

Linear animations develop at a constant rate and appear uninteresting and crude to users. To enhance animation effects, Core Animation includes a CAMediaTimingFunction class. It offers more sophisticated control over animation timings. You can use this class to create customized timing functions. It also features a small selection of preset functions. You can use these by dropping in a named preset function as a constant value with a kCAMediaTimingFunction prefix.

The EaseOut curve starts quickly and ends slowly. Applied to a swipe animation, it creates an impression of deceleration. The view moves in quickly and gradually

slows down before stopping. This is a natural-looking curve, with a relaxed and unhurried feel.

The EaseIn curve works the opposite way, starting slowly and speeding up before snapping to a stop. This is not a natural effect — the animation stops suddenly, as if the animated object has hit a wall.

The EaseInEaseOut is a mix of the other effects. Movement starts slowly, speeds up in the middle of the transition, and slows down just before the animation stops. It conveys an urgent impression, suitable for business and productivity applications.

To use timing functions, call the setTimingFunction method on an animation object. You can initialize the CAMediaTimingFunction object with a named preset by using the functionWithName: method. See the documentation for more on the CAMediaTimingFunction Class Reference.

Control Animations with Preset Timing Functions

① Reload the ViewSwitcherController project used in the previous example and then click ViewSwitcherViewController.m.

② Find the timingFunction object in touchesBegan:.

③ Set the timing function to kCAMediaTimingFunctionEaseIn.

④ Click Build and Run to build and run the application.

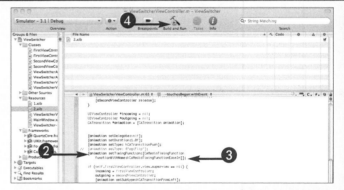

⑤ Tap/click the screen to run the transition.

⑥ Observe how the transition starts slowly and ends suddenly.

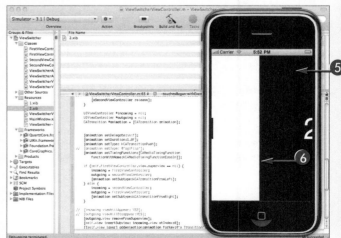

7 In Xcode, return to ViewSwitcherViewController.m.

8 Set the timing function to kCAMediaTimingFunctionEase InEaseOut.

9 Click Build and Run to build and run the application.

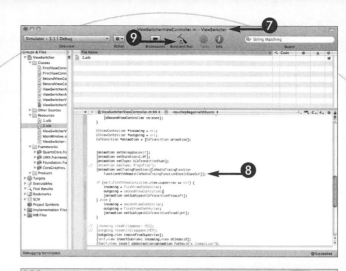

10 Tap/click anywhere on the screen to run the transition.

11 Observe how the transition starts and ends slowly, speeding up in the middle.

12 Optionally, change the timing function to kCAMediaTimingFunctionEaseOut and kCAMediaTimingFunctionLinear and then review how this affects the transition.

13 Optionally, change the timing duration and then review how this affects the feel of the transition, with the different timing functions.

The view transition is controlled by a preset timing function.

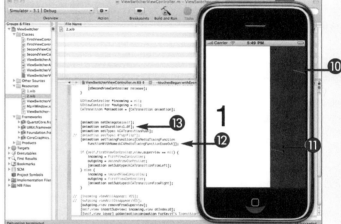

Extra

CATransitions and UIView animations use different code and have different features. However, UIView includes its own set of preset transitions. These are identical to the CATransitions but use a different prefix — for example, UIViewAnimationCurveEaseIn. To set the timing function, use setAnimationCurve on the UIView.

Unlike CATransitions, UIView animations are arranged in blocks. The block starts with beginAnimations: and ends with commitAnimations:. To use a timing curve, you must place setAnimationCurve inside a block. Outside a block, UIView animation methods do nothing.

UIView animations include further features, such as delays, auto-reverse, and repeat counts. For example, setAnimationRepeatCount: 5.0 repeats an animation five times. You can combine this feature with timing functions to create more eye-catching effects. Repeating and auto-reversing an animation by using the EaseInEaseOut function makes it bounce, wobble, or jiggle. The effect can be unsubtle if it is overused, but it can add interest to transitions when used sparingly.

Create a Bounce Effect with a Custom Timing Function

You can create customized timing functions for finer control over transitions. Bounce animation effects are an attractive feature that appears in Springboard and in some of the built-in applications on the iPhone. There is no preset bounce timing function, but you can easily create one. Instead of using one of the preset timing functions, you can generate a customized function with the `initWithControlPoints:` method.

`initWithControlPoints:` takes four floats: c1x, c1y, c2x, and c2y. These values set Bézier spline handles for the animation timing function, not absolute xy values. The timing function always starts at 0% and ends at 100%. You can use the Bézier values to set how the timing function develops between these points.

Animating Bézier curves numerically is not an intuitive process, but you can use a simple technique to make it more manageable. Set c1x and c2x so they total 1; for example, set c1x to 0.4, and set c2x to 0.6. You can then use these values as time percentages. In this example, point 1 is reached after 40% of the duration and point 2 after 60%.

You can then use the y values as approximate settings for the depth of the effect at each x point. For example, if c1y = 0 and c2y = 0.5, the effect starts very slowly, reaches 50% at 60% of the duration, and then 100% at 100% of the duration.

To create a bounce effect, set cy2 to more than 1. This creates a curve that overshoots at the second point and then returns to 1 when the animation ends. A small value for cy2 creates a small, natural-looking overshoot. A larger value creates an extreme effect.

Create a Bounce Effect with a Custom Timing Function

① Reload the ViewSwitcherController project used in the previous example and then click ViewSwitcherViewController.m.

Note: *You can find the CABounceView project on the website for this book: www.wiley.com/go/ iphonedevelopmentvb.*

② Find the `timingFunction` object in `touchesBegan`.

③ Replace the preset timing function with `initWithControlPoints:`.

④ Set the values to `0.5 :1.0 :0.5 :1.05`.

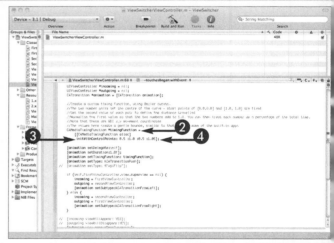

⑤ Click Build and Run to build and run the application.

⑥ Tap/click the screen to review the subtle bounce effect.

7 In Xcode, return to ViewSwitcherViewController.m.

8 Change the previous values to :0.7 :0.0 :0.3 :1.5.

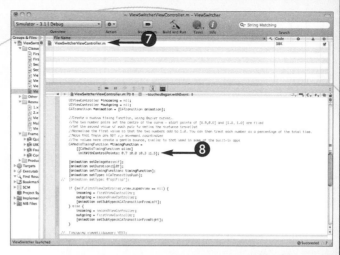

9 Click Build and Run to build and run the application.

10 Tap/click the screen to review the more extreme bounce effect.

11 Optionally, experiment with other values and durations.

The view transition is controlled by a custom timing function.

Extra

You can specify a delegate object to create even more sophisticated animation effects. The CAAnimation class includes animationDidStart and animationDidStop: finished methods. animationDidStart is triggered when the animation begins. You can use this to synchronize independent but related animations among different objects. Often, the delegate object is self, but you can add the animationDidStart method to a separate object, and it will run the method on demand.

animationDidStop: finished: returns a Boolean that tells the delegate whether the animation completed successfully. If it is (finished == NO), the animation was paused or interrupted. You can use animationDidStop: to trigger a cascade of animations; as each animation ends, it can trigger a new animation in a different object. It can also show or hide visible objects or create some other response.

If you need to trigger different methods, you can change the messages that are sent. Use setAnimationWillStartSelector: and setAnimationDidStopSelector: to change the selector.

Transform
a View

You can transform views and view objects to create sophisticated animation effects as well as improve the visual impact of your application. Animations can be triggered at any time for any reason. They do not have to be applied to complete views. You can transform and animate any visible object, including buttons, switches, sliders, images, map views, and webviews. You can also animate complete view trees by sending animation commands to the root view of the tree. Other objects in the tree are animated automatically.

Animations are often used to add interest to the interface. For example, iPhone alerts are animated to make them appear to grow out of the screen, with a subtle bounce effect. The size of the alert box expands from nothing, overshoots, shrinks slightly, and then springs back again to the final size.

You can animate objects by modifying their properties, including the center position, and by applying *affine transformations.* Affine transformations use complicated matrix-based math to set the size, rotation, and position of an object. Helper methods are available to hide the math and make transformations easier to use. Custom animations can be managed by using an NSTimer timer, set to run an animation update method on every timer tick.

This example animates an image and a switch by modifying their center position properties to bounce them off the bottom of the screen. It also applies affine scaling transforms to squash them as they rebound. The transform expands the width while shrinking the height, creating a very simple simulation of elastic deformation.

Transform information is held in a CGAffineTransform data structure and applied to the objects by using the setTransform method. For more on setting up and using affine transforms, see Chapter 8.

Transform a View

1. Create a new project by using the View-based Template and then save it as ViewTransformer.

Note: You can find the ViewTransformer project on the website for this book: www.wiley.com/go/iphonedevelopmentvb.

2. Open ViewTransformerViewController.h and then add instances of UISwitch and UIImageView to the interface.

3. Add a counter, two floats to set the x and y deformation values for each visible object, and two integers to set their vertical positions.

4. Add a CGAffineTransform variable to hold the transform information and then add IBOutlet declarations to the two visible objects.

5. Open ViewTransformerViewController.xib in Interface Builder.

6. Add a UIImageView and a UISwitch object to the main view and then assign an image to the ImageView.

Note: You can assign any small image to the ImageView. *This example uses a red-and-white-checked ball.*

7. Link the objects to their corresponding outlets.

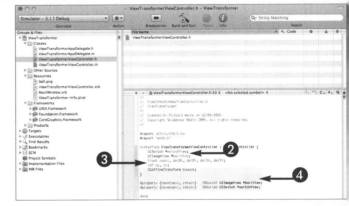

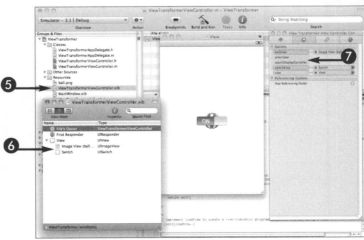

⑧ In ViewTransformerController.m, declare π as a constant.

⑨ Synthesize the two visible object views.

⑩ Find `viewDidLoad`, uncomment it if necessary, and then add code to implement an `NSTimer`, with a 50Hz repeat rate, triggering a custom method called `doTimer:`.

⑪ Add a `doTimer:` method and then begin to fill it out with math to create a bounce effect, moving the center position of each view with the `setCenter:` method.

Note: `setCenter:` *takes a* `CGPoint` *structure as its input. Use* `CGPointMake` *to convert a pair of coordinates into a* `CGPoint`.

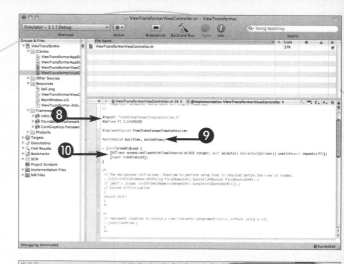

⑫ Add code to calculate the elastic deformation effect, stretching and squashing each axis slightly when the object is bouncing.

⑬ Add code to convert the calculated transformation into a transformation object that can be plugged into `CGAffineTransform` and then use `setTransform:` to apply the transformation object to one of the view objects.

Note: *The* `CGAffineTransformScale` *method is a convenient way to transform x,y scaling factors into a single scaling transform.*

⑭ Repeat step 13, applying the transform to the other object.

⑮ Click Build and Run to build and run the application.

It shows two objects bouncing, subtly squashed as they rebound from the bottom of the screen.

Extra

You can use view transformations to add interest to games and to extend your application with contextual options that appear and disappear as required. Game tokens and tiles can be animated so they drop into position individually from the top of the screen, with optional bounce effects. This would be a flamboyant option for a productivity application, but more subtle animations, with entire views that glide into position from the bottom or side of the screen, can be used in almost any context.

You can use animation movements and transformations to create effects that are more flexible than those possible with modal or preset transformations; for example, views that slide in to cover just part of the screen and slide out when dismissed.

Views and objects remain active while they are being animated. In this example, the switch continues to work as a switch. It could be connected to an application feature and then used in the usual way.

Using transformations effectively is as much a design problem as a coding challenge. Your application should use them to add value for the user and to enhance user interest and involvement. Animations can easily become distracting. Add them only where there is a clear user benefit.

119

Add Audio and Vibration Alerts

Music player features are an important benefit of the iPhone and iPod. However, the audio layer is complex. It is possible to synthesize custom sounds via digital signal processing or play back and mix samples. You can use these features to add audio effects to your applications.

Synthesizing and processing sound is not straightforward. However, adding audio alerts to your application is relatively easy. Various solutions are available. One of the simplest and most effective is to use the AVAudioPlayer class. Each AVAudioPlayer object can be initialized with a sound file from the file system when your application loads. To play a sound file, send a [play] message to the object. You can also start the sound from different index points by setting the currentTime property.

To initialize a sound file, create an AVAudioPlayer object and then pass it a URL that points to a file. To create the URL, create a path object that points to the required file

and then initialize a URL object from it. For more on files and paths, see Chapter 7. You can simplify this process by writing a custom method to encapsulate this process and convert a file name to a URL that can be passed to AVAudioPlayer directly. This example creates a path explicitly to demonstrate the steps.

Vibration alerts use a separate part of the audio layer. You can create a vibration alert at any point in your application by using AudioServicesPlaySystemSound (k_SystemSoundID_Vibrate);. This uses the AudioToolbox framework. You will need to include this, with the AVFoundation framework, in your application when you build it. In the 3.1 SDK, the AudioToolbox is included in the list of frameworks that can be added by choosing Add→Existing Files in Xcode.

AVFoundation does not appear in this list. It can be manually found at /Developer/Platforms/iPhoneOS.platform/Developer/SDKs/iPhoneOS3.1.sdk/System/Library/Frameworks/AVFoundationFramework.

Add Audio and Vibration Alerts

① Create a project by using the View-based Template and then save it as AlertSound.

② Find or create an MP3 file, drag it to your project's folder in the Finder, and then drag it to the Resources folder in the Groups & Files pane.

The file is added to the project, and a link is created to it.

③ Right-click on the Frameworks folder in Groups & Files, choose Add→Existing Frameworks from the pop-up menu, and then add the AudioToolbox framework.

④ Repeat step 3, click Add Other, and then navigate to the path given above for the AVFoundation framework.

Note: *In later versions of the SDK, the AVFoundation framework may be in a different location or it may be added to the main list of frameworks.*

⑤ Click AlertSoundViewController.h.

⑥ Add the AVAudioPlayer class.

⑦ Add an instance of AVAudioPlayer.

⑧ Add a property declaration for the instance.

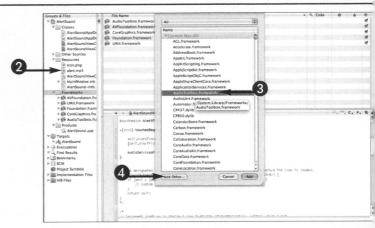

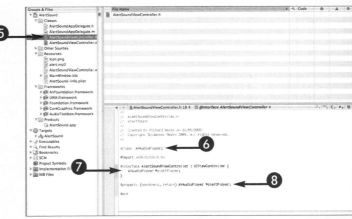

⑨ Synthesize the AVAudioPlayer object.

⑩ Find ViewDidLoad and then add code to convert the file name to a path.

⑪ Add code to convert the path to a system URL.

⑫ Add code to load the AVAudioPlayer object with the file specified by the URL and then use the prepareToPlay method to make it ready for playback.

ote: *This is boilerplate initialization code. You can reuse it, with appropriate minor changes, whenever you need to initialize an AVAudioPlayer object.*

⑬ Add a touchesBegan: method.

⑭ Add code to initialize the play position and to run the play method on the AVAudioPlayer object.

⑮ Optionally, add code to trigger a vibration alert.

⑯ Click Build and Run to build and run the application.

The alert sound plays when the user taps the screen.

ote: *This example shows an optional modified nib file. The design of the nib does not affect playback.*

ote: *You can find the AlertSound project on the website for this book: www.wiley.com/go/ iphonedevelopmentvb.*

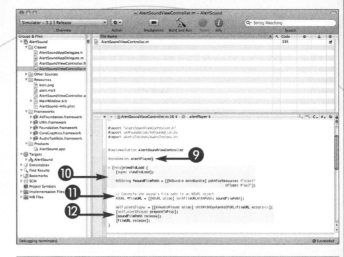

Extra

You can use AVAudioPlayer to mix sounds automatically. The iPhone has two separate audio channels. One can play compressed MP3 and AAC sounds via a built-in hardware decoder. The other plays uncompressed audio from the iPhone's file system.

The hardware decoder can only play one sound at a time. If you want to mix compressed sounds, you must add your own decoder routines and then stream them to a lower level of the audio layer.

However, multiple instances of AVAudioPlayer can be called to simultaneously play an indefinite number of uncompressed sound files. Uncompressed formats include AIFF and WAV. To mix sounds, create two or more AVSoundPlayer objects, initialize them with files, and then trigger playback of each object with a [play] message.

It would be useful to be able to play system sounds on demand. Unfortunately, the system sounds are not available directly, and the official documentation does not list file names or locations. To play system sounds, you must find copies online and then add those copies to your application. You can also use other sound effects to create customized alerts — for example, from the Freesound archive at www.freesound.org.

Create an Interface without Using Interface Builder

You can create an open-ended and responsive custom interface under code control without using Interface Builder. Custom interfaces are potentially far more flexible than the relatively simple views that can be created in Interface Builder. Your application can show buttons, sliders, and images or hide them at any time. They can be made to move, flash, rotate, or change color — with or without custom animations.

Objects can be hidden by rearranging the view hierarchy or they can be created and released on demand, freeing their memory for reuse. They can also have their targets and actions reassigned dynamically so different methods are triggered at different times.

You must solve two problems to create a custom interface. The first is memory management. It is often useful to pre-define an array of pointers for dynamic objects, link them to objects when they are created, and then reset them to `nil` when the objects are released. This adds a small overhead to the root view controller's header file but simplifies other parts of the code.

The other problem is ergonomic design and layout. Interface Builder's key advantage is visual design, guaranteeing good aesthetics. Dynamic interfaces are harder to lay out. You have to build and run the code repeatedly to check its appearance. You can simplify this process by creating code to automate spacing, centering, and alignment.

Assembling a coherent user experience can be an interesting challenge. Interfaces with movement, animation, and dynamic features push the boundaries of established design but can be more rewarding to develop and use.

This example demonstrates a very simple dynamic interface. Code added to `loadView` creates a background view with a rotating button. The spinning button creates another button when touched and deletes it when touched again. The second button displays an alert.

Creating an Interface without Interface Builder

① Create a new project by using the View-based Template and then save it as CreateViews.

Note: *You can find the CreateViews project on the website for this book: www.wiley.com/go/ iphonedevelopmentvb.*

② Open CreateViewViewController.xib in Interface Builder.

③ Delete the view, save the file, and then quit Interface Builder.

④ Open CreateViewsViewController.h in Xcode.

⑤ Add two `UIButtons` and a `UIView` to the interface.

⑥ Add property declarations for both buttons and the view.

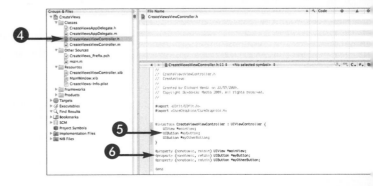

7 Open CreateViewsViewController.m, synthesize the view declared in the header, and then add two global float variables.

8 Find `loadView` and uncomment it and then add code to create a view under program control.

9 Add code to create a button under program control and then add it to the view hierarchy.

10 Add code to create a timer and to implement a timer method that produces a rotation animation effect by using the global floats as counters.

11 Add code to implement a `makeAButton:` method that adds another button under program control.

12 Add code to implement a `buttonClicked:` method that changes the direction and color of the original button and triggers the `makeAButton:` method.

13 Add code to show an alert when the second button is clicked.

14 Click Build and Run to build and run the application.

The application shows two buttons under program control. One button rotates; the other appears and disappears under the control of the first button and displays an alert when clicked.

Extra

You can use the `addTarget:` method to define the messages sent by a visible object. For example, `[aButton addTarget:self action:@selector(aMethod:) forControlEvents: UIControlEventTouchDown];` sets `aButton` so it triggers `aMethod:` when the user first touches it. The `addTarget` property sets the target object. If you set this to `self`, you can add `aMethod` to the original file. You can also point `addTarget:` to a different object if you need to route the message elsewhere:

```
aMethod: (id) sender {
//Code for aMethod: goes here
}
```

`aMethod` is not identical to `aMethod:`. In Objective-C, these are completely different and unrelated method names. If you include the colon, you can use `(id) sender` to report the identity of the object that sent the message and to read its properties.

Introducing UITableView

You can use the `UITableView` class to display scrolling lists and to add menu-like navigation trees to your application. Many of the iPhone's built-in applications, including Settings and Contacts, use table views. Table views are highly customizable.

Multicolumn tables are not supported, but table *cells* — individual items in the table list — can show text and images and navigation arrows. Cells can also display optional *accessory views* — extra preset graphics used for navigation and editing.

Data Sources and Cells

Table views use a *data source*. The data source defines the number of items in a table, the number of subsections, and the contents of each cell. When the table is initialized, the view controller asks the data source for this information. A selection of methods is available to load these settings into the controller. For example:

```
-(NSInteger) numberOfSectionsInTableView:
   (UITableView *)tableView
{return 3;}
```

This initializes the controller with three subsections. Depending on the application, these methods can read data dynamically from the data source or can return simple constants, as shown here. The data source can be an array, a set of nested arrays, or some other object. It takes two parameters — an *index path* and a *row*. The index path is an instance of `NSIndexPath` and selects a unique cell in the table tree structure. `index Path.row` selects the current cell in the current table. The row is the number of the cell in the table.

Each cell is an instance of the `UITableViewCell` cell view class. To save memory, only visible cells are instantiated; for example, a table with hundreds or thousands of entries may only require a handful of cell views. A `dequeueReusable`

`CellWithIdentifier:` method returns cells that are already in memory for reuse. To set the contents of a cell, implement the `cellForRowAtIndexPath:` method. This method is called automatically for each visible cell. You do not need to loop through the cells manually to initialize them. Instead, add code to recycle a cell where possible or to create a new cell when it is needed. For example:

```
UITableView *cell = [thisTableView
   dequeueReusableCellWithIdentifier:
   CellIdentifier];
if (cell == nil) {
 cell = [[[UITableViewCell alloc] initWithStyle:U
 ITableViewCellStyleDefault
 reuseIdentifier:CellIdentifier] autorelease];
}
```

You can then read data from the data source for the cell's index path and row and set one or more cell attributes, such as the cell's text field:

```
cell.textLabel.text = [aStringArray objectAtIndex:
   indexPath.row];
```

This assigns the text for that cell from a data source — in this example, an array of strings.

Grouped Tables

Tables can be split into *sections*. Each section is a subtable selected with a section index. Some methods expose the section index directly. Alternatively, use `[indexPath section]`.

Use the `numberOfSectionsInTableView:` method to set the number of sections. You can set individual headers and footers for each section by using the `titleForHeader InSection:` and `titleForFooterInSection:` methods.

Tables offer two *styles* — *grouped* or *plain*. You can set this property in Interface Builder or by using the

`initWithFrame: style` method when creating a table view programmatically. You cannot change the style after initialization. Plain tables are rendered as a list of cells with bold text that extend across the display. Floating headers and footers appear as white text on gray and are rendered in a smaller font than the default cell text. Grouped tables embed rounded cells within a gray frame. Headers and footers are rendered in the frame area.

Cell Styles and Accessory Views

By default, cells include a main text label. Optionally, you can add a detail text label, which is rendered in a smaller font than the default cell text, and an image view. Four UITableViewStyle presets render these features in different ways; for example, UITableViewCellStyle Subtitle displays main and detail text and an image, while UITableViewCellStyleDefault does not display the detail label. For example illustrations of every style, see the Standard Styles for Table-View Cells section in the "Table View Programming Guide" for iPhone OS in the Apple documentation. Use initWithStyle: reuseIdentifier: to set a style when a cell is created. You cannot change the style of an existing cell.

Accessory views include a chevron, a check mark, and a disclosure chevron control, which can be used to trigger an action. You can add any one of these to a cell by setting its accessoryType property to the appropriate accessory constant — for example, UITableViewCellAccessory Checkmark. For the full list, see the UITableViewCell Class Reference documentation. Cells also display separate add/ delete/reorder accessory views when the table is in editing mode. These features automatically appear and disappear when you are editing.

Optionally, you can customize cells to display colored text and backgrounds, multi-line styled text, and control objects, such as switches, buttons, and sliders. For example, you can create a custom cell design with almost any combination of features and then load it from a nib file on demand.

Table Editing

Editing features for adding, removing, and rearranging cells are built into UITableView but must be enabled explicitly. Calling setEditing: animated: enables and disables edit mode, showing editing accessories.

Implement the commitEditingStyle: method to receive editing updates from the table. You should modify the data in the data source as required and call the reloadData method on the table to refresh it.

UITableView Navigation

You can use UITableView for navigation as is by using view-switching techniques described in Chapter 5 to show and hide subviews when a table cell is tapped. However, Apple's User Interface guidelines suggest that you should always combine a UITableView with a UINavigation Controller. The navigation controller automates view switching and animation. It displays a Back button when the user switches views and automatically switches back to the superview when the user taps it.

You do not need to add a Back button to the nib file or create it programmatically. However, you must set each view's title property; the navigation controller reads title to generate the button. Optionally, you can also add a button at the right of the navigation bar to implement custom features. The title string font or size cannot be changed, and the length is very limited.

You can implement table view navigation in two ways. The least efficient is to create a separate controller subclass for each view in the tree. This is a valid option for trees with a small number of table views but is cumbersome for more complex trees.

A more efficient option is to create a subclass for each level in the tree. For example, the root table may lead to a number of second-level tables, which are instances of a single controller class that is initialized with unique data. These can lead to a number of third-level instances, which may be a different controller class, and so on.

You can then use the same code to load a number of different tables by allocating an appropriate view controller when the user taps a cell to select the next level, initializing its data source and title and calling pushViewController: to push it onto the view controller stack to display it. For an example, see the MultiView application later in this chapter.

Create a Table View and Fill It with a List

Y ou can create a skeleton for an application with a table view by creating a new project with the Navigation-based Application template in Xcode. The template creates two nibs — one with a navigation controller and the other with a `UITableView`. It also links a root view controller to the table view and adds method stubs to the controller.

To implement a simple list, customize the method stubs to read data from a data source and pass it to the table cells. In this example, the data source is an `NSArray`. The array is initialized with a list of planet names in `viewDidLoad` in the view controller.

By default, when you build and run the template, it displays an empty list. To initialize the template with data, you must edit two methods: `numberOfRowsInSection:`

and `cellForRowAtIndexPath:`. `numberOfSectionsIn TableView:` returns 1 because the table in this example has a single section. This method does not need to be changed. `numberOfRowsInSection:` sets the number of rows in the table. In the template, it is set to 0. You must edit it to return the number of items in the data source array. Finally, `cellForRowAtIndexPath:` creates or recycles new cells as needed and sets each cell's label text to match the corresponding string in the data source array. By default, it returns empty cells. You must edit it to set each cell's text label, using `cell.textLabel.text = [mylist objectAtIndex: indexPath.row];` to select and read a string from the data source array.

This simple example does not implement editing or navigation. Cells are highlighted automatically when a user taps them, but tapping a cell does not trigger an action method.

Create a Table View and Fill It with a List

① In Xcode, choose File→New Project.

② Click the Navigation-based Application template and then save it as Simple List.

Note: You can find the Simple List project on the website for this book: www. wiley.com/go/iphonedevelopmentvb.

③ Click RootViewController.h.

④ Add an `NSArray` to the interface to create a data source for the controller.

⑤ Declare the array as a property and then save the file.

⑥ Click RootViewController.m.

⑦ Synthesize the array declared in the header.

⑧ Find and uncomment `viewDidLoad`.

⑨ Add code to initialize an array with a list of strings, to assign the contents to the data source array, and to release the original array.

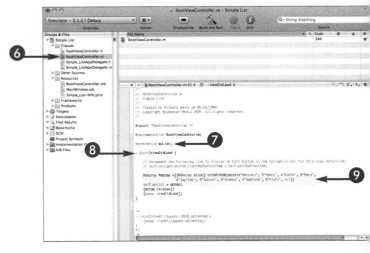

0 Scroll down to find the table view methods in the template.

1 Edit the `numberOfRowsIn Section:` method to return the number of items in the data source array.

2 Add code to the `cellForRowAt IndexPath:` method to set the text label of each cell to one of the strings in the data source selected by the index path row and then save the file.

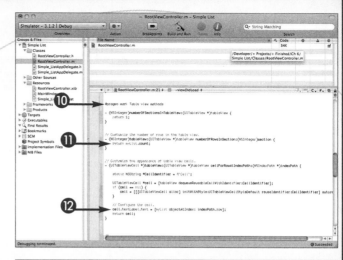

3 Click Build and Run to build and run the application.

● The application loads and displays a table view from a data source array.

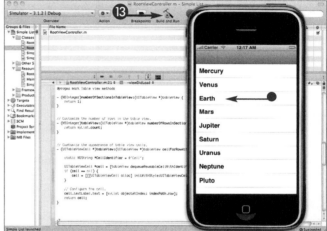

Customize Cell Traits

You can customize a cell's font, text style, text color, and size by setting its properties. The UITableViewCell class includes a selection of properties that you can customize with simple assignments. The cell text is a UILabel object. You must access the most common properties indirectly via the label object. For example:

```
cell.font = ["Some font"];
```

This is not recommended. The correct code is:

```
cell.textLabel.font = [UIFont fontWithName:
 @"Courier" size: 36.0];
```

Because the text fields are labels, you can access all the properties of a UILabel. For example, you can set a drop shadow:

```
cell.textLabel.shadowColor = ["Some color"];
cell.textLabel.shadowOffset =
 CGSizeMake(someOffsetX, someOffsetY);
```

If you are using one of the cell styles that includes a detail view, you can set its properties in a similar way:

```
cell.detailTextLabel.font = ["Some font"];
```

You cannot set a cell's background color directly. Both of the following have no effect:

```
cell.backgroundColor = ["Some color"];
cell.textLabel.backgroundColor = ["Some color"]
```

To customize the background color of individual cells, you must remodel the entire cell, as shown in the example presented later in this chapter. To change the background color of every cell in a table, change the background color of the table itself, as described in the Extra section on the facing page.

Because cells are returned individually, you can set different traits for every cell or change traits to indicate groupings. For example, you can color-code an alphabetized list or change one or more properties in every n^{th} cell to create sections.

Customize Cell Traits

① In the Finder, press Option and then drag and drop the Simple List project folder to make a copy.

② Rename the copied folder as ListWithTraits.

Note: *You can find the ListWithTraits project on the website for this book: www.wiley.com/go/ iphonedevelopmentvb.*

③ Double-click the Simple List. xcodeproj file to open it in Xcode.

Note: *The project name remains Simple List, even though the containing folder has changed. This does not affect the original project folder. Unfortunately, there is no simple way to rename a project in Xcode.*

④ Click RootViewController.m.

⑤ Scroll down to find the cellFor RowAtIndexPath: method.

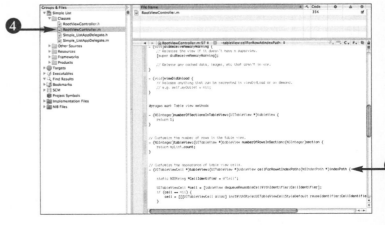

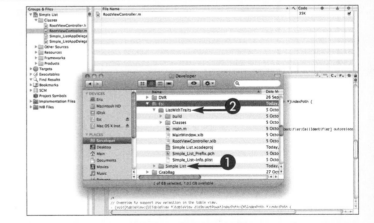

6 Add code to set each cell's text color and font.

Note: `UIColor` *is a color object.* `blueColor` *is a pre-defined color mix.*

7 Add code to change the text alignment mode and to center the text within the cell.

8 Add code to add a drop shadow with a small offset.

Note: `CGSizeMake` *returns a* `size` *object, used here to define the drop shadow offset.*

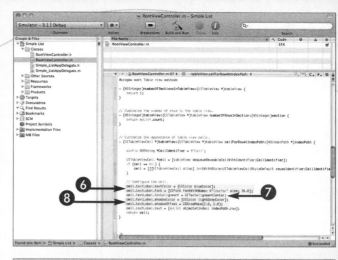

9 Click Build and Run to build and run the application.

● The application displays the data source list, with applied text effects.

Add Images
to Cells

I n addition to text, you can add images to cells to display extra information about items in the list or for purely decorative reasons. For example, you can use images to create virtual LEDs by using color and lit/unlit effects to indicate the status of list entries. You can also switch images when the user taps a cell to create customized highlight and selection effects.

Cells configured with the default UITableViewCellStyle Default style or UITableViewCellStyleSubtitle style include a blank UIImageView object. To add an image to a cell, load and assign it to this image view. The image view area is a square, with dimensions equal to the cell row height. Images are scaled automatically to fit into this area. You can change this behavior by setting the image view's contentMode property to one of the

pre-defined UIViewContentMode constants, defined in the UIView Class Reference.

To load and assign an image, you can use the standard code for retrieving a UIImage from your application bundle:

```
cell.imageView.image = [UIImage imageWith
              ContentsOfFile:
              [NSBundle mainBundle]
          pathForResource:
          @"animage"
          ofType: @"png"
          inDirectory: @"/"]];
```

You can also load images from other file locations in the iPhone or use the iPhone's graphics frameworks, as described in Chapter 8, to create custom images on demand.

Add Images to Cells

① In the Finder, press Option and then drag and drop the Simple List project folder to make a copy.

② Rename the copied folder ListWithImage.

Note: You can find the ListWithImage project on the website for this book: www.wiley.com/go/iphonedevelopmentvb.

③ In a photo editor of your choice, create a 20 × 20 graphic image.

Note: This example uses PNG transparency. This is optional. For cells with the default white background, you can save your image on white.

④ Save the image as a PNG file to the new project folder.

Note: The file name is arbitrary. In this example, the file is saved as tinyblueblur.png.

⑤ In the Finder, double-click Simple List. xcodeproj to open the project in Xcode.

⑥ Right-click on the Resources folder. Choose Add→Existing Files and then navigate to the PNG file. Click it to add it to the project. Do not copy it to the project.

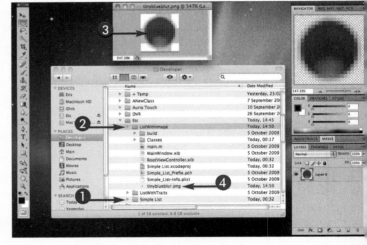

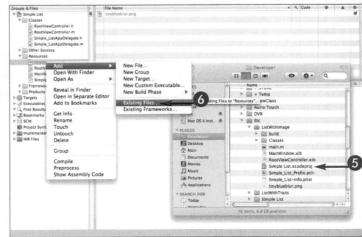

7 Click RootViewController.m.

8 Scroll down to the `cellForRow AtIndexPath:` method.

9 Add code to load the PNG image and to assign it to the cell's image view and then save the file.

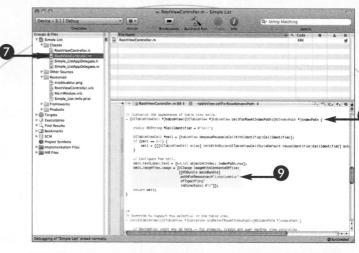

10 Click Build and Run to build and run the application.

● The application loads the PNG image and adds it to the image view built into every cell in the list.

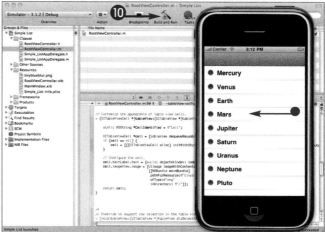

Extra

To change cell row height, implement the `heightForRowAtIndexPath:` method. For example:

```
-(CGFloat)tableView: (UITableView *)tableView heightForRowAtIndexPath: (NSIndexPath *)
 indexPath
{return 100;}
```

This sets the height of every cell to 100 points. Heights are set in points, not pixels. You can use this method to create a table of cells of varying heights by returning different heights for different paths.

The image view in a cell is a standard instance of `UIImageView`, with all its features. For example, you can animate the image in a cell by loading a series of flip-book images into an `NSArray` and assigning it to the image view's `animationImages` property:

```
cell.imageView.animationImages = anAnimationArray;
```

Add Check Marks and Disclosures to Cells

You can add an accessory view to a cell to create a status indicator or to imply that the cell is part of a menu tree and will respond when tapped.

There are four types of accessory views. `UITableViewCellAccessoryNone` is the default and does not display an accessory. `UITableViewCellAccessoryDisclosureIndicator` displays a rightward-facing chevron. You can use it in navigation tables to suggest that the cell leads to another table or view when tapped. `UITableViewCellAccessoryDetailDisclosureButton` is a rightward-facing chevron in a circular button. You can use it to suggest that the cell leads to a configuration, settings, or a preferences view. The button is a separate instance of `UIButton`, added as a subview. It responds to touches independently, inside its own active area within the cell, and displays a simple animation when tapped.

`UITableViewCellAccessoryCheckmark` is a simple check mark. You can use it to indicate that a cell is selected for some task or application feature.

To display an accessory view in a cell, set its `accessoryType` property within the `cellForRowAtIndexPath:` method. For example:

```
cell.accessoryType = UITableViewCellAccessory
 CheckMark;
```

This adds a check mark to the cell.

This example implements check-marking for individual cells. The cell status is held in a mutable array as a string. In this example, only `YES` and `NO` strings are used to enable and disable the check mark for each cell.

When a user taps a cell, the table calls the `didSelectRowAtIndexPath:` method. This method is commented out in the template. To add cell selection features, uncomment it and then add code to update the data source and the display. In this example, the code toggles the status string in the `checkList` array and calls `reloadData` on the table to refresh the display.

Add Check Marks and Disclosures to Cells

1 In the Finder, press Option and then drag and drop the Simple List project folder to make a copy and rename it ListWithAccessories.

2 Double-click Simple List.xcodeproj to load it in Xcode.

3 Click RootViewController.h.

4 Add a mutable array to the interface and then declare it as a property.

5 Click ViewController.m and then synthesize the new array property.

6 Add a mutable initialization array, with default status strings for each cell.

Note: *To pre-select cells so they have a check mark, when the application loads, set one or more array strings to* YES.

7 Add code to assign the initialization array to the `checkList` array.

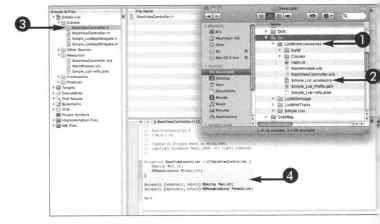

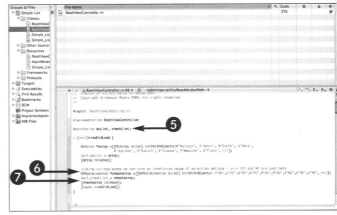

⑧ Scroll down to the `cellForRowAt IndexPath:` method.

⑨ Add code to read the cell's status from the `checkList` array and display a check mark accessory if the cell is selected.

⑩ Add code to disable conventional cell selection.

Note: *This disables the default blue highlight that appears when a user taps a cell.*

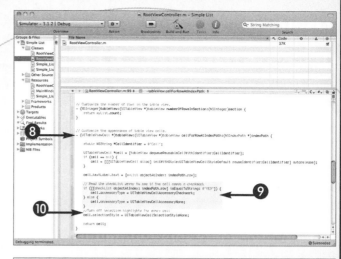

⑪ Scroll down to find the `didSelectRowAtIndexPath:` method and then uncomment it.

⑫ Add code to toggle the cell status string when a user taps a cell.

⑬ Add code to refresh the table and to display the new cell status.

⑭ Click Build and Run to build and run the application.

● The application displays a check mark by the side of each cell when a user taps it and removes the check mark when a user taps the cell again.

Note: *You can find the ListWithAccessories project on the website for this book: www.wiley.com/go/ iphonedevelopmentvb.*

Extra

Accessory views are useful but limited. You can use them to indicate binary yes/no and on/off status options and to add navigation prompts for menus. However, you cannot use them for cells with more than two possible states.

You can use the image view options described later in this chapter to create more sophisticated effects — for example, selecting between two or more images to indicate different types of cell status. Unfortunately, the position of the image view is fixed at the left and cannot be customized.

For a wider range of effects, you can customize the views used within the cell, either by re-allocating them programmatically or by loading one or more custom cell designs from a nib file. For more details, see the next two examples.

Working with Table Editing and Customized Cells

You can use the editing features built into UITableView to implement cell deletion, addition, and reordering. You can also customize cells to enhance their impact, add extra features, and improve their usability. Many iPhone applications use cells in the simplest possible way. You can create more advanced effects, with better user appeal, by creating your own customized designs for cells.

Table Selection

When a user taps a cell, the table view calls the didSelectRowAtIndexPath: method. This method is included in the Navigation-based Application template but is commented out. To enable selection, uncomment it and then add code that responds to the user's cell choice; for example, add a selection marker to the cell.

You must use this method to implement table navigation. Add code to load another view controller, initialize it with setup information, and then push it onto the controller stack:

```
[self.navigationController pushViewController:
  theNextViewController animated: YES];
```

This creates the familiar menu-like slide-in view-switching effect used in many of the iPhone's built-in applications. If the next view is another table view, you must initialize its data source before you display it. For an example, see the multiview switching sample application later in this chapter.

Table Editing

You can enable table editing by sending the table view a setEditing: message:

```
[aTableView setEditing: YES animated: YES];
```

By default, this slides in a delete icon at the left of the cell. If a user taps the button, a separate delete confirmation button, labeled delete, appears at the right of the cell. Tapping the confirmation button triggers the commitEditingStyle: forRowAtIndexPath: method.

To edit a table, you must add, delete, or exchange items in the data source; for example, you can delete an item by calling the deleteRowsAtIndexPaths: method on a data source array. You can then refresh the table display by calling [aTableView reloadData];.

Edits can be made on one cell at a time or they can be *batched*. In batched editing, the data source should be updated continually within the commitEditingStyle: method, with calls to standard add/delete/exchange NSArray methods. However, the table view is only refreshed when the

user signals that editing is complete — for example, by clicking a Done button.

You must maintain separate insertion and deletion arrays, with a list of index paths for each item. When batched editing ends, your application should call the insertSections: withRowAnimation:, and deleteSections: withRowAnimation: methods, passing the insertion and deletion arrays. For example:

```
[tableView beginUpdates];
[tableView insertRowsAtIndexPaths:
  insertIndexArray withRowAnimation:
  UITableViewAnimationFade];
[tableView deleteRowsAtIndexPaths:
  deleteIndexArray withRowAnimation:
  UITableViewAnimationFade];
[tableView endUpdates];
```

The beginUpdates and endUpdates calls set the start and end of an animation block and must be included, even when animation is disabled.

Customizing Cells

The `UITableViewCell` class has limited customizability. For more advanced effects, you can modify the cell's view tree directly, adding extra elements as needed. *Tagging* is a key concept for this type of editing. A tag is an arbitrary number added to a subview that can identify it. You can set a tag for any `UIView` object, including all its subclasses:

```
[thisViewObject setTag: 321];
```

You can then access the tagged view within another object — such as a cell — by using:

```
[cell viewWithTag: 321];
```

This searches the view tree and returns a pointer to the view object with the specified tag. You can use tagging to search any composite `UIView` object. You do not need to know the structure of the view tree or the index number of each view in the tree. However, you must keep track of the class of each tagged object so you can access its properties.

Adding and Changing New Cell Views

For example, to add a new `UILabel` to a cell:

```
UILabel *thisLabel = [[UILabel alloc] init];
[thisLabel setTag: 111];
[cell addSubview: thisLabel];
[thisLabel release];
```

You can then retrieve the tagged label:

```
UILabel *cellLabel = (UILabel *)[cell viewWithTag: 111];
cellLabel.someProperty = somePropertyValue;
```

The first line of this code retrieves the tagged label and reminds your application that it is an instance of `UILabel`. This is the only way to restore the class of a customized view. If you do not include this step, the retrieved view remains a generic instance of `UIView` and you cannot access all its properties.

Loading a Cell Design from a Nib File

You can add new views to cells programmatically by using `alloc`, `init`, and `addSubview`. However, you can simplify the design process by creating a complete cell design in Interface Builder. Interface Builder includes a `TableViewCell` in its list of objects. To create a customized cell, create a new empty object in Interface Builder, drag an instance of `UITableViewCell` to it, and then add further objects — such as a blank background view, a label, or a button — to build a view tree for the cell. Optionally, you can tag some of the objects for later access.

You can then load the cell from a nib file:

```
[[NSBundle mainBundle] loadNibNamed:
  @"myCellNib" owner: self options: nil];
```

To enable links to the cell's properties, you must create a separate instance of `UITableViewCell` as a named `IBOutlet` property in the class interface and then link the cell design to the named outlet property in Interface Builder.

You can link objects in cells to a controller as you typically would. For example, if your cell includes a `UIButton`, create a `buttonPressed:` method in your controller and then link the button to it in Interface Builder. When the application runs, any cell button a user taps triggers `buttonPressed:`.

Create
Color-Coded Cells

You can use cell color-coding in a table to improve the appearance of cells and to indicate cell status. The default all-white color scheme is ideal for tables with large fonts. If you decrease the font size, an all-white background becomes harder to read. You can increase clarity by alternating colors in the table. White and light gray are popular choices, as is the alternating white and light blue scheme used in many OS X applications. You can also use colors to indicate cell status and cell groupings. Subtle background shadings can be an effective way to indicate that cells are grouped — without using table sections.

Although you can set a table's background color with `tableView.backgroundColor = [UIColor aColor];`, this sets the background color of every cell. Setting the background of individual cells is more complex. One solution is to extend `cellForRowAtIndexPath:` to set

the background color of the cell's root view and add a new `UILabel` with a transparent background color. Without this customization, the default `UILabel` object hides the cell background.

The new label must be the correct size within the cell. Use `initWithFrame:` to set the dimensions as a `rect` — a standard rectangle object with an x,y offset from its superview, which is the surrounding cell, and a width and height. To make a `rect`, use the `CGRectMake` function, which is part of the graphics library:

```
UILabelView *newLabel = [[UILabel alloc]
  initiWithFrame: CGRectMake(xOffset, yOffset,
  width, height)];
```

You must also tag the cell so you can set its text label separately, set a clear background color, and set a font and size. To re-create the default table font:

```
[newLabel setFont: [UIFont
  boldSystemFontOfSize: 20];
```

Create Color-Coded Cells

① In the Finder, press Option and then drag and drop the Simple List project folder to make a copy. Rename the folder ListWithColors. Double-click Simple List. xcodeproj to load it in Xcode.

Note: *You can find the ListWithColors project on the website for this book: www. wiley.com/go/iphonedevelopmentvb.*

② Click RootViewController.m.

③ Scroll down to the `cellForRowAt IndexPath:` method.

④ Optionally, add code to set the default background color.

Note: *This creates a light gray background for the entire table.*

⑤ Add code to tag the root view in the cell.

⑥ Add code to create a new `UILabel` for the cell, re-creating the default frame size, with a slight indent.

⑦ Add code to set a clear background color and to re-create the default table font.

⑧ Add code to tag the label, add it to the cell, and then release it.

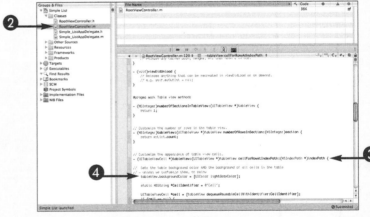

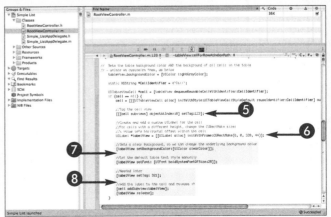

9 Add code to retrieve the background view by using a tag.

10 Add code to set the color of the background view, creating alternating colors calculated by using the index path row.

11 Add code to retrieve the cell's new UILabel.

12 Add code to set the text of the UILabel.

Note: You must create a new UILabel and add it to the cell. These steps are essential because the label's clear background color allows the cell's background color to show through.

13 Click Build and Run to build and run the application.

● The application displays cells with alternating gray and white background colors.

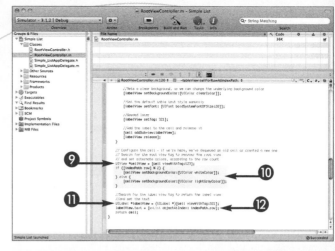

Apply It

To create alternating cell colors:

```
UIView *cellView [cell viewWithTag: someTag];
If ([indexPath row] % 2 {
[cellView setBackgroundColor: [UIColor aColor];
} else {
[cellView setBackgroundColor: [UIColor anotherColor];
}
```

You must set the cell's tag when it is first created:

```
[[cell subViews: objectAtIndex: 0] setTag: someTag];
```

Add Sliders to Cells

You can add controls by inserting them into the cell's view tree when the cell is created. For example, to add a slider, allocate a pointer at the start of the `cellForRowAtIndexPath:` method: `UISlider *sliderView;`

You can then create a slider and assign it to the cell:

```
sliderView = [[UISlider alloc] initWithFrame:
 CGRectMake(xOffset, yOffset, width, height)];
```

The `xOffset` and `yOffset` values set the position within the cell. `width` sets the width of the slider. For a slider, `height` is redundant but must be included anyway.

To assign a target method action for a control object:

```
[sliderView addTarget:self action:@selector
 (theTargetMethod:) forControlEvents:
 UIControlEventValueChanged];
```

This is equivalent to linking the slider to an `IBAction` method in Interface Builder. When the user moves the slider, `theTargetMethod:` is called.

To retrieve a pointer to the cell that triggered the method:

```
UITableViewCell *thisCell = (UITableViewCell *)
 [sender superview];
```

This returns the superview of the slider, which is the surrounding cell. This code assumes that the cell is the root of its own view tree.

You can identify the cell in various ways. This example reads the cell label to identify the cell:

```
NSString *cellText = thisCell.textLabel.text;
```

It copies the cell text to the navigation controller title field as an indicator. You can also read the index path for each cell directly:

```
NSIndexPath *thisIndexPath =
 [indexPathForCell: thisCell];
```

This example does not implement a full auxiliary data source. The settings are temporary and for display only.

Add Sliders to Cells

1 In the Finder, press Option and then drag and drop the Simple List project folder to make a copy. Rename the folder ListWithControls. Double-click Simple List.xcodeproj to load it in Xcode.

Note: *You can find the ListWithControls project on the website for this book: www.wiley. com/go/iphonedevelopmentvb.*

2 Click RootViewController.m.

3 Scroll down to the `cellForRowAt IndexPath:` method.

4 Add code to create a pointer to a `UISlider`.

5 Add code to set the default cell selection style to `None` so the cell is not highlighted when a user taps it.

6 Add code to create a new slider and to initialize it.

7 Add code to set a target action method for the slider called `sliderChanged:`.

8 Add code to insert the slider into the cell's view tree and to release the slider.

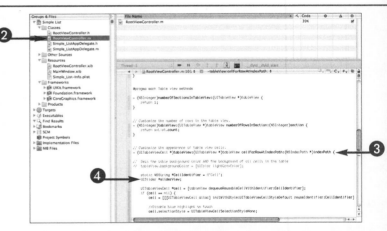

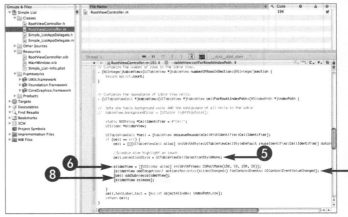

9 Add the `sliderChanged:` method.

10 Add code to retrieve a pointer to the cell that was modified and to read the label in the cell.

11 Add code to retrieve a pointer to the slider.

12 Add code to set the title bar with the name of the modified cell and the slider value.

Note: `self` *is the view controller, which is initialized as an instance of a navigation controller in the template.*

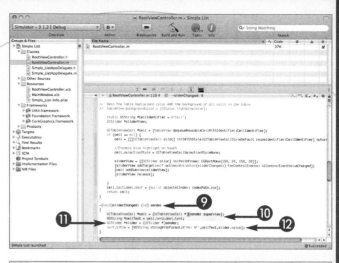

13 Click Build and Run to build and run the application.

● The application displays a list of cells with sliders, and moving a slider updates the title bar.

Note: Because the application does not maintain a separate data source for the sliders, adding more cells to the example creates unpredictable results.

Extra

You cannot update controls in cells directly; for example, do not try to set the value for a slider in a given cell. Objects inside cells are temporary and can be recycled. When a cell is recycled, all visible properties should be re-initialized with new data.

To do this, create an auxiliary data source array to store control values. Add an assignment from the data source to a control's property in `cellForRowAtIndexPath:`. For example:

```
sliderView.value = [myAuxiliaryDataArray objectAtIndex: indexPath.row];
```

This sets a slider's value from a control array. When your code changes one or more control values, call `[table reloadData];` to refresh the entire table. This updates all the visible values in the table automatically.

In the other direction — when the user changes the value of a control — you must update the auxiliary data source in the target action method. Otherwise, the slider, switch, or another control that is visible on the display will not be connected to the underlying data.

Load a Cell Template from a Nib File

To customize a cell, you can design a single instance of UITableViewCell in Interface Builder. Create a new file by using the Empty template in Interface Builder and then save it, adding it to your project. Add an instance of UITableViewCell from the Library. Expand by adding extra features to its view tree as required.

Cells are almost infinitely customizable. Cell width is fixed at 320 pixels, and only one column is available. Although it is possible to create multicolumn tables using customized cells, Apple's User Interface guidelines do not support this.

To access objects in the tree from your code without creating links to them, tag them in Interface Builder. Many objects include a tag field. Tag values are saved with the nib and can be accessed from your code.

This example creates a simple cell design with three elements. A UIView provides a colored background fill, a UILabel provides static text, and a UIButton Rounded Rect Button provides interaction. An IBAction button Pressed: method is used to receive button touch events and is assigned to the button in the nib in Interface Builder.

The cell is allocated and loaded implicitly. A cell pointer called tvCell is declared in the header as an outlet and then a link is created between the table view cell and tvCell in Interface Builder. Because of the link, the code automatically loads tvCell with the contents of the nib.

Another hidden feature is that you must assign File's Owner in the cell nib to the RootViewController class in the template. Do this before creating links to the nib's contents.

Load a Cell Template from a Nib File

① In the Finder, press Option and then drag and drop the Simple List project folder to make a copy. Rename the folder NibCell List. Double-click Simple List.xcodeproj to load it in Xcode.

Note: You can find the NibCell List project on the website for this book: www.wiley.com/go/iphonedevelopmentvb.

② Click RootViewController.h.

③ Add an instance of UITableView Cell declared as an IBOutlet.

④ Declare the instance as a property. Add a buttonPressed: IBAction method. Save the file.

⑤ Add code to assign a string identifier to each cell and to load a cell from a nib file if required.

Note: This identifier should match the identifier for the cell view in the nib file added in step 11 below.

⑥ Add code to access the UILabel in each cell and to set its text.

⑦ Add code to access the UIButton in each cell, to set the button title, and to align the title to the center of the button.

⑧ Add code to implement the buttonPressed: method and then add code to read the title of the button that triggered the method and to set the title bar.

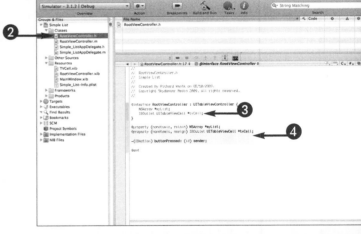

9 Double-click RootViewController.xib to load it in Interface Builder. Choose File→New to load a new Interface Builder template.

0 Click Cocoa Touch and Empty, click the Choose button, and then save the new nib file to the project folder as TVCell.xib. Click the Simple List check box and then click Add to add it to the project.

1 Add a Table View Cell to the new nib file.

2 In the Attributes pane in the Inspector window, set the Identifier to myTVCell to match the cell identifier in the code.

3 Add a UIView, a UIButton, and a UILabel. Click the UILabel, and in the Attributes pane, set its tag to 222 to match the tag in the code. Set the tag for the UIButton to 111 to match the tag in the code.

4 Click File's Owner.

5 In the Identity pane in the Inspector window, set the Class to RootView Controller in the drop-down menu.

The type field changes from NSObject to RootViewController.

6 In the Connections pane, drag a link from the Table View Cell to the tvCell IBOutlet in File's Owner. Link the TouchDown event from the button to the buttonPressed: method in File's Owner. Save the file.

Click Build and Run to build and run the application.

● The application loads and displays a table with customized cells with attributes loaded from the data source. When the buttons are tapped, they update the title bar.

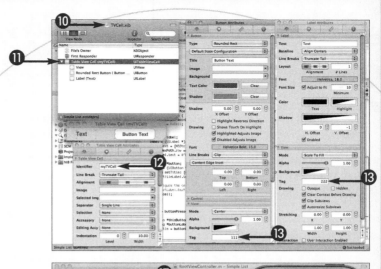

Extra

This example assigns a target action method for button events in Interface Builder. Alternatively, you can call the `addTarget:` method on each button whenever a cell is created in `cellForRowAtIndexPath::`

```
UIButton *button;
Button = (UIButton *)[cell viewWithTag: tagForAButton];
[button addTarget:self action:@selector(theTargetMethod:)
  forControlEvents: UIControlTouchDown];
```

When you assign a method to a button in Interface Builder, every button in the table triggers the same method. If you use code, each button can trigger a different method. You can also change methods as cells are updated — for example, to call one method from highlighted cells and a different method from other cells. Optionally, you may need to add extra arrays to the data source to manage user interaction with cell and object states.

Add and Delete Cells

Y ou can create editable tables to enable users to add and delete cells from a table. To implement editing, add buttons, switches, or other controls to enable the user to enter edit mode. This example adds Add and Delete buttons to the navigation bar. You can also display buttons on a toolbar. In this example, add and delete features are implemented differently. When the user taps the Delete button, the table enters editing mode by sending the `setEditing:` message to the table:

```
[self.tableView setEditing: YES animated: YES];
```

When `animated` is `NO`, editing controls appear instantly. When it is `YES`, controls slide in from the left of the table.

By default, editing mode displays a delete view at the left of every cell. If a user taps the view, it rotates and a Delete confirmation button appears at the right of the cell. You do not need to add code to implement these animations.

Table views also include a built-in swipe-to-delete feature. When a user drags a finger across a cell, the table displays a red Delete confirmation button. In both cases, tapping the Delete confirmation triggers the `commitEditingStyle:` method. To implement the deletion:

```
[tableView deleteRowsAtIndexPaths:[NSArray
  arrayWithObject: indexPath]withRowAnimation:
  UITableViewRowAnimationFade];
[tableView reloadData];
```

`deleteRowsAtIndexPaths:` takes an array of index paths to allow for batch deletion. This example does not support batch deletion, so `[NSArray arrayWithObject indexPath]` converts the index path into a single array.

This example implements a very simple Add option. When the user taps the Add button, it appends a single entry with a preset title to the data source and calls `[tableView reloadData];` to refresh the table.

Add and Delete Cells

① In the Finder, press Option and then drag and drop the Simple List project folder to make a copy. Rename the folder Edit Simple List. Double-click Simple List.xcodeproj to load it in Xcode.

Note: *You can find the Edit Simple List project on the website for this book: www.wiley.com/go/iphonedevelopmentvb.*

② Click RootViewController.h.

③ Add the `UITableViewDelegate` protocol to the controller header.

Note: *This is optional here but is essential if you want to experiment further with table view delegate methods.*

④ Change both of the `NSArray` declarations to `NSMutableArray`.

Note: *An `NSArray` is static. You must use an `NSMutable Array` whenever you need to add and remove items.*

⑤ Click RootViewController.m, find `viewDidLoad`, and then change the initialization `NSArray` to an `NSMutableArray`.

⑥ Add code to add a Delete button to the navigation bar.

⑦ Add code to add an Add button to the navigation bar.

Note: *Both buttons use an action selector to choose the method that is triggered when the button is tapped. In this example, `enterDeleteMode` and `enterAdd Mode` methods are triggered.*

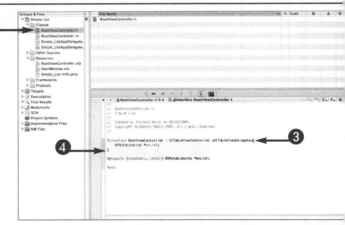

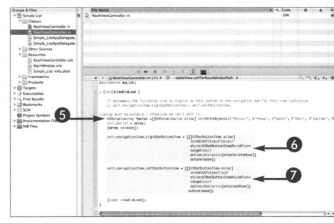

8 Add code to implement the enterDelete Mode method, appending a blank entry to the data source array and reloading the table to refresh it.

9 Add code to implement the enterDelete Mode method, changing the right button title to Cancel, setting it to trigger an exitDeleteMode method, and enabling editing with animation.

10 Add code to implement the exitDelete Mode method, renaming the right button Delete, setting it to trigger the enter DeleteMode method, and disabling editing mode on the table.

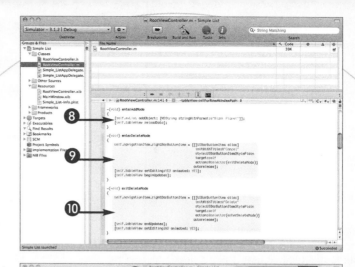

11 Scroll down to find the commitEditing Style: method and then uncomment it.

12 Add code to delete the selected item from the data source.

13 Add code to reload the table to refresh the display.

14 Add code to exit delete mode.

15 Click Build and Run to build and run the application.

● When the Delete button is tapped, delete options appear with a Cancel option. When the Add button is tapped, the application adds a blank cell to the table.

Note: For clarity, in this example, the table has been set to display data in the grouped format in Interface Builder. This does not affect editing. The grouped format does not pad the end of the table with empty cells.

Extra

Editing is highly customizable. To change the default red delete icon to a green insertion icon, add the <UITable ViewDelegate> protocol to the table view controller and implement the tableView: editingStyleForRow AtIndexPath: method to return UITableViewCellEditingStyleInsert. You can also return UITableView CellEditingStyleNone to disable editing for that cell and hide the editing icons. This method takes index path information, so you can use it to set the editing mode for individual cells.

To change the text in the Delete confirmation button for some or all cells:

```
-(NSString *)tableView: (UITableView *) tableView
  titleForDeleteConfirmationButtonForRowAtIndexPath: (NSIndexPath *) indexPath
{return @"A different string"}
```

Create Moveable Cells

You can move cells by entering edit mode to display reordering buttons. Reordering buttons slide in from the right of the display. There is no separate reordering option or editing style.

When the user taps and holds a cell's reordering button, it is redrawn with a drop shadow. The user can drag the cell to a new position in the table and then release it to confirm the move.

To implement reordering, include the `moveRowAtIndexPath:` method in your code. If this method is not present, reordering is disabled. When it is included, reordering buttons appear automatically when the table enters edit mode.

You can implement cell deletion and reordering in the same application. Deletion triggers the `commitEditingStyle:` method. Reordering triggers the `moveRowAtIndexPath:` method. These methods work independently.

For clarity, this example does not implement deletion. It removes the Delete button and disables automated cell indentation in editing mode. To hide the Delete button, the `editingStyleForRowAtIndexPath` method is implemented. It returns `UITableViewCellEditingStyleNone`, which removes the button. To disable indentation, the `shouldIndentWhileEditing` method is implemented and returns `NO`.

You do not need to call `[tableView reloadData];` to refresh the table after a move. The move reorders the table cells automatically. However, you must update the data source in the `moveRowAtIndexPath:` method. The method passes a `fromIndex` and `toIndex` to indicate source and destination indices. The simplest and most efficient way to implement a move is:

```
NSString *cellString = [[aDataSourceArray
  objectAtIndex: fromIndexPath.row] retain];
[aDataSourceArray removeObjectAtIndex:
  fromIndexPath.row];
[aDataSourceArray insertObjectAtIndex:
  cellString atIndex: toIndexPath.row];
[cellString release];
```

If the data source does not hold strings, modify the code accordingly.

Create Moveable Cells

① In the Finder, press Option and then drag and drop the Simple List project folder to make a copy. Rename the folder Reorder Simple List. Double-click Simple List.xcodeproj to load it in Xcode.

Note: *You can find the Reorder Simple List project on the website for this book: www.wiley.com/go/iphonedevelopmentvb.*

② Click RootViewController.h.

③ Change both of the `NSArray` declarations to `NSMutableArray`.

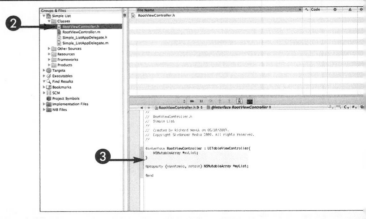

④ Click RootViewController.m, and in `viewDidLoad`, change the initialization array to an `NSMutableArray`.

⑤ Add a call to a new `exitReorderMode` method to initialize reordering.

Note: *The compiler warning here is for information only — it does not affect compilation.*

6 Implement an `enterReorderMode` method. Add code to create a navigation bar button and name it Done. Assign `exitReorderMode` as the target action, enable table editing, and then set the table view delegate.

7 Implement the `exitReorderMode` method. Add code to create a navigation bar button and name it Move. Assign `enterReorderMode` as the target action and then disable table editing.

8 Implement the `editingStyleForRowAt IndexPath` method to hide the Delete button in editing mode.

9 Implement the `shouldIndentWhile Editing` method to disable indents in edit mode.

10 Implement the `moveRowAtIndexPath:` method.

11 Add code to move entries in the data source by using `fromIndex` and `toIndex`.

12 Click Build and Run to build and run the application.

● When the Move button is tapped, the application displays reorder buttons next to each cell. When a cell's button is tapped, the cell floats and can be moved up and down the table.

Note: *The active area around a reorder button is not implemented reliably, and cells do not always float when the button is tapped. This is a bug in the table view.*

Extra

You can enable editing and move options selectively by implementing the optional `canEdit` and `canMove` methods. For example:

```
- (BOOL)tableView:(UITableView *)tableView
  canEditRowAtIndexPath:(NSIndexPath *)
  indexPath
{return NO;}
```

This disables editing for every cell. Similarly,

```
- (BOOL)tableView:(UITableView *)tableView
  canMoveRowAtIndexPath:(NSIndexPath *)
  indexPath
{return NO;}
```

This disables reordering for every cell. These methods are called once for every visible cell. Use an auxiliary

data source indexed by the `indexPath` — or some other conditional test — to enable and disable editing and reordering for individual cells.

In theory, to implement these methods, you must add the `UITableViewDataSource` and `UITableViewDelegate` protocols to your view controller; otherwise, they remain undefined.

In practice, they work even if you do not. This is a bug in the current 3.1.2 version of Xcode and may — or may not — be fixed in later versions.

However, to implement them, you must explicitly set a delegate for the table view.

Create Sections in Tables

Y ou can split tables into sections to group items and improve clarity. Tables display sections as sublists. The grouped table style shows sections as discrete units. The plain style shows them sequentially within the same list. Both styles support headers and footers. The grouped style shows headers and footers before and after the table in the surrounding frame. The plain style displays floating headers and footers in a smaller font on a gray background. When the user scrolls past the header, it sticks to the top of the display, and the remainder of the section scrolls under it.

Use the `numberOfSectionsInTableView:` method to set the total number of sections. Your data source must return a count of items for each section. Use this in the `numberOfRowsInSection:` method to set the length of each section.

To set a header for each section, implement the `titleFor HeaderInSection:` method. Typically, you can use a switch statement to select a title from the data source. For very simple tables, you can hardwire the section headers into your code.

The `cellForRowAtIndexPath:` method — used to fill cells with data — must be able to switch between sections to select the cell data. You can use a switch statement to do this or you can set up your data source as an array of arrays and use `[indexPath section];` as a selection index that chooses one array from the collection. An array of arrays is often the most efficient solution.

This example fills three sections with data from three separate arrays and adds floating headers. You must add the `titleForHeaderInSection:` method manually because it is not included in the template. The other methods are already present.

Create Sections in Tables

① In the Finder, press Option and then drag and drop the Simple List project folder to make a copy. Rename the folder ListWithSections. Double-click Simple List.xcodeproj to load it in Xcode.

Note: *You can find the ListWithSections project on the website for this book: www.wiley.com/go/ iphonedevelopmentvb.*

② Click RootViewController.m.

③ Remove the data source array code in `viewDidLoad`.

④ Add three array definitions to create data sources for three sections.

Note: *This code uses the #define directive to create inline code for the arrays. Alternatively, you could create three array pointer variables in the header and then assign data to them in `viewDidLoad` or one of the other initialization methods.*

⑤ Scroll down to find the table view methods, and in `numberOfSectionsInTableView:`, add code to return 3.

⑥ In `numberOfRowsInSection:`, add code to return the number of items in each data array.

⑦ Add the `titleForHeaderInSection:` method and then add code to return a different string for each section.

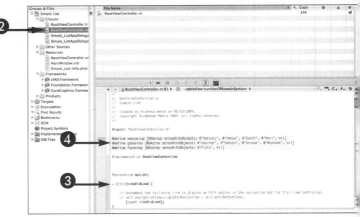

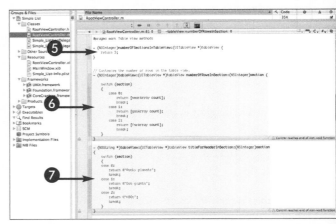

146

8 In `cellForRowAtIndexPath:`, add code to set the data source array for each section.

Note: *This code loads the cells for each section with data from a different array. Because cell contents are assigned dynamically, you must implement section selection in this method.*

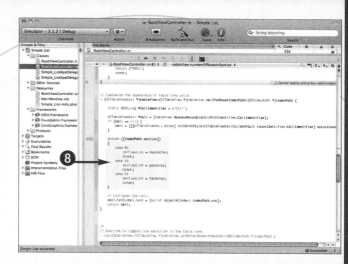

9 Click Build and Run to build and run the application.

● The application displays a table with three sections. Each section has a floating header.

Extra

You can control the spacing of headers and footers in two ways. The simplest and most efficient option is to set the table's `sectionHeaderHeight` and `sectionFooterHeight` properties. Heights are in points and are the same for every section.

For customized control of header and footer heights, implement the `heightForFooterInSection:` and `heightForHeaderInSection:` methods. These override the default properties. By switching on the section number, you can return different sizes for different sections.

You can add an *index* — a vertical list of quick links — by implementing the `sectionIndexTitlesForTableView:` method. This method returns an array of strings, which should be set to the section headers. The table view floats the strings in a list, rendered in a small font, at the right of the table. Tapping an entry in the index scrolls the table to that section. An index is particularly useful for long lists that are split into alphabetized sections. For example:

```
#define alphabetArray [NSArray arrayWithObjects: @"A", @"B"... @"Y", @"Z", nil]
- (NSArray *) sectionIndexTitlesForTableView: (UITableView *)
{return alphabetArray;}
```

This creates an A to Z index. Not all letters are shown here; you must explicitly include the full list in your code.

Introducing Pickers

You can use pickers to display a rotating table on a virtual rotating wheel, called a *component*. The user can rotate the picker to select a single item from the table. As the picker spins, it generates a click. An optional translucent center marker indicates the selected item.

When dropped into a view, a picker has a fixed height of 215 pixels and fills the width of the screen. It is not possible to modify these dimensions in Interface Builder or by setting the picker's properties in code.

Unlike table views, pickers can display more than one component at a time. Columns are customizable; you can set the width of each component.

Pickers can be used to select an item from a list. Items can appear as text or graphics and can be refreshed dynamically to display changing content. Because of the limited height, a picker is a good way to display a list in a small space. Pickers are limited only by memory and can display hundreds of items. However, picker-scrolling is somewhat tedious; 50 items is a realistic limit for users.

Pickers and Tables

Internally, the UIPickerView class is closely related to UITableView. Picker components are similar to sections. To set the number of component wheels in a picker:

```
-(NSInteger) numberOfComponentsInPickerView:
   (UIPickerView *) pickerView
{return anInteger;}
```

To set the number of items in a component:

```
-(NSInteger)pickerView: (UIPickerView *)
  pickerView
 numberOfRowsInComponent: (NSInteger) component
[return anInteger;}
```

By including a switch statement for component, you can give each component a different number of items. Items may not align across components. You can set the row height for a component with rowHeightForComponent:. This changes the spacing between rows; it does not change the text or graphic size for each row item.

The titleForRow: forComponent: method is equivalent to cellForRowAtIndexPath: and reads a text string to set the label for each row. You should add the UIPickerViewDataSource and UIPickerView Delegate protocols to your controller to include these methods, and you must set an explicit picker delegate to implement them. Typically, this is self when the methods are included in the controller, but it may be some other object.

Pickers, Selections, and View Recycling

Pickers do not automatically recycle views that are not visible. There is no equivalent to the dequeueReusableCellWith Identifier: method available for table views.

It is possible to ignore recycling and keep all views in memory, but this is wasteful. For more efficient results, your code must implement customized recycling features. Use the didSelectRow: InComponent: method to return the currently selected item, calculate which views should be

queued or released, and queue or release them. You should also use this method to return a picker selection.

You can also query a picker object to find the currently selected row with selectedRow: InComponent:. This method can be run at any time to return a picker selection. However, there is no way to test if the picker is in motion, so you should use didSelectRow: InComponent:; it triggers when the picker stops and is guaranteed to be stable.

Date and Time Pickers

UIDatePicker is a simplified class related to UIPicker View and optimized for date and time displays. It shows a picker with a fixed number of components, depending on the mode. The four modes are Time, which displays hours and minutes and an optional AM/PM marker; Date, which displays months, days, and years; DateAndTime, which displays both the time and date; and CountDownTimer, which displays an hour and minute counter. Modes are prefixed with UIDatePickerMode; for example, Count DownTimer would be UIDatePickerModeCount DownTimer. You can set the mode with a simple assignment to the datePickerMode property:

```
thisPicker.datePickerMode =
  UIDatePickerModeDateAndTime;
```

The mode is not fixed and can be updated at any time.

Date pickers do not automatically show the current date and time. You should initialize a picker with a date and time before displaying it. To load the current date and time:

```
NSDate *now [[NSDate alloc] init];
thisPicker.date = now;
[now release];
```

Date pickers use the iPhone's locale setting to select a calendar and set the day, month, and year order. Implementing support for a full set of international calendars is complex. Many applications only support the Gregorian (Western) calendar. You can set a picker's calendar with the calendar property. This defaults to the user's selection, which may not be Western.

Setting the Date and Time

To set an arbitrary date and time, allocate an instance of NSDate and then fill it with NSDateComponents:

```
NSDateComponents *comps = [NSDateComponents alloc] init]
[comps setYear: 1963]; [comps setMonth: 1]; [comps setDay: 15];
[comps setHour: 17]; [comps setMinute: 10]; [comps setSecond: 23];
NSDate *oldDate = [gregorian dateFromComponents: comps];
thisPicker.date = oldDate;
[comps release];
```

To set a countdown time, set the picker's countDownDuration property by using an NSTimeInterval in seconds. You must implement the timer action by using an NSTimer; for details, see Chapter 9.

Customizing Pickers

It is possible to resize pickers, move pickers, and create horizontal pickers. However, these options are not built into the picker view class — all require tricks. For example, you can clip the sides of the picker by moving it into an intermediate view and clicking the ClipSubviews check box for the view in Interface Builder. You can use this technique to create a number of parallel thin dials.

Resizing a picker is more complex. It is possible to change the height of a picker by editing a nib file with a text editor. To rotate and scale a picker, you can use *affine transforms* — scaling and rotation routines — to literally rotate and scale the picker image. Affine transforms are part of the iPhone's graphics library. For more, see Chapter 8.

Create a Multicolumn Picker

You can use pickers to display static lists. However, picker data can also be updated dynamically. This example implements a simple times table application with two wheels. The first wheel sets a number. The second wheel displays up to 30 multiples of that number. As the user spins the first wheel, the numbers in the second wheel update automatically. The second wheel is for display only; the user can scroll up and down to review the list, but the second wheel does not trigger any further action. The width of each wheel is customized to enhance the display.

To create a picker application, add a picker to a view in Interface Builder. You can position the picker within the view by dragging it vertically. You cannot set the width or height. To connect the picker to your application, add the

`UIPickerViewDelegate` and `UIPickerViewDataSource` protocols to your controller header. Create an `IBOutlet` to a picker object and then link it to the picker in Interface Builder. Set the picker object delegate to `self` when the view loads. You can now add various picker-related methods to your code. If you do not implement a minimal set of methods, the picker is not displayed.

To refresh the picker after an update:

```
[thisPicker reloadAllComponents];
```

This cycles through every row in the picker, changing its contents. To set the contents, use the `titleForRow:forComponent:` method to return a string for each item.

By default, a virtual plastic cover marks the selected row in the picker. You can disable this feature:

```
thisPicker.showsSelectionIndicator = NO;
```

Create a Multicolumn Picker

① Create a new project with the View-based Application template and then save it as SimplePicker.

Note: *You can find the SimplePicker project on the website for this book: www.wiley.com/go/iphonedevelopmentvb.*

② Click SimplePickerViewController.h.

③ Add the `UIPickerViewDelegate` and `UIPicker ViewDataSource` methods to the header.

④ Add a pointer to an `IBOutlet` for a `UIPicker View` and then declare the pointer as a property.

⑤ Synthesize the picker pointer. Add an integer variable for the times table multiplicand. Uncomment `viewDidLoad` and then add code to set the picker delegate to `self`.

⑥ Add code to set the number of components and the number of items in each component.

Note: *This code returns a constant. To set a different number of items for each component, add a conditional or a switch statement for the component number and use it to return different values.*

⑦ Add code to set the content of each item, using a conditional statement to select the content for each component.

⑧ Add code to set the width of each component, using another conditional statement.

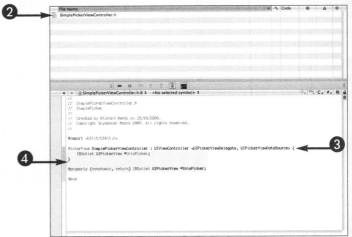

9 Add code to respond to row selections by updating the multiplication factor and refreshing the table.

10 Add code to set the row height.

Note: *This code returns the same row height for both components. To set different row heights, use a conditional or switch statement.*

11 Double-click SimplePickerView Controller.xib to open it in Interface Builder. Drag and drop a UIPicker View from the Library to the view. Optionally, move the picker position so it is vertically centered in the view.

Note: *The default picker view is loaded with static data that shows a list of locations around San Francisco. This is for display only.*

12 Click File's Owner.

13 Add links from the picker to the thisPicker IBOutlet and to the delegate and datasource outlets.

Note: *The delegate and datasource outlets are pre-defined and appear in this list automatically.*

14 Click Build and Run to build and run the application.

● The application displays a picker with two components. Changing the selection in the first component automatically updates the items in the second component.

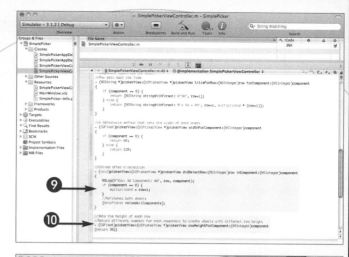

Extra

Default picker rows are instances of `UILabel`. For customized picker graphics, add this method:

```
-(UIView *)pickerView:(UIPickerView *)pickerView viewForRow:(NSInteger)row
forComponent:(NSInteger)component
reusingView: (UIView *)view
```

You can use this method to return any subclass — including a custom subclass — of `UIView`. For example, if it returns `UIImageView` objects, the picker displays images. You can use this method to fill pickers with sliders, buttons, and switches. However, fixed images and text are typically more useful.

Potentially, you can design one or more customized views in Interface Builder and then load them into the picker from a nib file. The default picker cells do not support color selections. You can use nib-loaded or programmatically generated views to add color.

Create a Date and Time Picker

You can use a date picker to select and show dates and times. Date pickers do not include a clock, calendar, or timer. To implement real-time features, you must build clock, timer, and calendar code around them. This example does not build a clock. It demonstrates the four different date picker modes, selected with a segmented switch. When the user changes the picker, it formats the setting and copies it to the console.

A picker's date property is read-write:

```
aDate = thisPicker.date; //Read the date from
  the picker settings
thisPicker.date = aDate; //Write a date to the
  picker
```

The Time, Date, and DateAndTime modes return a valid date string. The CountDownTimer mode returns a fixed date of Dec 02, 0002, and a time after 12:00 AM set by the timer count.

UIDatePicker is a relatively simple object. However, date and time formats are complex. The iPhone includes support

for the Gregorian (Western) calendar and for Islamic, Japanese, Chinese, Hebrew, and Buddhist calendars.

Converting a given date and time into a locale-appropriate string that automatically renders the date into a user's local calendar is simple: Use an NSDateFormatter object. For example:

```
NSDateFormatter *dateFormatter =
  [[NSDateFormatter alloc] init];
[dateFormatter setTimeStyle:
  NSDateFormatterMediumStyle];
[dateFormatter setDateStyle:
  NSDateFormatterMediumStyle];
aDateString = [dateFormatter stringFromDate:
  thisPicker.date];
[dateFormatter release];
```

This sets aDateString with a readable date and time. Use NSDateFormatterStyleNoStyle to leave a field blank. To show a time zone, set the time style to NSDateFormatterFullStyle.

Loading the date and time with valid date and time elements is more complex. You must use NSDateComponents, as described on the previous page.

Create a Date and Time Picker

1. Create a new project with the View-based Application template and then save it as DatePicker.

Note: You can find the DatePicker project on the website for this book: www.wiley.com/go/iphonedevelopmentvb.

2. Click DatePickerViewController.h.

3. Add an IBOutlet to a UIDatePicker and then declare the picker as a property.

4. Add segmentChanged: and pickerChanged: IBAction methods.

5. Synthesize the picker.

6. Find and uncomment viewDidLoad.

7. Add code to initialize the picker with the current date and time.

8. Implement segmentChanged: to respond to taps on a segmented switch and then add code to reload the picker with the current date and time and to read the switch state and set the picker mode.

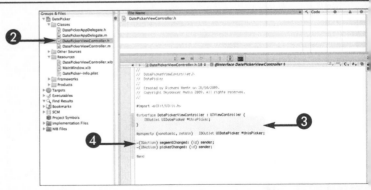

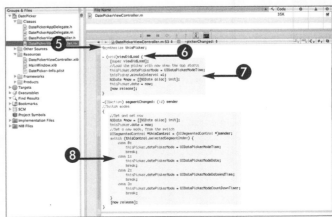

9. Implement the `pickerChanged:` method, add code to read the time and date selected on the picker, and then copy the date and time to the console.

10. Double-click DateViewPickerController.xib to load it in Interface Builder and then drag and drop a UIDatePicker and a UISegmentedControl from the Library into the empty view.

11. Link the picker in the view to the thisPicker IBOutlet.

12. Link the value changed message from the picker to the pickerChanged: method and the valueChanged: message from the segmented controller to the segmentChanged: method and then save the file.

13. Click Build and Run to build and run the application.

14. In Xcode, choose Run→Console to display the console.

● The picker displays the current date and time. The segmented control changes picker modes. When the picker selection is changed, it is copied to a string in the console window.

Extra

For more control over date and time information, create an instance of NSCalendar:

```
NSCalendar *thisCalendar [[NSCalendar alloc] initWithCalendarIdentifier: NSGregorianCalendar];
```

You can then use NSDateComponents to split an NSDate object into the day, month, year, weekday, hour, minute, and second fields.

NSDateComponents is not filled automatically from an NSDate. You must specify the fields you need explicitly by using *calendar unit* constants to select each calendar item — days, months, etc. For details, see the list in the NSCalendar reference documentation. For example:

```
NSDateComponents *theseComponents = [thisCalendar components: NSDayCalendarUnit fromDate:
  today];
NSInteger day = [theseComponents day];
```

This returns only the day number. If you do not include a calendar unit in the list of components, the corresponding property in your instance of NSDateComponents is not returned.

Create a Multiview Navigation-Based Application

You can use the Navigation-based Application template as the starting point for a menu-like multiview application. The template is not complete, and you must add extra features to create a full application. However, it includes a basic selection of features that can easily be extended.

The key principle of a multiview application built from table views is controller class management. It would be possible — but very inefficient — to create a separate class for every view in the application. It is simpler and more efficient to create generic classes that can be initialized with content as required.

Creating a multiview application is a four-step process. Create a new class for the next view level. Design a nib for the new class. Implement special features in the code if required. Add code to a selection method — typically

didSelectRowAtIndexPath: — to load an instance of the next class in the hierarchy, prime its data source with data, and display it.

This example uses three classes to manage 17 views. A root view class lists three planets. A moon view class lists each planet's moons. A final view class displays a string that could be filled with information about each moon. Each class below the root view is primed with content by the class above it. When the user taps a cell, the controller loads an instance of the next class from a nib file, primes its data source, and calls:

```
[self.navigationController pushViewController:
   nextController animated: YES];
```

The navigation controller automatically animates the switch to the next view. It also adds a Back button so the user can return to the previous view.

Create a Multiview Navigation-Based Application

① In Xcode, choose File→New Project.

② Click the Navigation-based Application template and then save it as MultiView.

Note: *You can find the MultiView project on the website for this book: www.wiley.com/go/iphonedevelopmentvb.*

③ Click RootViewController.h.

④ Add a pointer to an NSArray, declare it as a property, and then save the file.

⑤ Click RootViewController.m and then import the header for a new controller class called MoonViewController.

Note: *This class is not yet part of the project. It is added in a later step.*

⑥ Create three local data source arrays. Synthesize myList and then find and uncomment viewDidLoad. Add code to load the arrays with data, set the first array as a data source for the table, and assign a title to the table.

⑦ Scroll down to find the table view methods.

⑧ Add code to set the number of cells in the table from the array count.

⑨ Add code to read a label for each cell from the data source array.

⑩ Add code to add a disclosure chevron to each cell.

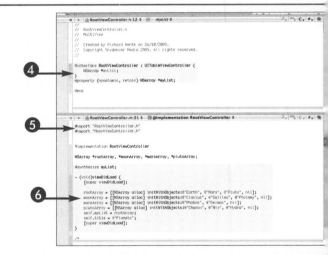

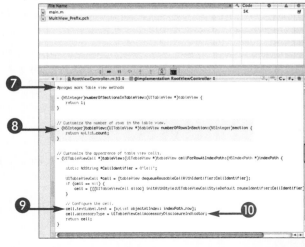

⑪ Uncomment
`didSelectRowAtIndexPath:`.

⑫ Add code to load an instance of `Moon ViewController` from its nib.

⑬ Add code to read the cell tapped by the user and to select and prime a data source array and title for the instance of `MoonViewController`.

⑭ Add code to push the instance of `MoonViewController` to the view stack and to animate a view switch and then save the file.

Note: *This code loads the next controller with data, sets the next navigation bar title, and implements a view switch.*

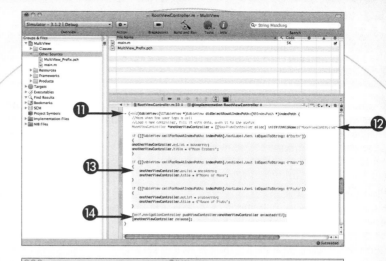

⑮ Right-click on the Classes folder in the Groups & Files pane and then choose Add→New File from the pop-up menu.

⑯ Click Cocoa Touch Class in the iPhone OS pane.

⑰ Click UIViewController subclass, and under options, click the With XIB for user interface check box.

⑱ Click Next and then save the file as MoonViewController.

A new `MoonViewController` class is added to the project. The class is a subclass of `UIViewController` and includes a nib file.

Note: *MoonViewController.xib is not automatically added to the Resources folder, but you can manually move it there.*

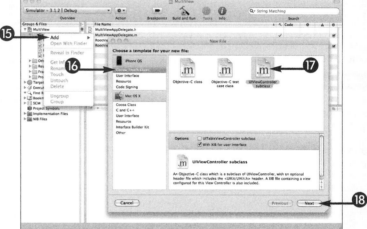

Extra

Controller classes can be reused as required. Typically, a root controller class handles the top level of view selection, and one or more subcontroller classes handle the remaining levels. First-level controllers are often generic. Final-view controllers are more likely to be specialized — for example, to implement specific features, display data, or set preferences and application controls. In outline, the hierarchy often looks like this:

```
root view controller  ➔  first level controller  ➔  one or more final views
```

It is possible in some applications to create a single generic controller class that can be used for every level. The common requirements for a controller are a nib name, a controller class name, a controller title — used by the navigation bar and its Back button — and a pointer to a data source. It is good design practice to minimize the number of different controller classes. The more generic the code, the more reliable it is and the more often it can be reused.

continued ➔

You can use the `didSelectRowAtIndexPath:` method to trigger a view switch to the next level. The template includes sample code in `didSelectRowAtIndexPath:`. However, the code is commented out. To implement view switching, uncomment the code and then replace the default controller class with your custom class.

There are many ways to implement view selection in `didSelectRowAtIndexPath:`. This example uses an indirect approach — it reads the label of the selected cell and then uses it to select data for the next view's data source. In a more complex application, you might load a full set of data for the entire application into an array of arrays, an `NSDictionary`, or even an SQLite database and then use the selected index path to select an entry and to prime the next view's content. It can be useful to detach

the data from a view controller class and to implement a separate model class exclusively for data management that can be accessed from any other class in the application.

This example creates a table skeleton but does not implement messaging across views. In a typical application, final views often manage preferences, application settings, or other user options. You can handle these by moving the data model for the application to a separate class or by using target action switching to trigger methods in objects other than the view controller.

The cells in this application use a disclosure/chevron accessory view to indicate that they display another view when tapped. You can use selective cell tagging, as described earlier in this chapter, to enable and disable accessory views for individual cells and to enable and disable navigation features for each cell.

Create a Multiview Navigation-Based Application *(continued)*

⑲ Click MoonViewController.h and then change the class to `UITableViewController`.

⑳ Add a pointer to an `NSArray` and then declare it as a property.

㉑ Click RootViewController.m. Copy the first three table view methods. Click MoonViewController.m and then paste the methods into the file.

㉒ Synthesize `myList` and then import the header for a new `FinalViewController` class that is created in a later step.

㉓ Add a new `didSelectRowAtIndexPath:` method and then add code to load an instance of a new `FinalViewController` class from a nib, set its title, and set a label property.

㉔ Double-click MoonViewController.xib to open it in Interface Builder.

㉕ Delete the default view and replace it with an instance of UITableView from the Library.

㉖ Link the dataSource and delegate outlets to File's Owner and then save the file.

Note: *This step connects the table view in the nib to the table view methods in the code. You do not need to add* IBAction *links to individual methods.*

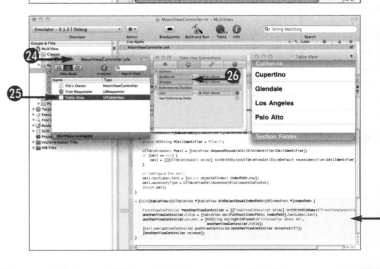

㉗ In Xcode, right-click on the Classes folder in the Groups & Files pane and then repeat steps 15–17 to add a new class called `FinalViewController` to the project.

Note: *FinalViewController.xib is not automatically added to the Resources folder, but you can manually move it there.*

㉘ Click FinalViewController.h. Add an `IBOutlet` to a label and add a string. Declare both as properties.

Note: *This class is a plain instance of `UIView Controller` and not a table view. Do not change its class.*

㉙ Click FinalViewController.m and then synthesize the label and the string.

㉚ Find and uncomment `viewDidLoad` and then add code to copy the string to the label outlet.

㉛ Double-click FinalViewController.xib to open it in Interface Builder. Add a UILabel to the default view. Optionally, center the view and increase its font size for clarity.

㉜ Link the UILabel to its corresponding outlet and then save the file.

㉝ Click Build and Run to build and run the application.

● The application displays a view tree with 17 elements on three levels. The user can tap cells to navigate through the tree. Back buttons for each view are automatically implanted by the navigation controller.

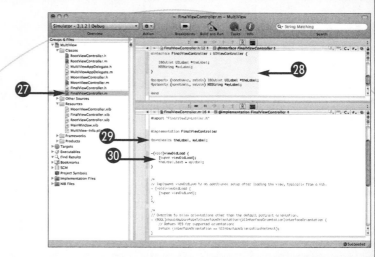

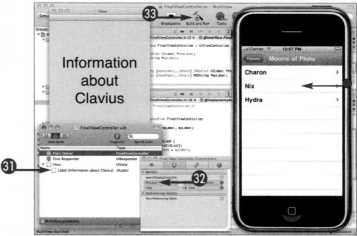

Extra

Because of a quirk or perhaps a bug, it is not always possible to access class properties that are declared as `IBOutlets`. In theory, it should be possible to set `FinalViewController`'s label text property directly from `MoonViewController`:

```
nextViewController.theLabel.text = aString;
```

Unfortunately, the label does nothing when it is loaded. As a work-around, the `FinalViewController` class includes an extra `myLabel` string property. `MoonViewController` sets `myLabel`. Code in `viewDidLoad` copies `myLabel` to `theLabel.text`. This sets the label correctly.

Using a single data source for most or all of the application can simplify data initialization and editing. It is good practice to create a unified and simple data scheme that can be accessed in a standardized way. For example, in this application, the view-switching selections are hardwired. This is adequate for a simple application but makes the code difficult to modify and reuse. Generalizing the view switching with selection methods instead of conditionals simplifies the code and makes it more efficient.

Working with Cocoa Data Types and Objective-C Variables

ocoa Touch offers a very rich set of features for working with data. You can use these features to simplify your applications and speed up the development cycle. Some of the features rely on the unique features of Objective-C and can also be used with conventional C-type variables.

Variables, Pointers, and Objects

Idiomatic Cocoa object allocation code can be complex. For example:

```
NSAClass *anInstance = [[NSAClass alloc]
  initWithConstants];
```

In words, this code calls the `alloc` method on `NSAClass` to return a block of memory that holds an instance of the class. The instance is initialized with one or more `Constants`.

`anInstance` is a pointer to the memory block. The leftmost `NSAClass` is a type declaration and tells the compiler the type of object `anInstance` points to. The compiler uses this information to calculate memory offsets when it accesses the properties of `anInstance`.

`anInstance` is not an object — it is a conventional C-type variable, which is a pointer to an object. The object exists in the memory pointed to by `anInstance`. When you release the memory, the object disappears; the pointer remains and can be reused.

Properties and Variable Scope

When you declare an object in a header, you split this code into two parts. The pointer is declared in the object header and added to the object's interface. However, the pointer remains `nil` until you allocate an object instance and assign it to the pointer. It is good practice to `alloc` and `init` in a single line. If you split `alloc` and `init`, test both for success.

Pointers do not have to be properties. You can declare a pointer anywhere in your code; for example, you can declare it at the start of the implementation section:

```
@implementation ThisClass
NSAClass *anInstance;
```

This pointer is visible to every method in the class but not visible to other objects. It is `nil` until you allocate and assign an instance of `NSAClass` to it.

If you declare a pointer inside a method, it is only visible inside that method:

```
-(void) aMethod {
NSAClass *anInstance;
//Code
}
```

The same rules apply to all conventional C-type objects, including `int`s, `BOOL`s, `float`s, and custom structures. You do not have to make every variable a property. It is legal to declare global variables that are visible to all methods beneath `@implementation` and to declare local method variables within the method code. Do not add these variables to the class header. Do not declare variables inside a conditional. The compiler cannot tell if the conditional code is called at runtime. It assumes variables are not visible outside the conditional scope:

```
if (someCondition)
  {
  int i = 10;
  i++;
  }
i = 0;
```

`i` is not defined outside the conditional, and the compiler throws an error on the last line.

Cocoa Touch Data Features

A key feature of Cocoa Touch is its exceptionally powerful data management features, which are far more sophisticated than those built into C, Java, and C++. These features offer pre-built solutions for common data management problems, including save and restore of the application state, undo/redo chains in arbitrary editing contexts, cut and paste, and both flat and relational databases. The iPhone also offers more general data management classes — with features for searching, listing, counting, modifying, and comparing objects — and object collections.

Dynamic Typing

You can use dynamic typing to assign properties to an object with an unknown class. This is a standard idiom in event-handling code. A handler method typically receives a sender object with the weakly typed placeholder `id` type, which is used when the type is not known at compilation:

```
-(void) anEventWasSentFrom: (id) sender
{
NSAclass *anInstance = (NSAclass *)sender;
}
```

This tells the compiler that both `anInstance` and `sender` are pointers to an `NSAclass` object. You should only use this technique when you are sure of `sender`'s type.

Essential Cocoa Data Objects

`NSArray` and `NSMutableArray` are sophisticated and powerful indexed arrays of arbitrary objects. You can assign any object type to any index and store different objects in the same array. `NSArray` is read-only. It offers simple indexed access and more sophisticated access options; for example, the `containsObject:` method tests if the array contains an object, and the `indexOfObject:` method performs a lookup and returns an object's index.

Use the `NSMutableArray` subclass for modifiable arrays. Methods are available for inserting and removing objects at a specific index, adding and removing objects from the end of the array, and replacing and swapping objects.

`NSDictionary` and `NSMutableDictionary` pair objects with keys. Pass a key to the dictionary to return an object. Objects do not have to be strings, so you can use a dictionary for arbitrary lists of settings or other application data. `NSMutableDictionary` includes methods for adding and deleting object-key pairs. Both dictionary types include the `keysSortedByValueUsingSelector:` method, which implements sorting via a custom method you write and returns a sorted list of keys in an array.

`NSSet`, `NSMutableSet`, and `NSCountedSet` support arbitrary unindexed object collections. `NSCountedSet` stores unique objects; when the `addObject:` method is called, it checks if the object already exists in the set. If so, `NSCountedSet` does not add it again but increments an internal counter, accessible through the `countFor Object:` method. `NSSet` can compare sets, checking for subsets, intersection, and equality. It also supports filtering through a `filteredSetUsingPredicate:` method that returns a subset based on a predicate selection.

Data Object Enumeration and Processing

`NSArray`, `NSDictionary`, and `NSSet` include efficient enumeration methods. You do not need to prepare a loop with an index counter or list keys explicitly. For example, to step through all the entries in a dictionary:

```
(for id key in aDictionary) {
 objectForKey = [aDictionary objectForKey:
 key];
 //Code to do something with objectForKey
}
```

Most data objects implement the `makeObjects PerformSelector:` method, which sends a selector message to every object. Use this feature to step through every item in a collection and process it with the selector.

Enter Text with a UITextField

You can use a `UITextField` to get a small amount of text — typically a single line — from the user. When the user taps the text field, a keyboard slides in from the bottom of the view. Typing on the keyboard adds text to the view. You can customize both the keyboard and the text field by setting the text field's properties or changing its default attributes in Interface Builder. Keyboard properties are listed in the `UIText InputTraits` Protocol Reference documentation and not in the documentation for `UITextField`.

To create a secure keyboard for passwords, click the Secure check box in Interface Builder or set the `secure TextEntry` property to YES. The `autoCorrectionType` property takes an auto-correction constant, such as `UITextAutoCorrectionTypeNo`. The `autocapital izationType` property takes an equivalent constant — for example, `UITextAutocapitalizationSentences`. Disable auto-correction and auto-capitalization for password input.

`keyboardAppearance` sets the color scheme of the keyboard. `UIKeyboardAppearanceDefault` selects a default light gray and blue scheme. `UIKeyboard AppearanceAlert` selects a charcoal and black color scheme. `keyboardType` is an essential property and defines the available keyboard type and layout. Set it to `UIKeyboardTypeNumberPad` for numeric input and then set `UIKeyboardTypePhonePad` for phone number input with # and * characters.

The `UIKeyboardTypeEmailAddress` and `UIKeyboard TypeURL` types include default www, .com, and @ characters. The default type is a plain ASCII keyboard, with built-in switching for special characters. `returnKeyType` is a related property and sets the return key. By default, this is Return but can be set to Go, Google, Next, Done, and other options by using a `UIReturnKeyType` constant prefix. These options are preset; you cannot set arbitrary text.

Call `resignFirstResponder` on the text view to hide the keyboard when the user taps the `return` key. This example displays two text fields with different properties. Text from each field is copied to a label for display.

Enter Text with a UITextField

① Create a new View-based Application template in Xcode and then save it as TextInput.

Note: You can find the TextInput project on the website for this book: www.wiley.com/go/iphonedevelopmentvb.

② Click TextInputViewController.h.

③ Add `IBOutlet`s for two text fields and two labels and then declare them as properties.

④ Add two `IBAction` methods and then save the file.

⑤ Click TextInputViewController.m and then synthesize the two text fields and two labels.

⑥ Find and uncomment `viewDidLoad` and then add code to set different attributes for each field.

⑦ Add code to implement a simple text view handler method.

⑧ Add code to implement a more complex text view handler method, suitable for multiple text views, and then save the file.

Note: You can use either technique in your own applications depending on requirements.

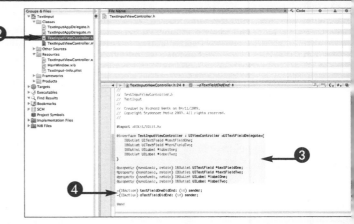

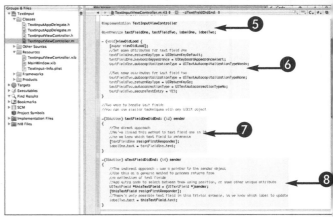

⑨ Double-click TextInputViewController.xib to open it in Interface Builder.

⑩ Drag and drop two UITextFields and two UILabels into the view.

Note: *Optionally, center and resize the labels and text fields. You can also preset some of their attributes by using the Attributes pane in the Inspector window.*

⑪ Link the labels and text fields to the corresponding outlets in the code.

⑫ Link each text field's Did End On Exit message to its corresponding IBAction and then save the file.

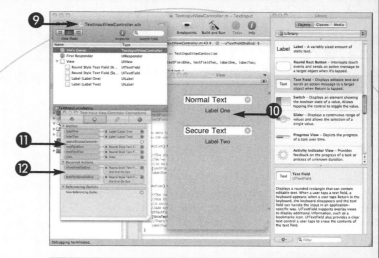

⑬ Click Build and Run to build and run the application.

● The application displays two text fields with different attributes. Clicking in a text field erases the existing text and displays a keyboard. Typing on the keyboard fills the text field. Clicking Return or Go dismisses the keyboard and displays entered text on an associated label.

Extra

There is no way to tag a `UITextField`. If your application has more than one text field, you can create separate value-changed methods to read the output from each field. This is an efficient approach when the text fields have very different functions and the methods that support them do not share code.

Alternatively, you can distinguish between two or more text fields in a single method by checking their position in the view:

```
UITextField *thisTextField = (UITextField *)
  sender;
if (thisTextField.frame.origin.y < aConstant)
  { \\Code for top text field }
else
  { \\Code for bottom text field}
```

You can use the `shouldChangeCharactersIn Range:` delegate method to control text input or to copy the text to another object as the user types. The method is called when the user types a new character and returns a `BOOL`, disabling the last character typed if `NO`. For example:

```
-(BOOL)textField: (UITextField *)textField
shouldChangeCharactersInRange: (NSRange)
  range
replacementString: (NSString *)string {
 NSMutableString *thisText = [NSMutableString
  stringWithString:textField.text];
 [thisText replaceCharactersInRange:
  range withString: string];
 return ([thisText length] <=6);
}
```

This limits the field to six characters. The delegate protocol is automatically adopted by `UITextField`; you do not need to add it explicitly.

Enter Multi-Line Text with a UITextView

You can use a `UITextView` to get multiple lines and paragraphs of text from the user and to edit existing text. `UITextView` implements automatic scrolling support. When the text extends beyond the visible area of the view, a scrollbar appears.

`UITextView` has two limitations. When the user taps the text area, the keyboard appears. However, the view area is not resized automatically, and the edit point may be hidden under the keyboard. To fix this, resize the text view when the keyboard appears. Use the `textViewDidBeginEditing:` method to set the bottom of the text view's frame above the top edge of the keyboard. On the iPhone, the keyboard is always a fixed size. Assuming the status bar is visible, the application is in portrait mode, and a navigation bar is included:

```
textView.frame = CGRectMake(0, 44, 320, 196);
 \\Keyboard visible, shortened text view
textView.frame = CGRectMake(0, 44, 320, 416);
 \\Keyboard hidden, text view fills the
 display
```

The other limitation is that there is no separate Done button. Tapping the Return key creates a new line, and you cannot use this key to hide the keyboard. Instead, you must embed the text view within a toolbar or navigation bar and then add a Done button. The user can tap the button after editing to dismiss the keyboard. Your code must hide the button and resize the text view again to its original dimensions. The simplest way to add and remove a Done button is by using code. Set the button's target action properties to trigger an `endEditing` method. You can add a button in Interface Builder, but it is more difficult to hide and reveal the button as needed.

Enter Multi-Line Text with a UITextView

1 Create a new View-based Application template in Xcode and then save it as TextView.

Note: *You can find the TextView project on the website for this book: www.wiley.com/go/iphonedevelopmentvb.*

2 Click TextViewViewController.h.

3 Add `IBOutlet`s for a text view and a navigation item and then add a pointer to a bar button item.

4 Declare all the items as properties and then save the file.

5 Click TextViewViewController.m and then synthesize the text view, the navigation item, and the bar button.

6 Find and uncomment `viewDidLoad`. Add code to set a navigation bar title. Optionally, add code to load the text view with the contents of a file.

Note: *If you do not add the file code, the text view displays the same default startup content whenever the application runs.*

7 Add code to implement `textViewDidBeginEditing:` to display a Done button so the user can end editing by triggering an `endEditing` method and to resize the text frame.

Note: *The `textViewDidBeginEditing:` method is called automatically by the text view. It is a delegate method, but you do not need to adopt its delegate protocol explicitly.*

8 Add code to implement an `endEditing` method for the Done button. Remove the button and restore the text view. Optionally, add code to save the text to a file. Save the file.

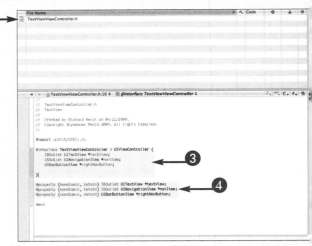

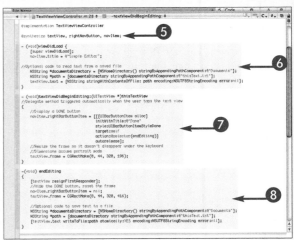

9. Double-click TextViewViewController.xib to open it in Interface Builder.

10. Drag and drop a navigation bar to the view and then drag and drop a navigation item onto the navigation bar.

11. Drag and drop a text view to the view.

Note: *The text view includes a block of default text. You can edit this text in the text view's attributes.*

12. Link the text view and the navigation item to their corresponding IBOutlets and then save the file.

13. Click Build and Run to build and run the application.

- The application displays an editable text view. During editing, a Done button appears. Tapping the Done button dismisses the text. Optionally, the application saves edited text and reloads it when it restarts.

Extra

You can preload a text view with text in Interface Builder in the Text field in the Attributes pane in the Inspector window. If you add text to this box, it resets the text view whenever the application loads.

To retain text between launches, you must save it to a file and reload it. Use code to create and retrieve a file in the Documents directory, as described later in this chapter. You can then use this path to save text:

```
[textView.text writeToFile: path atomically:
 YES encoding: NSUTF8StringEncoding error:
 nil];
```

Or reload it:

```
textView.text = [NSString
 stringWithContentsOfFile: path encoding:
 NSUTF8StringEncoding error: nil];
```

You can use file reloading to implement an undo feature, triggered by a button tap, or some other user action.

The dataDetectorTypes property enables automatic recognition of URLs and phone numbers. Use this to enable automatic underlining of links and phone numbers:

```
textView.dataDetectorTypes =
 UIDataDetectorTypeAll;
```

to enable automatic underlining of links and phone numbers. Tapping on a link terminates your application and loads the Safari browser. Tapping on a phone number loads the phone application. Detection only works if the text view's editable property is set to NO. Users can also tap and hold to pop-up a menu of options for the data type (such as save to the Address Book or copy to the Clipboard).

Introducing the
iPhone File System

For security reasons, your application does not have access to the iPhone's native file system and is limited to file access within its own protected sandbox. Files within the sandbox use a path system. Before you access a file, you must generate its path. You can initialize many of the standard Cocoa data types, including NSString, NSData, NSArray, and NSDictionary, with data loaded from a file at a path. You can also write their contents to a file at a path.

For convenience, file-handling features are built into these classes. You can also use the NSFileHandle class,

which offers more traditional binary read-write access to and from an instance of NSData, to implement file reads and writes with optional pointer support.

Because of the sandbox and the different contexts in which your application can access files, there is more than one technique for file access. You must use one technique to read files installed with your application and another to implement read-write file access. There is also more than one way to specify a file path.

Reading Files from the Application Bundle

When you add a file to your project in Xcode, it is automatically bundled with the application's installer. To find a path to a file, use [NSBundle mainBundle] to retrieve a reference to the application's bundle path and use pathForResource: to define the name and file type. For example, to find the path to a file called default.jpg:

```
NSString *thePath = [[NSBundle mainBundle] pathForResource:@"default" ofType: @"jpg"];
```

Files bundled with the installer are read-only. To change them, your application must load them and save them to the Documents folder. Bundles do not support subdirectories.

The Documents Folder and the Library Folder

Your application can access Documents, the only read-write folder in its bundle created when the application is installed. Use Documents as your application's main file area.

Your application should save important files to a folder named Documents, which is created when the application is installed. Subfolders must be created within Documents. Files saved to the Documents folder are backed up by iTunes.

You can also use NSCachesDirectory cached data and NSApplicationSupportDirectory for temporary data. Files in the cache are synced. Application support files may disappear at any time — even when your application is running.

To find the path to the Documents folder, use the NSHome Directory() function to find the application's home directory and append Documents to the string it returns:

```
NSString *docDirectory = [NSHomeDirectory()
  stringByAppendingPathComponent: @"Documents"];
```

You can then append a file name and extension to find the path to a named file. You can also use:

```
NSArray *paths = NSSearchPathForDirectoriesInDomains
  (NSDocumentDirectory, NSUserDomainMask, YES);
NSString *aPath = [paths objectAtIndex: 0];
```

File Paths and URLs

Path strings are not character strings. NSString includes a collection of methods for creating, editing, and combining path strings. For example, use stringByAppending PathComponent: to add a file name to a path. Use these methods when creating paths because they include extra code to handle unusual path characters and deal with other special conditions that are missed by conventional string operations.

Optionally, you can use a URL instead of a path to specify a file — typically to simplify access to paths defined relative to a root directory. Many of the data read-write methods built into Cocoa for file access can also work with a URL. Use the NSURL class to create a URL object and the fileURLWithPath: method to specify a file.

Using a File Manager

To create, delete, rename, and list files, use `NSFileManager`. An instance of `NSFileManager` points to a directory and allows directory operations. To create an instance:

```
NSFileManager *fileManager =
  [NSFileManager defaultManager];
```

You can then use file manager methods to modify files at a given path. To rename a file, move it from a source path to a destination path:

```
[fileManager moveItemAtPath:
  sourcePath toPath: destinationPath error: nil];
```

To delete a file, remove it:

```
[fileManager removeItemAtPath: aPath error: nil];
```

To list the files in a directory, create a path to the directory and use:

```
NSArray *directoryArray = [fileManager
  contentsOfDirectoryAtPath: aDirectoryPath
  error: nil];
```

This reads the directory into an array of `NSStrings`. You can display the list of files on the console with `NSLog`:

```
NSLog (@"Directory contents: %@",
  directoryArray];
```

You can also use the array as a data source for a table view.

`NSFileManager` also includes methods for checking the attributes of a file, checking whether it exists, for comparing the contents of files, and for creating symbolic links. See the NSFileManager Class Reference documentation for details.

Saving and Loading Photo Files

You cannot use file operations to access the photo or media libraries. To save an image to the photo library, use the `UIImageWriteToSavedPhotosAlbum:` method. To load an image, you must use a `UIImagePickerView`. See Chapter 9 for more on browsing the camera library.

To save an image to the Documents folder, convert it to an instance of `NSData`. `NSData` is a generic binary object and includes conversion methods to and from common data types. For example, to save an image as a PNG file:

```
NSData *imageData = [NSData dataWithData:
  UIImagePNGRepresentation(imageView)];
```

You can then save the data using `NSData`'s built-in method:

```
[imageData writeToFile:
  aPath atomically: YES];
```

The `atomically` parameter triggers a two-stage write that protects existing files from errors and accidental corruption.

To load an image from the Documents folder, create a path to the image and use:

```
UIImage *thisImage =
  [imageWithContentsOfFile: aPath];
```

Files in the Simulator

When you compile an application, it is bundled and copied to Users/<*Your Username*>/Library/Application Support/iPhone Simulator/User/Applications/<UID>/.

The UID is a unique character and number string and is generated automatically for each compilation. Bundles do not have text names — the UID is the only recognizable identifier. To find your bundle, select the Details view in the Finder and then click the Date Modified column heading to sort the directory with the newest folder at the top of the list. To examine data written by your application, look in the Documents subdirectory. To view the contents of the application bundle, right-click on the app file and then choose Show Package Contents from the pop-up menu.

Bundles are never deleted by Xcode, and the Applications directory can become very full. This does not affect the Simulator, but it can waste disk space. To clean the directory, drag old bundles to the trash.

Create and Manipulate Files

File management on the iPhone is straightforward. This example is a list of boilerplate code items that you can copy and paste into your own applications. It illustrates how to create, rename, copy, and delete files in the Documents directory using an instance of `NSFile Manager`. It also sends directory listings to the console for confirmation. To read and write files, use the methods built into the Cocoa Touch data classes — `NSArray`, `NSDictionary`, `NSData`, `NSString`, `NSNumber`, and `NSDate`. Use `initWithContentsOfFile:` to load data and `writeToFile:` to write data. You do not need to create a file manager for read and write operations.

To create a file path, begin by finding the Documents directory by using:

```
NSString *docDirectory = [NSHomeDirectory()
  stringByAppendingPathComponent: @"Documents"];
```

or

```
NSArray *paths = NSSearchPathForDirectories
  InDomains(NSDocumentDirectory, NSUserDomain,
  YES);
```

```
NSString *docDirectory = [paths objectAt
  Index: 0];
```

Although the second technique is preferred, the first technique is simpler. You can use the second technique to check for the existence of Documents. If the directory does not exist, `[paths count]` will be zero. If you create the documents string inside a conditional test, it will be undefined outside it. You must create a blank string outside the conditional and assign the documents path inside it. To define a file path, use `stringByAppendingPathComponent`:

```
NSString *filePath = [docDirectory
  stringByAppendingPathComponent: @"aFileName.
  txt"];
```

To rename, delete, and copy files, create a file manager:

```
NSFileManager *fileManager = [NSFileManager
  defaultManager];
```

Call the `moveItemAtPath:`, `removeItemAtPath:`, and `copyItemAtPath:` methods on the file manager with a file path to rename, delete, and copy files.

Create and Manipulate Files

① Create a new View-based Application template in Xcode and then save it as NSFileManager.

② Click NSFileManagerViewController.m.

③ Find and uncomment `viewDidLoad` and then add code to initialize a file manager.

④ Add code to get the Documents directory path.

⑤ Add code to create a file path and write a file at that path by using `NSString`'s built-in write method.

Optionally, add code to log the write operation to the console.

⑥ Add code to list the contents of the Documents directory to the console to confirm that a file has been written.

⑦ Add code to read in the file and to output its contents to the console for additional confirmation.

⑧ Add code to write another file and to list the directory again for confirmation.

⑨ Add code to copy the newest file to a third file and to list the directory.

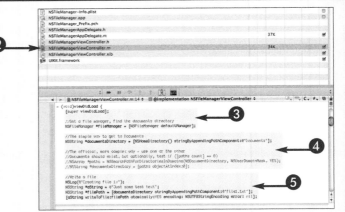

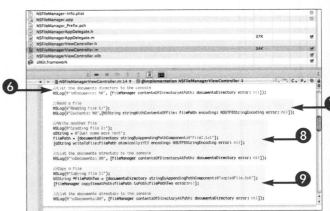

⑩ Add code to rename the file created in step 8 and list the directory for confirmation.

⑪ Add code to create a directory enumerator.

⑫ Add code to use the directory enumerator to step through all files in the documents directory, deleting them.

⑬ Add code to list the directory to the console for confirmation.

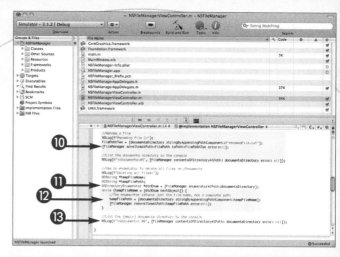

⑭ Click Build and Run to build and run the application.

⑮ Choose Run→Console in Xcode to show the Debugger Console window.

● The application creates, loads, copies, renames, and deletes a small collection of files in the Documents directory and lists the files in the directory after each operation.

Note: You can find the NSFileManager project on the website for this book: www.wiley.com/ go/iphonedevelopmentvb.

Extra

You can use a *directory enumerator* — a variable that lists files in a directory in order — to step through the files in a directory:

```
NSString *tempFileName;
NSString *tempFilePath;
NSDirectoryEnumerator *dirEnum = [aFileManager enumeratorAtPath: documentsDirectoryPath];
while (tempFilName = [dirEnum nextObject]) {
  tempFilePath = [documentsDirectoryPath stringByAppendingPathComponent: tempFileName];
  //Process the selected file
}
```

The enumerator returns file names but not full file paths. You must prepend the documents directory path to get the complete file path. You can use this feature to list files, perform a global delete, or copy files between subdirectories with a few lines of code. The enumerator also steps through all subdirectories.

To return a list of items in a directory without accessing subdirectories, use `contentsOfDirectoryAtPath:`. This returns an array of file names. You can then create and run an enumerator on the array to enumerate only the files at that path.

Work with NSDictionary

NSDictionary is a versatile data storage class. You can use it to create paired relationships between objects and *keys* — string identifiers — to implement data searches and fast lookup of arbitrary lists. Where an array uses a numeric index as a key, NSDictionary uses an arbitrary string. The critical lookup methods are valueForKey: and objectForKey:, which search the dictionary for a keystring and return a value or an object:

```
anObject = [myDictionary objectForKey:
  @"aKeyString"];
```

Data in NSDictionary is read-only. Use NSMutable Dictionary when you need to add and remove items. Optionally, you can define an initial capacity with dictionaryWithCapacity: or initWithCapacity:. This pre-allocates memory for a dictionary with a set number of items. This is not a hard limit — you can add further items as needed. However, pre-allocation is slightly faster. Use setObject: forKey: or setValue: forKey: to add items to the dictionary. You can use *fast enumeration* — simplified key listing — to step through every key in the dictionary:

```
for (id key in aDictionary) {
  objectForKey = [aDictionary objectForKey: key];
  //Process objectForKey as needed
}
```

The example code demonstrates an alternative enumeration technique by using an *enumerator object* — a separate object that performs explicit key enumeration. Either technique is valid. Objects can potentially be of any type.

This example implements a mutable dictionary for text strings. Two text fields define a key and a corresponding value. Add a key-value pair to the dictionary by clicking the write button. Search the dictionary for a key by clicking read. A list to console button lists all key-value pairs by calling the description method.

Work with NSDictionary

1. Create a new View-based Application template in Xcode and then save it as NSDictionary.

2. Click NSDictionaryViewController.h.

3. Add a pointer for NSMutableDictionary and IBOutlets for two text fields.

4. Declare all the items as properties. Add IBAction methods for three buttons. Save the file.

5. In NSDictionaryViewController.m, synthesize the properties. Find and uncomment viewDidLoad. Add code to allocate and initialize a dictionary and then add two object/key pairs.

6. Implement writeKey and readKey and then optionally add code to display <Not found> in readKey when a key is not in the dictionary.

7. Add code to implement the listToConsole method, calling description on the dictionary.

8. Add code to implement the textFieldShould Return: delegate method for the text fields, to resign First Responder status, and to hide the keyboard on return and then save the file.

Note: *This method is called by both text fields. To trigger this method correctly, you must set the delegate of each text field to File's Owner in Interface Builder.*

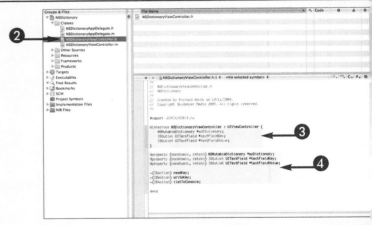

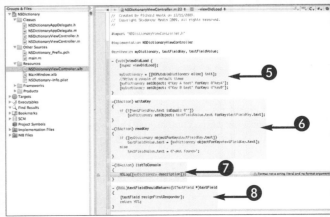

9 Double-click NSDictionaryViewController.xib to open it in Interface Builder and then drag and drop three buttons, two text fields, and two labels from the Library to the view window.

10 Set default keyboard attributes for each text field in the Attributes pane in the Inspector window. Set Capitalize to None and Correction to No. Set the Clear Button attribute to Is always visible in the drop-down menu and deselect the Clear When Editing Begins check box.

11 Lay out the items in the view and then name the buttons, labels, and text fields as shown.

12 Link touchDown events from the buttons to their corresponding IBAction methods. Link the delegate outlet from each text field to File's Owner. Link the text fields to their corresponding IBOutlets. Save the file.

Note: *The buttons are deliberately placed in the lower half of the display to hide them when the keyboard is visible. This simplifies operation and prevents them from claiming First Responder status from the keyboard.*

13 Click Build and Run to build and run the application.

14 Test the application by reading and writing key-value pairs.

15 In Xcode, choose Run→Console to show the console and then review the output when the list to console button is tapped.

● The application adds key-value pairs to the dictionary and can list the contents of the dictionary to the console.

Note: *You can find the NSDictionary project on the website for this book: www.wiley.com/go/ iphonedevelopmentvb.*

Extra

NSDictionary has many uses. A simple application is a language dictionary, which pairs words with description strings. You can use this feature to localize an application for different regions, storing different text strings in different instances of NSDictionary, loading a different dictionary for each locale, and using key definitions, such as kAlertTextNetworkError, to select and display them at runtime.

More complex applications can store a list of variables selected by key. You can use this feature to simplify development. Instead of declaring a variable in a header and synthesizing it in the implementation, you can add it to your application by defining a new key. This is not an efficient solution for high-performance applications because the key lookup adds significant overhead. But it can be a practical way to group related variables in an application where performance is not critical because NSDictionary implements its own disk methods. You can use it to save and reload groups of variables by adding just a few lines of code.

Dictionaries can be nested indefinitely to create complex tree-like data structures with built-in searching.

Work with Cut and Paste

You can add cut and paste features to your application in two ways. Cut and paste is built into UITextView and UITextField and works automatically without extra code. In other contexts, you can implement cut and paste manually with two supporting classes and links to the iPhone's message responder system. UIPasteBoard holds temporary data and is similar to NSDictionary. Instead of a valueForKey:, use valueForPasteboardType:. Convenience methods are defined for strings, images, URLs, and colors. Use [UIPasteboard generalPasteboard] to allow other applications to read pasted data.

If you quit your application and start another, the pasteboard contains someString, ready for pasting.

The UIMenuController class displays a pop-up menu with Cut, Copy, Paste, and Select commands. You cannot change the list of items, but you can use the update method to enable or disable each menu item as needed. The class is a singleton class. Use the sharedMenu Controller method to get the single instance.

To show or hide the menu, set the menuVisible property. Call a setMenuVisible: Animated: method for an optional preset animation. You must also set the target view or its superview as First Responder and implement the canBecomeFirstResponder: method to return YES. The menu appears in a target rect in a selected view, set with the setTargetRect: InView: method. Typically, you can copy the rect data from a target object's frame or bounds.

Work with Cut and Paste

① Create a new project in Xcode by using the View-based Application template and then save it as CutAndPaste.

② Click CutAndPasteViewController.h.

③ Add IBOutlet pointers to two text fields. Declare them as properties. Save the file.

④ In CutAndPasteViewController.m, synthesize the properties and then add an integer, a Boolean to track paste state, and a pointer to a UIPasteboard object.

⑤ Add a touchesBegan: method, add code to grab firstResponder status, and create a pointer to a UIMenuController and then add code to retrieve the touch object.

⑥ Add code to hit-test the touch position against the text labels, and if the touch is inside either label, set an appropriate menu target rect and paste state and display the menu.

⑦ Add code to implement the canPerformAction: method to select the items that appear in the menu.

Note: *This example implements context menu switching by using the* pasteState *variable.*

⑧ Add code to implement a cut method that copies the top label text to the pasteboard and updates the label.

⑨ Add code to implement a copy method that copies the top label text to the pasteboard.

⑩ Add code to implement a paste method that copies the pasteboard to the bottom label.

Note: *You must implement a method for every visible menu item.*

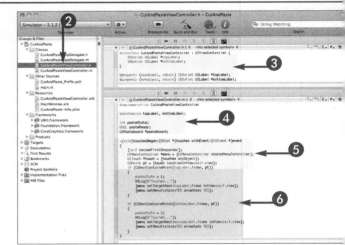

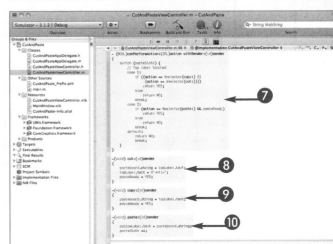

11. Add code to implement the `canBecomeFirstResponder` method to return YES.

12. Find and uncomment `viewDidLoad`. Add code to initialize the paste state variables and retrieve a pointer to the system pasteboard. Save the file.

13. Double-click CutAndPasteView Controller.xib to open it in Interface Builder and then add two UILabels to the view.

14. Link the labels to their corresponding IBOutlets and then save the file.

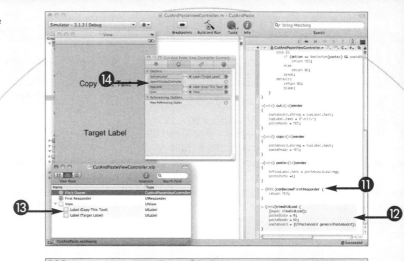

15. Click Build and Run to build and run the application.

16. Test it by clicking the top label to cut or copy and the bottom label to paste.

Note: *If the pasteboard is empty, the paste option does not appear.*

● The application displays a selection of cut, paste, and copy floating menus, depending on its state, and implements cut, copy, and paste user actions.

Note: *You can find the CutAndPaste project on the website for this book: www.wiley.com/go/iphonedevelopmentvb.*

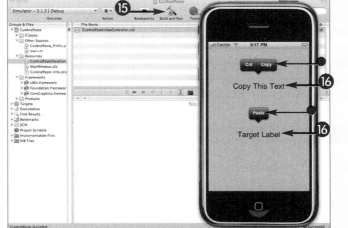

Extra

To make a menu appear, you must do three things that are not mentioned in the documentation. First, the view controller must become `firstResponder`. Second, you must implement the `canBecomeFirstResponder` method in your controller and return YES. Finally, to select the visible items on the menu, you must implement `canPerformAction:` and return YES or NO to select the items that appear on the menu.

Each item is a selector. To find a list of the available selectors, see the `UIResponderStandardEditActions` Protocol Reference documentation. For example:

```
-(BOOL)canPerformAction: (SEL)action withSender: (id) sender {
  if (action == @selector(copy:)) return YES
  else return NO; }
```

This displays a menu with only the copy option. Use this method to display different menu options in different application states. The example code creates a menu with Cut and Copy for the top label and Paste for the bottom label.

You must implement a method for each selector; otherwise, the application will crash. Typically, these methods implement cut, copy, and paste features by using the pasteboard.

The pasteboard is very versatile and can store multiple items of different types, including sets, dictionaries, and arrays. You can use this feature to cut, copy, and paste entire objects.

Save and Load Objects with NSKeyedArchiver

Many Cocoa Touch objects do not include load and save methods. However, you can use the NSKeyedArchiver class to save them and NSKeyedUnarchiver to reload them. For simple saving:

```
[NSKeyedArchiver archiveRootObject: anObject
  toFile: path];
```

This method returns NO if the file write fails. anObject can be a single object or it can be the root of an object tree. Saving the root object saves the entire tree. All property values are saved in the file. path is a standard file path. To reload the object:

```
anObject = [NSKeyedUnarchiver unarchiveObject
  WithFile: path];
```

This reads the saved data from the file and loads the object. You can load multiple copies of a saved object from a single file to duplicate it.

You can also save arbitrary objects and properties by encoding them into an instance of NSMutableData, used as a temporary file buffer. To use a buffer, create an instance of NSMutableData, create a named instance of NSKeyedArchiver, and use one or more of the encoding methods to add data. You can encode Cocoa Touch objects and more basic data types, including numbers and strings. Each encoding method adds a block of binary to the NSMutableData object, building up a complete archive that can be saved to disk. For example:

```
[thisArchiver encodeObject: anObject ForKey:
  @"aKey"];
//Add extra encode calls for other objects and
  data as needed
[thisArchiver finishEncoding]; //Finalize the
  binary
[thisMutableDataObject writeToFile: aPath
  atomically: YES]; //Write it to disk
```

To recover the data, load the archive into an NSData object and then call corresponding decode methods to recover the items that were added.

This example uses the first technique to save, recover, and display two copies of a UILabel object.

Save and Load Objects with NSKeyedArchiver

① Create a new View-based Application template in Xcode and then save it as NSKeyedArchiver.

Note: You can find the NSKeyedArchiver project on the website for this book: www.wiley.com/go/iphonedevelopmentvb.

② Click NSKeyedArchiverViewController.h.

③ Add two pointers to UILabel objects at the start of the implementation and then save the file.

④ Click NSKeyedArchiverViewController.m. Find and uncomment viewDidLoad. Add code to create a new UILabel and set some of its properties.

⑤ Add code to find the Documents directory, to create a path to a file in the directory, and to save the label object.

⑥ Add code to change some of the label's properties.

⑦ Add code to display the label.

Note: The saved label and the visible label now have different label text and different background colors.

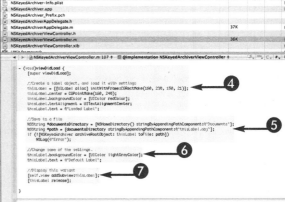

8. Add code to implement a `touchesBegan:` method, triggered when the user taps the screen, and then add code to remove the visible label from the display.

9. Add code to load the saved label and to display it.

10. Add code to load another copy of the saved label, to change its position, and to display it.

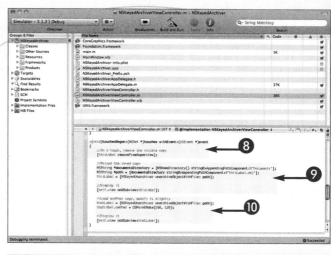

11. Click Build and Run to build and run the application.

● When the application loads, it creates and saves a label object to a file and displays a modified version. When the user taps the screen, the modified label disappears and two copies of the original saved label appear, retrieved from the file.

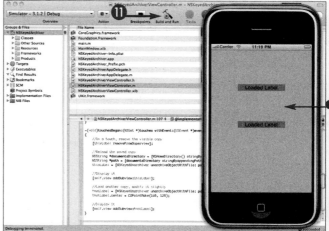

Extra

You can use key information to search an archive for specific items without having to decode and recover every saved item. A key is a unique string that identifies an item. For example, you might archive a series of objects:

```
[thisArchiver encodeObject: objectA ForKey: @"aKey"];
[thisArchiver encodeObject: objectB ForKey: @"bKey"];
```

Then, call `finishEncoding` and write them to disk.

To read one object from the collection, load the archive into a data object, initialize an unarchiver with the data, and decode the single object:

```
NSData *recoveredData = [NSData dataWithContentsOfFile: aPath];
NSKeyedUnarchiver *anUnarchiver =
  [[NSKeyedUnarchiver alloc] initForReadingWithData: recoveredData];
objectBRecovered = [anUnarchiver decodeObjectForKey: @"bKey"];
```

You can use `NSKeyedArchiver` to archive custom objects. However, you must implement the `encodeWith Coder:` and `initWithCoder:` methods within your object. These methods take an instance of a translation class called `NSCoder`. For an example, see later in this chapter.

Create and Change
Application Preferences

You can use a *settings bundle* to define application preferences. The user can change preferences in two ways. When you build and install an application with a settings bundle, it appears automatically in the iPhone's built-in Settings app as a multiview table, displaying items and subitems defined in the bundle. You do not need to write code to display this table.

However, you must add code to read the preferences from the settings bundle when your application starts. Optionally, you can also add code to your application to display the preferences and allow the user to change them, typically in a special view.

To add a settings bundle, choose File→New File in Xcode, choose Resource, and then choose Settings Bundle. Save the bundle with the default name. A new item called Settings Bundle appears in the Groups & Files pane in Xcode.

The default settings file includes four items: a group name, a text label called name, a switch, and a slider. Click the Root.plist file in Xcode to display an editor. Remove items by right-clicking on them and then choosing Cut from the pop-up menu. Add items by right-clicking on them and then choosing Add Row from the pop-up menu. Cut and paste items to move them up and down the list; you cannot drag and drop them. Whenever you edit Root.plist, you must delete and re-install the application. Otherwise, the new settings are ignored. To access the preferences from your application, create a pointer to an NSUserDefaults object.

```
NSUserDefaults *myDefaults = [NSUserDefaults
  standardUserDefaults];
```

You can then access myDefaults as an NSDictionary, using valueForKey: and <Type>ForKeyTitle: methods to read items and set<type>: for Key: methods to change them.

Create and Change Application Preferences

① Create a new project by using the View-based Application template and then save it as AppSettings. Right-click on AppSettings. Choose Add→New File. Click Resource in the iPhone OS pane.

Note: You can find the AppSettings project on the website for this book: www.wiley.com/go/iphone developmentvb.

② Click Settings Bundle.

③ Click Next and then save the file with the default Settings.bundle name.

A new Settings.bundle item is added to the project.

④ Click Settings.bundle and then click Root.plist.

⑤ Click Root to reveal its contents. Right-click on Root and then choose Add Row to add a new string. Set the Key to Title and the Value to AppSettings.

⑥ Click Item 0 to reveal its contents and then click the Title value to change it to This is a Group Header.

⑦ Change the Title of Item 2 to This is a Switch and then deselect its DefaultValue check box. Change the DefaultValue of Item 3 to 0.33. Save the file.

⑧ Click Build and Run to build and run the application and then quit the application and then load the built-in Settings application.

● Tapping/clicking AppSettings displays the edited defaults.

9 Click AppSettingsViewController.h and then add a pointer to a switch and a pointer to a slider, declare them as properties, and add two `IBAction` methods.

10 Click AppSettingsViewController.m. Add code to synthesize the pointers. Add a pointer to an `NSUserDefaults` object. In `viewDidLoad`, add code to initialize the pointer to `NSUserDefaults`, read settings from the preferences file, and set the values of the slider and switch.

11 Add code to implement the `switchChanged:` and `sliderChanged:` methods and then write updated settings to the preferences plist through the `NSUserDefaults` object.

Note: You must use the appropriate `<type>forKey:` to read a preference and a `set<type>:for Key:` to write a preference.

12 Double-click AppSettingsViewController.xib. Add a slider and a switch and then link their valueChanged messages to the code methods and their outlets to the IBOutlets. Save the file.

13 Click Build and Run to build and run the application. Change the slider and the switch. Quit and then reload the application.

● The application loads and displays two preferences settings. Changing the settings saves them automatically. The application reloads the settings when it starts.

14 Quit the application and then start the built-in Settings application.

● The updated preferences appear in the Settings application.

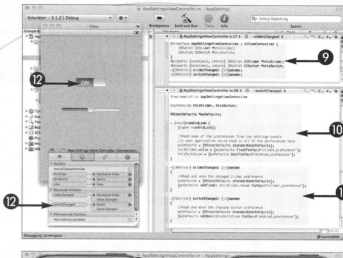

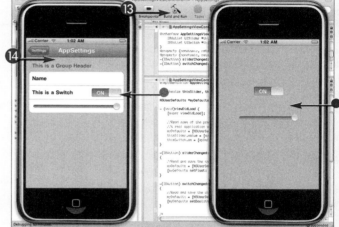

Extra

For information about the elements and options you can use in the plist, see the "Settings Application Schema" reference in the documentation. You can add the following items: editable text fields, read-only titles, toggle switches, sliders, and multivalue items.

Use multivalue items to select one item from an array of arbitrary values of any type. You must add a descriptive `Title` string for each item. You must also add a `Title` string at the root of the plist. The `Title` sets the name of your application that is displayed in Settings.

You can set auto-correction, secure, and auto-capitalization options for the keyboard used to edit a text preference in Settings. There is no way to auto-dismiss the keyboard.

For each preference item, you must include four subitems: a `Type` to define the item type, a `Title` for the item, a unique `Key` string, and a `DefaultValue`. You can add other subitems as required.

Two special item types provide extended features. `PSGroupSpecifier` splits the preference list into named sections. `PSChildPaneSpecifier` creates a link to a further plist file. Do not include the .plist extension in the file name.

Remember to save the plist manually before building — it is not saved automatically when you click Build and Run.

Save and Reload an Application State with NSCoder

For a simple application with very little data, you can save data in the preferences and settings plist, as demonstrated in the previous example.

For a more complex application, you can use the read and write methods built into the Cocoa Touch data classes. However, these methods are limited to supported data objects — NSArray, NSDictionary, NSData, NSString, NSNumber, and NSDate — and their mutable subclasses.

An application state typically uses one or more custom objects. To save and reload these, you must implement a *coder* — an instance of NSCoder used to translate data to and from the file system. To implement a coder, add two standard methods to your custom objects. encodeWith Coder: returns a coder object, packed with data, using one of the methods listed in the NSCoder Class Reference documentation. You must translate all the properties in your object into one of the supported classes and data types by using one statement for each property:

```
[coder encodeFloat: self.aFloatProperty
   forKey:@"aFloat"];
[coder encodeObject: self.anObject
   forKey:@"anObject"];
```

Save and Reload an Application State with NSCoder

① Create a new project in Xcode by using the View-based Application template and then save it as AppSaveRestore. Right-click on Classes, choose Add→New File, and then choose Cocoa Touch Class. Click the Objective-C class item and then choose NSObject. Click Next and then save the new class as aClass.

② Click aClass.h. Add a string and a float to the header and declare them as properties. Add encodeWithCoder: and initWithCoder: methods. Save the file.

③ Click aClass.m. Synthesize the properties. Implement the encodeWithCoder: method. Add code to encode the float and the string properties in a coder object.

④ Implement initWithCoder: and then add code to retrieve the properties from decoder.

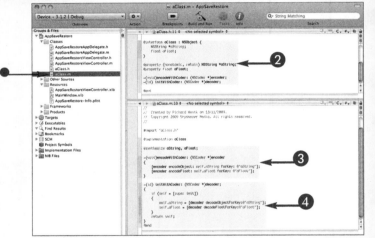

⑤ Click AppSaveRestoreViewController.h. Add IBOutlets to a slider and a text field. Add a pointer to an instance of aClass. Add a pointer to a string. Declare the new items as properties.

⑥ Add four IBAction methods for text return, slider change, save, and load operations and then save the file.

⑦ Click AppSaveRestoreViewController.m. Synthesize the properties. Find and uncomment viewDidLoad. Add code to create an instance of aClass and to reload a saved file if it exists.

⑧ Add code to implement saveState to write aClass to disk via a keyed archiver, which indirectly calls encodeWithCoder:.

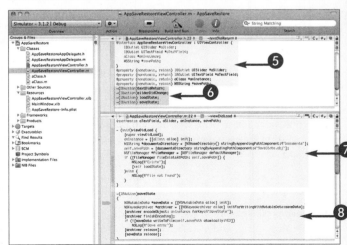

Note: *You must also* `#import aClass.h` *at the top of the file to include* `aClass` *in the project.*

9 Implement a `loadState` method to reload the saved data.

Note: *You must release the existing instance of* `aClass` *before reloading it from disk.*

10 Implement `sliderDidChange` and `textDidReturn` to update the data in `aClass` when the user makes a change.

11 Add a slider, a text field, and two buttons to the view and then optionally arrange them and improve the appearance of the view.

12 Link the slider and the text field to the two IBOutlets and the buttons, the text field, and the slider to their corresponding IBActions and then save the file.

13 In AppSaveAndRestoreAppDelegate.m, add and implement `applicationWill Terminate:`, calling `saveState` on the view controller to save the application state.

14 Click Build and Run to build and run the application.

15 Test it by operating the slider and text field, clicking Save and Restore to implement manual save and restore, and quitting and restarting the application to verify that settings are saved and restored automatically.

The application implements manual and automatic save and restore of an object that stores the application state.

Note: *You can find the AppSaveRestore project on the website for this book: www.wiley. com/go/iphonedevelopmentvb.*

Extra

You can save data whenever it changes. This is the preferred option for smaller applications. However, if your application is very active with many large objects, this can create significant overhead. A more efficient option is to save data when the application quits. The ideal location for write-out code is the `applicationWillTerminate:` method in the application delegate file. This method is not implemented in the standard Xcode templates, so you must manually add it. Your application should take no more than a couple of seconds to save data.

If you are encoding and decoding objects, be aware that objects returned by `decodeObjectForKey:` are auto-released. You must retain these objects; otherwise, they can disappear without warning, creating random crashes that are impossible to trace:

```
anObject = [[unarchiver decodeObjectForKey: @"aKey"] retain];
```

Use the `self = [super init]` option in a subclass of `NSObject`. In a subclass of an object that already implements `initWithCoder:`, replace it with `self = [super initWithCoder: decoder]`.

Introducing
Core Data

From OS 3.0 onward, iPhone OS includes the Core Data framework, which offers efficient classes for managing arbitrary data collections. You can use Core Data to build, save, and load arbitrary multiple-linked data structures, including databases. Searching, sorting, filtering, and data persistence are built into the framework. Core Data is ideal for implementing the model section of an application. It includes support for table views.

Core Data is a complex framework with advanced features, suitable for intermediate and advanced developers. A complete description is beyond the scope of this book. For novice developers, Xcode includes two application templates with Core Data features. You can use the Navigation-based Core Data Application template

to implement a table-based project with a simple editable database. Data in the database is saved automatically when the application terminates and is reloaded when it restarts.

Core Data is optional and incurs development and performance overhead. If your application is built around a static data model — for example, a simple game with a fixed number of tokens and game objects — it is more efficient to use arrays, dictionaries, and other limited conventional data types. Core Data is ideal for managing objects with many properties and interlinked relationships — for example, postings from multiple authors on a live messaging system or large collections of objects with many properties, such as a media library.

Basic Concepts

Core Data uses three primary data structures. A *managed object* is a container for a collection of data. The data is defined by one or more *entities*, each of which has a list of *attributes* — individual data items. Attributes can be part of the entity or they can link to attributes in other entities through a *relationship,* which can link or substitute data items across objects.

Managed objects are created, edited, saved, and reloaded using a *context*. A context is a single scratch pad area with methods for loading objects, saving or discarding them after edits, and maintaining an undo/redo list. You can use more than one context at a time. However, for simplicity and clarity, newcomers to Core Data should use a single context in each application.

A *persistent store* stores objects when they are not being edited. Typically, objects are stored to the iPhone's file system. However, Core Data also implements caching. The persistent store works in an abstracted and semiautomated way, saving objects to an SQLite database or an *atomic binary* collection of objects. You do not need to access the database directly.

To move data from the persistent store to the context, perform a *fetch request*. This returns an NSArray of entities that match the request's parameters. You can use *predicates* — search strings and qualifiers — and sorting to refine your search and fill the array with a list of entities selected by ordering or by searching for some feature or value in their attributes.

Faulting

Faulting is used to limit the objects in memory. By default, objects are represented with placeholders that do not contain attribute data. Objects are only loaded when their attributes are accessed. If you try to access an attribute in an object that is

not loaded, a *fault* fires. Faulting is transparent — the object is loaded for you and its attributes become accessible. However, you can customize fault handling to add your own features; for example, to *batch* load and *prefetch* objects for efficiency.

Key Core Data Classes

Managed objects are instances of the `NSManagedObject` class. Entities, attributes, and relationships are managed in Xcode by using an *object graph* editor, which reads and writes *data model* files with the xcdatamodel extension. The editor is built into Xcode. It displays entities and relationships graphically.

`NSManagedObjectContext` creates a context. The methods for this class manage object interactions, including fetch requests, object insertions and deletions, undo/redo, and save to a persistent store. Advanced developers can create multiple contexts and use the `mergeChangesFromContextDidSaveNotification:` method to automatically merge changes.

Persistent data is stored in an `NSPersistentStore`, which is managed with the `NSPersistentStore Coordinator` class. Use these classes to select a store type: binary, SQLite, or in-memory. The Core Data templates in Xcode define and manage a store for your application automatically and also include built-in save and restore features. When you add entities to a context, the template code automatically saves them when your application terminates.

`NSEntityDescription` describes and manages entities. The methods built into `NSEntityDescription` manage entities as objects; for example, copying and comparing entities and listing their properties. You cannot use this class to set the attributes of individual entity instances. Use the `insertNewObjectForEntity Name:` method to add an entity to a context. Use the `propertiesByName:` method to return a dictionary of properties for a named entity.

`NSFetchedResultsController` is a hybrid class designed to work with cells in a `UITableView`. It takes a fetch request for an entity and returns a sorted array that can be used to fill cells, indexed with a path index. Optionally, the fetch request can include a predicate. The class includes delegate methods that can update a table automatically whenever the underlying data is changed by other code or by a table edit.

Reading and Setting Attributes

A key feature of Core Data is that getters for entity properties are pre-defined. You can access them without pre-declaring them. For example, if you perform a fetch request that returns `anEntityArray` with a list of entities that match the search criteria, you read `anAttribute` for an entity selected by an array index:

```
aProperty = [[anEntityArray objectAtIndex: arrayIndex] anAttribute];
```

`NSFetchedResultsController` returns an array of objects that can be accessed by a cell index path and a managed object pointer. You can use key-value coding to read properties from this managed object directly:

```
aProperty = [aManagedObject valueForKey: @"anAttribute"];
```

Data Model Migration

If you change an application's object graph, Core Data returns an error unless you *migrate* the data in the persistent store to the new data model. Migration is an advanced topic that is outside the scope of this book. However, you can implement automatic lightweight migration, suitable for migrating minor changes, with a few lines of code. See the "Lightweight Migration" topic in the "Introduction to Core Data Model Versioning Data Migration Programming Guide" in the documentation.

Working with the Core Data Templates

Only the Navigation-based Application and the Window-based Application templates include a Core Data option. You can load the Core Data templates in two ways. Select either template and then click the Use Core Data for storage check box. Alternatively, navigate to Developer/Platforms/iPhoneOS.platform/Developer/ Library/Xcode/Project Templates/Application.

The Navigation-based Application and the Window-based Application templates include separate folders, which contain the Core Data templates. Move them to the Application folder, and they will appear in the main template window when you create a new project.

Create a Simple Core Data Application

This example demonstrates how to extend the Navigation-based Core Data Application template with a new feature. The template implements a minimal application that captures a time stamp when the user taps a button and supports cell deletion. However, it is built around a complete Core Data skeleton that reads, displays, saves, and loads data by using Core Data features.

You can extend or change the model to display other kinds of data in each cell. This example adds a new `FirstRun` entity with a single attribute called `initialDate`. `initialDate` is set once when the application runs for the first time. Subsequent time stamps read `initialDate` and calculate and display a time offset in seconds from the first run date.

The template's application delegate includes setup and teardown features for a Core Data context, with save/restore codes that write and read the data to a persistent store. You do not need to edit these features. They will continue to work if you change the data model.

To create the `FirstRun` entity, edit the application's xcdatamodel file by using Xcode's built-in editor. The editor includes two main areas. At the bottom of the display is a *diagram view,* with a visual representation of the entities in the model. Relationships are shown as visible links. Across the center of the display is a *browser view* that display entities, attributes, and properties. From left to right, the entity list shows a list of entities in the model; the property/attribute list shows the properties of a selected entity; and an inspector shows editable details for each item. You can use the inspector to set a data type for each attribute.

Use the editor to add the `FirstRun` entity, add a new `initialDate` attribute to FirstRun, and then set its data type to `date`, which makes it an instance of `NSDate`.

Create a Simple Core Data Application

① In Xcode, choose File→New Project and then click the Navigation-based Application template.

② Click the Use Core Data for storage check box, click Choose, and then save the file as CoreData NavBased.

③ Review the files created by the template and note the extra xcdatamodel file in the Resources folder, which only appears in a Core Data project.

④ Optionally, review the contents of the other files, including the Application Delegate.

Note: *Do not change the code in the Application Delegate.*

⑤ Click CoreData_NavBased.xcdatamodel and review the features of the data model editor.

⑥ Click the Event entity and note how the contents of the rightmost pane change to show its attributes.

⑦ Click the timeStamp attribute.

⑧ Click the Type drop-down menu. Note how you can set the data type of the attribute and minimum, maximum, and default values. For this example, leave these items unchanged.

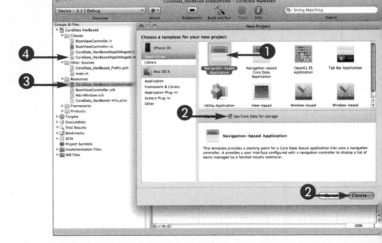

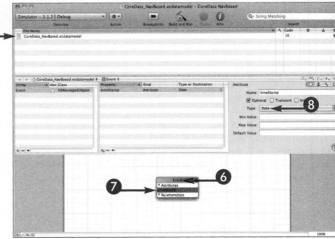

9 Right-click in the graph area to display a pop-up menu and then choose Add Entity.

A new entity appears in the graph area.

10 Double-click the title bar of the new entity and change the title to FirstRun.

11 Right-click in the graph area again to display the pop-up menu and then choose Add Attribute.

A new attribute is added to FirstRun.

12 In the Inspector window, set the new attribute's name to initialDate and its type to Date and then choose File→Save in the main menu to save the file.

13 Click RootViewController.h.

14 Add a new `NSDate appInitialDate` pointer.

15 Declare the pointer as a property and then save the file.

Note: You can find the CoreData NavBased project on the website for this book: www.wiley.com/go/iphonedevelopmentvb.

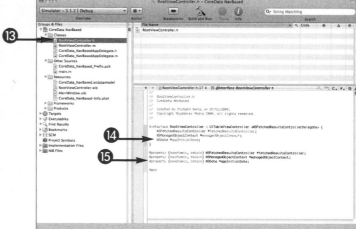

Extra

If you need to save and load objects but do not need to search them, link them, or define relationships between property fields, a Core Data solution may be unnecessarily complex. A simpler solution may be saving and loading by using `NSKeyedArchiver`. For details, see the example presented earlier in this chapter.

While Core Data may appear complex, in practice, an entity has some similarities to an object, with a slightly simplified property mechanism. A key difference is that entities do not support methods. However, they do support fetch requests, fetched properties, and relationships. This example implements fetch requests in code. You can also build them into the data model by right-clicking on an entity and then choosing Add Fetch Request from the pop-up menu. Name the fetch request and then click Edit Predicate to set predicate information — for example, to return values within, equal to, or outside a given data range. Fetch requests are not displayed on the diagram view. However, you can access them from your code by name.

continued ➔

You can customize the code in the template to implement support for the new features with a relatively small number of changes. The most significant changes are in the viewDidLoad method. You must add code to create a fetch request for FirstRun, return the results of the request, and count the number of items. If the count is zero, this is the application's first run, and you must add a new instance of FirstRun to the context and set its initialDate property. Otherwise, load the previously saved data from initialDate, and set a global appInitialDate property that can be accessed by other methods in the project.

The insertNewObject method in the template uses the [entity name] method to return a name. Because this modified example uses two entities, you must hardwire the Event entity name into the code so you can select it here to set it to Event.

If your data model is simple, it is good practice to hardwire entity names into code for clarity. In a more complex application, you may need to select entities with index numbers or implement some other directory-like option. Elsewhere in the template, entity names are hardwired.

To update the cell code to display a time difference, add new code to the cellForRowAtIndexPath: method. In this example, the description method in the template creates a string that adds a time zone code to the end of the displayed string. Added code strips the time zone characters from the string and replaces them with a time offset in seconds.

This example does not implement migration. If you make further changes to the data model, the application will crash. To run the application with a new data model, delete it from the Simulator or test handset and then re-install it. This deletes any saved data.

Create a Simple Core Data Application (continued)

⑯ In RootViewController.m, synthesize the properties declared in the header file.

⑰ Add local variables for the class: a fetch request, an entity description, an array, a date, a string, and a time interval.

⑱ Add code to initialize and run a fetch request on the FirstRun entity.

Note: *The template creates a context called* managedObjectContext. *You can use this context as is.*

⑲ Add code to check the results of the fetch request, test if a FirstRun entity already exists, and create it if necessary.

⑳ Add code to run another request to retrieve the initialDate attribute in FirstRun and copy it to the appInitialDate property.

㉑ In the insertNewObject method, replace [entity name] with @"Event".

Note: *Now that there are two entities in the model, this is used to specify an entity unambiguously.*

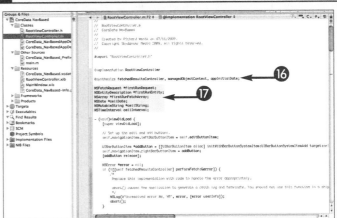

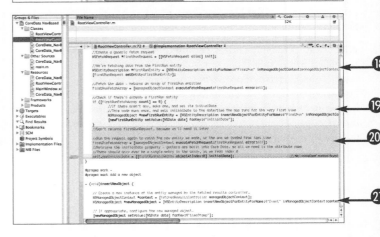

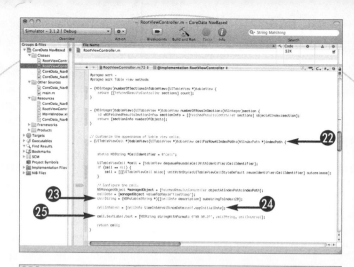

22 Scroll down to find the `cellForRowAt IndexPath:` method.

23 Add code to strip the last characters from the end of the default time string for the cell.

24 Add code to calculate the time interval from the time the application was first run by using the `appInitalDate` property.

25 Add code to add the time interval to the cell string and to display the string.

26 Click Build and Run to build and run the application.

27 Test it by adding and removing items from the table.

28 Quit and restart the application to confirm that the first runtime is saved permanently and restored when the application starts.

● The application displays a modified time stamp based on a first runtime saved and retrieved from the persistent store.

Chapter 7: Working with Text and Data

Extra

You can use Core Data to implement user permissions, to allow access to application features, to implement a time-limited demo, and so on. However, if a user can gain access to the iPhone's file system, the user can delete your application's data store. Deleting an application manually also deletes the data store.

Because there is no way to check if a data store has been removed or edited, the most secure way to manage application access data — including user permissions — is to keep data on a website, separate from the iPhone. The Foundation and Core Foundation frameworks and the App Kit framework, introduced briefly in Chapter 10, include features that are ideal for user permission control. You should use these features instead of Core Data to implement mission-critical application security. This has the obvious disadvantage that security features assume that Internet access is available.

An alternative solution is to offer your application with an encrypted permissions file. Core Data does not support encryption directly, but you can use it to store arbitrary binary objects and implement them with hashing, public key encryption, CRC (cycling redundancy check) coding, or some other encryption technology. You can build encryption around each iPhone's unique ID:

```
NSString *udid = [[UIDevice currentDevice] uniqueIdentifier];
```

Introducing XML

XML is a text-based extensible format for data exchange. You can use XML to save and load application data and to read data created by other applications. Many common file operations on the iPhone use XML implicitly. When you use them, they just work, and you do not need to work with the XML content directly. Others require explicit XML support.

An XML document typically consists of nested tagged fields. The tag names are arbitrary, and the tagged content is also arbitrary. Loading data from the document is called *parsing*. Typically, as the document is parsed, some or all of its data is copied into a machine-readable form.

A simple example application for XML is an Address Book. An entry in the Address Book includes first and last names, a phone number, an email address, and an address. A key advantage of XML is that each of these items can be repeated, with optional attributes; for example, the phone number field can include home, work mobile, and other numbers. The email field can include multiple addresses. Compared to a fixed-format Address Book, an XML database is *extensible* — items and data can be added indefinitely.

However, to implement the Address Book, each added feature requires its own code. One of the challenges of explicit XML development is balancing unique code with reusable code and managing the mappings between XML items and a working data model.

XML is a complex topic. This is a short introduction. For full details, see various online sources, such as the XML technology pages at www.w3.org/standards/xml.

Tree-Based and Event-Based Parsing

XML data is arranged in a hierarchy. A tree-based parser reads an XML document and converts it into a machine-readable tree structure. Typically, the entire tree is held in memory at the same time. An event-based parser reads a document and triggers processing methods that handle each item in the file. Event-based parsing uses less memory but requires more complex code.

The iPhone supports two types of XML parsing. Event-based parsing is available with the `NSXMLParser` class. As the parser works through the document, delegate methods are called for each type of item in the file. `NSXMLParser` does not process the data or attempt to assemble it into a tree. Limited tree-based parsing is built into the file support in `NSDictionary` and `NSArray`. When you `writeToFile:atomically:`, the data is saved as XML and can be read with a single `initWith ContentsOfFile:` or `initWithContentsOfURL:` call.

Key XML Features

A complete XML file is called a *document*. Documents consist of nested *elements*. Each element is a named data block, defined between symmetrical tags. For example:

```
<planet>
 <planetName>Earth</planetName>
 <planetMoon>
   <moonName>Moon</moonName>
 </planetMoon>
 <planetType>Rocky and wet</planetType>
</planet>
```

Attributes are optional subfields added to an element. You can use attributes to distinguish between two related elements or to add extra information to an element:

```
<phone location = "mobile">123 456 7890</phone>
<phone location = "home">098 765 4321</phone>
```

Elements and attributes are collected in a *namespace*. Namespaces are used to prevent naming collisions in files from multiple sources that may have identical element and attribute names. A document namespace is often defined at the top of a file by using an `xmlns` tag. Individual items can also be assigned to different namespaces as needed.

Data definitions can be implicit or explicit. If the data format is implicit and unlikely to change — for example, if you are the designer of the XML format — you can hardwire the names of elements and attributes into your code and make assumptions about the order in which they appear. This simplifies initial coding but can make maintenance and expansion more difficult.

For more advanced XML parsing, you can use a *Document Type Definition,* also known as a DTD. A DTD lists elements, attributes, and relationships explicitly. You can use this information to build an XML model dynamically, without knowing the format beforehand. DTD information can be included in an external file:

```
<!DOCTYPE planets SYSTEM "planets.dtd">
```

or listed inline at the start of a document:

```
<!DOCTYPE planets [
 <!ELEMENT planet (planetName, planetMoon,
 planetType)>
 <!ELEMENT planetName (#CDATA)>
 <!ELEMENT planetMoon (moonName)>
```

and so on, until the final closing]>. The #CDATA block defines literal text. NSXMLParser supports DTD definitions.

Using NSXMLParser

You must initialize an instance of NSXMLParser by loading it from a file or a URL. After initialization, the parser triggers a delegate method for each type of item it encounters in a file. For example, parser: didStart Document: is called at the start of each document; parser: didStartElement: is called at the beginning of each element; and so on.

NSXMLParser splits the file into its XML parts but does not do any further processing. You must add code to add delegate method to process each item. You can use the methods to assemble a tree, to list items, or to look for specific content. If you know the names and relationships of the XML elements, the parser code typically includes a list of switch items, with separately named case statements for each.

A list of associated methods, such as parser: found AttributeDeclarationWithName:, supports DTD parsing. If your application implements DTD, use these methods to create a memory model before using parsing the document data.

Memory Management

Memory management becomes critical when you are using NSXMLParser. The simplest and least efficient option is to build a complete document tree in memory. This is unrealistic for longer documents, which are more likely to be searched as needed rather than retained and edited. Because of this, parsed items may or may not need to be retained. You must take extra care to release items when they are no longer needed. Given the complexity of XML, it is good practice to use Xcode's Zombie and Leaks tools, introduced in Chapter 1, to check for memory leaks.

Bypassing NSXMLParser

In OS X, Core Data supports XML as a persistent store type. For performance reasons, this is not available on the iPhone. However, you can use the file methods in NSArray and NSDictionary to read and write XML to and from objects in your application without explicit parsing. You can also use the CFPropertyList library to read and write XML property lists without explicit parsing. Typically, you should only use NSXMLParser to load data from an existing XML file created by another application.

Work with NSXMLParser

You can use NSXMLParser to build a simple XML file lister. Because it is not tied to a specific XML DTD, you can use this application as the basis of a simple XML checker and display the contents of files generated by XML write methods. In a typical application, element names are tested in order to trigger specific actions. You can add this feature to the skeleton as needed.

To parse a file, create an NSXMLParser instance, initialize it with a file, and then call the parse method on it. If there is an error, the parser returns NO. Optionally, you can use

`[[parser parserError] localizedDescription];`

to retrieve an error string with an error code. Error codes are listed toward the end of the NSXMLParser Class Reference documentation. The listing is implemented with NSXMLParser's delegate methods. parser: DidStart Document: and parserDidEndDocument: are triggered at the start and end of the file. didStartElement: is triggered when the parser encounters a new element. A corresponding parser: didEndElement: method is available but implemented as a stub. parser: didStart Element: returns an attribute's NSDictionary. A key enumerator cycles through every key to list the associated value.

Work with NSXMLParser

① In a text editor, create an XML file and then save it as planets.xml.

② Create a new View-based Application template in Xcode. Save it as XMLParser. Right-click on Resources and choose Add→Existing File from the pop-up menu. Navigate to the XML file, select it, and then add it to the project, copying it into the project folder if necessary.

③ Click XMLParserViewController.h.

④ Add an IBOutlet to a text view. Declare it as a property. Save the file.

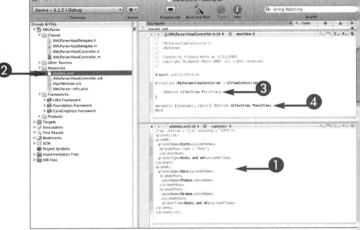

⑤ Click XMLParserViewController.m and then synthesize the text view and add local variable pointers to instances of NSXMLParser and NSEnumerator.

⑥ Find and uncomment viewDidLoad and then add code to load the target XML file from the application bundle, to initialize the parser, to set default processing options to the simplest configuration, and to parse the file.

Note: *You must set the parser delegate to* self *to implement the delegate methods.*

⑦ Add code to report success or failure and return an error code if necessary.

⑧ Add code to implement a local addString: method, which appends text to the text view with an optional new line.

Note: *This is a custom method. It is not a delegate method of the text view or the parser.*

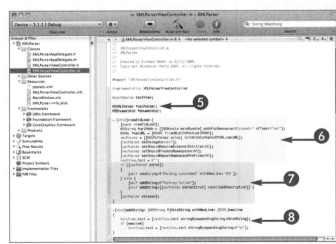

9 Implement `parserDidStart Document:` and `parserDidEnd Document:` delegate methods with code to display messages on the text view.

10 Implement the `didStartElement:` method and then copy the name of the new element to the text view to list it with a colon indicator.

11 Add an enumerator to list all the element's attributes from the returned attribute dictionary.

12 Implement the `foundCharacters:` method. Strip whitespace from the characters and list them. Save the file.

Note: The `didEndElement:` *and* `foundIgnorableWhitespace:` *methods are both ignorable.*

13 Click XMLParserViewController.xib to open it in Interface Builder and then add a text view to the view.

14 Link the text view to its IBOutlet and then save the file.

15 Click Build and Run to build and run the project.

● The parser lists the elements and attributes in an XML file to the text view.

Note: You can find the XMLParser project on the website for this book: www. wiley.com/go/iphonedevelopmentvb.

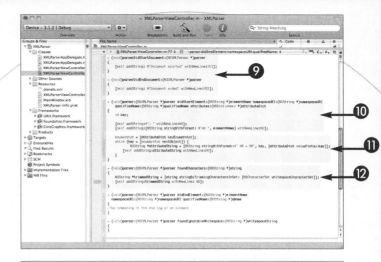

Extra

Whitespace is a common problem for XML. This example uses a character filtering feature built into `NSString` to remove some of the whitespace captured in the `foundCharacters:` method:

```
trimmedString = [sourceString stringByTrimmingCharactersInSet: [NSCharacterSet
  whitespaceCharacterSet]];
```

This strips all the common whitespace characters. However, to illustrate a typical whitespace issue, one problem has been left unsolved: If the closing tag for an element is on a new line, the new line is copied to the output.

Various solutions are possible. However, the example demonstrates that `NSXMLParser` does not parse cleanly. You may need to add substantial extra code to retrieve clean character data from your input file.

`NSXMLParser` includes a method called `foundIgnorableWhitespace:`, but this method does not appear to find whitespace — or anything else.

Copying Files to and from the iPhone

Your application may need to implement a file import and export option; for example, you can allow users to play files captured in an audio recorder on another computer.

Unfortunately, the sandbox system makes direct file access impossible. There is no way to read and write files to and from your application using the Finder, Windows Explorer, or a Linux equivalent. Apple has also disabled email attachments. However, you can implement various official and unofficial work-arounds.

Some solutions may eliminate your application from the App Store. For example, in 2009, a free application called iPhone Explorer offered its own file exchange API. Applications could include the API to offer iPhone Explorer support for direct USB file access on both OS X and Windows. iPhone Explorer is still available at www.iphone-explorer.com, but in late 2009, Apple excluded compatible applications from the App Store, and the API is no longer available.

Using iTunes and USB

iTunes does not sync applications you install on your iPhone for testing and thus does not save or restore their data. If you install an application from the App Store, you can load, uncompress, and examine an application's .ipa file after sync by looking in the <*Username*>/Music/iTunes/ Mobile Applications folder. To decompress an .ipa file, copy it to another location, rename it as a ZIP file, and then open it with Archive Utility on a Mac or an equivalent Windows utility. You can use this technique to examine data saved by commercial applications and for testing. It is not a practical solution for user file export.

Using the Photo Library

You can use `UIImageWriteToSavedPhotosAlbum:` to write images to the photo library and copy them via iTunes. An indirect solution for file copying is to save arbitrary data into a PNG-format file. You can then copy this file to and from the iPhone. To create a PNG, you must pad the data with extra bytes to make it fit into a rectangular format. You will also need to write a file extractor on the target computer, so this approach is not ideal.

Using the Simple FTP Example Code and HTTP GET

The OS 3.1 SDK includes a sample FTP application built around the `NSURLConnection CFFTPStream` classes. You can use this sample code to add a simple FTP server to your application, implementing uploading and downloading to and from a remote URL.

Experienced developers can extend this code to build a minimal but functional web server into an application. According to Apple, downloading from a URL "is discouraged." The `NSURLDownload` class, which implements downloading in OS X, is not available on the iPhone. However, `NSURLConnection` implements `HTTP GET`, which can be used for relatively simple downloads. For a practical example, see Chapter 10.

For experienced developers, an open-source project called cocoahttpserver offers an alternative pre-built iPhone HTTP server that can be built into any application. For details, see http://code.google.com/p/cocoahttpserver.

Using CFNetwork

You can use the CFNetServices API to implement a complete remote file browser in your application, allowing file copying in both directions. This is an intermediate-to-advanced project. Details are outside the scope of this book, and Apple's documentation for CFNetServices is not comprehensive. However, from the user's viewpoint, this option can be the simplest, and it has been implemented in a small number of applications.

Handle Errors with NSError

You can use NSError to trap error messages generated by file operations and system functions and optionally to run an error handler method to attempt recovery. NSError is not an abstract class; you can use it directly without creating an instance.

The simplest way to implement error handling is to create a reference to NSError and pass the pointer to the error parameter in a file operation. Because the parameter is a pointer, you must prefix an ampersand:

```
NSError *error;
[string writeToFilePath: path atomically:
  YES encoding: anEncoding error: &error];
```

If error is non-zero, you can take action by printing an error message to the console or displaying an alert.

A more compact option is to include the result of the method within a conditional. A successful run returns YES; an unsuccessful run returns NO:

```
if (![string writeToFilePath: path
  atomically: YES encoding:
  anEncoding error: &error])
{\\handle an error}
else
{\\optionally, handle the no-error condition}
```

To get an error string from an error string, use [error localizedDescription];. Error strings are not informative; they include a numerical code and a generic verbal description. There is no simple way to convert this information into a definitive text string. [error localizedFailureReason]; displays more information for certain errors but returns nil for others.

More detailed descriptions for each code are listed in various header files. Error codes include a *domain*, which specifies which part of the operating system — Cocoa, the Mach Kernel, or POSIX — raised the error. To find a description, you must check one or more header files associated with the domain. Details are listed in the Error Handling Programming Guide documentation.

Handle Errors with NSError

① In the Finder, create a copy of the TextView example. Rename it NSError. In TextViewController.m, add a pointer to an NSError object.

Note: *You can find the NSError project on the website for this book: www.wiley.com/ go/iphonedevelopmentvb.*

② In ViewDidLoad, add code to implement support for NSError reporting.

③ In endEditing, add code to implement support for NSError, writing success/fail messages to NSLog.

④ Make a deliberate mistake in the name of the Documents directory.

⑤ Click Build and Run then change the text in the view.

⑥ Tap the Done button to save a file.

⑦ In Xcode, choose Run→Console to display the console.

● The file does not save correctly. The application logs an error on the console.

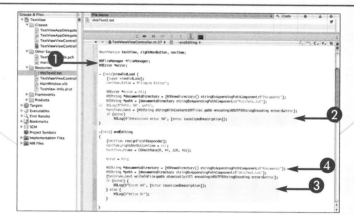

Introducing Graphics and Animation

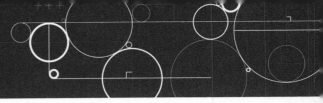

On the iPhone and iPod family, you can use three different dedicated graphics frameworks to create static and moving images: Core Graphics, Quartz Core, and OpenGL ES. A separate but related Core Animation framework automates animation effects that can be applied to views and graphic objects.

The frameworks include powerful features for creating, managing, updating, and drawing graphic objects. You can use the frameworks for traditional graphical applications, including games. You can also use them for creating interfaces with customized features, such as animated or button graphics generated with code.

Each framework is ideal for different applications, and you can simplify development by choosing the appropriate framework for a task — for example, choosing Core Graphics to create a simple gradient fill background for a view and OpenGL ES for a game with morphing animated 3-D objects.

Graphics and UIKit

UIKit includes links to all the graphics frameworks. You can embed images created with the graphics frameworks in UIKit view objects and then apply some of the graphic animation features to UIKit views. UIKit uses the graphics frameworks internally. Buttons, sliders, and other visible objects are drawn and animated by using calls to the Core Graphics and Quartz Core frameworks.

The visible parts of a view are held in one or more layer objects. You can access a layer object by calling the [layer] method on a view. You can then scale, rotate, and move the graphic content of the view by using the methods available in Core Animation and manipulate its content by using the functions in Core Graphics.

UIKit includes a library of general functions for creating and managing graphics. A *context* is a destination for graphics.

You can use a selection of `UIGraphics` functions in UIKit to read and set a context for your application. You can also read information from a context and then save it as a PNG or JPEG file.

Animation

There is more than one way to create animations on the iPhone. You can animate UIKit view objects directly by updating their properties. You can apply scaling, rotation, and translation to layers embedded in a view by using Core Graphics. You can also create more complex effects with OpenGL ES.

For intermediate effects, Core Animation, also known as Quartz Core in the documentation, offers a rich collection of animation management objects that can be applied to layer in a view. Core Animation simplifies animations with an object-oriented approach. Your code specifies a list of animated properties, a sequence of transformations, and a set of timing curves and animation events. Core Animation automatically calculates the required transforms over the specified time periods and then applies them to the target layers. Animations can be looped, repeated, or played once. The framework also includes delegate methods that can trigger arbitrary events when an animation begins or ends.

Core Animation is not as open-ended as OpenGL ES. The list of properties that can be animated is limited, and there is no support for arbitrary 3-D objects. However, it is a good solution for simple games with sprite-like objects and for animated user interfaces. All the animations in the iPhone's built-in applications, including the bounce, zoom, and fade effects, are created with Core Animation.

Core Graphics

Core Graphics, also known as Quartz 2D in the documentation, provides a library of functions and data structures for 2-D bitmap and vector graphics, with very basic support for z-axis rotations and zooms. You can use Core Graphics to create relatively simple shapes and images, rendered with a single color, a gradient fill, or a tiled texture. *Primitives* — basic graphic building blocks — include arcs, rectangles, and arbitrary vector paths. Fonts are supported. Helper functions, such as `CGPointMake` and `CGRectMake`, are included to simplify coordinate geometry and point management.

Contexts can support multiple independent layers, with variable opacity and clipping paths. Primitives can be combined into composite objects called *transparency layers*. In spite of the name, transparency layers are not necessarily transparent — they are grouped objects.

Layers can be modified with an *affine transform*, which applies a matrix transformation to the layer to scale it, rotate it, or move it. Core Graphics includes methods for managing and modifying a layer's matrix independently of the graphics within it. You can draw graphics into a view by adding Core Graphics code to a customized `drawRect:` method in a subclassed `UIView`.

OpenGL ES

OpenGL ES is a limited subset of the OpenGL graphics system used on desktop computers. It uses a server-based model that is initialized with a stream of vertex and color data, modified by camera settings, and is ideal for complex 3-D animations. An API called EAGL creates an interface between the OpenGL ES server subsystem, with optional framebuffers and a display context. On the iPhone and iPod, graphics acceleration hardware increases the performance of OpenGL ES. Game performance can be comparable to that of a basic desktop computer, albeit within the smaller pixel dimensions of the iPhone's display.

The iPhone 3GS uses an updated version of OpenGL ES code written for older hardware runs on the 3GS, but code written for the new and improved OpenGL ES 2.0 platform

will not run on older models. Xcode includes an OpenGL ES Application template, set up to run the newer version of OpenGL ES by default. To develop for the older version of OpenGL ES, you must modify this template by hand.

OpenGL is not a straightforward technology; the API and the underlying programming models are somewhat complex. For experienced OpenGL developers, OpenGL ES lacks many familiar features.

For beginners, vertex, color, and framebuffer management are challenging because developers must handle all the elements in a scene as efficiently as possible — for example, by supplying an explicit vertex count and removing redundant vertices from objects.

Touch Events and Coordinate Systems

The graphics frameworks do not process touch events directly. To create touchable graphic objects, you must attach them to a view and then use the `view` property and `locationInView:` method returned by the `touches Began:` and `touchesMoved:` methods or add customized hit-test code.

Each graphics framework uses a different coordinate system. For UIKit objects, point 0,0 is at the top left of the

screen. For Core Graphics objects, point 0,0 is at the bottom left, except when graphics are being drawn directly into a view. Core Graphics objects also use view- and layer-based local graphics systems — one relative to the top-left point of the object itself and another relative to the top-left point of a super object — the object above it in the view or layer hierarchy. OpenGL ES uses yet another coordinate system — point 0,0,0 is at the center of the screen.

Create a Context for Graphics

The Core Graphics framework draws into a *context*, not into a view. As a simplified programming model, you can think of a context as an area of memory with defined dimensions and properties, read and written by the Core Graphics drawing commands. Before you can draw into a view, you must retrieve its context or create a new one and then store it in a CGContextRef data type.

You can read a context for graphics by subclassing a view and then adding code to implement a customized drawRect: method. Code in drawRect: can retrieve the default context by calling the UIGraphicsGetCurrentContext function.

To create graphics, fill the drawRect: method with graphics commands that reference the context. You can find a complete list of commands in the CGContext Class Reference in the documentation. Optionally, you can create animated graphics by changing their properties and then calling drawRect: repeatedly.

To create a custom UIView subclass, create a project with the View-based Application template. Add a new instance of UIView to the project and then give it a unique name. Assign the new name to the default UIView in the nib by using Interface Builder. When the view loads, it automatically runs code in the new subclass with your customized drawRect: method.

You can also trigger drawRect: on demand by calling it directly from within the view. However, this can be unreliable — the rect context is not necessarily passed as it should be. A safer solution is to call setNeeds Display from the view controller rather than in the view — typically [self.view setNeedsDisplay];.

This triggers a refresh of the view and then calls drawRect: indirectly, with a guaranteed context.

Create a Context for Graphics

1 Create a new project with the View-based Application template and then save it as Context.

Note: *You can find the Context project on the website for this book: www.wiley.com/go/iphonedevelopmentvb.*

2 Right-click on the Classes folder in the Groups & Files pane and then choose Add→New File from the pop-up menu.

3 Click Cocoa Touch Class and then click Objective-C Class.

4 Select UIView from the Subclass drop-down menu and then save the new class as DrawView.

5 Double-click ContextViewController.xib to open it in Interface Builder.

6 Click the view object.

7 Click the Identity tab in the Inspector window.

8 Assign the DrawView class to the view by using the drop-down menu in the Class Identity pane and then save the file.

Note: *This step assigns code in the DrawView class to the view object in the nib.*

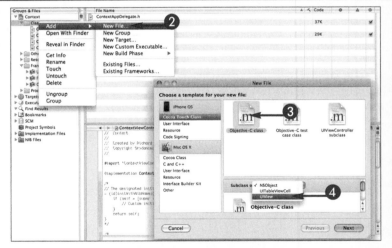

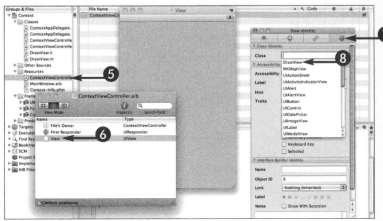

⑨ Click DrawView.m.

⑩ Find the `drawRect:` method and then add code to retrieve the default context.

⑪ Add code to clear the context, resetting it to black.

⑫ Optionally, add code to draw a test rectangle by using the `CGFillRect` function and then save the file.

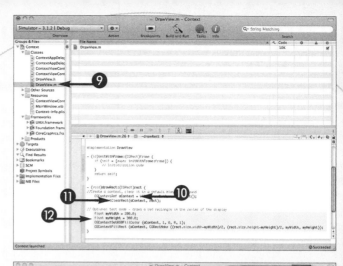

⑬ Click Build and Run to build and run the application.

● The `drawRect:` method retrieves the context and clears the view's default gray background, replacing it with black. Optionally, it also adds a red test rectangle to the center of the view.

Extra

UIGraphicsGetCurrentContext is ideal for getting a context from a view. However, you can also create contexts manually and then save their contents to disk or copy them for display — for example, to implement an image editor.

The CGPDFContextCreate function creates a PDF file, which can optionally be saved to the iPhone's file system. As you write graphics to the file, the contents are updated. The CGBitmapContextCreate function creates a simple bitmap with fixed dimensions and resolution. You can display the bitmap in a view by using CGBitMapContextCreateImage and CGContextDrawImage:

```
myImage = CGBitmapContextCreateImage (aBitmapContext);
CGContextDrawImage (aViewContext, aBoundingBox, myImage);
```

Custom contexts use a lower-left origin coordinate system. View-based contexts use an upper-left origin.

Create a Simple Animation with drawRect:

Y ou can create simple animations by calling the drawRect: method with a timer and then updating the size, position, color, or other property of graphic items in a view at each timer tick. This method is ideal for minimal animations with one or two moving objects. It is not recommended for more complex animations because the performance of drawRect: is very limited.

To create an animation loop, initialize a timer in the view controller and then add a selector that calls an update method on every timer tick. Add [self.view setNeeds Display]; to the update method. This calls drawRect: automatically every time the timer fires. For more on setting up an NSTimer, see Chapter 9.

You can then customize the drawRect: method in your view subclass to draw new objects on every timer tick, move one or more existing objects, or change other object properties. You can define local variables inside drawRect: to remember position, size, and other information. For example, to move an object vertically, you can create a local my_Y variable, increment it automatically every time drawRect: is called, and then use modulo division to keep it within the limits of the display.

This example uses a simple loop to draw 500 ellipses, with random positions, sizes, and colors. It also demonstrates the difference in performance between the Simulator and the iPhone hardware. On a typical MacBook or MacBook Pro, the code runs at the full timer rate of 20 updates per second. On a real device, the update rate drops to around 3 frames per second (fps).

Create a Simple Animation with drawRect:

① Open the Context project created in the previous example.

② Find drawRect:.

③ Add code to create a loop for 500 objects.

④ Add code to set a random fill color for each object as well as draw a filled ellipse with a random position and dimensions and then save the file.

Note: *The* random *function returns a large random number. You can scale the number within a range with modulo division or scale it to a float number between 0 and 1 by multiplying it and dividing it by a constant.*

⑤ Click ContextViewController.m.

⑥ Find and uncomment the viewDidLoad method.

⑦ Add code to create a timer object, triggering a fireTimer: method 20 times per second.

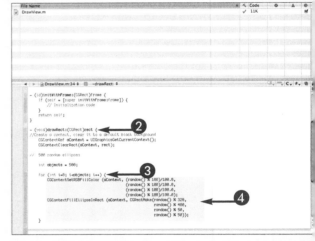

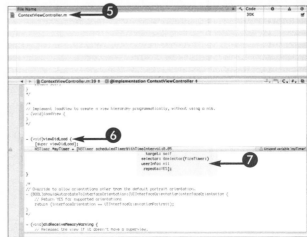

8 Add a `fireTimer:` method.

9 Add code to call the `setNeedsDisplayMethod` and then save the file.

Note: `setNeedsDisplay` *automatically calls* `drawRect:` *in the view.*

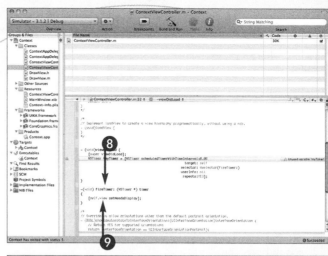

10 Click Build and Run to build and run the project.

● The application fills the view with 500 random ellipses, updated at the timer rate.

Extra

`CGContext` commands use a rendering model. A context is more than a block of memory — it also implies an interface with a physical or virtual output device. In Mac OS X, you can use `CGContext` commands to print a document to a printer. The iPhone does not support a printer, but advanced concepts included in the `CGContext` rendering model still apply. For example, you can enable anti-aliasing for smoother output, enable font smoothing, and set interpolation options for image scaling.

You can draw to more than one context in `drawRect:`. Use `UIGraphicsPushContext(aContext)` to draw to a second context and `UIGraphicsPopContext` to retrieve the original context. You can push an almost-indefinite number of contexts onto the stack, but you must balance each stack push with a stack pop. For examples, see later in this chapter.

Introducing Paths

Paths are a key feature of the CGContext graphics library. You can use a path to trace an arbitrary outline. A selection of functions for drawing simple paths, including rectangles, arcs, and ellipses, is pre-defined. You can also create custom paths with arbitrary shapes.

Paths are objects that are assembled from points, linked by lines, and can be closed, open, and noncontiguous, with many disconnected subpaths. Lines can be curved, with optional Bézier and quadratic controls, or straight. You can begin and end a path anywhere within a context's drawing rectangle. Only one path can be active in a context at a time, but you can create and draw paths sequentially as well as store multiple paths in a context to draw repeated shapes.

A path is an invisible shape, not a visible graphic. To render the shape into a graphic, you must paint the path. You can paint paths to render their outlines and to create filled areas. You can set a line pattern, a separate line color, and a fill color. You can control how overlapping colored areas merge by setting a blending mode.

Building a Path

You can build a path in two ways. The CGContext library includes a selection of path functions to create lines, arcs, and other shapes. Call CGContextBeginPath to start a path and — optionally — CGContextClosePath to end it. Within the path, you can move the drawing point with CGContextMoveToPoint. Drawing functions include CGAddLineToPoint, CGAddCurveToPoint, CGContextAddArc, and others. For a complete list, see the CGContext Class Reference documentation.

When you paint a path created with these functions, it is deleted. You can create persistent path objects by calling functions in the CGPath library. The drawing functions are identical to those in the CGContext library, but they begin with the CGPath prefix — for example, CGPathAddLineToPoint.

The start and end functions are different. Use CGPathCreateMutable to begin the path and CGCloseSubpath to end it. To add the finished path to the graphics context, use CGContextAddPath.

Adding Shapes and Curves

Paths include a current draw location. You can set this directly with CGPathMoveToPoint and CGContextMoveToPoint. When you add a shape, the draw location is updated to the last drawn point in the shape. When you add two lines to a path, the second line automatically begins where the first line ends.

You can add rectangles and ellipses by using CGContextAddRect and CGContextAddEllipseInRect. A separate CGContextAddRects function adds an array of rectangles. This function is a good way to draw a grid of cells. It is not suited for multicolored graphics — all rectangles in the array are painted and filled with the same color.

When you draw an arc, a straight line segment is added from the current draw location to the start of the arc. To create independent arcs, you must create an arc, paint it, create the next arc, paint it, and so on. CGContextAddArc implicitly calls the CGContextMoveToPoint function, so you do not need to use CGContextMoveToPoint to set the initial drawing location.

Use CGContextAddCurveToPoint to create a Bézier curve with two control points. This function takes six coordinates altogether — a pair for the end and a pair for each control point. Use CGContextAddQuadCurveToPoint to create a simpler quadratic curve with a single point. Control points use absolute, not relative, coordinates. You must add the endpoint of the curved line to them. They are invisible and are not painted.

Paths can be filled and stroked with separate colors. Stroking the path traces its outline. Filling it colors in the area within the outline. You can define colors by using either RGB (red, blue, green) values or CMYK (cyan, magenta, yellow, black) values. The valid range for each color component is 0.0 to 1.0. An alpha coefficient sets transparency — use 1.0 for block colors with no transparency. You also can set the transparency for the entire path independently with CGContextSetAlpha.

The iPhone supports color spaces, including RGB, CMYK, Lab, and indexed. The default is RGB. For CMYK, Lab, or other colors, you select a color space with CGContext SetFillColorSpace.

By default, paths are painted so they cover the background, with transparency set by the current alpha value. You can create more sophisticated effects by selecting a blending mode to combine the foreground and the background in more creative ways. The list of available modes is similar to those built into image-editing software, such as Adobe Photoshop and Gimp.

You can use blending modes to combine the foreground and the background to show only the lightest or darkest colors and areas and to create extreme effects that radically transform colors by using the difference and exclusion blend modes. For a complete list of available blending modes see the CGBlendMode definitions in the CGContext documentation.

The Current Transformation Matrix

The Current Transformation Matrix (CTM) applies fixed rotation, translation, and scaling factors to the current context. This affects the dimensions and orientation of all paths in the context.

You can manipulate the CTM to move, rotate, or shrink and expand the graphics in a context. For example, CGContextRotateCTM rotates all the graphics in a context by a given angle. You can use this for animation effects, changing the CTM dynamically and redrawing the graphics. You can also use it to compensate for different coordinate systems — for example, by setting the y-scaling to –1 to invert the context coordinates with an optional translation to re-center the graphics. The CTM is always present and active, but its default values have no visible effect.

Clipping

You can use a path to define a clipping area for a context. Graphics outside the path are not painted. To create a clipping path, begin the path with CGContextBeginPath, add one or more shape, line, or curve functions to create an outline, and then end the path with CGContextClosePath. Enable the clipping with CGContextClip. Clipping areas do not have to be contiguous, and — like all graphic content — they can be animated. You can use clipping to produce static cutouts or to create moving windows on top of background graphics. Although the Quartz 2D framework is typically used for simple static graphics, creatively working with clipping, coloring, and shape control can create more sophisticated animated effects.

Hit Testing Graphics

Use CGContextPathContainsPoint to check if a coordinate is inside the current path. The test refers to the current color fill mode.

If a fill mode is enabled, the test checks if the coordinate is inside the path outline. If stroke mode is active, the test checks if the point is close to the outline.

Create a Path

Y ou can use CGContext path commands to define the shape of a path and create arbitrary shapes, with almost unlimited complexity. Paths are like the movements of an imaginary pen in the context space. The pen can draw lines, curves, and a small library of preset shapes. It can be picked up and moved to a new drawing position — paths do not have to be contiguous.

Use CGContextBeginPath(aContext) to start a new path. Optionally, call CGContextClosePath to end a path. This function draws a line from the current drawing position to the start of the path. If you do not close a path, it remains open. If you fill an open path with color, the fill function implicitly closes it.

Use the CGContextMoveToPoint function to set a new drawing position for a path, using absolute coordinates within the context. You can call this function as often as you need, to move the virtual pen around the context space.

Use CGContextAddLineToPoint to draw a straight line from the current draw position to a new draw position. CGContextAddCurveToPoint draws a curved line, shaped by two control points. The control point positions are defined in absolute context space. To specify relative coordinates for the control points, use offsets. For example, if the line ends at x,y, you can specify the curve.

```
CGContextAddCurveToPoint (aContext,
  x+firstControlX, y+firstControlY,
  x+secondControlX, y+secondControlY,
  x, y);
```

Use CGContextAddRect to create a rectangular path segment at a given position, with given dimensions. Like CGContextAddArc, which draws an arc, it includes an implicit call to CGContextMoveToPoint to move the drawing position. This example creates a path with lines, curves, and a surrounding rectangle.

① Create a new project by using the View-based Application template and then save it as Path.

Note: *You can find the Path project on the website for this book: www.wiley.com/go/ iphonedevelopmentvb.*

② Right-click on the Classes folder and then add a new custom UIView subclass called DrawView.

③ Double-click PathViewController.xib to open it in Interface Builder and then click the view object.

④ Assign the DrawView class to the view by using the drop-down menu in the Class Identity pane and then save the file.

⑤ Click PathViewController.m.

⑥ Find the drawRect: method. Add code to retrieve the drawing context, to clear it, and to begin a path.

⑦ Add code to create a polygon path, using a loop to draw multiple straight lines, calculating the endpoints of each with simple trigonometry.

⑧ Add code to declare the variables used in the loop calculations.

Note: *This example demonstrates how to create a path programmatically, creating multiple line segments under code control.*

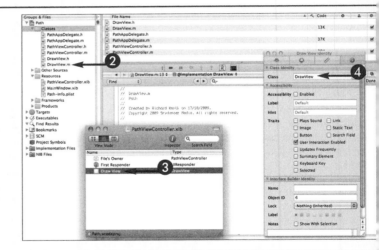

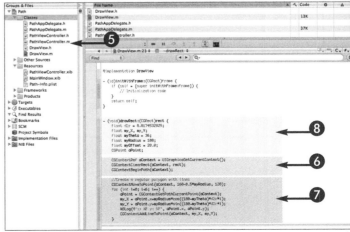

9 Make another copy of the the loop added in step 7 below it.

10 Change the values in the `CGContext MoveToPoint` call to move the drawing position lower down the display.

11 Add code to draw curves instead of line segments, using relative coordinates for the curve control points.

12 Add code for a bounding rectangle, inset from the edge of the display area, and then add code to stroke the path with a thin white line to make it visible.

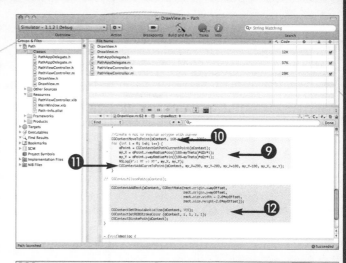

13 Click Build and Run to build and run the application.

● The application draws three subpaths: one with straight lines, one with curved lines, and a bounding rectangle. The paths are stroked with a thin white line.

Extra

The Core Graphics library supports a number of data structures for handling points, rectangles, and dimensions. Some of the `CGContext` functions expect specific data structures rather than lists of naked floats. The `CGGeometry` library includes a list of convenience functions for packing floats into these data structures.

`CGPointMake` takes two floats and converts them into a `CGPoint` coordinate, with separate x and y values. `CGRectMake` takes four floats and converts them into a `CGRect`, with a top-left origin `CGPoint`, a width, and a height. `CGSizeMake` takes two floats and converts them into a `CGSize`, with a width and a height.

For example, to pass a `CGRect` to the `CGContextAddRect` function:

```
CGContextAddRect (aContext, CGRectMake(x, y, size, width));
```

The CGGeometry library also includes methods for finding the geometric relationship between two rectangles, for comparing points and rectangles, and for checking if a point or rectangle is inside another rectangle.

Paint a Path

Y ou can paint a path to create lines and color fills. Until you paint a path, it is invisible. When you paint a path, the path is released. To paint it again, you must define it again — in full. You can also store it as a path object and then paint the object.

You can stroke a path to paint its outline or fill it to cover its area with color. The CGContextSetShouldAntiAlias function can enable anti-aliasing, creating smoother output.

Use CGContextStrokePath to stroke a path. Optionally, you can set the stroke width with CGContextSetLine Width and the stroke color with CGContextSetRGB StrokeColor. Lines can be enhanced with a *dash pattern* to create dashed and textured effects.

To define a dash pattern:

```
CGFloat aDashPattern[]={1.0, 2.0, 1.0...};
CGContextSetLineDash (aContext, phase,
  aDashPattern, count);
```

phase is a pattern offset and sets the starting point in the dash pattern array. count is the number of items in the

array. The array holds a sequence of line widths, in pixels, defining the pattern.

You can set how lines are joined by setting CGContextSetLineJoin, passing it one of the CGLineJoin constants defined in the CGContext reference in the documentation. Miter joins create a sharp corner, round joins smooth the join point, and beveled joins square the corner. Similarly, you can control how line ends are drawn by passing constants to CGContext SetLineCap to create butt, rounded, and square ends.

To fill a path, use CGContextEOFillPath or CGContext FillPath. If there are multiple enclosed areas within the path, these functions fill them in different ways. CGContext EOFillPath alternates between filling enclosed areas and not filling them from the center outward. CGContextFill Path calculates path crossings in a more sophisticated way. CGContextEOFillPath typically leaves unfilled areas, while CGContextFillPath is more likely to completely fill the area within a path outline.

Paint a Path

① Open the Path project created in the previous example.

② Find the drawRect: method in DrawView.m.

③ Add code to enable anti-aliasing.

④ Add code to the end of the first group of drawing commands to set a line width of 2.0 pixels.

⑤ Add code to set a red RGB stroke color, with no transparency.

⑥ Add code to stroke the path.

Note: *This destroys and releases the path. Subsequent calls to a paint function in* drawRect: *will not draw the path again. You must begin a new path after every paint command.*

```
- (void)drawRect:(CGRect)rect {                    ②
    float d2r = 0.0174532925;
    float my_X, my_Y;
    float myTheta = 36;
    float myRadius = 100;
    float myOffset = 20.0;
    CGPoint aPoint;

    CGContextRef aContext = UIGraphicsGetCurrentContext();
    CGContextClearRect(aContext, rect);
    CGContextBeginPath(aContext);
    CGContextSetShouldAntialias(aContext, YES);     ③

    //Create a regular polygon with lines
    CGContextMoveToPoint(aContext, 160-0.5*myRadius, 120);
    for (int i=0; i<6; i++) {
        aPoint = CGContextGetPathCurrentPoint(aContext);
        my_X = aPoint.x+myRadius*cos((180-myTheta)*d2r*i);
        my_Y = aPoint.y+myRadius*sin((180-myTheta)*d2r*i);
        NSLog(@"x: %f y: %f", aPoint.x, aPoint.y);
        CGContextAddLineToPoint(aContext, my_X, my_Y);
    }
    CGContextSetLineWidth(aContext, 2);
    CGContextSetRGBStrokeColor (aContext, 1, 0, 0, 1);
    CGContextStrokePath(aContext);

    //Create a not so regular polygon with curves
```

```
    float d2r = 0.0174532925;
    float my_X, my_Y;
    float myTheta = 36;
    float myRadius = 100;
    float myOffset = 20.0;
    CGPoint aPoint;

    CGContextRef aContext = UIGraphicsGetCurrentContext();
    CGContextClearRect(aContext, rect);
    CGContextBeginPath(aContext);
    CGContextSetShouldAntialias(aContext, YES);

    //Create a regular polygon with lines
    CGContextMoveToPoint(aContext, 160-0.5*myRadius, 120);
    for (int i=0; i<6; i++) {
        aPoint = CGContextGetPathCurrentPoint(aContext);
        my_X = aPoint.x+myRadius*cos((180-myTheta)*d2r*i);
        my_Y = aPoint.y+myRadius*sin((180-myTheta)*d2r*i);
        NSLog(@"x: %f y: %f", aPoint.x, aPoint.y);
        CGContextAddLineToPoint(aContext, my_X, my_Y);
    }
    CGContextSetLineWidth(aContext, 2);                    ④
    CGContextSetRGBStrokeColor (aContext, 1, 0, 0, 1);    ⑤
    CGContextStrokePath(aContext);                        ⑥
```

7 Add code to begin a new path before the second set of path commands.

8 Add code to set a green fill color.

9 Add code to paint the path using `EOFillPath`.

10 Add code to begin a new path before the third set of drawing commands.

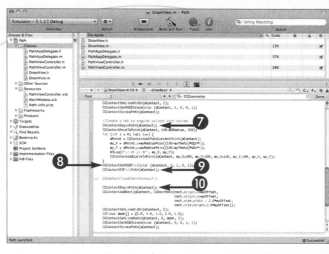

11 Add code to set the line width to 5.0 pixels and then add code to create a dashed pattern for the third path.

12 Add code to apply the pattern and then set a blue stroke color.

13 Add code to stroke the path.

14 Click Build and Run to build and run the application.

● The application paints each path with a different color and paint option.

Create a Clipping Path

With a clipping path, you can limit path painting to a fixed area. You can use clipping to paint graphics inside a subwindow or subarea — for example, to render graphics inside a button, leaving the area around it unchanged.

To create a clipping path, define a path in the usual way. Clipping paths can be any shape, and you can use all the standard path creation functions to define them. Like normal paths, clipping paths do not have to be contiguous. You can clip multiple areas within a context.

To apply the clipping, call CGContextClip. This generates a clipping mask for the context. Subsequent paint commands intersect the mask. Areas within the mask are painted; areas outside the mask are not. You

can also call a selection of clipping functions to create rectangular areas. For example, CGContextClipToRect creates a clipping rectangle and includes an implicit call to CGContextClip.

Typically, you add a clipping path at the start of drawRect: to clip all subsequent painting. To leave some paths unclipped, call CGContextClip after they are painted. Paths painted before a CGContextClip call are drawn without clipping.

Clipping is cumulative. If you call CGContextClip more than once, the clipping area becomes the intersection of both calls. A second call can shrink the clipping area but cannot expand it or remove it.

Create a Clipping Path

① Open the Path project saved in the previous example.

② Find the drawRect: method in DrawView.m.

③ Add code to create a new circular path in the center of the display, the width of the display.

④ Add CGContextClip to set the path as a clipping path.

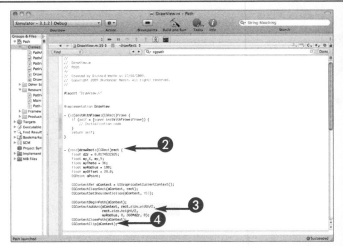

⑤ Click Build and Run to build and run the application.

● The new path clips the shapes in the example. The shapes are not painted outside the clipping area. The clipping path is not stroked or filled and remains invisible.

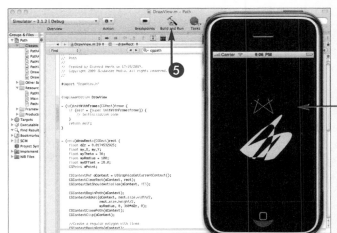

6 Place comment marks around the new clipping path to inactivate it.

7 Copy its code, paste it before the dashed rectangular path, and then uncomment the copy.

8 Make the clipping circle slightly wider so it extends beyond the display.

Note: *For clarity, this example uses a code summary feature in Xcode to minimize the for/next loops and replace them with dots. To activate this feature, highlight a block of code and then click in the gray sidebar to the left of the code window.*

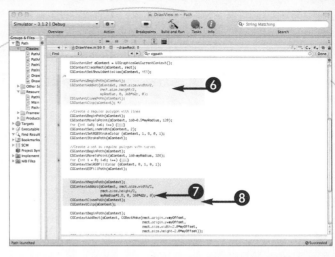

9 Click Build and Run to build and run the application.

● Paths drawn before the clipping path is defined are not clipped, only the rectangular path drawn after it is clipped.

You can use `CGContextClipToMask` to clip an image from a file or any other `CGImageRef` object. Mask clipping is more sophisticated than path clipping because it can include transparency information. You can use mask clipping for *feathering*, which is softening the edge of a clipped area. Because a `CGImage` can be generated from a bitmapped context, which can in turn reference path information in a view context, you can use this technique to feather any path. You can also save and load masks to disk — for example, to create brushstroked frame effects around a view.

You can apply multiple independent clipping areas to multiple paths by calling `CGContextSaveGState` before creating a new clipping path and then painting one or more paths inside it. Call `CGContextRestoreGState` to restore the previous path. Saving a state saves all the graphics settings for a context, including fill and stroke colors, line widths, and dash patterns. The save and restore functions use a stack mechanism. You can save more than one state, as long as you balance each save with a restore.

Create a Reusable Path Object

You can define paths as objects without adding them to the context for drawing. There is no simple way to save a path to a file as a series of points, so you cannot use this feature to create a library of useful shapes. However, you can use *affine transformations* to repeat paths with scaling, rotation, or movement to create graphic effects that might otherwise be difficult to code.

Path objects are instances of the `CGPathRef` data type. You must use manual memory management when working with path objects. You cannot `alloc` a path, but you must call `CGPathRelease` to release it when it is no longer required. You can also call `CGPathRetain` to increase a path's retain count.

Path objects use functions in the `CGPath` library. To create a path instance, call `CGPathCreateMutable`. You can copy a path with `CGPathCreateCopy` to create a fixed path that cannot be changed or `CGPathCreate MutableCopy` to create a copy that can be extended.

The `CGPath` library includes a set of path functions for adding to a path. These are almost identical to those in the `CGContext` library; for example, `CGPathAddArc` adds an arc, `CGPathAddRect` adds a rectangle, `CGPathAdd CurveToPoint` adds a curve, and so on. When calling these functions, you must pass a path object and an instance of an affine transform. To modify a path without using an affine transform, set the transform field to `NULL`. For example:

```
CGPathAddRect (myPath, NULL, CGRectMake,
  topLeftX, topLeftY, width, height);
```

This adds a rectangle to `myPath`. Subject to memory availability, you can create an unlimited number of path objects and modify and paint them independently.

To add a path object to a context, call `CGContextAddPath (aContext, myPath);`.

You can then fill and stroke the path in the usual way.

Create a Reusable Path Object

① Create a new project with the View-based Application template and then save it as Path2.

Note: *You can find the Path2 project on the website for this book: www.wiley.com/go/ iphonedevelopmentvb.*

② Right-click on the Classes folder and then add a new custom UIView subclass called DrawView.

③ Double-click Path2ViewController.xib to open it in Interface Builder and then click the view object.

④ Assign the DrawView class to the view by using the drop-down menu in the Class Identity pane and then save the file.

⑤ Find `drawRect:` and then add code to retrieve a context, to clear the context, and to apply anti-aliasing.

⑥ Add code to create a mutable path object.

⑦ Add code to add a rectangle to the path object.

⑧ Add code to add the path object to the context.

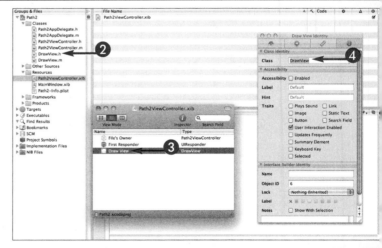

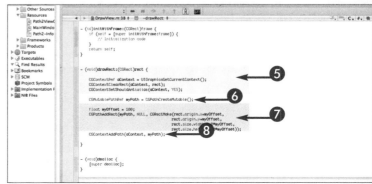

9 Add code to set a line width and a red stroke color.

10 Add code to paint the path.

11 Add code to release the path object.

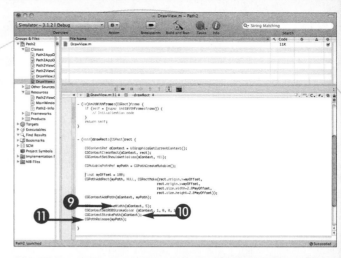

12 Click Build and Run to build and run the application.

● The application builds the path object, assigns it to the context, and then paints it.

Extra

The CGPath library includes functions for comparing paths and for testing points in paths. Call CGPathEqualTo Path to check if two paths are identical. CGPathContainsPoint tests if a point is inside the filled area of a path. CGPathGetBoundingBox returns the rect that surrounds a path.

Although there is no simple CGPathSave or CGPathLoad function, you can use CGPathApply to examine and list the points in a path as well as the connections between them. CGPathApply calls a custom applier function for each point. You can create an applier function that lists each CGPathElementType in the path, with its associated type. Path elements are constants and are defined in the CGPath reference documentation. Assembling a complete path manager from these function calls is not entirely straightforward, and you may find it easier to create a simplified alternative system for saving and loading shapes by using your own alternative data structures.

Using Affine Transforms

Y ou can use affine transforms to scale, rotate, and move paths. Affine transforms are defined with a `CGAffineTransform` data type and manipulated with functions in the `CGAffineTransform` library.

Affine transforms use matrix math to implement geometrical transformations. You can set the transformation matrix directly by using `CGAffineTransformMake` followed by a list of six floats. However, the matrix math is challenging and difficult to work with directly. The `CGAffineTransform` library includes helper functions to calculate the matrix coefficients for you when you want to apply a scaling factor, rotation, or translation. For example, `CGTransformMake Rotation` takes a float in radians and returns a matrix that creates the corresponding rotation. Similarly, `CGTransform MakeScale` and `CGTransformMakeTranslation` return a scaling matrix and a translation matrix, respectively.

There is only one kind of transform object. A rotation of 0.0, a translation of (0.0, 0.0), and a scaling factor of 1.0 all return the same unit matrix that does nothing.

You can modify transforms by calling a modifier function on an existing transform. For example, `CGAffine TransformTranslate` applies a further translation to an existing transform. However, to combine different transforms, use `CGTransformConcat`. This takes two transforms as input parameters and then multiplies their matrices together. For null transforms, use `NULL` in place of a transform object. You can undo translations by using `CGAffineTransformInvert` to create an anti-transform that exactly cancels an input transform.

You can transform points, sizes, and `rects` by applying convenience functions; for example, `CGRectApply AffineTransform` creates a set of transformed `rect` coefficients from an input rect.

The path creation functions in the `CGPath` library take a pointer to a transform as one of their parameters. You can use a different transform for each path and subpath. When you include a transform, you must prefix it with `&` to return the pointer.

Using Affine Transforms

1. Open the Path2 project saved in the previous example.

2. Find `drawRect:` and then add a constant to convert degrees to radians.

3. Add a null transform matrix by creating a rotation of zero.

Note: *This creates a base reference matrix for further transformations.*

4. Move the `CGPathRelease` function call from the end of `drawRect:` to the position shown so the initial path is released as soon as it is no longer needed.

5. Add code to start a for-next loop and create multiple paths.

6. Add a pointer to a transform in the `CGPathAddRect` function.

Note: *Do not use the null transform. Use a different name, as defined shortly.*

7. Close the for-next loop.

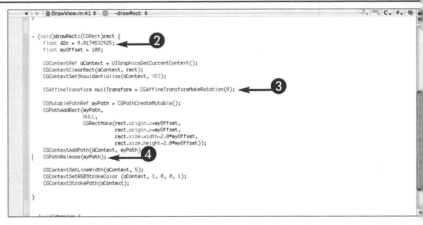

8 Create a scaling transform based on the null transform.

9 Create a rotation transform based on the null transform.

10 Concatenate the two transforms to create a combined transform for the `CGPathAddRect` function.

Note: *You could also use* `CGAffineTransform MakeRotation` *and* `CGAffineTransform Scale` *to create the two transforms. However, code that refers to a null transform can easily be changed to create a non-null base transform for both operations.*

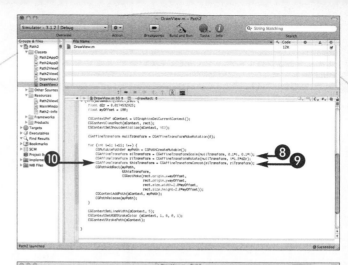

11 Click Build and Run to build and run the application.

● The application adds the same path ten times, applying a different transform each time. Scaling and rotation are calculated relative to the top-left origin.

Extra

Transforms are specified relative to the context origin. If you apply a scale transform to shrink a path, it shrinks toward the top left of the context. Similarly, if you apply a rotation, the path rotates relative to the origin.

It is often more useful to apply transforms relative to some other point, such as the center of the display or the center of the path. To keep transforms centered, you must apply a compensating translation to the geometric center of a path. This is easy to calculate for rectangles and other regular paths.

To find a rectangle surrounding an arbitrary curved path, use the `CGPathGetBoundingBox` function. You can then center the rectangle with simple trigonometry.

Transforms are noncommutative; the order of rotation, translation, and scaling is important. You should rotate and scale a path first and then apply a translation to move it to the required center point — allowing for the fact that scaling a path moves its geometric center point.

Using the Current Transformation Matrix

The Current Transformation Matrix (CTM) applies a global transform to the drawing context. You can use the CTM to create global scaling effects and translations to compensate for movement or windowing — for example, to draw to a subwindow in a view without having to refer to the subwindow's coordinates for every point in a path. You can also use it to invert coordinate systems or to re-center them. For example, translating by the context height and scaling the y-coordinate by –1.0 is equivalent to mapping a top-left origin to a bottom-left origin. Translating by half the screen width and screen height is equivalent to moving the origin to the center of the display.

There is only one CTM, and it is stored with the graphics state. To apply different transformations — for example, to flip an image but leave path coordinates unchanged — you can push a graphics state, change the CTM, and then pop the graphics state to restore it.

The CTM is equivalent to a single fixed affine transform that is attached to the context. All points in a context are affected equally. You can use further affine transforms to modify individual paths. The two transforms are cumulative but are applied independently.

To apply a CTM transform, call the CTM functions in the CGContext library, passing the context and the required parameters. For example:

```
CGContextTranslateCTM (myContext, xoffset,
  yoffset);
```

This will translate every point in the view by the x and y offsets. Similarly, CGContextRotateCTM applies a rotation in radians and CGContextScaleCTM scales the context. You can apply a separate affine transform to the entire CTM with CGContextConcatCTM.

You can use an animation timer to change the CTM dynamically. This example uses a timer to create a simple animated bounce effect with an applied transformation.

Using the Current Transformation Matrix

1. Create a new project with the View-based Application template and then save it as CTM.

Note: *You can find the CTM project on the website for this book: www.wiley.com/go/iphonedevelopmentvb.*

2. Right-click on the Classes folder and then add a new custom UIView subclass called DrawView.

3. Double-click GradientViewController.xib to open it in Interface Builder and then click the view object.

4. Assign the DrawView class to the view using the drop-down menu in the Class Identity pane and then save the file.

5. In viewDidLoad in CTMViewController.m, add an animation timer.

6. Add a call to the setNeedsDisplay method, triggered by the timer.

7. Find drawRect: in DrawView.m, add a float to create a drawing offset for a centered rectangle, and then add another float to create a variable CTM offset.

8. Add code to retrieve the context, to clear it, and to enable anti-aliasing.

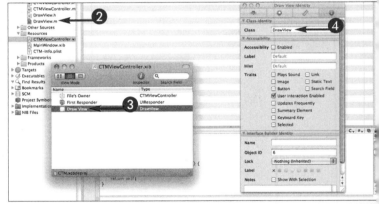

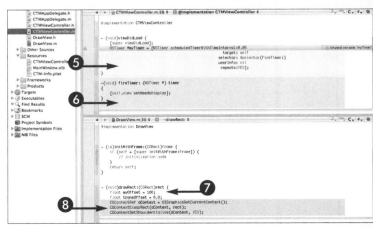

9 Add code to create a float constant that converts degrees to radians.

10 Increment the variable CTM offset.

Note: As the timer runs, the offset is incremented at each timer tick.

11 Add code to convert the offset into a variable CTM translation.

Note: The output of the sine function multiplied by 100 automatically limits the translation distance to +/– 100.

12 Add code to draw and stroke a centered rectangle.

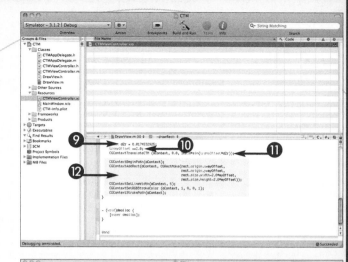

13 Click Build and Run to build and run the application.

● The application draws a moving rectangle. The drawing coordinates of the rectangle are fixed. A variable CTM translation moves it on the display.

Note: The sample code for this example includes two other simple CTM applications: a rotation animation and a static change of origin.

<hr>

Extra

Like affine transforms, the CTM applies transforms with respect to the context origin. By default, this means that rotations operate around the origin — typically the top left — and not around the center of the display.

To rotate objects around the center of the display, use the CTM to translate the origin to the center. You can then draw objects around the center by using both positive and negative coordinates. For example, drawing a path between (-50.0,0.0) and (50.0, 0.0) creates a line across the center of the display. Rotating this line spins it around the center.

For many applications, you can solve this problem more easily by using layers, as described earlier in this chapter.

Create Color

You can use the RGB system to set fill and stroke colors. For example, `CGContextSetRGBFill Color` takes four floating point numbers between 0.0 and 1.0 and specifies red, green, and blue and alpha/transparency values for a path's fill color.

This is the simplest way to set color and is adequate for most applications. However, the iPhone has inherited a selection of color management features from Mac OS X. When you use color in a more advanced way — for example, to create gradient fills or a palette of named colors — these features become important.

A *color space* is a mapping between an array of floats and a visible color. For example, in the RGB color space, the first three floats specify red, green, and blue components, respectively. In the CMYK color space, four floats specify cyan, magenta, yellow, and black components. There is also a gray color space, with a single grayscale lightness value. The last float in every color space is an alpha value for transparency control.

In the `CGContext` library, convenience fill and stroke functions are available in pre-defined RGB, CMYK, and Gray color spaces. For example:

```
CGContextSetGrayFillColor (aContext, 0.5,
  1.0);
```

This sets a mid-gray fill color. The Gray color space takes a single component to set a grayscale brightness.

You can use other less common color spaces, such as a Lab or indexed color, by creating a custom `CGColorSpace Ref` object and adding one of the `CGColorSpaceCreate` functions to select a target space.

Create one or more named `CGColorRef` objects to define colors within that space. Define the colors by passing a list of component values in an array. You can then paint with that color by calling `CGContextSetStrokeColor WithColor` and `CGContextSetFillColorWithColor`. Color space and color objects should be released when no longer needed.

Create Color

① Create a new project with the View-based Application template and then save it as Colors.

Note: *You can find the Colors project on the website for this book: www.wiley.com/go/iphonedevelopmentvb.*

② Right-click on the Classes folder and then add a new custom UIView subclass called DrawView.

③ Double-click ColorsViewController.xib to open it and then click the view object.

④ Assign the DrawView class to the view by using the drop-down menu in the Class Identity pane and then save the file.

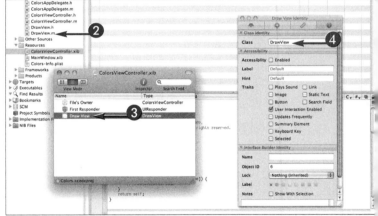

⑤ Click DrawView.m. Find the `drawRect:` method. Add code to retrieve the graphics context, to clear it, and to enable anti-aliasing.

⑥ Add code to create a rectangular path.

⑦ Add code to stroke it with 100% magenta in the CMYK color space.

⑧ Add code to create a smaller rectangular path and then add code to stroke it with 100% brightness in the Gray color space.

Note: *This example creates white.*

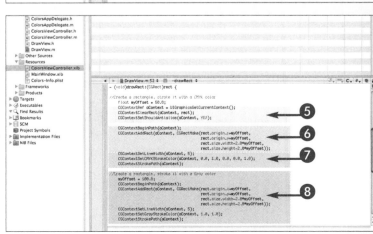

9 Add code to create an array with three color components, plus alpha, that can be used to define a color in the RGB color space.

Note: *This example creates 100% green.*

10 Add code to create a color space reference to a new RGB color space.

11 Add code to create a named reference to a color within that color space.

12 Add code to create and stroke a rectangle, using the named color, and then release the color.

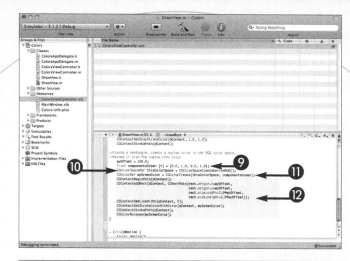

13 Click Build and Run to build and run the application.

● The application draws three rectangles, stroked with colors selected from three different color spaces.

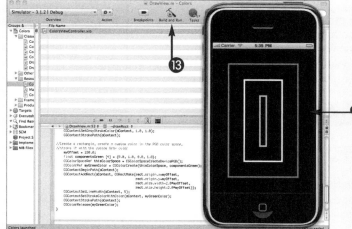

Extra

You can mix colors from different color spaces in the same context. All colors — whatever their space — are mapped to indices on the iPhone's display. When you stroke or fill a path, the iPhone maps the current components through a function in the color space to create an absolute display color. This mapping is done automatically.

The process is complex, but the results are simple: You can mix RGB, CMYK, and Gray convenience functions in the same `drawRect:` call. You can also create named custom colors by using any color space and use them to paint paths in the same context.

Color spaces can be device-independent to provide reliable color across a range of output devices. On the iPhone, professional color management is not a key feature. The convenience functions use device color, with a simple default mapping between indices and display color.

The CGColorSpace Reference documentation includes a list of functions for working with calibrated color. These are currently redundant on the iPhone. However, if a hardware calibration accessory becomes available, you can use these functions to implement color management features.

Create Color Gradients

You can create arbitrary color gradients and then use them to fill arbitrary areas by calling the CGContextDrawLinearGradient and CGContext DrawRadialGradient functions. To create a gradient, use the functions in the CGGradient library.

CGGradientCreateWithColorComponents creates a gradient from an array of component float values. You must pass the function to a CGColorSpaceRef object so it can convert the floats into device colors. You must also supply a locations array with an entry for each color. *Locations* define the bunching of the spread. They should add up to 1.0. For example, {0.0, 0.5, 1.0} creates a smooth gradient between three colors. {0.0, 0.1, 1.0} creates a sharp step between the first two colors, with a much smoother gradient to the final color.

Gradients are drawn between start and endpoints, filling the area between them. Optionally, you can extend the fill

from the endpoints in either direction. This continues the fill, using the start and end colors. Gradients ignore the current path but can be limited by their start and endpoints. Use CGContextDrawLinearGradient to draw a linear gradient. This fills the area perpendicular to a line between the start and endpoints. Add the kCGGradientDrawsBeforeStartLocation constant to the drawing options parameter to extend the fill beyond the start point. Similarly, the kCGGradientDraws BeforeEndLocation constant extends it in the other direction, beyond the endpoint.

Use CGContextDrawRadialGradient to draw a circular gradient. This function takes two points and two radii and then interpolates a fill between the two circles they define. You can use the extension constants to continue drawing the colors at either end of the gradient, creating expanding or decreasing circles in the selected directions. If either circle shrinks until its radius is 0, drawing stops.

Create Color Gradients

1 Create a new project with the View-based Application template and then save it as Gradient.

Note: *You can find the Gradient project on the website for this book: www.wiley.com/go/ iphonedevelopmentvb.*

2 Right-click on the Classes folder and then add a new custom UIView subclass called DrawView.

3 Double-click GradientViewController.xib to open it in Interface Builder and then click the view object.

4 Assign the DrawView class to the view by using the drop-down menu in the Class Identity pane and then save the file.

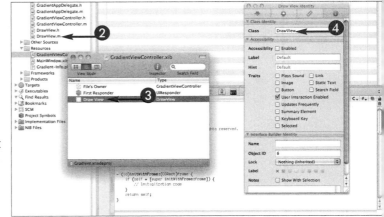

5 Click DrawView.m. Find the drawRect: method. Add code to create start and end fill points.

6 Add code to retrieve the graphics context, clear it, and enable anti-aliasing.

7 Add code to create a color space object, selecting RGB color in device space.

8 Add code to define a gradient with three locations and three sets of RGB color components.

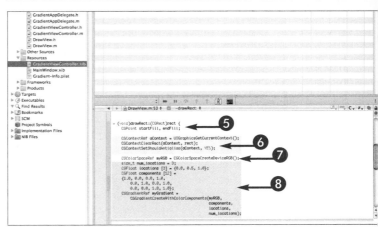

9 Add code to save the graphics state.

Note: *This saves the current clipping path, which is null.*

10 Add code to create a rectangular clipping path.

11 Add code to draw the gradient.

12 Add code to restore the graphics state and draw a separate radial fill with two circular points.

Note: *Restoring the graphics state restores the null clipping path and guarantees that the radial fill is not clipped.*

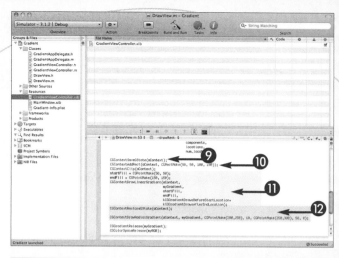

13 Add code to release the gradient and color space objects.

14 Click Build and Run to build and run the application.

● The application draws a rectangular clipping area filled with a gradient as well as a separate radial gradient between two circles.

Extra

There is no built-in function for filling or stroking a path with a gradient. When you apply a gradient, it fills its rectangular or radial area. It may extend beyond that area to fill the entire context.

To limit a gradient to a path area, set the path to clip the context. For example:

```
//<Create a path here>
CGContextClip(aContext);
CGContextDrawLinearGradient(aContext, aGradient, startPoint, EndPoint, 0);
```

Stroking a path with a gradient is far more complex. A relatively manageable but limited solution is to clip the path area, fill it with the gradient, and then fill a slightly smaller area with the background color. Use an affine transform to shrink the path before the final fill. You will need to translate the scale center point to the geometric center of the path, calculated from `CGPathGetBoundingBox`.

If the background contains complex graphics, you can draw the gradient path to a separate bitmap context and then use a blending mode to superimpose it on the background.

Add a Bitmap Image

You can load a bitmapped image directly into a context. Images can be loaded from disk or they can be painted as paths. The context does not have to be visible — you can load images and paint to a spare context that you keep off-screen. You can then paint the image data to the context or blend it with data in the current context.

If your project requires one or more static images, it is easier and quicker to use `UIImageView` image objects, as described in Chapter 4. Loading an image into a context is more complex than loading a `UIImageView`. The data is loaded from a file as binary, interpreted to create an image object, and then drawn into the context. This is slower and less efficient than loading an image into a view, but it gives you more control over color rendering

and blending options, transforms, and data management. To load image data from a file, pass a file path to `CGDataProviderRef`, which is a reference to a data provider object. A *data provider* reads data of a specified type from a specified file path. The type is included for type checking. Data is not interpreted by the provider.

Use `CGImageCreateWithPNGDataProvider` to interpret the data as a PNG file and `CGImageCreateWithJPGDataProvider` to interpret it as a JPEG. To interpret data as a raw bitmap in a color space, use `CGImageCreate`.

The output from all these functions is a `CGImageRef` object, which refers to a `CGImage`. You can pass the `CGImageRef` to a drawing function, such as `CGContextDrawImage`, to draw the image into the context.

Add a Bitmap Image

① Create a new project with the View-based Application template and then save it as Bitmap.

Note: *You can find the Bitmap project on the website for this book: www.wiley.com/go/iphonedevelopmentvb.*

② Right-click on the Classes folder and then add a new custom UIView subclass called DrawView.

③ Double-click BitmapViewController.xib to open it in Interface Builder and then click the view object.

④ Assign the DrawView class to the view by using the drop-down menu in the Class Identity pane and then save the file.

⑤ Click DrawView.m. Find the `drawRect:` method. Add code to declare a CGImageRef.

⑥ Add code to create a string file path for a file called bitmap.png.

⑦ Right-click on the Resources folder and then add a file called bitmap.png to the project.

Note: *You can use any suitable PNG file with a resolution smaller than 1024 × 1024. Ideally, the file should have a resolution of 480 × 320 pixels, but this is not essential.*

⑧ Add code to create a data provider object, to load it from the file, to interpret the data as a PNG file to create an image, and to release the data provider.

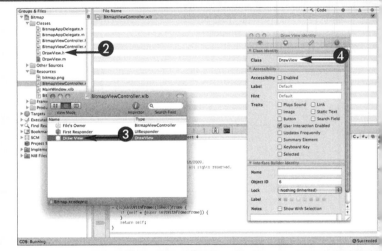

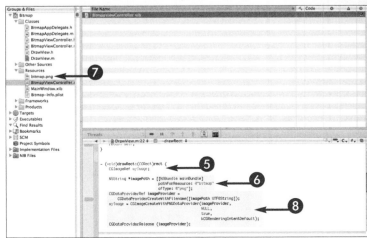

9 Add code to retrieve the current drawing context and clear it.

10 Add code to flip the image vertically.

Note: *The default coordinate system for loaded files uses a bottom-left origin. This CTM transformation adjusts the image so it displays correctly in a top-left origin, view-based context.*

11 Add code to draw the image in the context and release it.

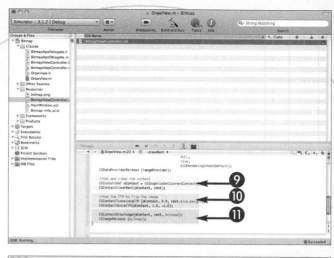

12 Click Build and Run to build and run the project.

● The application loads a bitmap from a file and then draws it in the context.

Note: *Optionally, you can add extra paths and drawing commands to paint more objects into the context, using the bitmap image as a background.*

Extra

To convert data from a context into an image — for example, to draw it into a different context — create a bitmap context by using the `CGBitMapContextCreate` function. Draw into the bitmap context in the usual way. The bitmap remains invisible, but all the path, stroke, fill, and other context features are active. Call `CGBitMapContext CreateImage` to return a `CGImageRef`. You can then draw the image referenced by the `CGImageRef` into your main context.

You can use `CGImageMaskCreate` with a data provider to load or create a mask — an image that hides or reveals underlying graphics. A mask is applied globally to a context. Typically, lighter areas hide graphics, while darker areas are more transparent. You can create very sophisticated effects with masking, including *chroma-keying* — often used in video to remove a fixed background color and place studio actors on a separate background. Quartz 2D does not support video, but you can use the same technique with still photos.

Create a Drop Shadow

You can add a drop shadow to any path to create the illusion of depth in a context. Drop shadow effects are part of the graphics state. After you initialize a drop shadow, all paths and objects are drawn with a shadow.

You can initialize a shadow and change its settings at any time by calling the `CGContextShadow` function. Typically, you call this function once before you begin creating paths to create a unified look for the context as a whole.

The function takes a size parameter and a blur factor. The size parameter is an instance of `CGSize` and sets a width and height offset for the shadow. For example:

```
shadowOffset = CGSizeMake(10, -10);
```

This creates a drop shadow effect to the bottom right of a path. The y offset is inverted because the drop shadow

function uses a bottom-left origin coordinate system. You can then pass the shadow offset to the shadow function:

```
CGContextShadow (thisContext, shadowOffset,
  blur factor);
```

The blur factor sets the width of the shadow blur. As a very approximate guideline, the total width of the blurred path is equal to the blur parameter. Values of 5 to 15 create a realistic, tight shadow. Larger values create a more diffuse, understated effect.

The default shadow is drawn in black, with 33% alpha. For the shadow to be visible, the background of the context must be light enough to show it clearly. Light gray and white are suitable background colors. Because the `CGContextClearRect` function clears a context to black, you must draw another `rect` filled with a lighter, different color before you add objects with a drop shadow.

Create a Drop Shadow

① Create a new project with the View-based Application template and then save it as Shadow.

Note: *You can find the Shadow project on the website for this book: www.wiley.com/go/iphonedevelopmentvb.*

② Right-click on the Classes folder and then add a new custom UIView subclass called DrawView.

③ Double-click ShadowViewController.xib to open it in Interface Builder and then click the view object.

④ Assign the DrawView class to the view by using the drop-down menu in the Class Identity pane and then save the file.

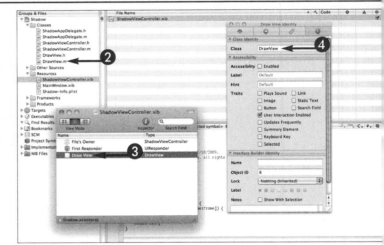

⑤ Find `drawRect:` in DrawView.m and then add a `CGSize` variable to control the shadow offset.

⑥ Add code to retrieve the context and enable anti-aliasing and then create a path the same size as the context.

⑦ Add code to enable the shadow effect.

⑧ Add code to fill the context with white.

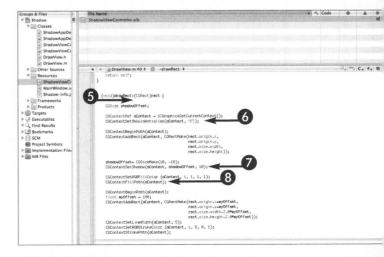

9 Add code to create a centered rectangular path.

10 Add code to stroke the path with red.

11 Add code to create a smaller rectangular path.

12 Add code to change the shadow offset and to stroke the path in green.

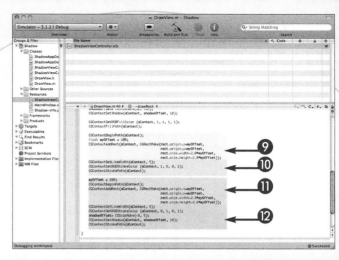

13 Click Build and Run to build and run the application.

● The application paints red and green rectangular paths, each with a different shadow offset.

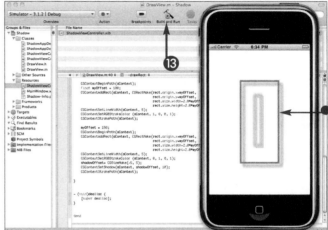

Extra

You can change the drop shadow color by calling `CGSetShadowWithColor`. For example:

```
CGContextSetShadowWithColor (thisContext, shadowOffset, blur, aColor);
```

`aColor` is a `CGColorRef`, defined earlier. Colored drop shadows create a soft and diffuse effect. You can also use a colored drop shadow to mimic a glow. Use yellow or white for the shadow on a dark background. Set the offset to (0,0) and then set a blur factor of 10 to 20.

You can enable and disable shadows in two ways. Because the shadow effect is part of the graphics state, you can disable it by saving the default graphics, drawing one or more shadowed objects, and then restoring the state. Remaining objects are drawn without shadows.

You can also use `CGContextSetShadowWithColor`, passing `NULL` as the shadow color. Shadow effects are somewhat processor-intensive. If your application needs to run efficiently, use the former method. Drawing `NULL` shadows wastes cycles.

Using Patterns

Y ou can use the `CGPatternCreate` function in the CGContext library to create repeating tiled graphics. Patterns are useful for background textures as well as for fill effects and are a global feature of a context, affecting all stroke and fill functions until changed.

The `CGPatternCreate` function provides a wrapper for a custom pattern drawing function that you must write yourself. `CGContextSetFillPattern` calls your drawing function repeatedly, automatically stepping the draw position across the context.

The drawing function is a general-purpose block of Objective-C code. Typically, patterns are assembled from filled and stroked paths, with colors. You can also load and paint images, either from disk or from some other source. For more sophisticated effects, you can create animated patterns by making one or more parameters in the drawing function variable, adding `CGContextSetFillPattern` to `drawRect:` and calling `drawRect:` repeatedly from a timer.

It is good practice to declare pattern size constants for the horizontal and vertical pattern dimensions and then use these constants in your drawing function and in `CGPatternCreate` to scale the pattern.

The drawing function is called via a callback, which you set using a `CGPatternCallbacks` data structure. Create an instance of `CGPatternCallbacks` with a reference to your drawing function and then pass a pointer to the reference when calling `CGPatternCreate`.

You can also apply a global pattern transform in `CGPatternCreate` and — optionally — a different transform within the drawing function. `CGPatternCreate` is an instance of `CGPatternRef`. Potentially, you can initialize more than one pattern and then pass it to `CGContextSetFillPattern` as required.

Using Patterns

① Create a new project with the View-based Application template and then save it as Pattern.

② Right-click on the Classes folder and then add a new custom UIView subclass called DrawView.

③ Double-click PatternViewController.xib to open it in Interface Builder and then click the view object.

④ Assign the DrawView class to the view by using the drop-down menu in the Class Identity pane and then save the file.

⑤ Click DrawView.m and then add horizontal and vertical pattern size constants.

⑥ Add code to create a pattern drawing function and then add code to define the size of the pattern, using the size constants, and to translate the pattern with an affine transform.

Note: *Typically, you must apply a translation to center the pattern in the display.*

⑦ Add code to create a path.

⑧ Add code to fill the path with a color.

Note: *You can use any number of paths and any number of colors in a drawing function.*

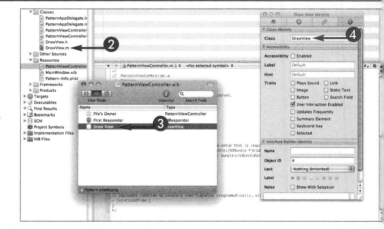

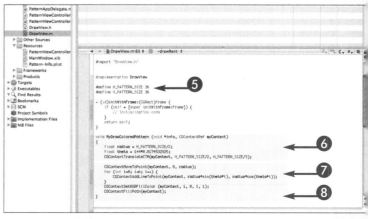

9 Find `drawRect:` and then add code to retrieve and clear the context as well as enable anti-aliasing.

10 Add code to declare pattern variables and constants and then save the graphics state.

Note: The `CGPatternCallbacks` function creates a callback object. You must initialize it with the name of your drawing function.

11 Add code to create a color space for the pattern and then assign it as a fill color for the context.

Note: You must call the `CGColorSpaceRelease` release function to explicitly release color space objects.

12 Add code to create a pattern object, set it as a fill source, paint the context `rect` with it, and restore the graphics state.

Note: This implementation is boilerplate code. You can copy it as is. The significant variables are the pattern size offsets and the name of the drawing function.

13 Click Build and Run to build and run the application.

● The application fills the context with a tiled pattern, created with a drawing function.

Note: You can find the Pattern project on the website for this book: www.wiley.com/go/iphonedevelopmentvb.

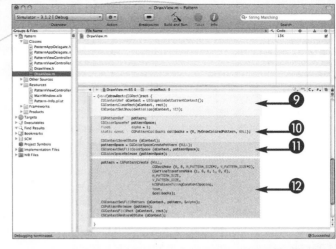

Using Transparency Layers

ransparency layers may not be transparent and are not drawn as layers. Instead, they are arbitrary groups of objects with shared properties. Typically, you can use a transparency layer to draw a drop shadow around the outside perimeter of a group of objects or to set a combined alpha value.

Without the transparency layer feature, drop shadows are added separately for each object. If two objects overlap, the shadow for the second object appears on top of the second object. This limits how objects can be displayed.

When both objects are painted as a transparency layer, their outer edges are combined and the shadow is drawn around them. If one object is inside another object, its drop shadow is not drawn at all.

You can combine any group of paths into a transparency layer by prefixing them:

`CGContextBeginTransparencyLayer(aContext, NULL);`

To mark the end of the layer:

`CGContextEndTransparencyLayer(aContext);`

Paths and objects between these calls are combined into a transparency layer.

Optionally, the `NULL` pointer can specify a `CFDictonary` object, with information about custom retain, release and copy, and equal-test callback methods, used for all objects in the layer. Typically, this feature is not used.

Internally, transparency layers are drawn to a separate context and composited into the original context with a transparent background — thus, the name. For maximum performance, keep the height and width of both contexts as small as possible.

Using Transparency Layers

1 Create a new project with the View-based Application template and then save it as TransparencyLayers.

Note: You can find the TransparencyLayers project on the website for this book: www.wiley.com/go/iphonedevelopmentvb.

2 Right-click on the Classes folder and then add the DrawView subclass. Double-click TransparencyLayersViewController.xib and then link the view object to the DrawView subclass in Interface Builder. Save the file.

3 In the `drawRect:` method in DrawView.m, add code to retrieve and initialize the context, add a drop shadow, and draw two separate-colored rectangles.

4 Click Build and Run to build and run the application.

● The application draws two colored rectangles. Each has a separate drop shadow.

5 Add code to begin a transparency layer before the first rectangle.

6 Add code to end a transparency layer after the second rectangle.

7 Click Build and Run to build and run the application.

● The application draws the two rectangles as a single object, with a single drop shadow around the combined perimeter.

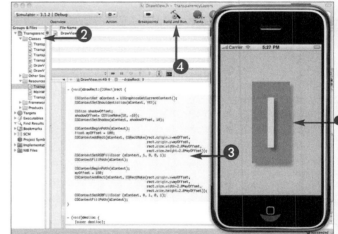

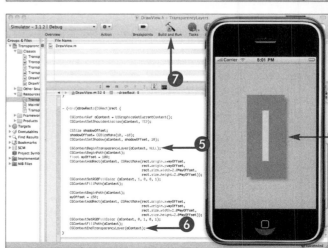

Using CGLayers

CGLayer is a general solution for optimized off-screen drawing and compositing. Typically, you can use CGLayer objects for pattern effects and layer blending.

Using a CGLayer object, you can draw a pattern once by using any of the usual path, stroke, and fill commands, cache it in the CGLayer, and then redraw it on demand. If the pattern is small enough, it is cached by the graphics hardware, dramatically improving efficiency.

You can draw the contents of a CGLayer at any position within a context. Setting a blending mode for the underlying context creates layer blending effects. For more complex effects, you can stack multiple CGLayer objects with different blending modes.

CGLayer objects are easy to work with. Call CGLayer CreateWithContext to create a new layer and CGLayerGetContext to retrieve its context. You can

then draw or paint to the context in the usual way. You can create as many CGLayer objects as your project needs and draw to them independently.

CGLayerCreateContext takes a source context parameter, which passes the current graphics state to the new layer so the CGLayer context inherits the properties of the source context.

To composite the layer into a context, call CGContext DrawLayerAtPoint. This composites the layer into the destination at the specified coordinates. Optionally, you can save and restore the graphics state around this function to add temporary effects, such as drop shadows or opacity control.

CGLayers use the bottom-left origin coordinate system. If you are compositing them with a view-based context, you must apply a transform to flip the coordinates; otherwise, the content is inverted.

Using CGLayers

① Create a new project with the View-based Application template and then save it as CGLayers.

Note: You can find the CGLayers project on the website for this book: www.wiley.com/go/iphonedevelopmentvb.

② Right-click on the Classes folder and then add the DrawView subclass. Double-click CGLayersView Controller.xib and then link the view object to the DrawView subclass in Interface Builder. Save the file.

③ In DrawView.m, define two pattern size constants.

④ In drawRect:, add code to create a CGLayer Ref and CGContextRef for a new layer and then add local constants to set the pattern size and a rotation angle used to draw a star.

⑤ Add code to retrieve and initialize the main context.

⑥ Add code to initialize and retrieve a CGLayer context as well as to fill it with a star shape.

Note: For efficiency, the CGLayer's size rect is the same size as the pattern.

⑦ Add code to step across the main context and draw multiple copies of the pattern.

⑧ Click Build and Run to build and run the application.

● The application draws multiple copies of the CGLayer in the view's context.

Note: The star is inverted because the code does not include a compensating transform to flip the CGLayer.

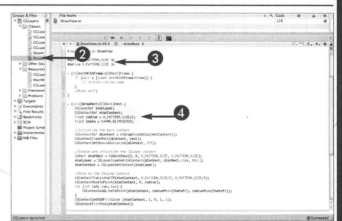

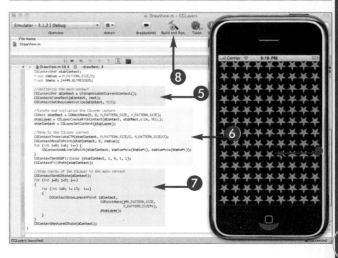

Introducing CALayer Objects

The CALayer class is part of the Core Animation framework. You can use it as a wrapper for graphics created by using the CGContext library to animate the position, rotation, and scaling of the graphics. You can also use it to simplify rotation, scaling, and translation transforms. CALayer is part of the QuartzCore framework. You must add this framework to your project to enable CALayer's features.

Bounds, Positioning, and Layer Geometry

Layers simplify transforms with an *anchor point*. By default, this is the center of the layer. Transforms are applied relative to the anchor point, so scale transforms and rotations do not need a compensating translation. You can change the anchor Point property to create other effects — for example, to rotate a hierarchy of layers around a common origin.

The layer position property defines the relationship between the layer and its super object — a view, a window, or another layer — depending how the layer was created. By default, position is set to the center of the super object so the layer is centered automatically. To move the layer within its super object, change position.

The layer is drawn around its anchorPoint, and changing anchorPoint also moves the layer. If you do not want the layer to move when you modify the anchor point, change position to compensate.

The bounds property is a CGRect and sets the width, height, and context origin of the layer relative to its own coordinates. The context origin is only used when you draw graphics into a layer by using the CGContext library. The size.width and size.height subproperties are set in absolute pixels and stretch and shrink the layer contents. You can use them instead of an affine scale transformation to expand or shrink the layer in either or both dimensions.

Layers, Contexts, and Other Content Sources

You can fill a layer with content in three ways. By default, all UIView object subclasses have an associated layer that holds their content. To access the layer, call the layer method on the object. For example:

```
CALayer *thisLayer = [self.view layer];
```

In a view, this controller returns the layer for the associated view. You can then change the layer properties to move, transform, or otherwise modify the view.

You can assign an image to a layer by setting its contents property:

```
thisLayer.contents = anImage;
```

Here, anImage is a CGImageRef object loaded from a file or copied from a bitmap context.

You can also implement one of the CALayer delegate methods to associate a context with a layer and paint paths and images into it. For example, use drawLayer: inContext:

```
-(void)drawLayer: (CALayer *)aLayer
  inContext:((CGContextRef) aContext)
{
  //Path drawing, filling, and stroking commands
  go here
}
```

Layers support a hierarchy, identical in principle to the view hierarchy introduced in Chapter 3. Each layer can have one or more sublayers held in an indexed array. All layers have a superlayer — except for the root layer, which is at the root of the tree. To add a sublayer, use the `addSublayer:` method. You can also insert a sublayer at an arbitrary index or above or below another specified sublayer by using the `insertSublayer:` method.

Use `removeFromSuperlayer` to remove a layer and `replaceSublayer: with:` to replace a layer with another. Applying a transform to a layer also transforms its sublayers. Moving a layer or changing its bounds also modifies the sublayers. Layers use local coordinates internally — for example, when drawing to a context associated with a layer. A layer's `position` property is set relative to its superlayer.

The default root layer of a `UIView` object uses the standard top-left origin coordinate system. Layers generated programmatically use a bottom-left origin.

You cannot add layers to a project in Interface Builder. However, you can create a UIView tree to access its layer objects to animate them.

Constraints, Clipping, and Gravity

You can center layers relative to their superlayer by adding a constraint: Create a constraint layout manager and then add one or more constraint attributes. For example:

```
thisLayer.layoutManager =
  [CAConstraintLayoutManager layoutManager];

[thisLayer addConstraint: [CAConstraint
  constraintWithAttribute: kCAConstraintMidX
  relativeTo: @"superlayer" attribute:
  kCAConstraintMidX];
```

This centers a layer horizontally relative to its sublayer. You can also set `MinX||Y` and `MaxX||Y` constraints to define minimum and maximum offsets from the surrounding superlayer.

To clip sublayers to the bounds of a superlayer, set its `masksToBounds` property to YES.

You can use *gravity* to control the positioning and scaling of content in a layer. By default, content is centered and is stretched or compressed to match the layer bounds. To change this, set the `contentsGravity` property by using one or more `kCAGravity` constants. `kCAGravityResizeAspect` maintains the content aspect ratio. `kCAGravityTop` moves the content to the top center of the bounds. For a full list, see the CALayer Class Reference documentation.

Layer Transforms

You can apply both 2-D and 3-D transforms to a layer. To create a 3-D transform, use the `CATransform3DMake AffineTransform` function in the Core Animation framework. The library includes functions for creating 3-D translation, scaling, and rotation transforms. You do not have to specify the transform matrix directly. You can assign the transform to a layer by setting its transform property:

```
thisLayer.transform = a3DTransform; //Uses the
  CATransform3D data structure
```

The CGContext library's 2-D transform functions use an incompatible data structure. To assign a 2-D transform, use the `setAffineTransform` convenience method to convert it to 3-D:

```
[thisLayer setAffineTransform: a2DTransform];
  //Uses the CGAffineTransform data structure
```

You can also set rotation, scaling, and translation indirectly by using `setValue: forKeyPath::`

```
[thisLayer setValue:[NSNumber numberWithInt:
  anAngle] forKeyPath: @"transform.rotation.x"];
```

You cannot set these fields directly. For example:

```
thisLayer.scale.z = aScaleFactor;
```

This generates a compiler error.

Fill and Animate a CALayer

Because every view has an associated layer, you can use the View-based Application template to create a simple layer animation. To animate a layer, change any of its animatable properties. You can do this by driving the animation with a timer or by handing over the animation to the Core Animation framework. A timer is ideal for simple effects. For complex animations, use Core Animation. It offers more sophisticated control of curves, timing, and trigger event management.

This example creates a simple two-stage animation driven by a timer. In the first stage, the layer bounds are initialized to zero and animated until the image fills the screen. In the second stage, an animated 3-D transform is applied and spins the layer in three dimensions. Layer

content is supplied from a file bundled with the application, which is read through a data provider object.

This example does not access a context, so it does not need a subclass of UIView. Instead, layer control code is added to the view controller. The code retrieves the layer for the default view object and assigns the loaded image to its contents property. It initializes a timer and triggers an animation method that applies the bounds scaling and rotation transform. The bounds setting and the transform are both layer properties and are updated with a simple assignment. A counter variable is incremented on each timer tick and controls the animation.

Layers are part of the Quartz Core framework. You must add this framework to any project that uses layers.

Fill and Animate a CALayer

1 Create a new project with the View-based Application template and then save it as Layers.

Note: *You can find the Layers project on the website for this book: www.wiley.com/go/iphonedevelopmentvb.*

2 Right-click on the Resources folder and then choose Add→Existing Files to import a PNG file into the project, copying it if necessary.

Note: *You can use any file with dimensions smaller than 1024 × 1024 pixels.*

3 Right-click on the Frameworks folder and then choose Add→Existing Frameworks from the pop-up menu.

4 Find the QuartzCore framework in the list and then click Add at the bottom right of the window to add it to the project.

5 In LayersViewController.h, import the headers for the QuartzCore framework and then save the file.

6 In LayersViewController.m, add four float variables to control the animation.

7 Add a CGRect variable.

8 Add a CALayer variable.

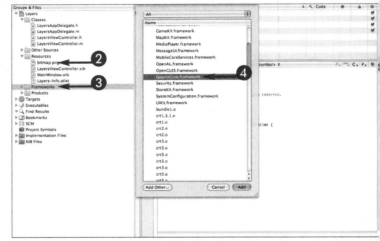

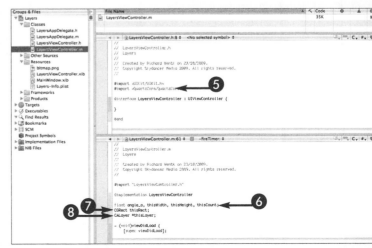

9 Uncomment `viewDidLoad` and then add code to create a data provider and use it to load the test image from disk into a `CGImageRef` object.

10 Add code to retrieve the view's layer object and set the image as the layer contents.

11 Add code to set the layer bounds to zero, to hide the image, and to prepare the initial animation phase.

12 Add code to create a timer that triggers a method called `fireTimer:`.

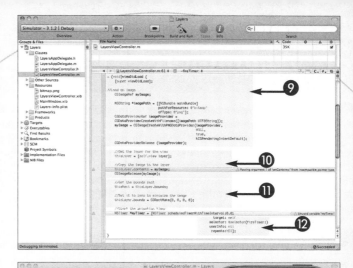

13 Add the `fireTimer:` method.

14 Add code to implement the first stage of the animation, increasing the bounds rectangle to zoom the image out from the center of the display.

15 Add code to implement the second stage of the animation, applying a 3-D rotation, animated with a changing angle.

16 Click Build and Run to build and run the application.

● The application loads an image from disk, zooms it out from the center of the display, and spins it in 3-D space.

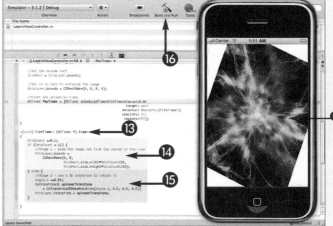

Working with
Core Animation

You can use Core Animation to create sophisticated, semiautomated animation effects. Core Animation includes an abstracted collection of objects and methods designed to simplify animation. You can use it to assemble animation effects that run automatically. For example, when a property is changed, an animation runs, and the property changes smoothly. You can also chain and group animations so they run simultaneously or one animation triggers another. You do not need to use a timer, calculate keyframes, or interpolate property states.

Animation objects are attached to layers in a *render tree* — a hierarchy of animation objects. To run an animation, call the addAnimation: forKey: method on a layer. Typically, you define an animation object's properties in full and then add it to a layer to run it.

Animation Types

The top-level animation class is CAAnimation, which creates animation objects and defines common properties, including a delegate, ...DidStart and ...DidStop delegate methods, and a removedOnCompletion property, which defines whether the animation is released automatically from the render tree when it completes. The CAProperty subclass adds cumulative and additive properties. For advanced animations, you can use it to apply an optional transform, calculated by using a separate function.

Typically, you do not use these classes directly but work with two specialized subclasses. CABasicAnimation is an animation object that interpolates between start and end values over a duration by using a defined timing function. To select the value, use animationWithKeyPath:. For example:

```
anAnimation = [CABasicAnimation
  animationWithKeyPath: @"aProperty"];
```

aProperty is any CALayer animatable property — for example, anchorPoint, bounds, or transform. For a full list of animatable properties, search for "animatable properties" in the documentation.

CAKeyFrameAnimation supports *keyframes* — discrete timing steps with associated property values. The keyTimes array sets the duration of each keyframe segment. Use CAKeyFrameAnimation to animate movement or other properties along a path object, passed via a CGPathRef. You can make moving objects rotate automatically to the path tangent by passing a rotation mode constant to the animation object's rotationMode property. You can also set a calculationMode property to control interpolation between keyframes. For example, kCAAnimationLinear calculates simple linear interpolation, kCAAnimationPaced calculates a smoothed interpolation, and kCAAnimation Discrete disables interpolation and creates step changes.

You can also use the CATransition class to create transition effects between layers. For more on transitions, see Chapter 5. In Mac OS X, you can use this class to create custom transitions by using the Core Filter framework. Unfortunately, filters are not supported on the iPhone. However, you can use this class to create layer switching effects within a view.

Implicit and Explicit Animation

According to the Core Animation documentation, animations are enabled by default. Changing a layer's properties should be equivalent to creating a basic animation between the old and new value, with a duration of 0.25 second.

Unfortunately, the documentation is incorrect. You can create implicit animations on a layer by referencing its UIView:

```
[UIView beginAnimations: nil context: nil];
self.view.layer.aLayerProperty = aNewValue;
[UIView commitAnimations];
```

However, layer-level implicit animation code that works correctly in Mac OS X does not work on the iPhone. For reliable results, define all animations explicitly.

Animation Values

Animation values cover a range of data types. To set a value for an animation, pass the parameter as an NSValue:

```
anAnimation.propertyValue =
  [NSValue valueWithAType: aValue];
```

aType supports the full range of Objective-C types and also includes convenience methods for returning

CGPoint, CGRect, CGSize, CGAffineTransform, and CATransform3D. For example, to animate a bounds rectangle between two rects:

```
anAnimation.fromValue =
  [NSValue valueWithCGRect: aStartRect];
anAnimation.toValue =
  [NSValue valueWithCGRect: anEndRect];
```

Layer Actions and Delegate Methods

Layer actions are methods triggered by a layer event: a change in a property, a change in the layer tree, or an explicit method call. For example, you can trigger a layer action by adding, removing, hiding, or showing a layer in the layer tree.

Typically, you can use layer actions to create a library of implicit animations. For example, you can trigger an animation whenever a layer is resized, to create a smooth change, or to add a bounce effect.

To add layer actions, set a delegate object for the layer and then implement the actionForLayer: forKey: method in the delegate. Because the method can be called by any object, use the placeholder id data type:

```
-(id<CAAction>)actionForLayer: (CALayer *)
  aLayer forKey: (NSString *) aKey
{
  //Add code here to trigger an animation
  //or perform any other task, as required
}
```

The <CAAction> statement defines a method that implicitly implements the CAAction protocol. You must return a CAAction object, or NULL, from the method — otherwise, the application will crash. A simple example of an application with a layer action method, named actionForLayer, is included on the website for this book: www.wiley.com/go/iphonedevelopmentvb.

Animations offer their own delegate methods. animationDidStart: is called when the animation begins. animationDidEnd: finished: is called when it completes. The finished: flag returns a Boolean value; if YES, the animation completed successfully.

You can use this method to trigger another animation or to create an animation dispatch controller that cycles between a number of different animations.

Duration, Speed, and Playback Mode

CALayer and all CAAnimation objects adopt properties defined in the CAMediaTiming protocol. You can use these properties to repeat animations, set a speed multiplier factor, and define a *fill mode* that sets the final result of the animation. For example, repeatDuration sets a time in seconds. The animation repeats until this

period expires. repeatCount sets a repetition counter. Setting fillMode to kCAFillModeForward fixes the animated object in its final state. Setting autoReverses to YES plays the animation backward when it completes. You can also set an optional beginTime to delay the start of the animation.

Animation Groups

To group animations so they run simultaneously, create an CAAnimationGroup object, passing it an array of basic or keyframe animation objects in its animations property. Individual animation durations are clipped by the duration of the group object. They are not scaled. You cannot set separate delegate methods for each animation, and the removeOnCompletion property is ignored.

Create an Animation with CABasicAnimation

Y ou can use `CABasicAnimation` to create simple animations that interpolate between two values over a specified duration using a fixed timing function. This example re-creates the animation example from earlier in this chapter. Using `CABasicAnimation` calls instead of a timer loop.

For simple animations, this technique requires more code. If your animation uses a single variable and does not need a complex timing function, incrementing the variable inside a timer-triggered method may be a more efficient solution.

However, Core Animation offers many more facilities and is easier to control. Using `CABasicAnimation`, you can set an absolute duration for the animation without having to calculate timing intervals and increments. You can also set precise initial and final values. For a smoother effect, you can use one of the timing function presets, such as `kCAMediaTimingFunctionEaseOut`. This example creates a smoothed bounds animation that starts quickly

and decelerates. When applied to a rotation, it varies the rotation speed.

You can also chain animations, creating a sequential animation dispatcher with the `animationDidStop:` method by using an animation state variable to select an animation. For more complex effects, you can replace the `CABasicAnimation` calls with `CAKeyFrameAnimation` calls, adding an optional timing or position path with keyframed values.

You cannot pre-define animations in a method, such as `viewDidLoad`, and call them inside the `animation DidStop:` method. If you do this, the application crashes because the `animationDidStop:` method is part of the animation object's support code.

In this example, animations are initialized and then called immediately by using the `addAnimation:` method. This adds the animation to the target layer's render tree and runs it immediately.

Create an Animation with CABasicAnimation

① Create a new project with the View-based Application template and then save it as Animation.

Note: You can find the Animation project on the website for this book: www.wiley.com/go/iphonedevelopmentvb.

② Right-click on Resources and then choose Add→Existing Files from the pop-up menu to add and copy a bitmap PNG file to the project.

③ Right-click on Frameworks and then choose Add→Existing Frameworks from the pop-up menu to add the QuartzCore framework to the project.

④ In AnimationViewController.h, import the Quartz Core headers and then save the file.

⑤ In AnimationViewController.m, add variables for an animation state variable, two `rects`, three 3-D transforms, a `CALayer`, three `CABasicAnimations`, and π.

⑥ Uncomment `viewDidLoad` and then add code to create a data provider object and load it with the bitmap image.

⑦ Add code to retrieve the view's layer object.

⑧ Add code to assign the bitmap image to the layer's contents.

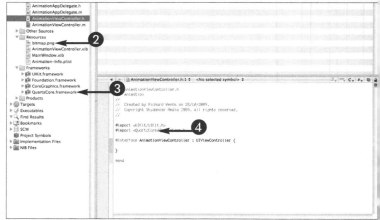

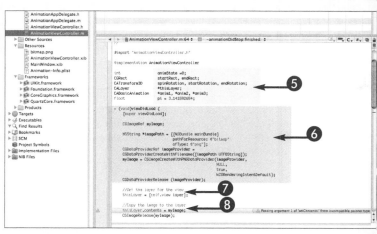

⑨ Add code to create an animation that expands the layer's bounds from the center of the screen until it fills the display, sets the delegate object to `self`, and loads and triggers the animation.

⑩ Add an `animationDidStop:` method with a case statement to select a response depending on `animState`.

⑪ Add code for an animation that creates the first half of a full rotation and updates the `animState` variable.

⑫ Add code for an animation that creates the second half of a full rotation and resets the `animState` variable so it loads and triggers the first rotation again.

⑬ Click Build and Run to build and run the application.

● The application runs three animations in sequence: a bounds zoom and a loop with two sequential half rotations.

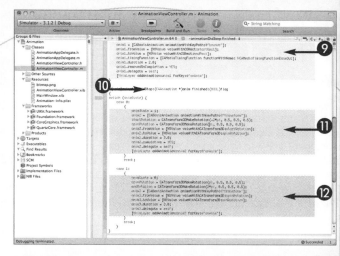

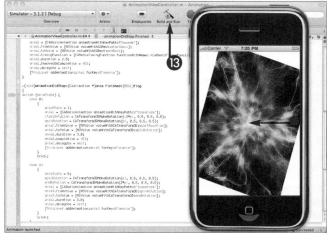

Extra

You cannot animate a 3-D affine transform by interpolating its angle from 0 to 2π. Internally, 0 and 2π are identical, so the animation does nothing. This example works around this problem by interpolating between -2π and π for an initial half-rotation and then interpolating again between π and 2π to complete the rotation. This is counterintuitive mathematically but creates the required result.

3-D rotations are complex. To handle them correctly, you should access the 3-D transform matrix directly and supply it with values calculated by using *quaternions*. Quaternion algebra is widely used in 3-D animation to manage rotations. Details are beyond the scope of this book. For a short introduction, see en.wikipedia.org/wiki/Quaternions_and_spatial_rotation.

Introducing OpenGL ES

OpenGL is an industry-standard graphics framework. OpenGL ES is a subset of OpenGL and is designed for small, mobile devices. You can use OpenGL ES in your applications to create high-performance animations, games, and customized user interface features. OpenGL ES can produce both 2-D and 3-D output and is hardware-accelerated. Many of the iPhone's graphics are created from underlying OpenGL ES calls.

OpenGL ES is somewhat complex and the available documentation is sparse. With OpenGL ES itself, there are no classes or class references, and the data structures and functions are unique to the graphics subsystem. The OpenGL standard is managed by the Khronos Group, an independent organization. For reference materials, visit the Khronos website at www.khronos.org. At the time of writing, the URL for OpenGL ES 1.1 reference pages is www.khronos.org/opengles/sdk/1.1/docs/man. For OpenGL ES 2.0, refer to www.khronos.org/opengles/sdk/docs/man.

OpenGL in Outline

OpenGL uses a set of graphics commands, defined as functions. Graphics commands are passed to a server, which processes the commands and draws output to a buffer. Some functions operate on the client side. The `glEnableClient State` function tells the server to enable one of its features so it can be used to interpret data. For example, `GL_VERTEX_ARRAY` tells the server to be ready to interpret arrays of vertex data, defining points in 3-D space. Similarly, `GL_COLOR_ARRAY` enables color support.

Data created by your application is passed to OpenGL by way of pre-defined pointer variables. You cannot set these pointers directly. To load them, use a pre-defined function. For example, the `glVertexPointer` function loads the server's vertex pointer with an array of vertex data. Similarly, `glColor Pointer` loads the color pointer with an array of color data.

To create output, use `glDrawArrays`. This function takes a pre-defined constant that controls how the vertex data is interpreted. `GL_TRIANGLES` interprets the vertices as independent triangles. `GL_POINTS` interprets them as independent points. `GL_TRIANGLE_STRIP` interprets them as a connected strip of triangles, with shared vertices. For the full list of options, see the reference documentation on the Khronos site.

Triangles and triangles strips are the two most efficient drawing options and should be used where possible. Creating optimized vertex lists is one of the challenges of OpenGL programming. For example, you can draw a cube as six independent squares or as a single triangle strip. The triangle strip solution is far more efficient but harder to generate.

Buffers, Contexts, and Cameras

Output is rendered to a *framebuffer* — an area of memory that can be copied to the display. The rendering process calculates the image by using a virtual camera. You can set a number of matrices to control the distance and aperture of the camera. Use the `glMatrixMode` function to select the matrix to modify; typically, you initialize the `GL_MODELVIEW` matrix to set the camera position and the `GL_PROJECTION` matrix to set the aperture and create perspective effects. You can use `glLoadIdentity` to reset a matrix. You can also use `glViewport` to set viewport geometry.

On the iPhone, OpenGL ES output is integrated into a view by using an `ESRender` class. This includes code to link the output from a framebuffer to a context, making it visible in a view. An instance of this class is pre-defined in the OpenGL ES Application template. The template also includes code that creates a set of buffer objects. A related `EAGLView` class manages animation timing.

OpenGL versus OpenGL ES

Because OpenGL ES is a subset of OpenGL, many familiar OpenGL functions are missing. If you are familiar with OpenGL, you will need to adjust to its less sophisticated feature set. If you are a beginner, you cannot copy and paste code from the many examples of OpenGL available online because it will not work without modifications.

Among the more obvious differences, `glBegin` and `glEnd` are not available. There are no immediate mode functions, such as `glRectf`. To create objects, load their

vertices into an array and then pass the array to one of the pre-defined pointers. There are no polynomial evaluation features. Less obviously, graphics memory is constrained on the iPhone. You cannot build and animate objects of arbitrary complexity.

A detailed list of differences is available on the Khronos website. The current URL is www.khronos.org/registry/gles/specs/1.1/es_cm_spec_1.1.12.pdf.

Open GL ES 1.1 and 2.0

The iPhone 3GS and third-generation iPod touch 16MB and 32MB models use the newer OpenGL ES 2.0 specification. This is a distinct new dialect of OpenGL, with significantly different features and a modified programming model.

OpenGL ES 1.1 is based on the OpenGL 1.5 specification. It assumes that objects and functions are fixed and pre-defined. OpenGL ES 2.0 is based on OpenGL 2.0. It assumes that parts of the graphics engine are programmable.

This is most obvious when working with textures and atmospheric effects, such as fog. OpenGL ES 1.1 includes a `glFog` function to render fog effects. In OpenGL ES 2.0, fog, textures, and other effects are created with *shader objects*, which allow developers to create graphic effects with custom source code. Shader development is beyond the scope of this book. For more, see the OpenGL ES 2.0 specifications at www.khronos.org/opengles/2_X.

Using the OpenGL ES Application Template

Some but not quite all of the essential features of an OpenGL ES application are included in the OpenGL ES Application template. This is a complex template, with some redundancy. By default, it produces graphics output for an iPhone 3GS and iPod touch running OpenGL ES 2.0. If you are developing for earlier iPhone and iPod touch devices, you must modify the template slightly before using it.

The template includes an `EAGLView` class and two rendering classes: `ES1Renderer` and `ES2Renderer`. The first is for original iPhone OpenGL ES 1.1 code. The

second is for OpenGL ES 2.0 code. To develop for OpenGL ES 1.1, open `EAGLView.m` and find the `initWithCoder` method. Comment out the following line:

```
renderer = [ES2Renderer alloc] init];
```

You can then add custom code to the `render` method in ES1Renderer.m.

To develop for OpenGL ES 2.0, leave the line uncommented and then add code to the `render` method in ES2Renderer.m.

OpenGL ES Animation Timing

The OpenGL ES Application template includes an animation timer that repeatedly calls the `render` method. To modify the animation rate, change the `NSTTimeInterval` value for the `NSTimer` object in EAGLView.m. The default is 60 frames per second. You can use OpenGL ES to draw static graphics by disabling the timer and calling the `render` method elsewhere.

A fast update rate creates performance constraints because the render method is called at every timer tick and calculates, loads, renders, and buffers the scene in full. You must optimize your code carefully to avoid dropped frames. However, in practice, you can often drop the frame rate to 30 Hz without obvious effects.

Create an OpenGL ES Animation

Y ou can use the OpenGL ES Application template as a framework for an OpenGL ES application. The template sets up a view, a layer, a context, and an animation timer and then automatically creates suitable buffer objects. To build your animation, add OpenGL ES to the render method in one of the ESRenderer classes. This example uses OpenGL ES 1.1, so you must comment out the ESRenderer2 selection in EAGLView.m to select the ES1Renderer class.

This is a complex example. It creates 50 random rotating triangles, each with a random color fill between the three vertices. OpenGL uses a center-origin coordinate system. Distances are specified in nominal unit values, not in pixels. In this example, the triangle vertices are randomized between –1.0 and +1.0 in all three dimensions.

Color values are specified as bytes, with four bytes for each color value: R, G, B, and alpha. To calculate suitable random values, two auxiliary randomization routines are defined at the start of the code.

A doInit flag is used to fill two arrays with random vertices and color values at the start of the render routine. The initialization is done once. Subsequent render cycles apply a varying glRotatef function to spin the triangles in 3-D space. The array vertices are not modified directly. Instead, the glRotatef function applies the OpenGL ES equivalent of an affine transformation before rendering the graphics. The rotation value is calculated by using a sin function, making the triangles sway slowly around the axes.

An optional glCullFace call removes triangles that are hidden behind other objects. This is not necessary in this example but is included for completeness. In a more complex scene, this function improves efficiency by removing polygons that are not visible from the camera position.

Create an OpenGL ES Animation

① Create a new project by using the OpenGL ES Application template and then save it as OpenGLDemo.

Note: *You can find the OpenGLDemo project on the website for this book: www.wiley.com/go/iphone developmentvb.*

② Click EAGLView.m.

③ Scroll down to find the initWithCoder: method.

④ Comment out the line that selects the ES2Renderer class and then save the file.

Note: *This selects the ES1Renderer class as the renderer.*

⑤ Click ES1Renderer.m and then add a constant to define the number of triangles.

⑥ Add a randomization function that creates a number in the range +1 to -1.

⑦ Add a randomization function that creates a number in the range 0 to 255.

Note: *For clarity, the prototype for these functions is defined above the code and not in the header file.*

⑧ Add code to create a vertex array, a color array, and an initialization flag.

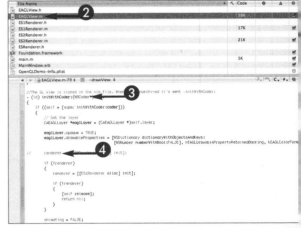

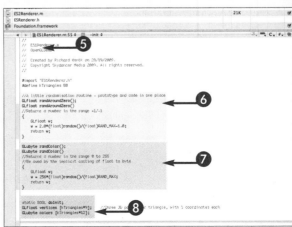

9 Find the `init` method to add code to initialize the `doInit` flag.

10 Find the render method to add four integers for loop control and four floats for rotation and position control.

11 Add a test for the initialization flag and a loop to fill the vertex array with random triangles.

12 Add a loop to fill the color array with random colors and code to clear the initialization flag.

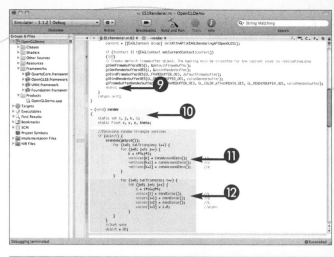

13 Add code to clear the scene and set a black background color.

14 Add code to set up a camera, to rotate the scene view, and to increment the position and rotation variables for the next frame.

15 Add code to assign the generated arrays to the input arrays in OpenGL ES and to draw the scene.

16 Click Build and Run to build and run the application.

● The application generates 50 random triangles and then animates them.

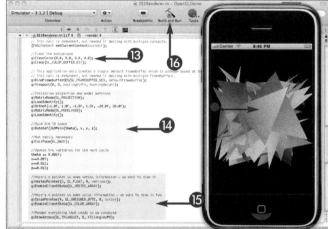

Extra

The OpenGL ES Application template includes code to create and manage a suitable collection of render buffers. The `EAGLView` class creates an instance of a `CAEAGLLayer`. This is a subclass of `CALayer`, with all its properties. You can use Core Animation to animate this layer's position, size, and rotation. Potentially, you can create more than one `CAEAGLayer` and composite multiple animations together — for example, to create multiple animated buttons in a view. However, composited performance can suffer.

`CAEAGLayer` features an optional `EAGLDrawable` protocol with a single `drawableProperties` object. This is an `NSDictionary` with two subproperties. `kEAGLDrawablePropertyColorFormat` defaults to 32-bit color. You can specify 16-bit color with the `kEAGLColorFormatRGB565` constant. This may improve performance for some applications.

`kEAGLDrawablePropertyRetainedBacking` takes a Boolean. When `YES`, the framebuffer is not cleared between frames. You can use this option to draw a single non-animated static frame into the `CAEAGLayer` by using OpenGL ES functions as an alternative to the Core Graphics drawing functions.

Introducing Media Types and Frameworks

You can use the frameworks in the iPhone's Media Layer to add music, video, and photo features to your application. The Media Layer includes the Core Graphics and OpenGL ES frameworks, described in Chapter 8, with added support for audio and video and for the built-in camera.

The Media Layer is a patchwork of classes and code libraries, with independent features and distinct coding interfaces. The older legacy frameworks are complex and difficult to work with. In recent iPhone OS updates, Apple added simplified frameworks for audio and video playback and recording and for access to media files in the iPod library on the iPhone.

You should use these newer frameworks where possible. They offer a minimal but adequate selection of basic media features, with sample code. However, if your application needs to process, generate, or edit audio or video, you should use the legacy frameworks. The simplest way to master these frameworks is to copy code from Apple's samples or from an open-source application, assuming licensing restrictions allow reuse.

Supported File Formats

The iPhone supports .m4v, .mp4, and .mov video file formats for files that implement H.264 Low-Complexity, standard Baseline Profile encoding, or MPEG-4 Simple Profile encoding, with AAC-LC audio up to 160 Kbps and 48 kHz stereo. The maximum bandwidth is 2.5 Mbps, with a maximum frame rate of 30 Hz and frame size of 640 × 480 pixels. For more on supported video specifications, see www.apple.com/ca/iphone/specs.html.

Audio file support includes lossy AAC 16 to 320 Kbps, with optional iTunes DRM, MP3 16 to 320 Kbps and VBR, and lossless WAV, AIFF, and Apple Lossless formats. Non-standard supported audio types include the legacy and speech-oriented µ-Law, A-Law, AMR, and ILBC formats, which offer relatively poor quality but are included for low-bandwidth recording and playback. There is no MIDI file support.

By default, AAC and MP3 files are played through a hardware decoder circuit. This circuit can only process a single audio stream at a time and cannot mix multiple AAC and MP3 streams. To mix compressed files, your application must implement its own software decoding and stream mixing.

Image file support includes PNG, TIFF, JPEG/JPG, GIF, and BMP files. Windows icon ICO, cursor CUR, and bitmap XBM files are also supported. A PDF API is available for viewing PDF files, with some limitations. The preferred format for images is PNG. You can use the `UIScrollView` object to implement scrolling and zooming of large files.

CoreAudio and the Audio Frameworks

CoreAudio is a collection of audio and music frameworks. It includes AVFoundation, which is a new framework that offers streamlined and simplified management of audio files. The new `AVAudioPlayer` and `AVAudioRecorder` classes dramatically simplify audio playback and recording. AVFoundation works with files recorded by the user, included with your application bundle, or streamed by an online service. It cannot play audio from the iPod library on the iPhone.

The remainder of the CoreAudio framework provides low-level audio support for buffer-based audio playback, synthesis, and processing. It includes the AudioToolbox framework for converting, streaming, and queuing audio. Audio processing is managed through the AudioUnit framework, which offers a collection of pre-built audio effects. On the iPhone, the base CoreAudio framework manages file types. The rest of the processing is done in AudioToolbox.

To access the iPod library, use the MediaPlayer framework. This framework was added in OS 3.0 and includes classes for picking media from the library, playing music and video, setting the playback volume, creating playlists and collections, and displaying artwork.

The MPMediaPickerController class is designed to slide in modally on top of an existing view. It displays a modified but familiar view of the iPod application's own item selection lists. Your application can use this class to get a user's selection of media from the Library before playing the files.

There is no way to copy Library items or play them through one or more AU processors. Items are accessed via a unique key, not via a file path or URL.

Effectively, the Library runs as a media server. Item requests are processed by the iPod application, which runs in the background.

Audio and video support are not handled consistently; it is not clear if they will be rationalized in future updates of the OS. The MPMoviePlayerController class can play video files from disk, selected via a URL, but it cannot play video files from the Library. As of iPhone OS 3.1, the MPMediaPickerController used for selecting media from the Library does not list video files. The MPMusicPlayerController is limited in the opposite way. It can play audio from the Library but cannot access audio files on disk that are bundled with your application, downloaded, or recorded by the user. You must use one of the other audio frameworks to play these audio files.

Using the Camera

The iPhone's camera uses a special UIKit class called UIImagePickerController. This class is included in Interface Builder's Library, and you can drag it onto a view in the usual way. It offers a pre-built navigation interface that can display images from the iPhone's camera roll. You can also configure it to load the camera interface and return a photo. On the iPhone 3GS, this class handles video recording. Somewhat unexpectedly, video and photo capture are treated as image selection events and are not managed by a separate camera or photo-capture class.

Navigation within UIImagePickerController is semiautomated. It is designed to be used modally, appearing as a pop-up that slides into view, offers the users a selection of features in a variety of pre-built views, and disappears when dismissed. You cannot build the controller into a framed subview, and you cannot customize its navigation features, change its toolbar, or modify its appearance. However, you can use buttons and other interface objects to invoke it from a separate view. The controller is associated with a UIImagePicker ControllerDelegate protocol. You can use this to customize its operation. For example, when it captures an image successfully, you can implement the didFinish PickingMediaWithInfo: method with code to save an image captured with the camera.

Editing Video

UIImagePickerController includes rudimentary features for topping and tailing a recorded video to remove unwanted content from the beginning and end of a recording. A separate UIVideoEditController class offers video recompression at various quality levels. You can use this class to trim and compress video recordings after they have been recorded with a UIImage PickerController. The editing features available in both classes are minimal. It is likely that future releases of the iPhone OS will offer more sophisticated video editing.

Display a Scrollable Large Image with UIScrollView

You can expand a scrollable view into a larger image with a UIScrollView object. A scroll view automatically creates scrollbars at the sides of the screen. The user can move around the image by dragging the scrollbars or by dragging the image directly. Properties include a deceleration constant and a bounce-effect Boolean. You can set these to control how dynamic and tactile you would like the scrolling feature to be.

The simplest way to use UIScrollView is to create a top-level UIScrollView nib in Interface Builder, add a UIView object in code, and then load it into the UIView with a UIImage.

Although UIScrollView can simplify the design of scrolling views, it has some significant limitations. It

supports an associated UIScrollViewDelegateProtocol. For example, you can add automated support for pinch and stretch events by implementing the viewForZoomingIn ScrollView method in the protocol, with a single line of code that returns the current scroll view. If you do not implement this method, zooming is disabled.

The default zooming feature has limited usefulness. It is linked internally to the UIView object that holds the image data. When the UIView's zoom is set by a zoom action, it cannot be reset to 1.0 to cancel the zoom. The only way to reset a zoom is to remove the UIView and then replace it with another UIView with the same content. It is often simpler to implement zooming manually, applying a CGAffine scaling transform to the underlying view and managing other features of the UIScrollView manually.

Display a Scrollable Large Image with UIScrollView

① In Xcode, create a new project with the View-based Application template and then save it as ScrollView.

② Click ScrollViewViewController.h.

③ Add the UIScrollViewDelegate protocol to the interface.

④ Add an IBOutlet with a named UIScroll View object. Add a UIImageView. Add property declarations for both objects. Add an IBAction method called zoomView. Save the file.

⑤ Find or design a large image file, right-click on the Resources folder, and then choose Add→ Existing Files to add the image file to the project.

⑥ In ScrollViewViewController.m, synthesize the ScrollView and the ImageView objects and then find the viewDidLoad method and uncomment it.

⑦ Add code to initialize the scroll view parameters, including its deceleration, bounce response, delegate, scroll indicator style, and zoom factors.

⑧ Add code to initialize the image view with your chosen image file, set the content size, center the view, and add the scroll view to the view hierarchy.

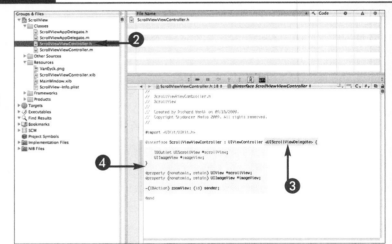

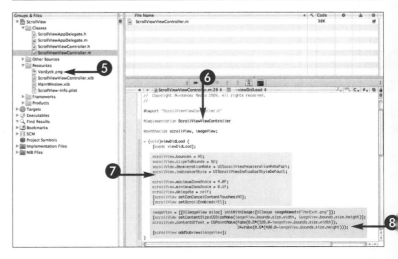

⑨ Create a `zoomView IBAction` method.

⑩ Add code to copy a pointer supplied by the sender from a slider object to a local slider instance and then read the slider value.

⑪ Add code to apply a scale transformation of the image view by using the slider value to set the scale.

⑫ Add code to center the image view in the scroll view and then save the file.

⑬ Double-click ScrollViewViewController.xib to open it in Interface Builder, add a scroll view and a toolbar to the view, and then add a slider to the toolbar.

Note: A bar button item is created automatically when the slider is added.

⑭ Link the `scrollView` outlet to the scroll view object.

⑮ Link the `zoomView IBAction` method to the `Value Changed` output of the slider and then save the file.

⑯ Click Build and Run to build and run the application.

● The application displays the image file in a scrolling window. The slider sets the zoom factor and automatically centers the image on the display.

Note: You can find the ScrollView project on the website for this book: www.wiley.com/go/ iphonedevelopmentvb.

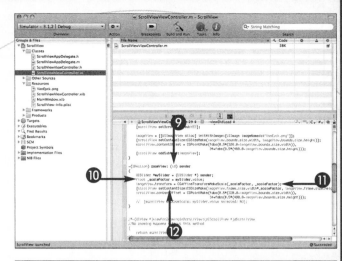

Extra

Although it is possible to access the internal view of a `UIScrollView`, this option is undocumented and cannot be used in apps developed for the App Store. A useful alternative is a custom class called `ZoomScrollView`, created by developer andreyvit. `ZoomScrollView` is open source, and you can use it freely in your own applications. Currently, the source is available on the github code-sharing site at http://github.com/andreyvit/ScrollingMadness.

`UIScrollView` monopolizes touch events and does not pass them to a view controller. To handle touch events, you must subclass `UIScrollView` and then override the touch events with custom implementations, passing them up the responder chain. For example:

```
-(void) touchesBegan touches withEvent: (UIEvent *) event {
  if(!self.dragging) {
    [self.nextResponder touchesBegan: touchesWithEvent: event];
  }
  [super touchesBegan: touches withEvent: event];
}
```

Using UIWebView to Display a PDF

You can use the `UIWebView` class to display images and PDF files as well as conventional web pages. When displaying a PDF, `UIWebView` creates pages automatically based on the pagination in the file. A user can shrink and zoom the content with pinch and stretch movements.

When compared with the features available in a full PDF reader, `UIWebView`'s PDF support is limited. There is no way to scroll to a specific page or to read and save the scroll position. Because of this limitation, there is no way to store the scroll position when your application quits. The webview always shows the first page of the document when it loads. There is also no way to save PDF files from the web to a local document folder. You can email files and links to yourself, but there is no Save As feature.

However, you can use `UIWebView` to display a short PDF, such as a help file with graphics, with your application bundle. PDFs are best viewed in landscape mode, so your application should implement auto-rotation.

For more sophisticated results, you can use the PDF features built into the CoreGraphics framework. With CoreGraphics, you can display a document page by page and also save graphics context as a PDF file. However, this framework is much more difficult to work with than `UIWebView`.

This example loads a very long PDF document into a `UIWebView` to demonstrate how easy it is to use the PDF display features — and also how limited the class is when used to display longer documents.

Use UIWebView to Display a PDF

① In Xcode, create a new project with the View-based Application template and then save it as WebViewPDF.

② Click WebViewPDFViewController.h.

③ Add an `IBOutlet` with a named `UIWebView` object to the interface.

④ Add a corresponding property declaration and then save the file.

⑤ Find or design a PDF file, right-click on the Resources folder, and then choose Add→ Existing Files to add the file to the project.

Note: *This example uses a file from PlanetPDF — www.planetpdf.com — but you can use any convenient PDF file.*

⑥ In WebViewPDFViewController.m, synthesize the `webView` object and then find the `viewDidLoadMethod` and uncomment it.

⑦ Add code to create a load request for the imported PDF file from a local URL specification and to auto-scale the pages to force them to fit into the display and then add code to load the request into the webview.

⑧ Edit the `shouldAutorotateToInterfaceOrientation` method to enable auto-rotation and then save the file.

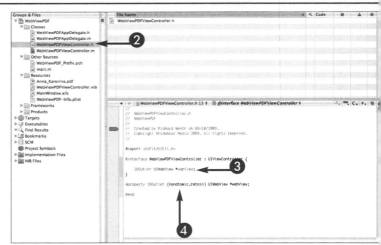

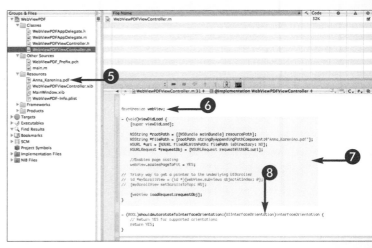

9 Double-click WebViewPDFViewController.xib to open it in Interface Builder.

10 Drag a Web View from the Library and then drop it on the main view.

Note: *You can display the Library by choosing Tools→Library.*

11 Link the Web View to the webView outlet in File's Owner and then save the file.

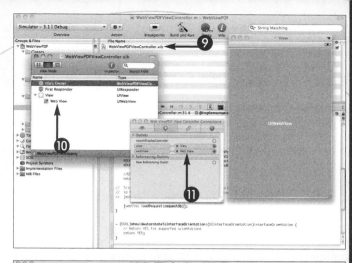

12 Click Build and Run to build and run the application.

● The PDF loads immediately and is displayed with page breaks. The user can scroll up and down the document and use pinch and stretch actions to change the magnification.

Note: *You can find the WebViewPDF project on the website for this book: www.wiley.com/go/ iphonedevelopmentvb.*

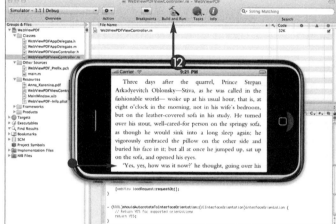

Extra

The scrollbars created by `UIWebView` suggest that it is built on top of an underlying scroll view. In fact, it includes an instance of a different but related class called `UIScroller`. `UIScroller` is an undocumented class, and you cannot change any of its properties in applications intended for the App Store. This is an unhelpful limitation because, by default, `UIWebView` implements features that you might prefer to disable — such as the `ScrollsToTop` option, which automatically scrolls content to the top of the file when the user taps the status bar.

You can access `UIScroller` unofficially in apps not intended for the App Store by using Objective-C's loose object binding to return a general-purpose pointer in an `id` object:

```
id myScroller = (id *) [webView.subviews objectAtIndex: 0];
```

This returns a pointer to the `UIScroller` object in `myScroller`. You can then disable `ScrollsToTop`:

```
[myScroller setScrollsToTop: NO];
```

Because this is an undocumented system feature, you cannot use this code for applications built for the App Store.

Browse the Camera Image Library

Y ou can use the UIImagePickerController class to select one or more items from the iPhone's and iPod's image library. To use the picker, create an instance, prepare its settings, and display it with presentModalViewController: Animated:.

The picker calls two delegate methods on exit — one for cancel events and one for selection events. To ensure the built-in navigation features work, add UIImagePicker ControllerDelegate and UINavigationController Delegate to your view controller's interface.

You can use UIImagePickerController to view the entire photo library or to select items from the camera roll and to take photos. To select a source, set the sourceType property by using one of the UIImagePickerController SourceType constants listed in the UIImagedPicker ControllerSourceType Class Reference documentation —

for example, UIImagePickerControllerSourceType SavedPhotosAlbum. Because not all iPhone and iPod models include a camera, you must use the isSource TypeAvailable method to check if a data source exists.

Use the imagePickerController: didFinishPicking MediaWithInfo: method to read information about a selected image. Information is returned in an NSDictionary collection, which includes both image data and supporting information, including the media type and URL. Metadata is not available. You can access the image data:

```
someImageView.image = [info objectForKey:
  UIImagePickerControllerOriginalImage];
```

To read the supporting data, change the key to one of the constants listed in the UIImagePickerControllerDelegate Protocol Reference. You must dismiss the picker when you have collected the information:

```
[myPicker dismissModalViewControllerAnimated:
  YES];
```

Browse the Camera Image Library

① In Xcode, create a new project with the View-based Application template and then save it as FilmRollBrowser.

② Click FilmRollBrowserViewController.h.

③ Add the UIImagePickerController Delegate and UINavigation ControllerDelegate protocols.

④ Add an IBOutlet with a named UIImage View object. Add a corresponding property declaration. Add an IBAction method called showFilmRoll. Save the file.

⑤ Click FilmRollBrowserViewController.m. Synthesize the image view. Optionally, uncomment viewDidLoad and add code to load the view with a default image.

⑥ Add code to implement showFilmRoll to test if a camera library is available and then create and initialize a UIImage PickerController object if it is.

⑦ Add code to display an alert if no camera or image library is available.

⑧ Add code to implement the didFinishPickingMediaWithInfo: method, to load the selected image into the background, and to dismiss the picker and then save the file.

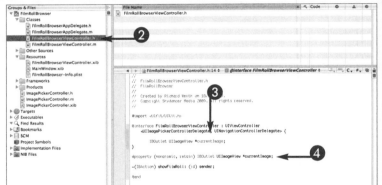

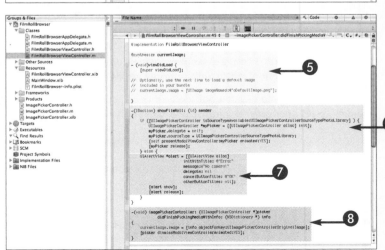

9 Double-click FilmRollBrowserViewController.xib to open it for editing in Interface Builder.

10 Add an Image View, a Toolbar, a Bar Button Item, and optionally two Flexible Space objects to the view by dragging them from the Library.

11 Resize the image view so it is not covered by the toolbar.

12 Create links from the image view in the interface to the image view outlet in File's Owner and from the toolbar button's sent action to the showFilm Roll: method, also in File's Owner, and then save the file.

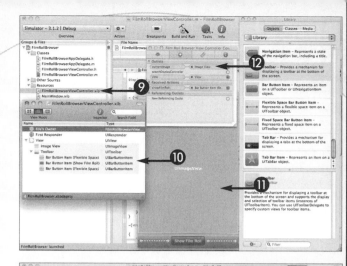

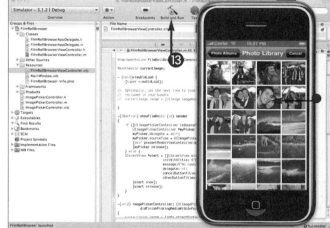

13 Click Build and Run to build and run the application.

● The application displays the image picker when the toolbar button is tapped, with full folder navigation. It updates the background image view when the user selects a photo in the picker.

Note: You can find the FilmRollBrowser project on the website for this book: www.wiley.com/go/iphonedevelopmentvb.

Extra

By default, cancel events dismiss the picker automatically. There is no need to implement imagePicker Controller: didCancel explicitly. However, you can override this method to add features that are triggered when the user cancels — for example, updating the contents of a controlling view or displaying a message. If you implement the didCancel method, you must include code to dismiss the picker controller.

As is usual with delegate methods, you can implement them in the calling class by setting the delegate to self or in a different object by setting the delegate accordingly.

On the Simulator, UIImagePickerController displays a preset collection of folders and photographs. It does not display images from your Mac's iPhoto collection. On a real handset, the UIImagePickerControllerSource TypePhotoLibrary source type displays all the photos and recorded videos on the device, organized into folders. The user can navigate through the folders to make a selection.

Using the Camera

Y ou can use the `UIImagePickerController` class to load the device's camera and to take photos. The camera is considered an image picker and is loaded and dismissed in the usual way apart from two differences. The first is that the source type is set to `UIImagePickerControllerSourceTypeCamera`. This source type tells the picker to load the camera interface instead of the usual photo picker view. The second is that you must extend the `didFinishPickingMediaWithInfo:` delegate method to save the photo. By default, the photo is returned as a `UIImage` object, but it is not saved to disk. You can save it by calling:

```
UIImageWriteToSavedPhotosAlbum ([info
  objectForKey:
  UIImagePickerControllerOriginalImage], self,
  nil, nil);
```

It can take a few seconds for the camera interface to appear, so it is good practice to show an activity indicator.

When used as a camera, `UIImagePickerController` does not seem to be completely reliable. You will get better results by allocating a single instance of the object when your application loads and releasing it when it quits rather than by creating and deleting an instance for every photo.

You can extend the camera feature by implementing extended options. If you load the camera with the `allowsEditing` property set to `YES`, the user can crop the photo with a floating bounding box. You can save the edited image with the `UIImagePickerController` `EditedImage` key. The camera captures images that are much larger than the 320×480 resolution of the display. If you copy an image from the camera or the image library directly to an image view, it will appear cropped and magnified. To compensate for this, you can apply a scaling transform to shrink the image dimensions to match those of the view.

Using the Camera

① In the Finder, make a copy of the FilmRollBrowser folder from the previous example and then rename it TakePhoto.

Note: *Changing the folder name does not change the file names. The files for this project reuse the FilmRollBrowser prefix.*

② In FilmRollBrowserViewController.h, add a new `IBAction` method called `takeAPhoto` and then save the file.

③ In FilmRollBrowserViewController.m, add a Boolean called `savePhoto` to set image browser and camera modes.

④ Find `viewDidLoad` and then add code to allocate a `UIImagePickerController` object.

Note: *This example creates a single instance of* `UIImagePicker` `Controller` *when the application loads, re-initializes it as needed, and then releases it when the application quits.*

⑤ Add code to `showFilmRoll` to set `savePhoto` to NO.

⑥ Add code to initialize the picker.

⑦ Add a new method called `takeAPhoto` and then copy the code from `showFilmRoll` to `takeAPhoto`.

⑧ Change the source type to `UIImagePickerController` `SourceTypeCamera`.

Note: *For clarity, this example uses two different methods with almost identical code for image selection and camera setup. For a production build, these methods would be combined.*

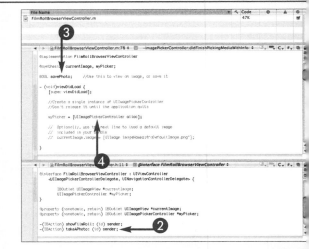

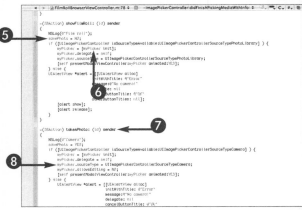

242

⑨ Find the `didFinishPickingMedia WithInfo:` method.

⑩ Add code to create a local copy of the returned image.

⑪ Add code to save the returned image and then save the file.

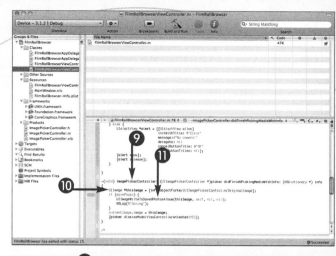

⑫ Double-click FilmRollBrowserViewController.xib to open it in Interface Builder. Add a new button to the toolbar, naming it Take a Photo. Delete one of the flexible space items so the two buttons are justified hard left and right.

⑬ Link the new Take a Photo button to the takeAPhoto method in File's Owner.

⑭ Click Build and Run to build and run the project and then test it by tapping the Take a Photo button.

Note: The camera is not available in the Simulator. You must test the project on a real device.

● The Take a Photo button loads a pre-built camera interface, with a preview as well as Retake and Use buttons. Clicking Use saves photos to the photo library.

Note: You can find the TakePhoto project on the website for this book: www.wiley.com/go/ iphonedevelopmentvb.

Extra

On the iPhone 3GS, you can use the camera to make video recordings. The code is very similar. You must add the kUTTypeMovie to the media types property array in `UIImagePickerController` and then check that the source is available before recording.

To save a video:

```
UISaveVideoAtPathToSavePhotosAlbum ([info objectForKey: UIImagePickerControllerOriginalImage],
    self, nil, nil);
```

For more advanced camera management, you can set the `cameraOverlayView` property to display a custom view and then use the `takePicture` method to trigger image capture. You can also supply a scaling factor to the `cameraViewTransform` property to create a preview zoom effect. This sets a zoom factor for the image capture preview but does not affect the camera.

Record and Play Back Audio

Y ou can use the AVAudioRecorder and AVAudio Player classes to record and play back an audio file. To use AVFoundation, you must add the framework to your project and then import its headers. AVFoundation uses constants defined in CoreAudio, so you must also add CoreAudio and its headers. Add both frameworks by right-clicking on the Frameworks folder in the Groups & Files pane in Xcode, choosing Add→Existing Frameworks from the pop-up menu, and then adding the frameworks from the list that appears.

To initialize a recorder object, create an instance of AVAudioRecorder, create an NSDictionary, load the dictionary with keys that set the audio format and recording quality, and then initialize the recorder with a URL to define a file name. You can then start recording:

```
[myRecorder  recordForDuration:
  (NSTimeInterval) <a duration in seconds>];
```

You can stop the recorder at any time with [myRecorder stop];. This saves the recorded file.

You can play the recorded file with an AVAudioPlayer by initializing it with the URL of the recording and calling:

```
[myPlayer prepareToPlay];
```

```
[myPlayer play];
```

This example creates a simple recorder and player with singleton instances of AVAudioRecorder and AVAudio Player allocated in viewDidLoad and released in dealloc. It saves recordings to the Documents folder, using the current date and time to generate a unique file name.

Record and Play Back Audio

① In Xcode, create a new project by using the View-based Application template and then save it as AudioRecorder.

② Add the CoreAudio and AVFoundation frameworks to the project.

③ Click AudioRecorderViewController.h. Import the headers for CoreAudio and AVFoundation. Add the AVAudioRecorderDelegate and AVAudioPlayerDelegate protocols.

④ Add an IBOutlet for a UILabel, an AVAudioRecorder object, an AVAudio Player object, and a URL object. Add the corresponding properties. Add start, stop, and play IBAction methods. Save the file.

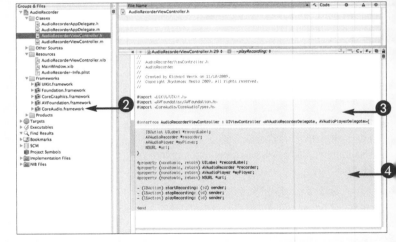

⑤ In AudioRecorderViewController.m, synthesize the properties from the interface. Add two Booleans to control recording and playback status. Add a macro definition for the application's Documents folder.

⑥ Add the startRecording IBAction method and then add code to update the recording button title and initialize a dictionary object with recording settings.

⑦ Add code to create a URL with a file name based on the current time and date.

⑧ Add code to initialize and start recording.

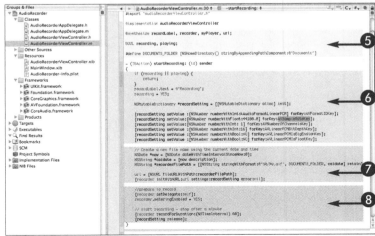

⑨ Add code to implement the `stopRecording` method, updating the Booleans and the label, and then add code to implement the delegate method, called when recording ends successfully.

⑩ Add code to implement the `playRecording` method, loading an `AVAudioPlayer` object with the recorded file. Add code to implement the delegate method, called when playback ends successfully.

⑪ Find and uncomment `viewDidLoad`. Add code to allocate the `AVAudioPlayer` and `AVAudio Recorder` objects. Save the file.

⑫ Double-click AudioRecorderViewController.xib to load it in Interface Builder. Add a label to the default view, add a toolbar, and then add three bar button items and two flexible spaces to the toolbar. Name the buttons Play, Stop, and Record. Optionally, set the label title to Stopped and center it in the view.

⑬ Click File's Owner, and on the Connections tab in the Inspector window, link the label with the label outlet.

⑭ Link the bar button items to their corresponding methods and then save the file.

⑮ Click Build and Run to build and run the project and then test it by tapping/clicking the Play, Record, and Stop buttons.

● The application records audio from the built-in microphone and then replays it.

Note: *This project works in the Simulator and uses the Mac's built-in microphone.*

Note: *You can find the AudioRecorder project on the website for this book: www.wiley.com/go/iphonedevelopmentvb.*

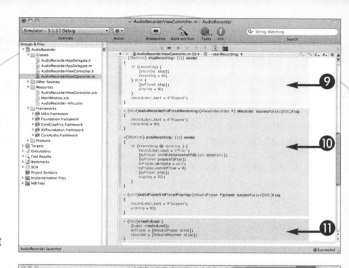

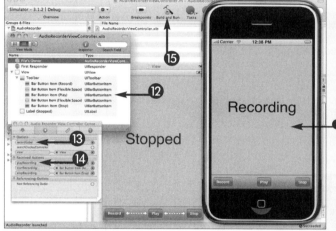

Extra

The iPhone's microphone is very poor, and recording audio at CD quality — 44.1 kHz sampling rate, 16 or 24 bits, two channels, linear PCM — is likely to waste memory. More realistic settings for speech are 22050 kHz, 8 bit, one channel, linear. WAV and AIF files are highly portable formats and can be played and edited by almost any audio software.

To use even less memory, you can record compressed audio to Apple's CAF format. Set the AVFormatIDKey to one of the following:

```
kAudioFormatAppleLossless // Apple Lossless
kAudioFormatiLBC //Compressed iLBC for low quality speech
kAudioFormatIMA4 //IMA4/ADPCM
```

There is no way to record MP3 files directly.

iPodTouch users must connect an external microphone to enable recording. iPhone users can also benefit from the higher quality offered by an external third-party microphone.

Introducing the
MediaPlayer Framework

Y ou can use the MediaPlayer framework to access content from the iPod library and to play videos and music. On the iPhone and iPod touch, the built-in iPod application runs continuously in the background. The MediaPlayer framework provides an interface to the iPod server. It offers music selection and playback via the MPMusicPlayerController class. Video playback is handled by the MPVideoPlayer Controller class, which is — somewhat surprisingly — not compatible with the iPod library.

The iPod Database

To play an item or a list of items, your application runs a query by using the MPMediaQuery class or displays an MPMediaPickerController. Queries use the familiar iTunes composer, genre, compilation, artist, and other fields to select content from the library. You can also use the MPMediaType constants to select media types, including music, audiobooks, and podcasts.

You can create queries under program control — for example, to play random selections or to step through all the work by a single artist or in a single genre. Queries do not display an interface. To allow users to specify query criteria, you must display a custom view with a list of query fields and options. Alternatively, your application can display an MPMedia PickerController — a modal view with a limited version of the iPod content selection interface.

Queries return a *collection,* which is an instance of the MPMedia ItemCollection class and is an array of MPMediaItem items. You can pass a collection directly to an MPMusicPlayer Controller for playback. Items include a unique library index, called a *persistent ID.* You can use this ID as a library access key. There is no direct file access to items in the library and no way to convert a persistent ID to a file path.

Issues and Limitations

Although the iPod application lists video content, video is ignored by the MPMediaPickerController. It is not listed as a media type, and users cannot select it. Unfortunately, video podcasts are not filtered in the same way. If you use the MPMedia PickerController, you should be aware that users can select video podcasts but that neither the MPMusicPlayer Controller nor the MPMoviewPlayerController class can play this selection. It is possible this limitation will be removed in future versions of the iPhone OS.

Using MPMusicPlayerController

You can use MPMusicPlayerController in two ways. Your application can create a link to the iPod player application through the iPodMusicPlayer method. In this mode, it works as a remote control for the main iPod player. When your application quits, the iPod continues playing the last selection.

You can specify a local music player with the applicationMusicPlayer method. This creates an independent player that ignores the state of the main iPod application. When your application quits, playback ends.

To load music into MPMusicPlayerController, you can pass a collection with the setQueueWithItem Collection method. You can also pass a query object directly by using the setQueueWithQuery: method. Both methods create a playback queue, filled with one or more selected items.

To start, stop, and pause playback and to skip forward and backward through items in the queue, use play, stop, pause, skipToNextItem, and SkipToPreviousItem methods. You can add these features to your application by creating a view with buttons that trigger these methods.

Using MPMoviePlayerController

MPMoviePlayerController does not support collections and items, and you cannot use it to play videos in the iPod library. However, you can use it to play video files from disk or from a remote URL. The initWith ContentURL: method initializes the player with video content. The play method plays the content, fading the screen to a background color — the default is black, but you can specify an alternative with the background Color property — and then running the movie. You can show or hide transport controls with the movieControl Mode property. The default option displays a full set of controls when the user touches the screen. However, your application can show a volume control only or hide the controls altogether.

Movies do not load instantly. If a play message is received before the player is ready, it displays a blank screen and a progress indicator. MPMoviePlayerController automatically switches the display orientation to landscape mode. Portrait mode playback is not supported. Your application should support auto-rotation to ensure that when movie playback ends and the movie player disappears, the underlying view is rotated correctly.

Player Notification Events

The music and video player classes both create notification events. There is no associated delegate protocol. For example, the music player posts the MPMusicPlayer ControllerPlaybackStateDidChange Notification when the playback state changes — for example, from play to stop. You can add custom handler methods by adding:

```
[[NSNotificationCenter defaultCenter]
 addObserver: self
 selector: (myMusicPlayerStateChangedCallback:)
 name: MPMusicPlayerControllerPlaybackStateDid
 ChangeNotification
 object: myPlayer];
```

Then, create a -(void) myMusicPlayerState ChangedCallback: (NSNotification *) notification method elsewhere to handle state changes. This code will call the myMusicPlayerState ChangedCallBack: method when the play state changes. You can implement further features in this method — for example, to change the highlighting on a button.

The notification names are constant, described in the documentation for the MPMusicPlayerController and MPVideoPlayerController class documentation. The callback method names are arbitrary.

Property Keys

You can use property keys to access metadata and other information about media items. Use the valueForProperty: method on an item to read the information, passing a key as an NSString. For example, MPMediaItemProperty PersistentID returns the persistent ID, MPMediaItemPropertyAlbumTitle returns a title, and so on. Use MPMedia ItemPropertyArtwork to return a UIImage object with the artwork.

Setting Audio Volume

You can set the playback volume in two ways. The Media Player class includes a collection of three functions that can display or hide a volume control in an alert box. These are functions, not methods. For example, to show the volume alert, call (void) MPVolumeSettingsAlert Show();.

Alternatively, your application can use the MPVolumeView class. This creates a visible object that can be embedded in a view tree. The sizeThatFits: method returns a CGSize for a surrounding view. You can add an MPVolume View to a view in Interface Builder. It is listed in the Classes list in Interface Builder's Library. You must link it to an MPVolumeView instance in code and then initialize it to display a volume slider.

Create a Video Player

Y ou can play a video from disk with the MPMoviePlayerController class. In the current 3.x version of iPhone OS, this class cannot play movies in the iPod library. It can play files downloaded from a URL or bundled with your app.

To use the player, allocate an instance, initialize it with a URL, and then send it a play message. When it begins playing, it automatically sets the display to a background color initialized in the player's properties, rotates the view orientation to landscape, and then runs the movie. Use the movieControlMode property to show or hide the standard player controls.

If the controls are hidden, the movie plays until it ends. The user has no control over playback and cannot end it early. A volume-only mode shows a volume control but no transport buttons. Typically, users prefer to have all

controls available. The scaling option can create a full-screen effect when playing video content originally encoded for cinema or TV playback. Cinema and TV screens do not use the 3:2 aspect ratio of the iPhone display. When scaling is enabled, the content can be stretched or squashed in one or two dimensions to fill the display without gaps.

MPMoviePlayerController uses notification messages instead of a delegate object. Three are available: ContentPreloadDidFinish, PlaybackDidFinish, and ScalingModeDidChange. All use the MPMoviePlayer prefix. You can convert notification messages into custom method calls by loading them into the default NSNotificationCenter object. The notification messages can then trigger a delegate-like method — for example, when the player stops at the end of playback.

Create a Video Player

① In Xcode, create a new project by using the View-based Application template and then save it as VideoPlayer.

② Add the MediaPlayer framework to the project.

③ Click AudioRecorderViewController.h and then import the headers for the MediaPlayer framework.

④ Add an MPMoviePlayerController object to the interface, with a corresponding property declaration. Add an IBAction playMovie method. Save the file.

⑤ Source a short movie in a compatible format. Add it to the project. Click the Copy items check box to copy the file to the project folder.

⑥ In VideoPlayerController.m, synthesize the movie player object and then add code to implement a playMovie method that begins playback.

⑦ Find and uncomment viewDidLoad and then add code to create a URL for the movie from the application folder, initialize the player, and then load the URL in the player.

⑧ Add code to convert the DidFinish notification into a trigger for a callback method that runs when the movie finishes.

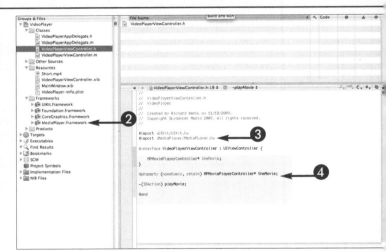

9 Add code to implement the callback method and clear the `DidFinish` notification.

10 Add code to support auto-rotation of the interface and then save the file.

11 Double-click VideoPlayerView Controller.xib to open it in Interface Builder. Add a button to trigger playback and then name it as shown. Optionally, increase the text size and set the auto-sizing properties so that the button supports auto-rotation.

12 Click File's Owner. Add a link from the button's Touch Down message to the playMovie IBAction method. Save the file.

13 Click Build and Run to build and run the project and then test it by tapping/clicking the button.

● The movie plays in landscape mode.

Movie controls appear when the user taps the screen.

Note: In the Simulator, the interface automatically rotates to landscape mode.

Note: You can find the VideoPlayer project on the website for this book: www. wiley.com/go/iphonedevelopmentvb.

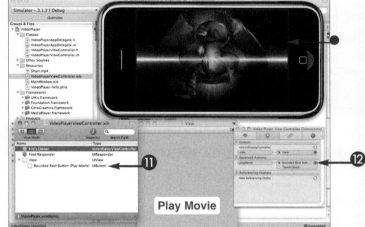

249

Extra

When you play video content in the Simulator, it uses the video codecs installed on your Mac. The iPhone and iPod touch offer a subset of these codecs, and video content that plays successfully on the Simulator may not be supported in hardware. If you are including video with your application, you should preview it on a real handset to ensure that it plays successfully. On an iPhone 3GS and video-equipped iPods, video captured from the camera will always play correctly.

When transcoding video for the iPhone, aim for a maximum stream rate of 1MB/s and a frame size of 480×320. Although the specification allows for a higher data rate and a frame size up to 640×480, the extra bandwidth is wasted on the iPhone's smaller display.

Access the Device's iPod Library

Y ou can use the `MPMediaPickerController` class to give users access to content in the iPod library on their devices. The picker appears as a modal view, with a simplified version of the main iPod content interface. The user can select different iPod content categories in the view and then select content in each category. You can initialize the picker so it returns as soon as a single item is selected or after multiple selections when the user taps the Done button. The picker automatically displays content lists in a table view, with accessory views to manage selections. It grays out items as the user selects them.

Items are returned as an `MPMediaItemCollection`. You can pass the collection directly to an `MPMusicPlayer Controller` for playback. In iPhone OS 3.1.x, the video category is not included in the picker, so there is no way to pick video content. Confusingly, users can still select video podcasts, but the `MPMusicPlayerController` cannot play video items, so it ignores them.

You can set one or more `MPMediaType` flags to pre-select the content displayed by the picker. The available types include `Music`, `Podcast`, `AudioBook`, and `AnyAudio` — defined with a common `MPMediaType` prefix — for example, `MPMediaTypePodcast`.

When the picker returns, it triggers one of two delegate methods — `mediaPicker: didPickMediaItems:` or `mediaPicker: didCancel:`. These methods are not automated, and you must hide and dismiss the picker in your code by implementing both methods and including `[myPicker dismissModalViewControllerAnimated: YES];` in each. Optionally, you can also set a title for the picker view by changing its `prompt` property.

This example uses the picker and the `MPMusicPlayer Controller` class to implement a simple playback application that plays single items or complete collections

Access the Device's iPod Library

① In Xcode, create a new project by using the View-based Application template and then save it as iPodAccess.

Note: *You can find the iPodAccess project on the website for this book: www.wiley.com/go/iphonedevelopmentvb.*

② Add the MediaPlayer framework to the project.

③ Click iPodAccessViewController.h. Import the headers for the MediaPlayer framework. Add the `MPMediaPickerControllerDelegate` protocol to the interface.

④ Add `MPMusicPlayerController` and `MPMediaPickerController` objects to the interface, with corresponding property declarations. Add `IBAction` methods for loading the picker view and for playing, pausing, and stopping the music player. Save the file.

⑤ In iPodAccessController.m, synthesize the objects in the interface.

⑥ Add code to implement an `accessThe Library` method that initializes and loads the content picker view.

⑦ Add code to implement the delegate method that dismisses the picker view and loads the music player with the returned collection.

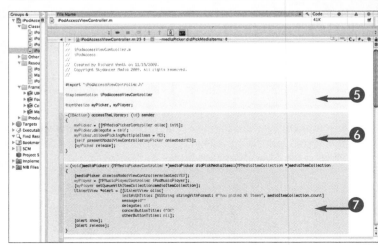

8 Add code to implement a `mediaPicker:...didCancel` method to dismiss the picker when the user cancels a selection.

9 Add methods to implement play, pause, and stop features for the music player and then save the file.

10 Double-click iPodAccessViewController.xib to open it in Interface Builder and then add a button to the view.

11 Add a toolbar. Add play, pause, and stop toolbar button items to the toolbar. Add flexible space items to the toolbar to justify the buttons.

Note: *You can set the play, pause, and stop button graphics by using the Identifier drop-down menu for each button in the Attributes tab in the Inspector window.*

12 Click File's Owner and then link the Rounded Rect Button to the accessTheLibrary method.

13 Link the play, pause, and stop buttons in the toolbar to their corresponding methods and then save the file.

14 Click Build and Run to build and run the application.

● The application loads an iPod content picker when the Rounded Rect Button is tapped. The selected content can be played with the transport buttons.

Note: *The iPod application is not available in the Simulator, and this illustration is a mockup of the result taken from an iPhone. You must test this project on an attached device.*

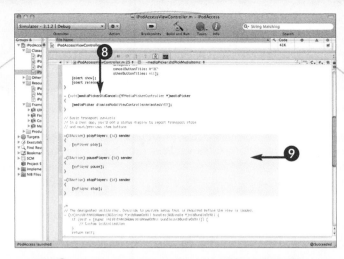

Extra

Instead of using the `MPMediaMediaPickerController` to select a collection, you can load the music player with a query by using the `setQueueWithQuery:` method, passing a preloaded query object. Queries are instances of the `MPMediaQuery` class. The class includes convenience methods for common query types, such as albums, artists, songs, and so on.

For narrower searches, use a *predicate*. A predicate is an instance of the `MPMediaPropertyPredicate` class. You can initialize a predicate with a value to select instances that match a certain search criterion. For example, `predicateWithValue:MPMediaItemArtist forProperty: @"Artist Name"` will return a list of items by an artist with the selected name.

You can use queries to search the iPod library programmatically. You can also use them to create a custom player, controlled by a custom view with simplified or expanded search options.

Schedule Events with Timers and Threads

You can manage repeated events by using a timer or with a subthread. These features are useful for animation loops, for measuring the time between events, for polling application states, and for running background tasks.

You can initialize a timer:

```
[NSTimer scheduledTimerWithTimeInterval:
 <time in seconds, as a float>
target:self
selector: @selector(aTimerMethod)
userInfo: nil
repeats: YES];
```

This triggers the `aTimerMethod` every `TimeInterval`. If `target` is not `self`, you can trigger a method in a different object. `aTimerMethod` must be implemented in the target object or the application will crash. To stop a timer — the documentation refers to this as invalidating the timer — create a named timer object, with initialization as shown previously, and call `[timerObject invalidate];` when it is no longer needed.

Threads offer a more complex collection of features. Threads run independently and asynchronously and are best used for background operations. The iPhone's UIKit framework does not support multi-threading.

You can create a thread by initializing an `NSThread` object with a selector, which will immediately detach and run independently.

Aside from physical memory, there is no limit on the number of different methods a subthread can trigger. You should create different methods for different subthread states — for example, `started`, `running`, and `exit`.

You must create an `NSAutoreleasePool` object at the start of every subthread to manage local memory. Release it just before the thread exits. Use `[NSThread exit];` to stop a subthread.

This example implements a subthread with a simple counter, running callback methods on the main thread to update the display. Examples of practical applications for threading include loading background data from a large file without locking the interface and polling a website to check for updates.

Schedule Events with Timers and Threads

1 In Xcode, create a new project by using the View-based Application template and then save it as Thread.

Note: *You can find the Thread project on the website for this book: www.wiley.com/go/iphonedevelopmentvb.*

2 Click ThreadViewController.h.

3 Add two named `IBOutlets` — one for a label and another for a button.

4 Add property declarations for both outlets. Add a `runThread IBAction` method. Save the file.

5 In ThreadViewController.m, synthesize the label and the button properties.

6 Add a Boolean to manage thread status and then lock the multi-threading to prevent multiple subthreads.

7 Add code for a `runThread IBAction` method that initializes and launches a subthread.

8 Add code for a `backgroundThread` method that implements a simple counter in the subthread, with a separate memory management pool and callbacks to the main thread.

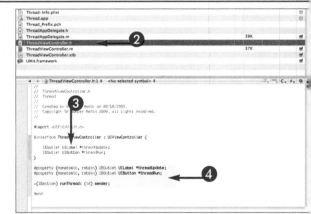

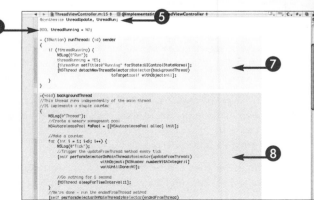

⑨ Add code to implement an update callback and then update the counter label while the thread is running.

⑩ Add code to implement a thread exit callback, to update the counter label and button title when the thread exits, and to reset the Boolean and then save the file.

Note: *You can add as many callbacks from a background thread as necessary. The names and features of the callback methods are arbitrary.*

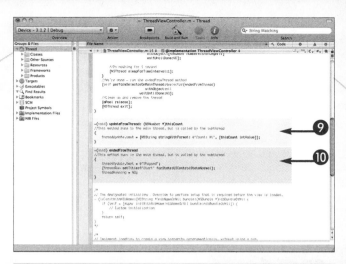

⑪ Double-click ThreadViewController.xib to open it in Interface Builder. Add a button and a label from the Library; label strings for these items will be set dynamically using code added below. Optionally, center and resize them in the view.

⑫ Link the label and button to their corresponding outlets in File's Owner.

⑬ Link the runThread: method in File's Owner to a Touch Down message from the button.

⑭ Click Build and Run to build and run the application and then test it by tapping/clicking the Start button.

● The label is updated from a counter run in a background thread and is automatically reset when the count ends.

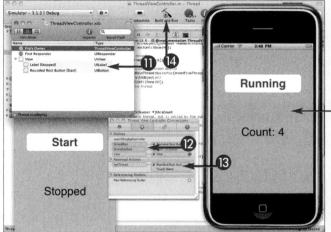

Extra

You can pass information from a subthread back to the main thread with

```
[self performSelectorOnMainThread:(aMethodInTheMainThread) withObject:(anObject)
    waitUntilDone: NO];
```

in the subthread. This immediately triggers `aMethodInTheMainThread`. If `waitUntilDone` is YES, the subthread waits until the method completes. Otherwise, execution continues. You can use this technique to update the interface indirectly by calling update code in the main thread.

When you attempt to pass values between a subthread and a main thread, you must convert them to objects. `NSNumber` objects require extra care. For example, to pass i as an int, use `[NSNumber numberWith Integer:i]` to convert it to an `NSNumber`. In the receiving method, use `[receivedNumber intValue]` to parse the incoming number as an int. Otherwise, the received number will be undefined.

Introducing the Address Book Frameworks

You can use the Address Book frameworks to read, search, and write to the Address Book database behind the Contacts application. The Address Book UI framework includes a small selection of picker objects and view controllers. You can add these to your projects to offer simplified access to the Address Book.

The Address Book framework offers low-level manipulation and processing of Address Book entries. You can use either framework to add and edit contacts and to search fields within Contacts for specific information.

Key Address Book UI Objects

The `ABPeoplePickerNavigationController` is almost identical to the top level of the Address Book. It lists groups and individuals. Users can tap on an individual's name to select it. You can initialize the controller so it returns a pointer to an individual's contact data or drills down automatically to show a page with a more detailed listing of contact information, which is implemented and managed by a different class. A navigation controller is built into this class and manages groups, subgroups, and drill-down, with minimal extra code.

At the next level, `ABPersonViewController` displays a person's contact details. You can set up `ABPeoplePicker NavigationController` to display this class automatically at the bottom of a drill-down or initialize it with data from a low-level search and display it separately.

You can use this class to filter the data — for example, to list only email addresses or phone numbers. When you enable filtering, unselected details are not displayed. This feature forces users to select specific data types.

You can also enable editing so users can modify contact information in your application without having to load the Contacts application.

The `ABNewPersonViewController` displays a blank dialog box. Users can fill in the fields to create a new contact. The controller must be associated with a navigation controller. Done and Cancel buttons are created automatically. When the user taps Done, the controller automatically adds the new details to the Address Book. The Cancel button dismisses the dialog box without saving the data.

`ABUnknownPersonViewController` is a hybrid class that combines some of the features of the person view with the new person view. You can initialize the view with preset data for any or all fields. Setting the `allowsAddingTo AddressBook` property to `YES` displays `Create New Contact` and `Add to Existing Contact` options.

You can use this class in various ways. For example, you can display contact information retrieved from an outside source, such as a Bluetooth transfer, so it can be reviewed, edited, and saved. If the contact information is a subfield, such as a new email address for an existing contact, this class can add it to existing information without opening an editing view.

Standard actions are also available. For example, when a user taps a phone number, your application can quit and pass the number to the iPhone application to initiate a call.

Frameworks and Delegates

To use these classes, you must add both the `Address BookUI` and the `AddressBook` frameworks to your project and import their headers. The frameworks are included in the standard list that appears when you right-click on Frameworks in Xcode and then choose Add→Existing Frameworks.

Many class features are devolved to delegate protocols. You must adopt and implement the delegate methods to add the functionality of these classes to your projects.

The Address Book framework is a low-level programmatic interface to the Address Book database. You can use it to implement custom features, such as searches, updates, summaries, and bulk data transfers.

The Address Book UI classes are not completely self-contained. You must use Address Book features to initialize them and to read, process, and — optionally — write contact data.

The Address Book framework uses Core Foundation objects and data types rather than Cocoa objects. There is some overlap; for example, `CFString` and `NSString` are almost synonymous. However, Core Foundation includes unique data types that have no direct Cocoa equivalents. Many are used in Address Book applications.

Core Foundation implements its own memory management features. Review the details at the Memory Management Programming Guide for Core Foundation in the documentation.

Key Data Types and Functions

`ABAddressBookRef` is a reference to a temporary scratch pad copy of the Address Book database. You must create a copy before you access the data and then either save the copy to confirm the changes or revert to ignore them:

```
addressBook = ABAddressBookCreate();
//Editing code goes here
ABAddressBookSave (addressBook, NULL);
//Or AddressBookRevert(addressBook) to revert
CFRelease(addressBook);
```

Functions are available for adding and removing records, counting records, and creating arrays of people or groups.

`ABRecord` provides an interface to records in the database. Each record has a unique ID. There are three essential `ABRecord` functions: `SetValue` for changing values, `CopyValue`, and `RemoveValue`. A fourth `CopyCompositeItem` function returns a string with a standard summary of the data in the record containing the prefix, suffix, organization, first name, and last name fields. You cannot select different fields. An `ABRecord` is not an individual contact entry; it is more like an access tool for data in the entry.

`ABPerson` is the primary data type and holds a complete set of contact data for an individual. You can create a new person by calling the `ABPersonCreate` function on a record. You can then add further details by using the `ABRecord` functions to set, copy, and remove values and labels. You can set an optional image for each person by using `ABPersonSetImageData`.

`ABGroup` implements grouping. Use `ABGroupAdd Member` to add a person to a group and `ABGroupRemove Member` to remove them. You can copy the members of a group to an array with `ABGroupCopyArrayOfAll Members`, with an optional `WithSortOrdering` suffix to sort the contacts by name.

Address Book Data

Address books hold many kinds of data, with duplicates; for example, some people may have more than one work phone number or email address. The Address Book data format is flexible enough to handle this requirement, at the cost of some complexity.

The primary properties are the Personal Information Properties — a set of constants that defines first name, last name, and other essential fields. These fields are single-valued. You can read and write them directly:

```
NSString *firstName = (NSString *)
  ABRecordCopyValue (aPerson,
  kABPersonFirstNameProperty);
```

Fields that may have duplicates are more complex. Each field has three subproperties — an *identifier*, which is a unique reference; an *index*, which is an array index; and a *label*, which defines the subfield type — for example, mobile or home for a phone number field. To read a subfield, create a temporary *multivalue object* — an object that can hold and reference more than one type of data — and use the identifier and label to select an array index and find the data. For sample code, see the PersonView example later in this chapter.

Using People Pickers

Y ou can use the ABPeoplePickerNavigation Controller class to list contact information in your application and to select individuals and groups. This example demonstrates the simple copying of data from a selected contact to labels in a view.

The people picker controller displays a navigable list of people and groups from the Address Book database. The picker is designed to work modally. To initialize and display a picker, allocate it, set a delegate, and then call presentModalViewController.

To handle returns, implement two delegate methods: peoplePickerNavigationControllerDidCancel: and shouldContinueAfterSelection:.

To process a cancel event, dismiss the modal view, release the picker, and perform any other cleanup that may be needed:

```
[self dismissModalViewControllerAnimated: YES];
```

shouldContinueAfterSelection: returns the selected person record when tapped and optionally allows drill-down to that person's contact details. To enable drill-down, return YES. To prevent drill-down, return NO and then release the picker.

To read a single-valued property:

```
aValue = (CastForType *)ABRecordCopyValue
   (person, kABPropertyConstant);
```

Using People Pickers

1. Create a new View-based Application template in Xcode and then save it as PeoplePicker.

2. Add the Address Book and Address Book UI frameworks to the project.

3. In the PeoplePickerViewController.h, #import the headers for the frameworks.

Note: This header adopts the ABPeoplePicker NavigationControllerDelegateProtocol in the interface.

4. Create four IBOutlet pointers to labels that will display first name, last name, email, and phone contact details. Declare them as properties. Save the file.

5. Click PeoplePickerViewController.m. Synthesize the four labels. Add a pointer to a people picker controller.

6. Add a touchesBegan: method and then add code to allocate, initialize, and display a people picker controller when the user taps the screen.

7. Implement the shouldContinue AfterSelectionon: method. Add code to dismiss the controller and to copy first name, last name, phone, and email information to the labels in the view. Add code to release the controller and to return NO, ending the contact selection process.

8. Implement the DidCancel: method to release and dismiss the controller when the user cancels.

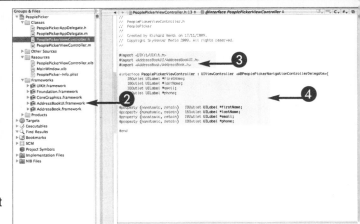

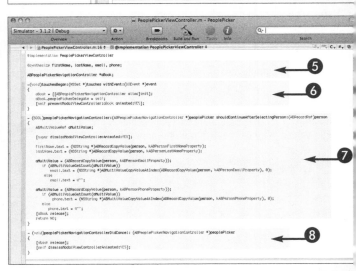

⑨ Double-click PeoplePickerViewController.xib to open it in Interface Builder. Add four labels to the view. Optionally, adjust their positions and attributes to improve the aesthetics of the view.

Note: *In this example, the top label displays a user prompt, and the other labels contain blank text. For simplicity, these startup defaults are set in Interface Builder rather than in code.*

⑩ Link the labels to their corresponding IBOutlets and then save the file.

⑪ Click Build and Run to build and run the application.

⑫ Test the application by tapping the screen.

A modal people picker controller appears.

⑬ Tap a name to select it.

● The application copies selected data from the contact to the labels in the view.

Note: *You can find the PeoplePicker project on the website for this book: www.wiley.com/go/iphonedevelopmentvb.*

Extra

This example assumes that returned multivalue arrays always have valid data in index 0. This is usually true but is not guaranteed. For improved reliability, you should use the alternative `shouldContinueAfterSelectionPerson: property: identifier:` method. This returns a selected property as well as a person. You can convert the unique identifier to an array index before reading the property. For sample code, see the next example.

Address Book projects can be difficult to test. The Simulator includes a small separate contacts list and does not display your Mac's contacts. To access your existing contacts, test projects on a handset. Any changes you make will be permanent and will be synced with your Mac when you next sync the device.

Many different data types are supported in the Address Book framework, and you must test all of them. If your application makes a wrong assumption about data types or multivalue fields, it will crash.

For multivalued properties, which may have more than one entry, you must use `ABMultiValueGetCount()` to test if fields are available before attempting to read them. Users often leave fields blank, so this test is not optional. Then, copy an item from the returned array:

```
aMultiValue = (ABRecordCopyValue(person, kABA
  MultiValueProperty));
if (ABMultiValueGetCount(aMultiValue)
aValue = (CastForType *)ABMultiValueCopyAt
  Index(ABRecordCopyValue (person, kABPropertyConstant), 0);
```

Show Contact Details and Filter Searches

You can use the drill-down feature in `ABPeoplePickerNavigationController` to display contact details. If the `shouldContinueAfterSelection:` method returns YES, the picker displays a person view that lists contact information.

You must implement the `shouldContinueAfterSelectionPerson: property: identifier:` method. This method is triggered when the user taps on a property. You can ignore the tap by returning YES or accept it by returning NO. If you accept it, add extra code to dismiss the picker and release it.

In this example, the returned property is tested to see if it is a mobile phone number. If it is, the picker is dismissed.

If not, the method returns YES, and the dialog box remains visible. You can use this feature to force a user to select a certain type of property.

You can further limit searches by calling `setDisplayedProperties:` on the picker before it appears, passing an array of properties. For a single property:

```
[aPicker setDisplayedProperties: [NSArray
  arrayWithObject: [NSNumber numberWithInt:
  kABPersonAProperty]]];
```

This nested code creates an array with a single integer property. If you add multiple entries to the array, multiple properties are displayed. This example demonstrates how both features together can be used to filter searches.

Show Contact Details and Filter Searches

❶ Copy or re-create the project from the previous example and then put it in a new folder named PersonView.

❷ In PeoplePickerViewController.h, add two `IBAction` methods to display phone numbers for a contact or all details and then save the file.

❸ In PeoplePickerViewController.m, replace the `touchesBegan:` method with a new `showAllDetails` method and then reuse the code in the method without changing it.

❹ Add a new `showPhoneOnly` method. Copy and paste the code from `showAllDetails`. Add new code to set the display properties to show phone numbers.

❺ To enable drill-down, cut the existing code from the `shouldContinueAfterSelectingPerson:` method and then replace it with a single line that returns YES.

❻ Add a new `shouldContinueAfterSelectingPerson: property: identifier:` method and then add code to convert an index for a multivalue variable into an index array.

❼ Paste the code and then move it inside a conditional that checks whether the returned property is a mobile phone number.

❽ Add code to the conditional to leave the picker controller active if the condition fails and then save the file.

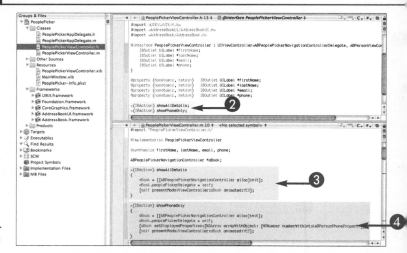

Note: This code dismisses the picker when a user selects a mobile phone number and leaves it in place if he or she selects any other property.

9 Double-click PeoplePickerViewController.xib to open it in Interface Builder.

10 Add two Rounded Rect Buttons to the view. Name and position them as shown. Optionally, remove the text prompt from the top label.

11 Link the Touch Down messages from the buttons to the corresponding IBAction methods.

Note: Because the labels do not contain text, the illustration shows their corner markers to indicate their positions.

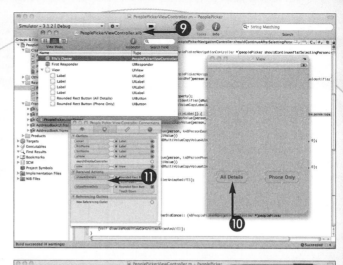

12 Click Build and Run to build and run the application.

13 Test the application by tapping/clicking the Phone Only button and selecting a contact.

● The application displays a person view with a filtered selection of properties. Optionally, it can display the full list if the user taps All Details.

Note: The application does not implement full type support. In All Details mode, selecting a non-string type, such as a date, will crash it. Because of the built-in type filtering, Phone Only mode does not have this limitation.

Note: You can find the PersonView project on the website for this book: www.wiley.com/go/iphonedevelopmentvb.

Add a New Contact

Y ou can use the `ABNewPersonViewController` and `ABUnknownPersonViewController` classes to display views that can add a new contact to the Address Book. To display the controller, create an instance and then set a delegate. Embed the controller inside a navigation controller and then present it modally.

This slides the new person view from the bottom of the screen. A single `didCompleteWithNewPerson:` method implements a return. Use it to dismiss the view and to release the navigation controller. The controller automatically creates a new person record and adds it to the Address Book. You do not need to add code for this.

`ABUnknownPersonViewController` is much more complex. You can initialize this controller with a record

that contains full or partial person data. You can also enable or disable automatic Address Book insertion.

When the controller loads, it displays Create New Contact and Add to Existing Contact options. The same record is used for both options. Create New Contact displays a new person view controller and updates the Address Book automatically. Add to Existing Contact displays a person picker, enables the user to select a contact, and combines the properties in the record with the existing properties.

The `didResolveToPerson:` method is triggered in both cases when a user taps the Done or the Cancel button. If Address Book updates are enabled, the class adds or updates a new contact automatically, so you do not need to add update code to this method. This example demonstrates code for both classes.

Add a New Contact

1 Create a new View-based Application template in Xcode and then save it as NewPerson.

2 Add the Address Book and Address Book UI frameworks to the project.

3 Click NewPersonViewController.h. `#import` the headers for the frameworks. Adopt the `ABUnknownperson ControllerDelegate` and `ABNewPerson ControllerDelegate` protocols in the interface. Create two `IBAction` methods to add a new person and to add an unknown person. Save the file.

4 In NewPersonViewController.m, create local variables for a navigation controller, an unknown person view controller, a new person view controller, and a person record reference.

5 Create an `IBAction` method to initialize and display an unknown person view controller by embedding it in a navigation controller.

6 Add code to implement the `didResolveTo Person:` method for the unknown person view controller, triggering a timer.

7 Implement the timer method to dismiss the unknown person view.

8 Implement the `ShouldPerformDefault ActionForPerson:` method to return `NO`.

9 Implement the `addNewPerson IBAction` method, initializing a new person view controller, and its `didCompleteWithNewPerson:` method so it dismisses, release the view, and then save the file.

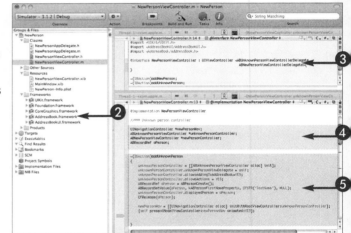

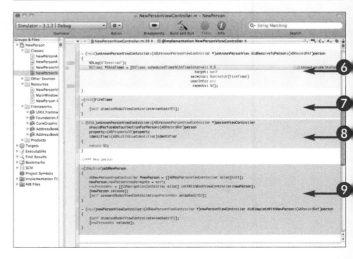

⑩ Double-click NewPersonViewController.xib to open it in Interface Builder, add two Rounded Rect Buttons to the view, and then name them as shown.

⑪ Link the labels to their corresponding IBOutlets and then save the file.

⑫ Click Build and Run to build and run the application. Test the application by tapping/ clicking the Add Unknown Person button.

The unknown person selection menu appears.

⑬ Tap Create New Contact.

A new contact appears, initialized with a test name. Tapping the Add New Person button shows a blank new person view, without initialization.

Note: *You can also experiment with the Add to Existing Contact option.*

Note: *You can find the NewPerson project on the website for this book: www.wiley.com/go/ iphonedevelopmentvb.*

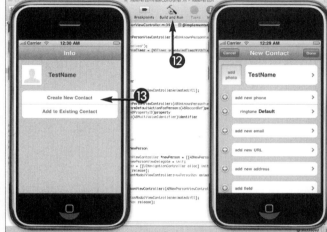

Extra

Although `ABUnknownPersonViewController` should be used modally with an associated navigation controller, dismissing the controller in the usual way does not always clear the view stack and reveal the original calling view, as it should.

In theory, the `dismissModalViewController:` method dismisses all views in a modal stack. In practice, calling the method on `self` after displaying an unknown person view controller can create random crashes and other problems.

This example includes a work-around — a timer fires, and the view is dismissed in a separate method. This eliminates the problem and creates an interesting double-animation effect.

`ABUnknownPersonView` allows *actions* — pre-defined property-based event triggers — for example, to load the email application when the user taps and email field.

To implement actions, add code to the `shouldPerformActionForPerson: property: identifier:` method. You should include this method with a `NO` return if you do not support this feature. Return `YES` for some or all properties to enable default actions — for example, to load the Phone application when the user taps a phone number.

Introducing Networking and Web Services

Although Apple does not encourage networked file access for security reasons, you can use two frameworks to add networking features to your applications.

The Foundation Framework offers three networking options. Direct URL file access is built into data classes such as `NSData`, `NSDictionary`, `NSArray`, and others. The `NSURLConnection` class offers byte-level download management. The OS X `NSDownload` class, which can download files directly to disk, is not available on the iPhone.

At a lower level, `NSNetServices` offers browsing of network domains and services as well as optional stream support for data and file access.

Intermediate and advanced developers can use the CFNetwork Framework, which offers low-level network programming for streaming, HTTP authentication, domain and service discover, and socket management.

Downloading Data from a URL

Cocoa minimizes the distinction between local and remote files. When data has a predictable URL, you can use this feature to initialize data objects with just a few lines of code. For example, to download an image from a web page into a `UIImage` object:

```
NSURL *url = [NSURL URLWithString:
  @"http://www.aurl.com/animage.png"];
UIImage *img = [UIImage imageWithData: [NSData
  dataWithContentsOfURL: url]];
```

To download arbitrary binary files of any type:

```
NSData *someData =
  [NSData dataWithContentsOfURL: url];
```

Save them to disk:

```
[someData writeToFile: path atomically: YES];
```

Here, `path` is a file path in your application's Documents folder. For more on the Documents folder and file paths, see Chapter 7. To use this technique, you must know the URL in advance. However, you can also download an HTML file as binary data and build a character parser around it to search for text or links. Potentially, you can use this approach to search entire websites, subject to bandwidth limitations.

You can also use this technique to download other data into your applications — for example, to add game weapons, new sounds, or new skins. Download arbitrary files as `NSData` and then save them with a suitable extension. For more complex data types, you can save them as an instance of `NSArray`, `NSDictionary`, `NSSet`, or `NSString` during development. You can then download them directly into new instances by using the URL loading methods built into these classes.

Using NSURLConnection

`NSURLConnection` and its associated `NSURL` classes are more challenging to work with. Simple downloads are relatively easy to implement, but authentication and cache management are less straightforward. The `NSURL` classes offer authentication features, explicit support for MIME file types, caching, and cookie management. You can use these features to add more sophisticated web-based support, including asynchronous file support, which does not pause an application while downloading. `NSURL` classes include an optional time-out monitor to report download failures.

To create a download, begin by creating an `NSURLRequest` and passing it an `NSURLConnection::`

```
NSURL *aRequest = [NSURLRequest requestWithURL:
  aURL cachePolicy: aCachePolicy timeoutInterval:
  anInterval];
NSURLConnection *aConnection = [[NSURLConnection
  alloc] initWithRequest: aRequest delegate: self];
```

All classes rely heavily on delegates. For example, to manage data reception, create an empty `NSData *receiveData` object and then implement the `connection:DidReceiveData:` method:

```
-(void)connection: (NSURLConnection *)connection
  didReceiveData: (NSData *)data
{ [receivedData appendData: data]; }
```

For a full list of classes and delegates, see the URL Loading System documentation.

Finding Services with NSNetService

For networked file and data access, use the Bonjour networking system. The NSNetservice API implements Bonjour features in the Foundation network. You can use Bonjour to find domains and services on a network and to pass data to them and from them. You can also *publish* services of your own — for example, to implement a web browser or FTP server or to allow file copying from the iPhone to a networked destination. Services exist in a *domain*. The domain of a local network is always local. — the final period is significant. Otherwise, you can ignore domains unless your application is publishing or accessing services on the Internet.

Use NSNetServiceBrowser to search for services in a domain. You must specify the services to search for — there is no wildcard list-all option. For a list of services, see www.dns-sd.org/servicetypes.html. To make a valid service string, prepend an underscore and append a

transport layer — usually TCP but occasionally UDP — with another underscore. For example, to look for web servers, use _http._tcp:

```
NSNetServiceBrowser *serviceBrowser =
  [[NSNetServiceBrowser alloc] init];
[serviceBrowser setDelegate:self];
[serviceBrowser searchForServicesOfType:
  @"_http._tcp" inDomain:@".local"];
```

The didFindService: moreComing: delegate method is triggered for each service found, returning an instance of NSNetService. If you know a service exists on the network, you can create an instance without searching:

```
aService = [[NSNetService alloc]
  initWithDomain: @"local." type: @"_http._tcp"
  name:serviceName];
```

Using Services

To use a service, you must resolve it to its return IP address and port information. Services attempt to resolve automatically. Two delegate methods netService DidResolveAddress: and netService: didNot Resolve: report success or failure. If a service resolves, you do not need to process it further. Optionally, you can create a mutable array of active services as a reference. If a service does not resolve, report an error to the user.

To send or receive data over a working service, call the getInputStream: ouputStream method on it:

```
NSInputStream *anInputStream;
NSOutputStream *anOutputStream;
[aService getInputStream: &anInputStream
  outputStream: &anOutputStream];
```

If you are using only input or output, set the other pointer to nil. The NSInputStream and NSOutputStream classes implement reading and writing of data. For example:

```
if ([anInputStream hasBytesAvailable])
uint8_t bytesRead = [anInputStream
  read:&aBuffer maxLength: numberOfBytesToRead];
```

The data format of the input and output streams is part of the service specification. It is up to you to implement low-level support for each service.

Other Network Features

The CFNetwork Framework reproduces many of the features of NSURLConnection but implements them with Core Foundation data types. The CFFTP API offers relatively straightforward FTP support. You do not need to search for or create an FTP service. You can create an FTP stream from a URL by calling the CFReadStreamCreateWith FTPURL or CFWriteStreamCreateWithFTPURL functions. The URL includes both the server and the file path. Sample code is available in the CFNetwork programming reference.

HTTP with optional authentication is also built-in but is slightly more challenging to work with.

Some network services require the iPhone's IP address. The [NSHost currentHost] call used to find the current IP address in OS X is implemented in the Simulator but is undocumented, and you cannot use it legally. It may also pause your application. Work-arounds are complex and access very low-level UNIX code. A number of legal solutions and discussions about iPhone IP address management can be found online — for example, by searching for "iPhone IP address."

Download Data from a URL

Many Cocoa Touch objects implement an `initWithContentsOfURL:` method. You can use this to initialize an object with data downloaded from the web.

The code is straightforward: Create a URL object from a string and then pass it to the `initWithContentsOfURL:` method. Optionally, you can download the data as raw binary into an `NSData` object and then pass it to an `initWithData:` method. This creates the same result but may offer extra decoding and copying features that are not otherwise available. It also implements URL downloading for objects that do not support it directly.

You must pay attention to file types and to coding. Different file types implement different decoding features. For example, the `UIImage` type supports TIF, JPEG GIF, PNG, BMP, ICO, CUR, and XBM file types. When you

download image binary into a data object and then pass it to `imageWithData:` for decoding, the file format is handled automatically. An unsupported format may cause a crash. To implement support for unsupported formats, you must write your own decoding code.

Similarly, the `initWithContentsOfURL` method built into `NSString` includes an encoding field, where you specify the encoding format — typically `NSUTF8String Encoding`. You cannot assume this format is correct. Non-Western websites may use a different encoding. Specifying the wrong encoding may cause crashes and other errors. This example implements file downloading for two elements: the source code of a web page and a GIF image. The URLs are hardwired into the code. The image appears in a `UIImageView`. The text is copied to a scrolling `UITextView`. It is not parsed for content or processed.

Download Data from a URL

① Create a new View-based Template application in Xcode and then save it as WebDownload.

Note: You can find the WebDownload project on the website for this book: www.wiley.com/go/iphonedevelopmentvb.

② Click WebDownloadViewController.h.

③ Create `IBOutlet` pointers to a text view and an image view.

④ Declare them as properties and then save the file.

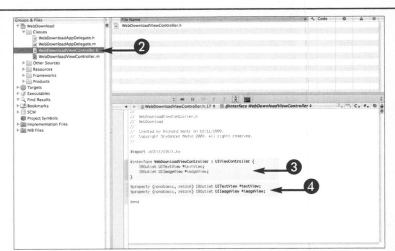

⑤ Click WebDownloadViewController.m.

⑥ Synthesize the text view and image view.

⑦ Find and uncomment `viewDidLoad` and then add code to create a URL, load the contents of the remote file into a string, copy the string to the text view assuming UTF8 encoding, and display the string in the text view.

⑧ Add code to download a GIF image and display it in the image view and then save the file.

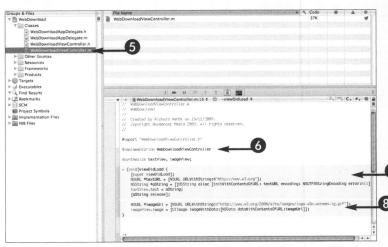

9 Double-click WebDownloadViewController.xib to open it in Interface Builder.

10 Add a UIImageView and a UITextView to the view.

11 Link the text view and image view to their corresponding IBOutlets and then save the file.

12 Click Build and Run to build and run the application.

● The application downloads and displays the source of a web page and a GIF image from the same site.

Note: *Downloads work transparently over Wi-Fi and over the cellular data network. If cellular data speeds are poor, there may be a pause before the data appears.*

Extra

Memory for data downloads is limited. If you attempt to download a large music or video file, expect memory warnings if the size is more than around 10MB. This limit depends on the memory footprint of the application and will be lower for memory-hungry applications. It is good practice to download data into objects that you allocate and release manually, perhaps after writing them to a file. Convenience methods and auto-release calls do not use memory efficiently.

Although some data objects offer an equivalent writeToURL: method, you cannot use this for simple uploads because it treats the URL as a named file. To upload data, you must implement a full solution that uses the CFFTP API or Bonjour services.

Networked data uploads can be useful on a LAN. You can use uploading to bypass the memory and disk limitations of the iPhone, saving entire objects to a temporary offline store. You cannot use this technique as general solution because users may not have access to a LAN and may not have a convenient disk server. But it can be a valid solution for data sharing for your own projects.

Launch Applications with URL Schemes

You can use URL schemes to terminate your application and launch another. On the iPhone, URL schemes are available for Safari, Google Maps, Mail, the Phone application, YouTube, iTunes, and the App Store. Developers can also create and publish custom URL schemes.

URL schemes add features to your application with very little coding effort. For example, you can direct a user to a page on the App Store with a couple of lines of code. You can also use URL schemes to share data between applications. For example, if you run a gaming site, you

can encode user and score information in a web URL and then upload it to your web server, bypassing the more complex data sharing needed with other techniques.

URL scheme calls are one-way only. They terminate your application and do not pause it. To return to your application, a user must restart it manually.

You can improve the user experience by calling on Address Book framework features to find contact data for email and SMS before you hand over execution to the next application.

Using a URL Scheme

URL scheme code is very simple. Use the identifiers on the facing page to select an application and prepare a string URL. Then, call the `openURL:` method on the current application. For example:

```
NSString *urlString = @"http://www.apple.com";
[[UIApplication sharedApplication] openURL:
  [NSURL URLWithString: urlString]];
```

This code terminates your application and loads Safari, showing Apple's home page.

You must pre-process strings with spaces and other characters to replace them with URL-compatible escape strings:

```
NSString *aString = @"A difficult string with
  spaces";
NSString *URLString = [aString
  stringByAddingPercentEscapesUsingEncoding:
  NSUTF8StringEncoding];
```

Each URL scheme offers different features. For example, the `sms:` scheme is very limited. You can select a phone number for the text, but you cannot include body text. The `mailto:` scheme supports body text, cc and bcc fields, and a range of other email features.

Not all devices support all schemes. For example, the iPod touch does not include the SMS application. Many URL schemes are not supported on the Simulator.

Creating a URL Scheme

You can allow other developers to launch your application by creating a custom URL scheme. Choose a unique string to define your scheme — for example, `launchMyApp`.

You can then add a new field to your application's `info.plist`. Click `info.plist` in Xcode and then right-click to add a new URL Types row. Expand Item 0, and set the URL Identifier to a reverse domain name, such as `com.mycompany.launchMyApp`. Add a new URL schemes item to Item 0. Expand its Item 0 in turn, and type in your launch string: **launchMyApp**.

To handle URL launches, add a `handleOpenURL:` method to your application delegate:

```
-(BOOL)application: (UIApplication *)application
  handleOpenURL: (NSURL *) url
{
// Process the URL string
}
```

Return `NO` to indicate an error. This hands control back to the calling application. Your application will not launch. Otherwise, return `YES`.

You must publicize your URL scheme to persuade other developers to adopt it by using your skill and ingenuity, as appropriate. There is no single definitive website or forum that lists all iPhone URL schemes, although http://wiki.akosma.com/IPhone_URL_Schemes is the most comprehensive to date.

Key Apple URL Schemes

SCHEME	APPLICATION	NOTES
http://	Safari	URLs are tested against other schemes automatically and may open other applications.
	YouTube	A YouTube URL
	iTunes	Copy and paste a Phobos server URL; for example: http://phobos.apple/com/webObjects/MZStore.woa/wa/viewAlbum.
	AppStore	Copy and paste an iTunes server URL; for example: http://iTunes.apple/com/webObjects/MZStore.woa/wa/viewSoftware.
maps://	Maps	Supports all the q= query features available on the Google Maps HTML server
tel:	Phone	Strings must not contain spaces or brackets. Dashes and + characters are supported.
sms:	SMS	String can include a phone number, formatted as above. Body text is not supported.
mailto:	Mail	Supports subject, body, cc, address, and other tags, as defined in RFC 2368

Selected Third-Party URL Schemes

New third-party schemes are released regularly. This is not a comprehensive list. For current details, see http://wiki.akosma.com/IPhone_URL_Schemes.

SCHEME	APPLICATION	NOTES
airsharing://	AirSharing	Launch only
appigonotebook://	Appigo Notebook	Launch only
ebay:	eBay	Launch only
fb://	Facebook	Supports various options. See iphonedevtools.com/?p=302.
comgoogleearth://	Google Earth	Launch only
irc//	ChatCo	Supports nicknames and room names
twinkle://	Twinkle	Use message=text&url=http://aUrl to set text and URL.
twit://	Twittelator	Supports a complete API. See www.stone.com/iPhone/Twittelator/Twittelator_API.html.
twitterific://	Twitterific	Use //post?message=%@", message]; to write a tweet.

Application Restart

You can use URL schemes to switch between your own applications. Switching is usually one way, but if you create custom URL schemes for all your applications and pack information about the calling application in the URL, you can switch to a second application and then restart the first application when a task is completed.

Introducing Keychains and Credentials

You can use the iPhone keychain to add security features to your applications — for example, to create usernames and passwords, to implement selective feature unlocking, or support time-limited demos. Data in the keychain is persistent. It remains available even if a user deletes and re-installs an application or restores it. It is also encrypted. The encryption has not yet been cracked.

Because the keychain is secure, it is a good location for sensitive user data and for important application settings. You can use it as a reliable persistent data store for arbitrary short strings and key-value pairs. It is not ideal for bulk data storage.

The Keychain on the iPhone

On Mac OS X, the keychain offers a single access point for secure features across all installed applications. The user can unlock all applications with a single confirmation.

On the iPhone, application sharing is disabled, and every application has a separate keychain. From OS 3.0 onward, limited sharing is possible, but it is difficult to implement and offers relatively limited benefits. If your application requires simple user/password control, credentials — described on the facing page — are a better solution.

The Keychain API

The keychain API is challenging. In outline, the keychain manages *items* — objects that allow access to a service or application — each of which has a collection of *attributes,* which contain security codes, passwords, and other details. The API uses C functions rather than object methods. Use `SecItemAdd` to add an item to the keychain, `SecItemCopy Matching` to find an item, `SecItemUpdate` to modify an item, and `SecItemUpdate` to delete an item.

The functions take a `CFDictionaryRef`, which is identical to and directly interchangeable with a pointer to an `NSDictionary`. The dictionary defines an item as an item class key-value pair, with optional further key-value pairs to define attributes. The class key defines the item type — a generic password, an Internet password, a certificate, or an *identity*, which is a certificate linked to a private key. Each type offers a different fixed library of attributes, such as creation date, access group, and others, defined by

constants. The constants are listed in full in the Keychain Services Reference documentation.

To search for an item using `SecItemCopyMatching`, create a dictionary with a class key-value pair and then add attribute key-value pairs and optional search key-value pairs to further refine the search. The search function can return more than one data type, so you must add another key-value pair to specify this type.

To create a simple user/password access system, you can ignore most of the API. However, you must still pack and unpack multiple dictionaries and handle various data type options. The API is powerful and configurable and can implement a data store for many kinds of secure transactions. However, it is overly complex for simple applications. Building a complete keychain access system is a significant challenge.

Sample Code and Worked Solutions

You can avoid duplicated effort by using sample code and worked solutions. If you need comprehensive keychain access, Apple's sample code includes a `GenericKeychain` application that implements a full solution. There are also code snippets throughout the documentation. Assembling a

working solution is still difficult, but using sample code is less difficult than starting from a blank template.

An open-source worked example is also available. See http://log.scifihifi.com/post/55837387/simple-iphone-keychain-code for details.

Working with Credentials

You can use *credentials* to simplify keychain access. Credentials are a feature of the NSURL classes and implement certificate- and password-based web security but can also be used in an application that does not access the web. The credentials mechanism provides a simple wrapper for keychain access and hides most of the complexity.

A credential is an object that holds security information. You can create credentials with a *trust* — a trust authentication held on a remote server. You can also create a credential with a certificate file. The simplest credential holds a username and password.

Credentials have three levels of *persistence*, which define how long the credential remains available: NSURL CredentialPersistenceSession saves the credential for as long as the application is running. NSURL CredentialPersistencePermanent saves the credential to the keychain. And None does not save the credential at all.

To create a username and password credential:

```
NSURLCredential *aCredential = [NSURLCredential
  credentialWithUser: @"aUserName" password:
  @"aPassword" persistence:
  NSURLCredentialPersistencePermanent];
```

Using Protection Spaces

Creating a credential does not store it in the keychain. To save it permanently, you must add it to a *protection space*. A protection space is designed to hold web server information. To create a protection space, allocate it and then use the initWithHost: method. You must use the method as a hostname, a port number, a protocol, an optional *realm*, which can be a web URL, and an *authentication method* constant, which defines a standard web security mode. Examples include server trust and HTTP basic; a full list with more detailed descriptions is available in the documentation.

To create a protection space for internal application use, leave most of the fields blank:

```
NSURLProtectionSpace *aPspace = [[NSURL
  ProtectionSpace alloc] initWithHost:
  @"anyHostName" port: 0 protocol: @"http"
  realm: nil authenticationMethod: nil];
```

To access the same protection space again, you must use identical property settings. You can, of course, fill in the fields with useful web-based information to create a protection space for web use.

The Credential Store

To save your credential, you must add it to a protection space. You cannot add it directly. Instead, you must use yet another object, called NSURLCredentialStorage, which is the wrapper for keychain access. To access credential storage:

```
allStorage = [NSURLCredentialStorage
  sharedCredentialSpace];
```

This returns the system's singleton shared credential storage object. To add a credential to a protection space and write it to the keychain:

```
[allStorage setCredential: aCredential
  forProtectionSpace: aPspace];
```

To retrieve it later, you must copy all the protection space's credentials to a dictionary and then use objectForKey: with a username to return a user's credential object:

```
NSDictionary *aDictionary = [allStorage
  credentialsForProtectionSpace: aPspace];
aCredential = [aDictionary objectForKey:
  @"aTextStringUserName"];
```

If the username is in the dictionary, aCredential holds a pointer to it; otherwise, it is nil. To recover a user's password, use the aCredential.password property to return a text string. You can then ask the user to confirm the password before unlocking secure features.

A protection space is an allocated object, so you must release it explicitly when it is no longer needed. This means you may need to re-create it before authenticating a username and release it afterward. As long as you use a standard set of properties, the same credentials will be available.

Credentials in the shared storage area are not shared between applications, even when they are in protection spaces with identical settings.

Add Secure Password Access with NSCredential

You can use NSCredential and its associated classes to implement user/password access control. This example implements a simple authentication scheme that saves credentials to the keychain, gets username and password pairs from a user by using two text fields, and tests them against the keychain.

The code implements a clear-all feature to remove all the credentials in the store and diagnostic logging to the console. With minor changes, the same code can store one or more secure key-value pair of strings for any application.

Parts of this example are similar to the NSDictionary example in Chapter 7. You can save time by copying it.

Add Secure Password Access with NSCredential

① Create a new project in Xcode and then save it as Credentials.

② In NSDictionaryViewController.h, add IBOutlets to two text fields and then declare the text fields as properties.

③ Add three IBAction methods to add a new user, to authenticate a user, and to clear all users and then save the file.

④ In NSDictionaryViewController.m, synthesize the text fields and then add local pointers to a credential, a protection space, a credential storage, and a dictionary.

⑤ Find and uncomment viewDidLoad and then add code to create a protection space, to create a pointer to the shared credential storage, and to list the number of saved credentials to the console.

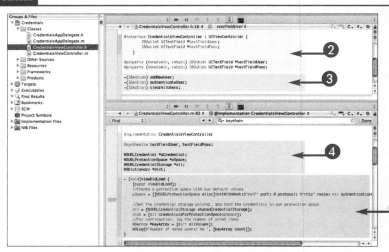

⑥ Implement the addNewUser IBAction method. Add code here to create a new credential for the name and password pair read in from the two text fields.

⑦ Implement authenticateUser IBAction and then add code to read a credential, to check it against the current name and password, and to create a success or failure alert.

⑧ Implement the clearAllUsers IBAction method and then add code to retrieve a dictionary with all stored credentials, to step through each item in the dictionary to delete it, and to log a confirmation to the console.

⑨ Implement a textFieldShould Return: delegate method for the two text fields to resign First Responder status and hide the keyboard.

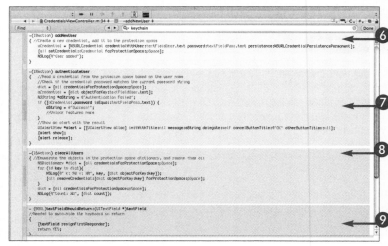

Note: *This method is used by both text fields. To enable this feature, you must link each text field's delegate outlet to File's Owner.*

⑩ Double-click CredentialsViewController.xib to open it in Interface Builder and then drag and drop three buttons, two text fields, and two labels from the Library to the view.

⑪ Set default keyboard attributes for each text field in the Attributes pane in Inspector. Set Capitalize to None and Correction to Now. Click the Clear When Editing Begins check box. Click the Secure check box for the password text field but not for the username text field.

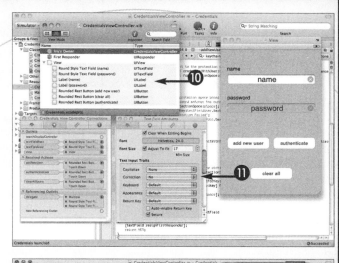

⑫ Lay out the items in the view and then name the buttons, labels, and text fields as shown.

⑬ Link touchDown events from the buttons to their corresponding IBAction methods. Link the delegate outlet from each text field to File's Owner. Link the text fields to their corresponding IBOutlets. Save the file.

⑭ Click Build and Run to build and run the application.

⑮ Test the application by adding usernames and passwords and authenticating valid and invalid combinations.

⑯ In Xcode, choose Run→Console to show the console and to review diagnostic output.

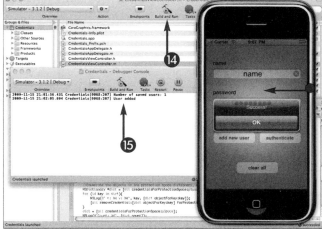

● The application saves pairs of usernames and passwords in the keychain. The data is saved permanently and can be accessed again after quitting and restarting. A clear-all option empties the keychain.

Note: *You can find the Credentials project on the website for this book: www.wiley.com/ go/iphonedevelopmentvb.*

Extra

You can use the credentials system to build permanent passwords into your application. For low-security passwords, such as keys to unlock game levels, the security of the keychain system is an unnecessary overhead, and you can hardwire the passwords into your application. For more secure authentication, you can use a remote web server to return a unique access code and save it with a user password.

If you — counterintuitively — save the password as the username and the secure code as the password, you can challenge the user for a password and use it to recover the access code from storage whenever you need to reauthenticate it remotely. Potentially, you can avoid passwords altogether, authenticating instead on an iPhone's unique ID. For more, see Chapter 7.

You can also hardwire passwords into your code and communicate them to users as needed. It is good practice to avoid including them as string literals.

Introducing Game Kit

Y ou can use Game Kit, introduced in OS 3.0, to create multiplayer games and share information between applications. Game Kit has three components: GKPeerPickerController, which manages connections; GKSession, which manages data transfer; and GKVoiceChatService, which implements voice chat over a network connection. Voice chat is optional. Peer picker and session objects are essential.

Game Kit is designed to work over Bluetooth. Internet connections using Wi-Fi or cellular data services are possible but require low-level programming of a server with sockets, managed via Bonjour. Peering via Bluetooth is much more straightforward.

Although Game Kit is ideal for games, it is relatively easy to create a Bluetooth text-messaging application or a swap tool for contact information. Data is split into small packets automatically and sent using two modes: *reliable*, which guarantees packet order and safe reception, and *unreliable*, which may drop packets but is significantly faster.

To transfer large files reliably, you must implement flow control and separate packet numbering and reassembly. You cannot use Game Kit to create a chat application that runs in the background and interrupts other applications when messages arrive. Because the iPhone does not support multi-tasking, Game Kit applications always run in the foreground and must be started and terminated manually.

Game Kit on the Simulator

The Simulator does not implement Bluetooth correctly and cannot pair with a handset. To test Bluetooth Game Kit features, you must use two handsets — two iPhones, two iPod touches, or one of each.

However, if you have two Macs, the Simulator can emulate a Bluetooth connection over Wi-Fi or Ethernet. You can use this to experiment with Game Kit without extra hardware, although you should always test commercial-grade applications on real devices.

Using GKPeerPickerController

The peer picker controller is a semiautomated object that can list and connect to other nearby handsets. To start a session, two or more users run a multiplayer application on their handsets. The peer picker controller in the application searches for nearby peers and lists them in a dialog box. Users can select one or more peers to add themselves to a game session.

To run the peer picker controller, allocate an instance, set a delegate to handle its delegate methods, and call [picker show];:

```
GKPeerPickerController *picker =
  [[GKPeerPickerController alloc] init];
picker.delegate = self;
picker.connectionType =
  GKPeerPickerConnectionTypeNearby;
[picker show];
```

This code creates and displays the picker dialog box and immediately starts searching for Bluetooth connections. To search for online connections, set connectionType to GKPeerPIckerConnectionTypeOnline. This property is a bitmask, and you can search for both types by ORing the two constants.

As the picker finds or fails to find a connection, it calls its delegate methods. The sessionForConnectionType: method must allocate and return a GKSession object that can be used for data transfer. When a session object is available, the picker calls didConnectPeer:. Typically, you use this method to dismiss the picker with [picker dismiss], clear its delegate, and initialize the session.

The peering process is somewhat random. The peer picker can create a session almost instantly or it can take a few minutes, irrespective of handset distance. A picker ControllerDidCancel: method is called if the user taps the Cancel button. This method dismisses the picker automatically. You must add code to release the picker's memory and disable its delegate.

Using GKSession

The `GKSession` object manages data transfers between peers. In the simplest possible case, you can send data to all peers:

```
[aSession sendDataToAllPeers: aDataObject withDataMode: GKSendDataModeUnreliable error: nil];
```

`aDataObject` is an instance of `NSData`, packed with the data you are sending. To receive data, implement the `receiveData:` method:

```
- (void) receiveData:(NSData *)data fromPeer:(NSString *)peer inSession: (GKSession *)session
  context:(void *)context
{
//Unpack or save the data here
}
```

This method is crucial but is not listed in the class documentation for `GKPeerPicker` or `GKSession`. You cannot transfer data without it. Do not implement significant data processing in `receiveData:`. When data requires complex processing, implement the processing elsewhere.

To send data to selected peers, use `sendData: toPeers:`, passing an array of `NSStrings` holding the target peer names. When receiving data, use the `peer` string to check the peer name if needed.

Packing and Unpacking Data

To transfer data, you must pack it and unpack it into an `NSData` object. `NSData` is designed for byte-level transfers. To transfer data structures, you can add C's `sizeof` function to return a data structure length and pass a pointer.

```
NSData *thisData = [[NSData alloc]
  initWithBytes: &aDataType length:
  sizeof(aDataType)];
```

Unpack the data in `receiveData::`

```
[data getBytes: &aDataType length:
  sizeof(aDataType)];
```

`aDataType` can be any C data type, including a structure.

To pack and unpack objects, use the `encodeWithCoder:` and `initWithCoder:` methods introduced in Chapter 7.

For game coding, keep data structures simple and short. The design of the data format is open and is your responsibility. A typical format is likely to include a short packet header with a type or target specification that defines a game event or game variable, followed by appropriate data. The receiver uses the header to update a variable or trigger a method.

You can use *key-value observing* to trigger methods automatically when game variables are updated remotely. Key-value observing (KVO) is an intermediate technique that enables objects to monitor properties, triggering an `observeValueForKeyPath:` method when the properties change. The method can then respond to the change — for example, by updating dependent properties. In a game, this could mean that changing a token position automatically triggers collision detection code.

KVO can be an efficient solution for game control. For details, see the "Key-Value Observing Programming Guide" in the documentation.

In a typical game, the same data model is maintained by all players. Each handset displays an individual view into the game space, controlled by an individual controller. But data is usually updated collectively so all players see the same game state at the same time.

This is relatively easy to manage in a two-player game but becomes more complex for open-ended game spaces with many players. As more players are added, lag times increase and data discrepancies can appear. To avoid this, set a conservative maximum limit on simultaneous play.

Using Voice Chat

Voice chat is relatively easy to implement. You must create an audio session to enable recording and playback and implement a `participantID` method to define participant names — you can reuse each peer's `peerID` string as an ID. The `GKVoiceChatService` class creates and reads data packets over a session connection and automatically routes the audio to and from the speaker and microphone via the audio session. For sample code, see the "Adding Voice Chat" chapter in the *Game Kit Programming Guide*.

Work with Game Kit

Y ou can use Game Kit to create a simple data exchange application. This example implements a minimal demonstration application that can link two or more handsets, sending and receiving data over a Bluetooth connection. To test the application, install it on two hardware handsets and run it simultaneously. When the user taps the screen, the application creates and displays a peer picker controller. The picker checks if Bluetooth is running. If not, it asks the user if he or she would like to enable it.

Once Bluetooth is working, the picker displays its search dialog box and runs its internal peering process. To create a session, two or more units in range must be displaying a picker at the same time. If the picker finds a possible peer, it adds it to a list on its display. To create a peering session,

two users must select each other. One peer only is asked to accept a connection. If the person accepts, a peering session is created by using a call to a delegate method.

These steps are automated and built into the picker controller. Once a session is running, the application dismisses the picker and implements session data exchange to read data from a slider and then transmits it to the other handset, where the remote slider moves in turn.

Two failure methods are implemented. `sessionDid FailWithError:` is triggered if the session connection drops or cannot be initialized correctly. It logs an error message to the console. `peerPickerControllerDid Cancel:` implements manual cancellation, dismissing the picker and cleaning up memory.

Work with Game Kit

① Create a new project in Xcode by using the View-based Application template and then save it as Game Kit.

② Click Game KitController.h and then add the peer picker controller and game kit session protocols to the header.

③ Add a pointer to a game session and an IBOutlet to a slider. Declare both as properties. Add a slider Changed: IBAction method triggered by slider updates. Save the file.

④ Synthesize the properties. Add a local float and a Boolean to manage the game state. Implement the slider Changed: method to pack and transmit the slider position via a game session — if a session is active.

Note: The gameOn Boolean disables the picker when a connection is active and re-enables it if a connection fails.

⑤ Add a touchesBegan: method to create, initialize, and display a peer picker when the user taps the screen.

⑥ Add code to implement the sessionForConnection Type: delegate method to return a valid session.

⑦ Add code to implement the didConnectPeer: method to initialize the session when the peer picker creates a connection and to dismiss and release the picker.

⑧ Add code to implement the peerPickerController DidCancel: and didFailWithError: methods to handle error conditions.

⑨ Implement the receiveData: method to receive and unpack a transmission and to update the slider position and then save the file.

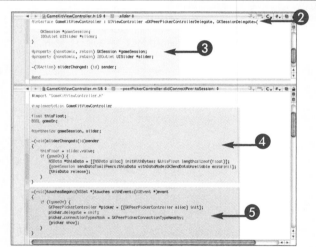

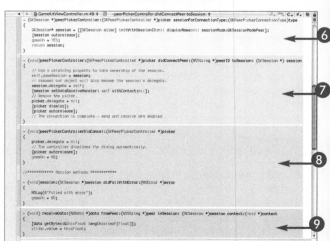

10. Double-click Game KitViewController.xib to open it in Interface Builder and then add a slider to the view.

11. Link the slider to its corresponding IBOutlet.

12. Link the slider's Value Changed message to the sliderChanged: IBAction method and then save the file.

13. Click Build and Run to build and run the application on two devices.

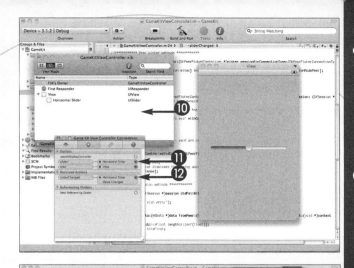

14. Test the application by tapping/clicking both screens, using the peer pickers to create a connection and moving the slider on both devices.

● The application displays a peer picker dialog box and creates a game session. Slider movements are copied between two or more devices.

Note: The Simulator can discover devices and list them in the peer picker table but cannot connect to them successfully.

Note: You can find the Game Kit project on the website for this book: www.wiley.com/go/iphonedevelopmentvb.

Extra

The picker list shows each unit's device name, as set in iTunes. This is often unhelpful because many users do not change the default names, so the peer picker is populated with a list of indistinguishable items — all named iPhone. You should add help information to your application to suggest more descriptive names.

By default, the peer picker does not time out. Bluetooth retransmissions drain the battery, so you should consider adding a timer that dismisses the picker automatically if a session is not completed within a set time.

Game Kit data transfer is bi-directional. There is no master or slave — the sliders move each other. Unless you distinguish between master and slave peers in your code, linked applications update each other automatically.

Apple includes a Game Kit application called GKTank in its sample code collection, which implements a complete two-player tank and obstacle game.

Internally, GKTank implements complex send and receive code, with application state and event information. It uses simple master/slave peering to distinguish between two players, using a random number to decide which player is which.

You can use the code in GKTank as a starting point for more complex games that exchange application state and event data.

If you run two Simulators on two Macs, they will connect over Wi-Fi.

Introducing the Accelerometer and Proximity Sensor

You can use the accelerometer and proximity sensor hardware built into iPhone to add novel and intuitive interactive features to your applications. For example, you can make games that respond to the orientation of the iPhone. The player can tilt the phone to control a rolling ball or set other game features. You can also use the accelerometer to create practical tools, such as a bubble level.

Accelerometer Applications

The accelerometer provides a tactile user experience. For most users, controlling an application by tilting the iPhone feels natural. For example, you can link the accelerometer to a view-switching method so the iPhone switches views when the user rotates it, shakes it, or taps it gently in one specific direction.

Many developers have concentrated on developing familiar applications, such as rolling ball games and simple novelty utilities. You can make your applications more appealing to users by approaching the accelerometer features more creatively — for example, by using the accelerometer to control a musical performance or to track physical movements to create networked sports games.

Acceleration and Gravity

The accelerometer reports two types of data. It responds to instantaneous movements and also reports the pitch, roll, and yaw of the iPhone. You can process this information to read the iPhone's orientation with respect to the ground. You can also read impulse events, such as side taps, nudges, and shakes. These are superimposed on the tilt values, which remain relatively steady.

The accelerometer reports the angle made by each of the handset's axes to nominal flat ground. The x-axis runs left and right across the iPhone's display, and the y-axis runs vertically through the center. The z-axis is perpendicular to the display. As you move the handset, the accelerometer reports the tilt of

each axis. The reference is an imaginary line to the ground, which passes through the center of the Earth. Values are nominally in the range +/− 1, but you should allow for some inaccuracies. The true range may be offset by up to 10%. The accelerometer does not report absolute rotation. To measure rotation, you must combine accelerometer readings with the compass built into the iPhone 3GS.

Instantaneous tap and shake values are superimposed on the tilt measurements. Vigorous shaking can produce values of +/− 3, although 2.5 is a more usual range. You can use values of around 1.5 to check for shake events.

The Proximity Sensor

The iPhone's proximity sensor is a separate hardware feature, independent of the accelerometer. The sensor is built into the case near the ear port at the top of the handset. It turns off the display during calls to save battery life. The sensor responds when an object is within a couple of inches of the sensor area. You can use it to trigger a response from the iPhone without touching the display. It is ideal for this kind of sporadic triggering but less ideal for extended contact. When the sensor is triggered, the iPhone's display blanks automatically and the touch screen is disabled.

Filtering and Noise Reduction

The output of the accelerometer is neither clean nor precise. It is calibrated so that 1G of acceleration produces an output of approximately +/− 1. However, the output suffers from noise and jitter. Values are accurate to no more than two decimal places.

You can set the rate at which the accelerometer returns data, but values remain inaccurate, even when they are reported less often. To maximize the useful information and minimize noise, you must filter the raw accelerometer data. You can do this in a variety of ways to emphasize and extract different data, depending on your application's requirements.

Low-Pass and High-Pass Filtering

Two standard filtering options are low-pass and high-pass filtering. They are not included in the accelerometer framework, so you must implement them yourself.

Low-pass filtering averages the accelerometer data. You can use low-pass filtering to remove jitter and noise, creating smooth and steady tilt readings. To create a simple low-pass filter, store previous values and then combine them with the current value using a weighting factor. For example:

```
x = acceleration.x*filterFactor +
    lastX(1.0-filterFactor)
lastX = x;
```

The smaller the weighting factor, the smoother the response. However, if the response is too smooth, it will lag behind the true value. The best way to fine-tune this factor is by experiment.

High-pass filtering removes steady values. You can use it to tilt information, leaving only taps and impulses. To implement a high-pass filter, you need to store the previous acceleration value:

```
x = filterFactor*(lastX + acceleration.x
    - lastAcceleration.x);
lastX = x;
```

Filtering is a complex topic. The challenge for iPhone developers is to create a user experience that feels smooth and accurate, even if it is not technically ideal. For most applications, this sample code should be adequate.

For more sophisticated and accurate filtering, see the `AccelerometerGraph` sample application in the Apple sample code collection. This implements tunable low-pass and high-pass filters, with optional value clamping to minimize noise and jitter.

Using the Proximity Sensor

You can access the sensor from the [UIDevice currentDevice] object. In outline, to turn on the sensor, you should set the proximityMonitoring Enabled property to YES. The sensor uses a notification mechanism rather than a delegate. You must add a callback by sending a message to the defaultCenter object, which is an instance of the NSNotification class.

You can then implement the callback method to read proximityState for the returned device object.

For example code, see the Accelerometer application on the website: www.wiley.com/go/iphonedevelopmentvb. Not every iPhone OS device includes the sensor. Your code should check that the sensor exists before adding the callback.

Using the Accelerometer

You can add accelerometer features to your application by using the acceleration classes and their associated objects, which are included in the UIKit framework. Accelerometer code is typically placed within a view controller object.

The elements of UIKit that manage the accelerometer are somewhat complex but are easy to handle in practice. The UIAccelerometer class defines the features of a master accelerometer object. Do not create instances of this class. Instead, you should access a pre-defined object named sharedAccelerometer. This is a *singleton* object — there is only ever one instance — shared between all threads and applications.

sharedAccelerometer has two properties that can be set: an update interval in seconds that specifies the update period and a delegate that sets an appropriate delegate object. Until you set a delegate, sharedAccelerometer

does nothing. Once you nominate a delegate, it begins sending messages at the specified interval.

To handle these messages in a view controller, set self as the delegate in the usual way. You will need to add the <UIAccelerometerDelegate> protocol to the controller's header to ensure that it can receive accelerometer messages. If your application has more than one view controller, you can create an extra class to implement the protocol in a separate object that can be read independently, with optional filtering features.

To read accelerometer information in the delegate, implement the accelerometer:didAccelerate method handler. Each message includes an instance of a UIAcceleration object. Copy the object to a local instance of UIAcceleration. You can then read the current x, y and z acceleration data. Optionally, you can also read a time stamp that is included in UIAcceleration.

Using the Accelerometer

① Create a new application by using the View-based Template and then save it as Accelerometer.

Note: You can find the Accelerometer project on the website for this book: www.wiley.com/go/iphonedevelopmentvb.

② Add the AccelerometerDelegate protocol to the application's view controller header.

③ Add label definitions to the view controller header to create three label objects — one for each axis.

④ Open Interface Builder, drag three labels onto the blank view, link them to the label definitions in the code, and then save the edited view.

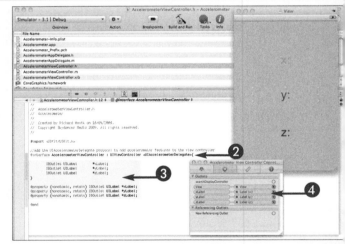

⑤ In Xcode, open the view controller implementation file and then synthesize the three labels.

⑥ Declare three private floats to store previous accelerometer values.

⑦ Declare constants for the update rate and the filter factor.

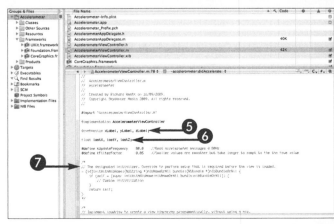

8. Find the `ViewDidLoad` method. If it is commented out, uncomment it. Add code to set the update interval and then nominate a delegate.

9. Optionally, add code to test if the proximity sensor is available and then set up a callback if it is.

10. Optionally, add code to process proximity sensor callbacks.

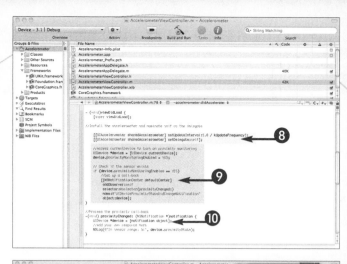

11. Add code to implement the accelerometer method to receive updates.

12. Add code to read the current values and then filter them.

Note: *Current values are returned in the acceleration object and read from* `acceleration.xyz`.

13. Add code to update the labels in the view and to save the new values for the next update.

14. Click Build and Run to build and run the application.

● The accelerometer values appear in the view and are updated when the handset is moved.

Note: *Acceleration features are not supported in the Simulator. You must test this example on a handset.*

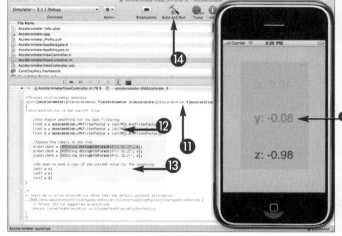

Extra

Although you can use the accelerometer to check for shake events, from iPhone OS 3.0 onward, you can also use the `motionEnded:` message. This is simpler to implement, but you cannot customize the sensitivity to test how hard the user is shaking his or her iPhone or count the number of shakes. If you need these extra features, you must derive this data from the accelerometer's output.

To check for shake events, add a handler for the `motionEnded:` method and make sure that it appears in your application's responder chain:

```
- (void)motionEnded:(UIEventSubtype)motion withEvent:(UIEvent *)event
{
  if (event.type == UIEventTypeMotion
      && event.subtype == UIEventSubtypeMotionShake )
   {
    // Handle shake events here
   }
}
```

Introducing
Location Services

ocation Services are built into the Core Location framework. Use this feature to add location-specific options to your applications. You can also link Location Services to the MapKit framework, which is an API for Google Maps. MapKit can draw maps in a view and annotate them with pins and other markers. When these options are combined with Location Services, you can add mapping, geo-tagging, and other map-based features to your applications.

Location Services relies on a combination of built-in GPS, Wi-Fi, and cellular information to estimate a location. The iPhone 3GS also features a compass, which can obtain heading information from the same framework. Older iPhone models do not include GPS and instead rely on cellular and Wi-Fi information. This is much less reliable and accurate than GPS, except in a limited selection of urban areas, but can provide a very approximate position fix. On the iPod touch, only Wi-Fi location is available.

Position Accuracy

Location Services returns an accuracy estimate and supports accuracy filtering. In certain mostly urban areas, Wi-Fi location fixes are supplied free to iPhone users from the Skyhook service. In other locations, accuracy is more limited. You can use the accuracy estimate to filter out the inaccurate position fixes that are generated when the framework returns its first position estimate. It is not unusual for the error on these first estimates to be a mile or more.

In theory, it is possible to receive a fix accurate to within 1 meter. In practice, the useful GPS accuracy is likely to be 50 meters. In ideal conditions, this may drop to 20 meters, but your application should not rely on this. When the iPhone is

used indoors in locations that do not offer a Wi-Fi location fix, the error will increase further — to 100 meters or more. GPS information may not be available at all indoors. For most applications, 100-meter accuracy is adequate.

If you use Location Services in your application, you should manage user expectations so users are aware of these limitations. If your application cannot get an accurate position fix within a reasonable time, it should time out and display an appropriate error message. For map-based applications, you can implement a circular estimated error display similar to that featured in the iPhone's built-in Google Maps application.

Altitude Information

The GPS unit can supply optional altitude information. As with the position fix, it is returned with an error calibrated in meters. If the error is negative, the measurement is invalid or GPS information is unavailable. Altitude information is rarely accurate to within 50 meters and often returns an error of more than 100 meters. Altitude monitoring remains more of a nominal feature than a useful one.

Applications for Location Services

The most popular applications with location support are commercial mapping and routing tools, designed to compete with the iPhone's built-in Google Maps application. While this sector is a buoyant market, solo developers are unlikely to have access to national or international routing and mapping databases. It is possible to implement limited routing features using the Google Maps API, but these fall short of the routing tools available on a commercial GPS device. Fortunately, popular but less intensive niches for location-aware applications remain open. Alternative possibilities include geocaching, photo tagging, and handheld GPS route management for hiking and camping. Location information is also ideal for social networking.

Power Requirements

Using Location Services places a significant drain on the iPhone's battery. Adding map tracking can drain a battery in around an hour, generating significant heat. It is good practice to turn off location tracking when it is not being used. This can create difficulties for users because useful applications often rely on continuous tracking. You can save power by running location services from a timer and updating location information once every minute or so. If location services are turned off the rest of the time, power drain becomes less of a problem.

By default, applications run with the system idle timer enabled. After a set period, the display dims and eventually blanks completely to save power. This prevents battery drain but also makes it difficult to use a mapping or location application, particularly while driving.

You can disable an application's idle timer by calling the `idleTimerDisabled` method on `UIApplication`. When the timer is disabled, the screen never blanks. This is practical for mapping and location tracking, but it dramatically shortens battery life.

To turn off the timer, add this line to the `applicationDid FinishLaunching` method in the application delegate:

```
[UIApplication sharedApplication].
   idleTimerDisabled = YES;
```

You should reset the value to `NO` when your application quits.

User Confirmation

If your application uses Location Services, the first time it runs in a session, the iPhone OS displays an alert asking the user to confirm access to the location features. The user can always decline this request. Users can turn off all location services in their preferences. Your application must include a conditional check to make sure that the user has allowed Location Services to run.

Using Location Manager Objects

On the iPhone 3GS, Core Location supports the hardware compass feature and returns a heading. The heading feature is closely related to the location tracker but operates independently. Both features rely on defining a `locationManager` object and nominating a delegate to receive updates from it.

To read the information, you must implement one or more of the methods defined in the Location Manager Delegate Protocol — for example, `didUpdateToLocation`, `didFailWithError`, or `didUpdateHeading`. Location and heading information are packed into `CLLocation` and `CLHeading` objects. You can read updated location and heading information from their properties.

Speed and Distance

The `CLLocation` class, which manages location information, includes a number of useful data structures and features. You can use these features to simplify a variety of location, distance, and speed calculations. For example, you can use `getDistanceFrom:` to calculate the distance between two locations. Two other useful properties are `speed` and `course`. `speed` returns a measured speed value in meters per second. `course` returns a calculated heading. You can use `course` as a limited substitute for the compass features in handsets that do not include a hardware compass, with the restriction that the handset must be moving for course calculations.

Usually, `CLLocation` objects are returned by Location Services, with individual latitude and longitude fields, and other data that describes accuracy and altitude. The `description` property returns all the location information packed into a text string in a convenient form that is ready for display. You can also initialize your own location objects with latitude and longitude settings as well as use `getDistanceFrom:` for custom distance calculations that are useful for navigation and mapping.

Get Your Location

You can use the Core Location framework to add location updates to your application and to read location information. Core Location uses a location manager object, which is an instance of the CLLocation Manager class. The location manager sends messages to a delegate. You can attach the location manager to a view controller, setting the delegate to self so the view controller receives the messages. To share location services among a number of different swapped views, create a separate delegate class.

When this application runs, the user is asked to confirm that location services can run. If the user has disabled location services, the locationServicesEnabled property will be FALSE. Your application should test for this condition before enabling position updates and optionally remind the user to enable location services.

A distance filter feature monitors the distance between current and previous location readings and suppresses

updates that are smaller than the filter setting. To disable this filter, set the value to the pre-defined constant kCLDistanceFilterNone.

You can also specify a target accuracy. Typically, you can set this to the pre-defined constant kCLLocation AccuracyBest. This does not guarantee good accuracy, but it forces Core Location to measure position as accurately as it can. To check the true accuracy, read the returned accuracy property.

Location information messages are passed to two methods: locationManager didFailWithError and location Manager didUpdateToLocation:FromLocation. You can use the former to report errors with an alert message. The latter method returns the current and previous locations in two instances of a CLLocation object. Messages arrive asynchronously whenever the hardware calculates a new position and the distance moved is greater than the distance filter setting.

Get Your Location

① Create a new application by using the View-based Template and then save it as Locator.

Note: You can find the Locator project on the website for this book: www.wiley.com/go/iphonedevelopmentvb.

② Add the CLLocationManagerDelegate protocol to the application's view controller header and then add an #import directive for CoreLocation.h.

③ Add label definitions to the view controller header to create label objects for latitude, longitude, accuracy, distance, and speed.

④ Open Interface Builder, drag five labels onto the blank view, link them to the label definitions in the code, and then save the edited view.

⑤ Right-click on Frameworks and then choose Add→ Existing Frameworks from the pop-up menu to select Core Location from the Frameworks list to add it to the project.

⑥ Open the view controller implementation file and then synthesize the label definitions in the view.

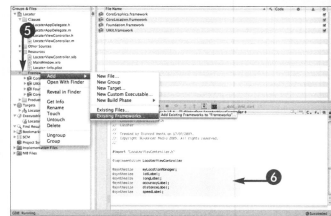

282

7 Find the `ViewDidLoad` method, and if it is commented out, uncomment it.

8 Add code to attach a location manager object to the view controller.

9 Add code to test if location services are available and to report an error if they are not.

10 Add code to nominate the view controller as the messaging delegate, set required distance filtering and accuracy properties, and enable location updates.

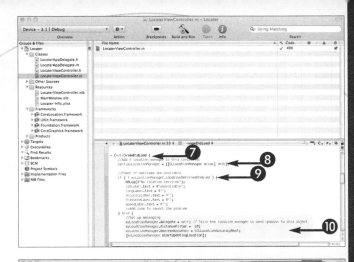

11 Optionally, add code to implement an error handler for location errors.

12 Add the `didUpdateTo:` method to receive location updates.

13 Add code to test for invalid updates with negative accuracy.

14 Add code to process location information updates and refresh the text labels in the view.

15 Click Build and Run to build and run the application.

The application receives position updates and displays them.

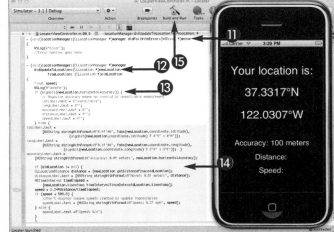

Note: Core Location in the Simulator returns a single update with the location of Apple's headquarters in Cupertino, California. To test the application properly, you must run it on a handset.

Extra

The location manager object returns an update as soon as `startUpdatingLocation` is called. You should ignore this first return. The first update is always an old location, with an old accuracy value, and is likely to be wrong. Your application should begin monitoring position and accuracy from the second update onward.

Outside of urban areas, updates will slowly converge on a user's true coordinates. It can be helpful to combine location services with MapKit, described later in this chapter. MapKit's location feature includes a clear visual display of a location, with an animated circle that displays the current estimated accuracy.

Returned locations are pairs of signed floats — positive for north and east. To convert latitude to a useful display string:

```
[NSString stringWithFormat:@"%.4f°@", fabs(newLocation.coordinate.latitude),
  signbit(newLocation.coordinate.latitude) ? @"S":@"N:)];
```

Replace `latitude` with `longitude` and N/S with E/W for an equivalent longitude string.

Introducing Google Maps and MapKit

You can use MapKit to add customized maps to your application with optional tags and annotations. MapKit uses many of the same frameworks and APIs as the built-in Maps application. It offers developers most of the same features, including the three standard map types: street, satellite, and combined. Your application can switch between map types at any time. Not all Google Maps features are supported. For example, StreetView is not available, and there is no built-in routing.

MapKit supports pins with annotations. Pins can be dropped at any map position, with a fixed optional animation effect that drops the pin from the top of the screen. Pins can use one of three preset colors. Apple's suggested color-coding assigns red to destination locations, green to starting points, and purple to user-specified points.

You can extend pins with callouts. By default, these appear as floating tags with a title and subtitle that appears when the pin is touched. However, you can customize pin graphics and callouts to create unique map effects.

GeoCoding is also included. You can use the GeoCoding lookup tools to search Google's online location database. This converts latitude and longitude into street addresses, with optional supporting information.

Optionally, your application can draw on the map in a separate layer to highlight features or display routes. Polylines and areas are not built into MapKit. However, you can add them to the map by using one of the iPhone's graphics frameworks.

MapKit and Core Location

MapKit and Core Location both offer location services, but there are significant differences between the frameworks. Core Location offers more features for reading and managing position information. You can turn positioning on and off to save power as well as read and set accuracy and error information for fine control. Generally, Core Location offers fine control over the hardware location features built into the iPhone. It also offers convenient methods for calculating speeds and distances.

MapKit hides many of these details. Your application can display a user's location. It appears with the same animated accuracy estimation circle display that appears in Maps, and it can be scrolled and resized by using built-in pinch, stretch, and drag features. These features are built into the map view. Your application does not need to implement them.

However, MapKit's location features are limited. Position updates run continually. Although your application can turn updates off, this removes the current position marker from the map. If no position fix is available, the map view `userLocation` property returns values of −180, −180. You must check for this error condition before using this property.

Adding the MapKit Framework

In the 3.1 SDK, you cannot add the MapKit framework to your project in the usual way because it is not included in the Existing Frameworks list that appears when you right-click on Frameworks in the Groups & Files windows. This is a bug in the SDK.

To add MapKit and other optional frameworks, choose Project→Add to Project from the main menu in Xcode,

navigate to /Developer/Platforms/SDKs/iPhoneSimulator3.1sdk/System/Library/Frameworks/MapKit.framework, and then click Add.

This location of the framework has moved continually through various updates of the SDK and may change again in the future. If the bug is not fixed, you can use Spotlight to search for its current whereabouts.

Map Views

You can quickly add a map to any application by adding an instance of `MKMapView` to a view by dragging and dropping it from the Library in Interface Builder. An `MKMapView` object — also known as a *map view* — immediately displays a map as soon as it loads. The user can scroll the map and use pinch and stretch actions to scale it.

To control the map from a view controller, add an outlet declaration to a map view in the view controller's header and then link to it in Interface Builder. Your application can

now change the map's display settings and enable or disable the animated current position marker.

To set a zoom factor and map center, your application must pass data to the map view by using a data structure called `MKCoordinateRegion`. This includes coordinates for the map's center and uses a substructure called `MKCoordinateSpan`, which sets the width and height of the displayed area in degrees.

MapKit Objects

You can create annotations, pins, callouts, and other effects by using a family of other MapKit objects and protocols. The MapKit framework is highly customizable. Pins and callouts are built into the framework, but your application can create more advanced effects by replacing the preset graphics with customized images.

The map view is supplemented with annotation objects and annotation views. *Annotation objects* store abstract information about an annotation, including its geographical

location and title. *Annotation views* generate graphics, including pins, callouts, and customized images.

If an annotation is visible on the map, a nominated delegate automatically triggers an annotation view method. This draws a pin or some other graphic at the annotation's position. If an annotation moves off the map, its corresponding view is saved in a buffer for recycling. This avoids alloc/release cycles and improves map performance.

Using Callouts and Annotations

To use pins, callouts, and customized annotation views, you must create a custom class that implements the `<MKAnnotation>` protocol. You can then use instances of this class to manage annotations.

The protocol defines title and subtitle text strings that appear in a callout. These are read-only properties and cannot be changed after an annotation object is created. They can only be set at initialization, so you must create a custom `init` method in your annotation class to manage string assignment.

You can add a pin to a map by creating an instance of an annotation object by using your custom `init` method to set its properties and calling `[mapView addAnnotation: myAnnotationObject];`.

This creates a default red pin with a callout. For more advanced pin control, you must implement the `mapView:viewForAnnotation:` method. To change pin color and turn on the animation effect, create an instance of the pre-defined `MKPinAnnotationView` object, set its properties, and then assign it as the method return. To implement pin recycling, use `dequeueReusableAnnotationViewWithIdentifier:`.

Another useful method is `calloutAccessoryControlTapped:`. This is called when the user taps a pin to display its callout. You can implement this method to add further features to your map, such as links to a webview. Full details of these and other methods are listed in the MKMapViewDelegate Protocol Reference in the documentation.

Display and Annotate a Map

Y ou can use MapKit to create a scrolling map that tracks a user's current position and displays an annotation pin. This example creates a map around the user's current location and then drops a single pin automatically. It uses a Core Location location manager object to return location information and manage updates.

A custom `DropPin` class is used to manage annotation objects. This implements the `<MKAnnotation>` protocol and uses a custom initialization method that sets the title of a pin's callout to an arbitrary string and its subtitle to latitude and longitude.

The map is created with an instance of an `MKMapView` object added in Interface Builder. To control the map, the map view is linked to an outlet, and various properties can then control its *span* — resolution, width, and height — and *region*, or position. A pin is created as an instance of `DropPin` at the current location and added to the map by using the `addAnnotation` method, called on the map view. This creates a default red pin. The `init` method sets the pin's title and subtitle to show You are here and the location.

Optionally, you can turn off location monitoring as soon as the pin drops by sending the `stopUpdatingLocation` message to the location manager. If you leave location monitoring turned on, the map will scroll and follow a user's location.

Display and Annotate a Map

① Create a new project by using the View-based Application template and then save it as MapView.

② Add the Core Location and MapKit frameworks to the project.

③ Add `#import` directives for MapKit and Core Location. Add `CLLocationManager Delegate` and the `MKMapView Delegate` protocols. Create instances of `CLLocationManager`, `MKMapView`, `MKCoordinateRegion`, and `MKCoordinateSpan` objects. Declare the `MKMapView` object as an `IBOutlet`.

④ Open Interface Builder, drag a MapView from the Library onto the main view, and then link it to the `MKMapView` object declared in the view controller.

⑤ Create a new class and name it `DropPin`.

⑥ Add the `MKAnnotation` delegate protocol to the header so the new class implements the protocol.

⑦ Create an `initWithCoordinate: andTitle` method for the class and then add `title` and `subtitle` properties — with associated getters.

Note: You can create any init method to assign strings to the two properties.

⑧ Add implementations for all the methods in the class implementation file.

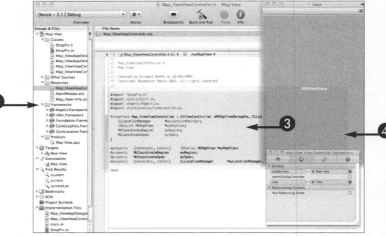

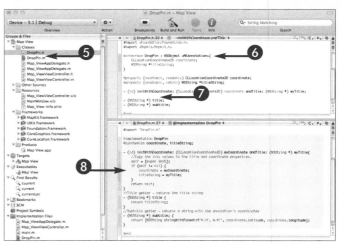

⑨ In the view controller implementation, synthesize the properties declared in the header.

Note: `pinDropped` *is an optional Boolean that can be used to monitor whether a pin has been dropped.*

⑩ In `viewDidLoad`, add code to implement a location manager and then attach it to the view controller.

⑪ Add code to set up and start location updates.

⑫ Add code to turn on the user location marker on the map view and to set the view controller as the map view delegate.

⑬ Add a `LocationManager` method.

⑭ Add code to set the map zoom factor so it displays individual streets and to center the map view on the current user location.

⑮ Add code to create an instance of `DropPin`, assign a title, and then call `addAnnotation` to add it to the map view.

⑯ Click Build and Run to build and run the application.

● The application drops a pin at the first location update and then annotates it with a brief message and a pair of coordinates.

Note: *In the Simulator, Core Location returns a single update with the location of Apple's headquarters in Cupertino, California. To test the application properly, you must run it on a handset.*

Note: *You can find the MapView project on the website for this book: www.wiley.com/go/iphonedevelopmentvb.*

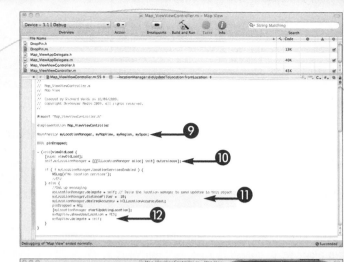

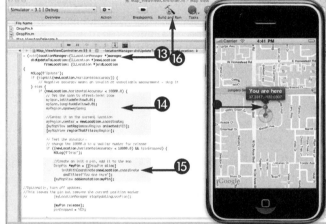

Extra

This example does not implement the `mapView:viewForAnnotation:` method. This method is triggered whenever an annotation is added to the map. It is an optional method but must be implemented to create custom graphics or to change the properties of the default `MKPinAnnotationView` class, including pin color and animation.

A typical implementation can appear complex because of the `dequeueReusableAnnotationViewWithIdentifier:` method. However, this simply implements automatic annotation view recycling. To aid recycling, annotation views can be grouped with an assigned name. Each view with the same name shares similar properties. An implementation typically checks for recycled views, uses one if available, or creates a new view.

You can hide specific annotation views by testing for a condition at the exit of `mapView:viewForAnnotation:` and returning `nil`. This is one possible way to show or hide annotations that share a common property, such as the location of friends, coworkers, or other specific location types.

Create an Application Icon and Badge

Y ou can make your application stand out in the App Store by adding a customized icon to the application bundle. Icons are a simple but effective way to improve the user experience. They are purely cosmetic, but graphic design is important on the iPhone, and it can be worth taking the time to design an appealing and attractive image for your project.

The iPhone OS automatically adds a glossy glass-like effect to icons. You do not need to create this effect yourself — it is added by Springboard.

You can also create a default load screen. As your application loads, this image zooms out of the center of the screen. It is replaced by your application's default view once the application starts running.

To add an icon, create a 57×57 PNG file in an image editor. Save it as Icon.png. Drag a copy to your application's project folder. From the Finder, drag the file to the Groups & Files pane in Xcode. Drop it in the Resources folder.

In the same folder, click the applicationname-info.plist file to edit it. Find the Icon file entry. Replace the blank field with Icon.png. File names are case-sensitive.

To add a default startup image, create a 320×480 PNG file in an image editor. Save it as Default.png with an initial capital. Drag a copy to your application's project folder and then drop the name in Xcode's Resources folder. The file is loaded automatically. You do not need to add it to your application's plist.

You can also add badges to your application. Numerical badges are created wtih a simple system call.

Create an Application Icon and Badge

① Create a new application by using the View-based Template and then save it as IconTest.

Note: *You can find the IconTest project on the website for this book: www.wiley.com/go/ iphonedevelopmentvb.*

② Design a 57×57 pixel Icon.png in an image editor, such as Adobe Photoshop or Gimp.

③ Design a 320×480 pixel Default.png file.

④ Save both files to the IconTest project folder.

⑤ In Xcode, add both files to the Resources folder in the project's Groups & Files pane.

Note: *You can add them by dragging and dropping them in the Resources folder from the Finder.*

⑥ Select the IconTest-info.plist file in the Resources folder.

⑦ Find the Icon file entry and then type **Icon.png** in the empty value field.

⑧ Click Build and Run to build and run the project.

● The application appears in Springboard with the customized icon. The Default.png file appears as a startup screen when the application runs.

Note: *If the Default.png image does not appear, choose Build→Clean in Xcode and then rebuild the project.*

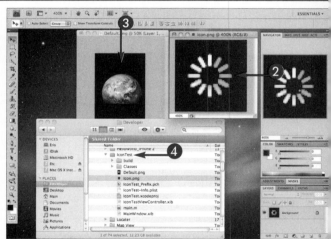

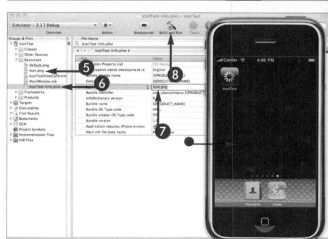

9 Click the IconTestViewController.m file in Xcode and then find the `ViewDidload` method and then add code to set the application badge.

10 Click Build and Run to build and run the project.

Note: *The code to set a badge can be placed anywhere in the application, except for main.m.*

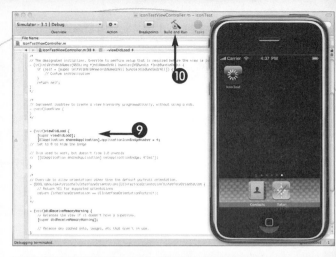

11 Quit the application.

12 After the application quits, a numbered badge number appears on the application icon.

Note: *To remove the badge under program control, use the same code to set the badge number to 0.*

Extra

Badges are most useful when they notify users of events, alerts, and messages when the application is not running. You cannot leave an application running in the background on the iPhone. However, you can use the Push Notification feature introduced in iPhone OS 3.0 to generate badges and user alerts automatically — but not to update applications with other information.

Push Notification requires client-side code in your application and server-side code in a separate web server. Client-side code samples are available in the Push Notification documentation. The server-side code is more complex.

In outline, your web server sends notifications to Apple's Push Notification Service, known as APNS. Each notification is sent to a unique token, which identifies a particular iPhone. The connection is secured via a Secure Sockets Layer (SSL) certificate.

APNS then generates notifications for individual iPhones. There is no global send option — your server must send out copies of the notification to every token in its database.

Your server must also collect tokens from users who sign up to the notification service, manage a token database, and generate notifications using PHP, Perl, or some other technology. Creating a working notification system is a significant undertaking.

Using C, Unix, and iPhone OS Functions

B elow the various frameworks, libraries, and object-oriented features, the iPhone runs a fairly standard variant of BSD Unix. Your application can access a variety of BSD and standard POSIX features with standard C function calls. You can add these to your code wherever you need them. Many functions are redundant or irrelevant on the iPhone. However, the list also includes string handling, line editing, and advanced math features that can be extremely useful. Objective-C is a superset of C. You can use C-language features anywhere in your application.

Using malloc() and free()

You can use

```
int *array = malloc (arraySize * sizeof(int));
// Use the array"
free (array);
```

instead of

```
NSMutableArray *array = [NSMutableArray alloc] initWithCapacity: arraySize];
//Use the array"
[array release];
```

The C version is faster because it avoids the Objective-C runtime overhead and also uses less memory. Cocoa object management is invaluable for dealing with complex object hierarchies, data structures, and assignment options, but for simple applications, plain C language is likely to be more efficient.

Using NSLog and NSString

NSLog and NString are similar to the C's variations on printf(). NSLog prints to the console, while NSString offers sophisticated string management. Both support all the standard printf() conversion codes:

FORMAT	MEANING
%@	Object
%d, %i	Signed int
%u	Unsigned int
%f	Float/double
%.nf	Displays n decimal places
%e	Float in scientific notation
%g	Automatically displays standard or scientific notation, as appropriate
%x, %X	Hex int, lowercase or uppercase
%b	Binary int
%p	Pointer
%c	ASCII character equivalent of int

NSLog and NSString can only print objects. Prepending a @ character converts whatever follows into an object. NSLog also supports description strings. You can use this feature to extend the range of printable formats. For example, NSLog (@"A string: %@", myNSString); is valid. The second @ tells NSLog to find the format from myNSString by requesting a description string. Many Cocoa objects support description strings, making it possible for NSLog to do more than print simple strings. You can print formatted strings directly by using NSLog. You do not have to create an NSString inside the NSLog call.

Unlike C's printf(), NSString includes UTF-16 multi-language support. The NSString class also implements an extensive collection of methods for initializing strings from URLs, file names, C strings, and plists, combining and splitting strings, and managing paragraphs.

You can use C's string features for very simple string processing. NSString is optimal for more complex string management.

Math Functions

In addition to simple standard trigonometric functions such as `sin()`, `cos()`, and `tan()`, the BSD library offers a selection of more advanced features.

Complex numbers

To use complex numbers, add `#import <complex.h>` to your application headers. This defines a new complex data type and declares `I` as the imaginary unit. You can then construct complex numbers as `double complex z = 1.23 + 3.45*I;`.

Available complex functions include complex conjugation, square roots, exponents, logarithms and powers, and complex trigonometric functions.

Distance function

`hypot(x, y)` is a Euclidean distance function that returns the distance between the origin and the pair of points specified. This function does not return the distance between two coordinates — `x` and `y` are single-valued, not coordinate pairs.

Advanced functions

`tgamma()` and `lgamma()` return the gamma function and its log, respectively. A set of Bessel functions is also available for calculating order 0 and order 1 functions of the first and second kind. For details, see the man page at `j0()`.

Cryptography and Random Numbers

BSD's original `rand()` function is a seedable generator with very poor randomness. The `random()` function was written to replace it with an improved generator that could still be primed with a seed. If the full `long` range is used, either function is adequate for simple games. If your application needs to mask the returned random number to leave only lower order bits, `rand()` may repeat; thus, `random()` is a better choice.

Both functions are adequate for simple ciphers but not for secure cryptography. A separate `arcrandom()` function implements the RC4 algorithm to generate cryptographically secure 32-bit keys.

Your application can also access the iPhone's Randomization Services. This is a managed source of randomness that reads from /dev/random and can return an array of random bytes by using `SecRandomCopy Bytes`. For details, see the Randomization Services Reference page in the Security framework documentation.

Two other libraries are available. The 3cc group implements block and stream ciphers by using the Common Crypto library. The 3ssl group implements OpenSSL to support the SSL and TLS protocols. Both are detailed and include a rich array of features that you can use to add secure cryptographic features to your applications using a variety of popular standards.

Threads and Process Management

All the thread and process management features built into Unix are available in the Core OS library. For example, you can force your application to quit by calling `kill(getpid(), SIGQUIT);`.

This sends a `SIGQUIT` signal to the operating system, which kills the process that your application is running in. It does not clean up your application's memory and does

not close open files, so this feature is more theoretically than practically useful. Root-level calls such as `reboot()` are available, but your applications do not run with root privileges, so they do nothing. Typically, your application should use the features of the `NSThread` class to manage threads via the operating system rather than attempting to control them directly.

Introducing the App Store

Y ou can use the App Store to distribute completed applications. Your applications can be free or you can set a price starting at 99 cents. Apple retains 30% of the in-store price and pays you the remaining 70%. Payments are calculated and made monthly to your bank account of choice. Currently, payments are collected per territory: North America, Europe, and so on. Payments are only made for a territory when the amount due is more than $150.

Apple reviews all applications before accepting them. The App Store uses the Apples iTunes Connect service at https://itunesconnect.apple.com. When you sign up for the Apple Developer Program, your Apple ID and password also allow access to the AppStore pages on iTunes Connect. These pages are for iPhone applications only — you cannot use them to sell music and media on iTunes. You must submit an application as a compressed bundle, built for distribution, and signed with a distribution certificate. See later in this appendix for more.

Creating Successful Applications

Apple's review process takes 14 days on average, and according to Apple, about 95% of applications are accepted. When you submit an application, it is tested for basic stability and functionality, and associated resources are checked for copyright ownership. You may be asked to confirm that you are the copyright holder of sounds and images that appear in your project.

Applications are rejected if they crash, do not work as stated, do not meet Apple's user interface guidelines, use undocumented Cocoa features or unsupported development environments, require excessive online bandwidth or use VoIP features without a licensing contract with a cellular provider, reuse code without an appropriate license, or conflict with the future plans of Apple or its cellular partners. You can improve your application's prospects by testing it thoroughly, making sure its interface design is consistent with Apple's design standard, and avoiding questionable code, development tools, and resources.

Application content is largely unrestricted. Applications do not need to be complex, impressive, or even notably useful. Books and music may be supplied in application form; pornographic or obscene content is not allowed, but games may include simulated violence. Applications are given age ratings to control access by minors. Ratings are calculated according to a checklist of features that appears during the submission process.

Financial, Legal, and Support Requirements

You must agree to support your applications. You can upload monthly updates if you need to, and you must supply a support email address and web page. You must also designate a local bank account for subscriber and user payments and accept Apple's distribution contracts. These are standard contracts and can be signed online in the Contracts and Legal section of iTunes Connect.

Some territories apply local sales taxes, either internationally or on applications created by residents. For example, sales in Japan are subject to a 20% withholding rate unless you complete a series of forms and submit them for approval to the Japanese government. You may need to supply further tax information for other territories.

The App Store offers a standard End User License Agreement (EULA) by default. If your application has special features or legal requirements, you can upload a revised agreement during submission.

Submitting Applications

You can use the Manage Your Applications feature on iTunes Connect to submit applications. If you have built and signed your application correctly, submission is relatively simple. You will need a large version of your project icon for marketing — this should be a 512 × 512 PNG file. You should create this first and then resize it to create the 57 × 57 PNG project icon. You will also need at least one 320 × 480 PNG screenshot and an SKU number, which is an arbitrary product number of your choice and must be different for each application.

Localization

You can improve your application's sales appeal by localizing it for different territories to provide local language support. To localize a nib file, right-click on it in the Groups & Files pane in Xcode, click the General tab at the top of the window, and then click the Make File Localizable button at the bottom of the page. To add extra languages, reopen the General tab and then click the new Add Localization button. Select a target language from the drop-down menu that appears. This creates a copy of the nib. Revise the labels in the new nib to the target language and then save the nib. Repeat this for all the languages you plan to support:

```
"welcome_key" = "Welcome!"
  //In the Localizable.strings file in en.proj
"welcome_key" = "Bienvenuto!"
  //In the Localizable.strings file in it.proj
```

Add the following code to the Application Delegate to run when the application loads:

```
NSUserDefaults *defaults = [NSUserDefaults
  standardUserDefaults];
NSArray *languages = [defaults objectForKey:
  @"AppleLanguages"];
NSString *currentLanguage = [languages
  objectAtIndex:0];
```

Use this to automatically replace the welcome_key with the string from the appropriate language, as specified in a user's iPhone preferences:

```
NSLocalizedString(@"welcome_key", @"");
```

Add other keys for other strings.

In-App Payments

From OS 3.0 onward, applications support in-app payments via the Store Kit framework. You can use them to add extra features to your applications that can be unlocked after payment or to supply further content.

The App Store lists your products, collects payments on your behalf, and keeps a record of products owned by individual users. It does not deliver or hold content. To supply content, you must either build it into your application and add code to unlock it after a successful purchase or make it available on a separate server. The server must communicate with the App Store to receive

payments receipts, check them for validity, and then implement a download feature for delivery of the content.

Because application data can be lost after a crash, Store Kit includes a restore feature that can retrieve details of previous purchases without billing a user again. Your application and optional server must be able to supply products again during a restore. To simplify development, you can test in-app features within a sandbox that runs independently of the main iTunes billing system and always authorizes purchases. You can create a test user for the sandbox by using the Manage Users page on iTunes Connect.

Build a Project for the App Store

X code does not include a distribution build target. You can create a distribution build by copying the release configuration and modifying it to add the required extra features. The distribution configuration is very similar but includes distribution code signing, a version number, an icon file, and an optional project identifier.

Once you have built a project for distribution, you cannot run it on your handset to test it because the code-signing features for distribution and provisioning use different certificates. However, a beta-testing feature called Ad Hoc Distribution is available for small groups of up to 100 testers. For details, see the description on the Developer Portal.

By default, all the Xcode templates use the Relative to Enclosing Group path option for the file links in Xcode.

If you copy a project to a different folder for backup, all the file paths are destroyed.

To solve this problem, open the Groups & Files pane and then right-click on Classes, Other Sources, and Resources in turn. Choose Get Info for each selection and then click the General tab. To set the Path Type option, click the Path Type drop-down menu and then choose Relative to Project. Paths are now relative to the project folder, and you can move or copy the folder to a different location on disk.

To create a compressed build folder for uploading to the App Store after a distribution build, click the product.app file under Products in the Groups & Files pane and then choose the Reveal in Finder option in the Tools drop-down menu. In the Finder, right-click on the .app file to compress it, making it ready for upload.

Build a Project for the App Store

① In Xcode, right-click on the project and then choose Get Info from the pop-up menu.

② Click the Configurations tab.

③ Click the word Release to select the Release configuration in the configuration list and then click Duplicate.

④ When Release copy appears, type **Distribution** to rename it.

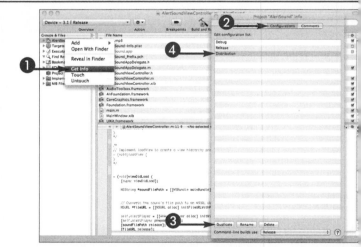

⑤ Click the Build tab to reveal the settings for the new Distribution build.

⑥ Navigate down to the Code Signing Identity entry.

⑦ If Any iPhone OS Device is not visible, click the Code Signing Identity triangle, right-click on iPhone Developer, and then choose iPhone Distribution from the pop-up menu.

Note: *This replaces the Developer code-signing profile with a Distribution profile. If you have not already created a Distribution profile, follow the instructions on the next page.*

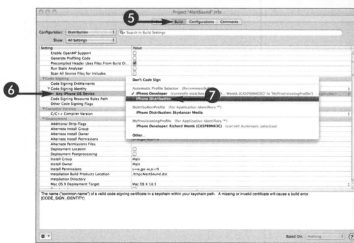

8. Right-click on the build target under the Targets header in Groups & Files.

9. Choose Get Info from the pop-up menu.

10. Click the Properties tab and then replace the generic identifier with a unique application name.

11. Define the application's icon file and version number.

12. Select the new Distribution configuration from the configuration menu and then build the project by choosing Build→Build.

13. Click the application product in the Products folder in Groups & Files.

14. Choose Reveal in Finder from the drop-down tools menu.

15. In the Finder, right-click on the .app file and then choose Compress *file name* from the pop-up menu.

The application is compressed, ready for uploading to the App Store.

Extra

Your application must be signed with a Distribution Certificate before you can submit it to the App Store. The Distribution Certificate is not the same as the Provisioning Certificate used for development. To create a certificate, load Keychain Access on your Mac and then create a certificate request on disk by using your email address and any name.

In the Certificates section of the Developer Program Portal, click the Distribution tab and then upload the request. Click Approve — if you are the Team Agent, you can ignore the email you receive — and then download the certificate.

In the Provisioning section of the Developer Program Portal, click the Distribution tab and then create and download a distribution provisioning certificate. Requests are approved immediately — you can reveal the Download button by refreshing the page. Download the certificate. Drag it onto Xcode to install it. You can now sign your applications during a distribution build for distribution.

Open Application Development

You can use open application development environments to create and run applications on your own iPhone and to see code created by other developers. There are two levels of open development. At the first level, you can continue to work in Xcode, using Apple's provisioning scheme to digitally sign your applications and limit them to your own handset.

At this level, you can expand your development skills by downloading, examining, and repurposing applications created by other developers and released with an open-source license. Custom frameworks are also available. You can also use alternative development toolkits and

environments that can speed up development. Some of these kits replace the iPhone's Objective-C and Cocoa programming model with different, simpler, and potentially more productive programming models.

At the second level, you can bypass Apple's restrictions and unlock the operating system of your device. This is known as *jailbreaking*. You can then access and interact with the iPhone's Unix-based operating system as well as installing and running your own applications without provisioning them. You can also install and run applications created by other developers.

Open-Source Applications

You can install open-source applications on your iPhone without restrictions. Most applications are supplied as complete Xcode-ready packages that you can download, unzip, build, and run. A good source for open applications is the www.theiphonedev.com website. One caveat is that open

applications are supplied with various licensing restrictions, such as the GPL (General Public License). If you repurpose code from an open application, licensing rules may force you to apply similar licensing restrictions to your project.

Alternative Development Toolkits

As the iPhone has become more popular, alternative development environments have begun to appear. The Objective-C and Cocoa development tools bundled with Xcode remain the most direct and efficient tools for iPhone application programming. But as the Android, BlackBerry, and Symbian platforms have developed their own application markets, developers have started to work with cross-platform development tools. These include the iPhone as an application target but also make it easy to convert an application so it works on Android, Blackberry, and other targets.

Nitobi PhoneGap

Nitobi PhoneGap is a JavaScript and HTML tool that offers cross-platform development on all the main mobile platforms and also makes it easy to repurpose applications for the web. It includes access to the iPhone's location, accelerometer, and Address Book features. It is free under an MIT (Massachusetts Institute of Technology) development license. Unfortunately, Apple sometimes refuses to accept a PhoneGap application in its App Store. For product details and download information, see www.nitobi.com/products/phonegap.

Appcelerator Titanium Mobile

Appcelerator is a cross-platform tool that supports iPhone, desktop, and Android development. It is based on HTML and JavaScript but also includes support for many of the iPhone's user interface and hardware features. The desktop version supports development in Python and Ruby. The iPhone version is limited to JavaScript, but it is possible that this may change in future releases. As of late 2009, Appcelerator remains in beta, with a free and open signup program. For information about the current state of the product, visit www.appcelerator.com.

Ansca Corona

The iPhone does not directly support Adobe's Flash technology. Corona is a development environment that enables Flash developers to create applications for the iPhone. It uses the Flash-like Lua language. Game and web developers can use Lua to move Flash games to the iPhone. For details, visit www.anscamobile.com/corona.

Opening Your iPhone

If you want to explore the iPhone further, moving beyond Apple's SDK and its alternatives, you will need to jailbreak it. Jailbreaking is not supported by Apple. Parts of the process may involve copying information from your iPhone. You must check local, state, and federal laws to make sure that making copies of this information is legal and does not break the terms and conditions of the iPhone or iPod user license.

Although jailbreaking tools are readily available online, you should be aware that jailbreaking is risky. At best, whenever Apple releases an update of the iPhone OS, you will lose your custom applications and will need to re-install them. At worst, Apple reserves the right to lock down the iPhone completely in future releases, eliminating jailbreaking completely. Both current and future jailbreaking attempts may render your iPhone permanently inoperable. Do not attempt to jailbreak your iPhone unless you accept these risks.

Jailbreaking tools continue to develop with each new release of the iPhone OS. There is no single definitive web source for jailbreaking utilities. You will need to search online for the most recent developments.

Open Development

Open development does not use Xcode. You should have experience with command-line compiler environments and practices before attempting it. You can download an alternative set of development tools from http://code.google.com/p/iphone-dev. With effort, it is possible to build the development environment on most platforms. Significant editing and assembly are required.

Do not attempt to use the alternative environment if you are not already an experienced developer. The iphone-dev project is aimed at developers who are familiar with command-line tools and understand how to load and build applications from a shared code repository. Unlike Xcode, it is not a click-and-go solution. However, if you can gain access to the repositories, you may be able to repurpose some of the code there for use in your own Xcode-based projects.

Cydia

Open developers have created a large alternative development community. There is an alternative open app store, called Cydia, which offers a wide selection of free applications. In 2009, it became possible for developers to sell applications on Cydia and receive payment via an Amazon or PayPal account.

SSH, Unix, and Open Installation

Apple's own SDK strictly limits access to the underlying iPhone OS. Applications cannot access files outside of their sandbox, and useful features built into Cocoa and the OS are not accessible via the SDK.

These limitations no longer apply to a jailbroken iPhone. This makes it possible to modify features of the OS and create applications with more powerful features than are possible with Apple's SDK. For example, an application called Springboard supports custom wallpaper backgrounds on the iPhone Dock and Desktop. It is also possible to modify the system font as well as access other key system settings.

These hidden features are not documented officially. However, code for many jailbroken projects is open and shared, and discussions about finding and using undocumented features are public. Experienced developers typically use collaborative development as a substitute for the formal documentation in the official SDK.

SSH is also available on a jailbroken iPhone. With SSH, you can use an external terminal application to connect to the iPhone and issue text commands to it. Once SSH is running, you can install an application package on the iPhone by copying the .app file to the /Applications directory and then setting its permissions to 0755 by using chmod.

Develop for the iPad

You can use the latest SDK — version 3.2 and later — to develop applications for the iPad as well as the iPhone and iPod touch. The iPad development environment is an extension of iPhone OS 3.1. Key features and concepts remain identical. You can use the examples in this book to understand the core OS classes of either platform. However, iPhone OS 3.2 adds a number of new classes and features that are exclusive to the iPad.

Key Similarities

All the key frameworks in OS 3.1 are supported on the iPad and can be used with minimal changes. Just like iPhone OS 3.1, OS 3.2 does not yet support multitasking. Apple's guidelines continue to state that applications must take full control of the display and manage all user interaction. Similarly, applications are still expected to launch and exit quickly, preferably saving and loading data invisibly, without an explicit save or load option.

The security sandbox, memory management issues, and memory limitations remain unchanged. Custom plug-ins and frameworks are not supported. The graphics hardware supports Open GL ES 2.0, with legacy support for Open GL ES 1. Hardware features include the Accelerometer, compass, Core Location, Wi-Fi, Bluetooth, a microphone, and a headphone socket.

Hardware Differences

The processor has been upgraded from an ARM CPU to a custom Apple design running at 1GHz. The effective performance is around one-and-a-half times that of an iPhone 3GS and two times that of an iPhone 3G. Up to 64GB of memory is available.

The iPad display is 768×1024 pixels. Future versions are likely to support other screen dimensions. In the preliminary beta SDK, external displays and projectors are supported, with arbitrary dimensions. Apple's first external display product offers a VGA output from a dock connector at 1024×768 pixels. This resolution may change in later releases. External displays are independent of the built-in display and can auto-detect resolution.

The first release of the iPad does not include a camera, but this is a key feature and is likely to appear in future models. The status of 3G/GSM voice hardware for telephone applications is not yet clear. VoIP (voice over IP) telephony is possible, subject to network restrictions.

Battery life is significantly improved. Power conservation is less of a challenge, and it is possible to run more hardware features simultaneously without excessive battery drain.

The iPad supports an external Apple or third-party keyboard. There is likely to be a much larger side market for external devices — music keyboards, media controllers, game hardware — for the iPad than the iPhone.

Backward Compatibility

All iPhone applications run on the iPad without changes. By default, they appear at the default 320×480 screen size inside a virtual frame surrounded by empty black space. Tapping a virtual 2X button expands the application to fill the iPad's display. This is a cosmetic screen zoom. The true resolution remains the same.

Backward compatibility makes it easy to develop basic iPad-compatible applications without an iPad. However, iPhone applications do not support the iPad's new hardware and software features.

Design Goals

The iPad is not just a larger iPod touch. The larger screen size, extended OS features, and faster processor mean that applications can include more features and display more options. The interface is more customizable, and developers can create unique interface features instead of assembling an interface from UIKit's limited selection of classes.

The iPhone is an ideal platform for simple apps with a single obvious key benefit. iPad applications can be more complex, with features rivaling those available on a desktop computer. Simplicity and aesthetic appeal remain essential design goals. A fundamental goal of the iPad is intuitive tactile computing. Users who want a rich and rewarding but streamlined and simple experience are a new key target audience. The planning and interface design of any project are even more critically important than they are for iPhone apps.

Changes to Windows and Views

The iPad user interface is based on iPhone's UIKit classes but has significant additions. A key change is that all applications must support every orientation. Although the orientation code introduced in Chapter 4 remains almost unchanged, support for non-portrait orientations is no longer optional. You must design views that support them.

The view system has been extended with new features. *Split views* allow the interface to be split into two custom views, which appear side by side. For example, a navigation-based application can now show two levels of navigation table views or a mix of table views and other elements. *Popovers* are pop-up views that can be used modally or non-modally to display application settings, tool palettes, menu options,

and navigation features. Unlike windows, they do not float and cannot be moved.

Popovers are dismissed by tapping on the background view. Conventional pop-up modal views remain available but now feature a *presentation style* option that configures whether the pop-up covers all or part of the view under it.

Where the iPhone offers a pre-designed keyboard for input, the iPad supports *custom input views* — views that slide in when first responder status is set, with a custom-designed combination of buttons or other features. *Input accessory views* display buttons and editing options that can be attached to a custom input view or to the existing keyboard.

Changes to Text and Graphics

At 132 ppi (pixels per inch), the display density is slightly lower than that of the iPhone's 162 ppi. Text and graphics are slightly less sharp. However, a completely new Core Text framework offers support for powerful text-rendering and layout features. Core Text can create text and layout effects comparable to or even better than those available in OS X. Text can be animated to create special effects or visually striking interfaces.

You can extend preset cut and paste features offered by the UIMenuController class, introduced in Chapter 7, with

custom options. A new UITextChecker class offers a built-in spell-checker with a customizable dictionary.

Path support has been simplified. The UIBezierPath class is a wrapper for the Core Graphics path functions and makes it easier to create, manage, draw, and fill both straight and curved paths and shapes.

PDF support has also been extended. It is now easier to create, display, save, and load PDF documents via a standard graphics context.

Changes to Event Handling

In iPhone OS 3.1, the touch system passes a set of touch events to an application for processing. In OS 3.2, a new UIGestureRecognizer class simplifies touch management with pre-defined subclasses that can recognize taps, pinches and stretches, pans and drags, swipes, rotations, and a new touch-and-hold gesture, also

known as a long press. You can add these classes to your application to respond to these gestures with notifications of your choice.

Because these gestures are pre-defined, they are now considered a standard feature in iPad development. Users will expect at least some of them to be available.

Changes to File Management

As on the iPhone, the ideal iPad app works with data without presenting the user with explicit save and load options. However, file support has been expanded. Applications can now register that they are able to open specific file types. For example, an email application can now link to helper applications to manage attachments. A new UIDocumentationInteractionController

class can implement basic pasteboard and preview features for files of an unknown type.

File sharing with desktop computers is now supported. Applications can make their internal sandbox directories available to a desktop computer. Users can copy files into and out of these directories without restriction.

Transition a Project to the iPad Simulator

Y ou can use the Xcode 3.2 SDK to develop for both the iPhone and the iPad. The SDK includes a new iPad Simulator. In the first seed release of the SDK, you can begin an iPad project by creating a standard iPhone project. You can then *transition* it to the new target. This modifies its nib files and forces it to run as a true full-screen iPad app.

Later releases of the SDK may support multiplatform development without transitioning. However, in the first seed release, a project created without transitioning runs inside an iPhone emulation frame in the iPad Simulator. The resolution is limited to the iPhone's 320 × 480 screen size. After transitioning the application's views, you can make full use of the iPad's full 768 × 1024 screen size, and add code to implement the iPad's new software features.

You cannot create iPad projects manually by resizing the views and windows in your project's nib files. Although Interface Builder includes new transitioning features of its own, you must use the transition tool in Xcode to successfully transition a project. Note that Interface Builder always displays iPad views at their full size, making it difficult to design views on Macs with smaller displays.

The iPad Simulator window runs at half the true resolution in portrait orientation and the full resolution in landscape orientation. You can rotate between orientations by choosing Hardware→Rotate Left/Right.

This example transitions the simple Hello World project from Chapter 3. It does not add any new code or implement full auto-rotation support but demonstrates how transitioning modifies a project's nib files to make them compatible with the iPad target.

Transition a Project to the iPad Simulator

① In the Finder, drag a copy of the HelloWorld project to a new folder.

Note: *This optional step leaves a safety copy of the original project as a backup.*

② Click HelloWorld.

③ In Xcode, choose Project→Transition.

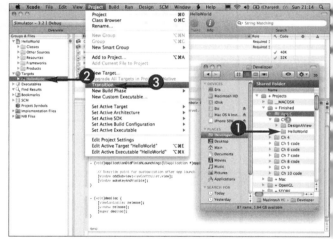

④ Click OK in the dialog box that opens.

Two new items appear in the Groups & Files pane: Resources-iPad and a new iPad target.

⑤ Delete the original Resources folder.

⑥ Delete the original target.

Note: *You can delete the folder and target by clicking them and pressing the Delete key or by right-clicking on them and then choosing Delete from the pop-up menu.*

Note: *These steps are essential and guarantee that Xcode compiles the project for the iPad.*

⑦ Double-click HelloWorldViewController.xib to open it in Interface Builder.

⑧ Double-click View to open it.

The view window has been resized to 768 × 1024.

Note: *For space and clarity, this figure shows only the central area in the view.*

⑨ Optionally, change and resize the text in the view to display a larger font.

⑩ Optionally, use the Placement buttons in the View Size pane in the Inspector window to center the text label.

⑪ Click the two solid red lines in the Autosizing area to enable auto-centering and to ensure the text remains centered for every orientation and then save the file.

⑫ Select OS 3.2 as the build target.

⑬ Click Build and Run to build and run the application.

● The transitioned project appears in the new iPad Simulator window.

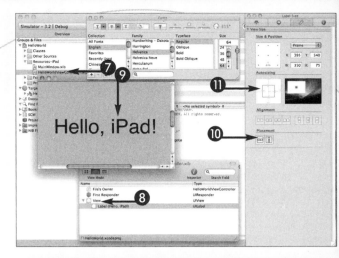

Extra

Apple's ultimate goal is to create a single unified development environment for both iPad and iPhone applications. In the 3.2 SDK, you cannot use the iPad's new software features in an iPhone project. Apple has stated that unified development will be possible in the future, which suggests that some or all of the new features in OS 3.2 may eventually find their way into iPhone apps. With a common code base and common features, unified development becomes a relatively trivial problem of reworking project nib files for both environments.

Until this universal development becomes possible, you must develop iPad and iPhone projects independently. It is easy to copy code but less easy to create interfaces that work equally well on both platforms with minor changes. The iPhone and iPad are idiomatically different and have different aims and target markets, making dual development a challenge for developers. The most promising opportunities are likely to come from apps that interact across both environments, taking advantage of the strengths of each, and not from projects that try to squeeze a near-identical experience into both platforms.

INDEX

INDEX

INDEX

INDEX

INDEX